Organized Labor
and the Mexican Revolution
under Lázaro Cárdenas

Organized Labor
and the Mexican Revolution
under Lázaro Cárdenas

By Joe C. Ashby

THE UNIVERSITY OF NORTH CAROLINA PRESS · CHAPEL HILL

To D. H. R.

Preface

Of the historic struggles of peripheral, colonial countries to overcome the difficulties imposed upon them by economic imperialism from without and economic liberalism from within, none is more moving than the Mexican battle during the Cárdenas era of the Mexican Revolution (1934–40) for the attainment of national sovereignty and a greater degree of economic independence. It is unquestionably true that "the government of Lázaro Cárdenas was the culminating moment of the Mexican Revolution."[1] In this new national statecraft, ". . . the trade union became an instrument for the reduction of power of private industry and for making the state the arbiter of the nation's economy."[2] At the same time, the labor movement exercised considerable power in national policy, thus becoming one of the principal agents of the state as workers achieved a more significant position in the evolution of Mexican social and economic life. There is a close parallel between the co-operation of organized labor and the chief executive in both Mexico and the United States during this period. A similar partnership was formed in Argentina a few years later.

The unique combination of the program of Mexican labor, the policies of the Cárdenas government, and the response of property

---

1. Jesús Silva Herzog, *La Revolución Mexicana en Crisis* (México, 1944), p. 18.
2. Frank Tannenbaum, *Mexico: The Struggle for Peace and Bread* (New York, 1950), p. 114.

owners—for the most part, foreigners—resulted, among other things, in the application of the agrarian laws to the Laguna cotton district, the expropriation of the National Railways Company, and, finally, in what was perhaps the outstanding event of the Mexican Revolution, oil expropriation. The power and influence of organized labor grew under the sponsorship of the Cárdenas régime, and the trade union, through the Mexican Confederation of Workers (C.T.M.) became an instrument of national economic policy. Toward the end of the Cárdenas era, the labor movement, largely under pressure of "outside forces," was apparently content to be only one segment in a "popular front" that attempted to consolidate the gains made in fulfilling some major provisions of the basic documents of the revolution, defending the national sovereignty of Mexico, and combating the growing Fascist threat.

In this epic struggle of human rights versus property rights, the Mexican labor movement, under the leadership of Vicente Lombardo Toledano, supported by Lázaro Cárdenas, was decisive. The organization that spoke for Mexican business enterprise said, "The labor theory of Cárdenas was to change the entire picture of worker-management relations in Mexico."[3] According to one labor historian, "With the inauguration of Lázaro Cárdenas as president of the country began an epoch never before equaled in importance in the public life of Mexico—in all aspects, economic and social."[4]

To examine the labor theory and to trace the development and the role of organized labor in Mexican economic policy during the Cárdenas régime are the purposes of this study. The relevance of such an inquiry for the present was pointed up by the late Professor Sanford Mosk when he wrote, ". . . what went on during the time of Cárdenas has had an indirect effect on the subsequent industrial development of Mexico."[5] Now an entire new series of studies has been undertaken on the role of organized labor in developing countries; but, with the exception of Robert J. Alexander's work, *Labor Relations in Argentina, Brazil and Chile*, these pertain primarily to the nations of Africa and Asia.[6]

3. Confederación de Cámeras Nacionales de Comercio e Industria de los Estados Unidos Mexicanos, *Análisis Económico Nacional 1934–1940* (México, 1940), p. 36.
4. Alfonso López Aparicio, *El Movimiento Obrero en México: Antecedentes, Desarrolo y Tendencias* (México, 1952), p. 213.
5. Sanford A. Mosk, *Industrial Revolution in Mexico* (Berkeley, 1950), p. 58.
6. Bruce H. Millen, *The Political Role of Labor in Developing Countries* (Washington, D.C., 1963); Wilbert E. Moore, *Industrialization and Labor: Social Aspects of Economic Development* (Ithaca, N.Y., 1951); Walter Galenson

Marjorie Clark's *Organized Labor in Mexico* remains the latest published scholarly work in English on the labor movement of Mexico,[7] although there are several good unpublished theses on certain limited phases of the topic which have been most useful in this study.[8] It is felt that a case study of Mexico just at the time she began her "breakthrough" into the stage of industrialization might make a worthwhile contribution to the new literature on the role of organized labor in developing countries. This view is reinforced by Miron Burgin's statement: "The urgency of more intensive research in the field of Latin American economic history thus becomes apparent. For it is only when the economic past of the Latin American countries is reconstructed that the process of current political and institutional development can be fully understood. It is likely that as a result of such studies many generalizations now current may have to be discarded or seriously modified."[9]

In appreciation of their influence in stimulating my interest in Latin America I should like to express my gratitude to Professors Ruth Allen, Lewis Hanke, and the late Professor Carlos Castañeda. Especially helpful during the course of research have been the comments of Professors Eastin Nelson and Merrill Rippy, both Latin-American scholars of the highest order. For aid and encouragement in making this book possible I am indebted to Dr. S. T. Keim, Jr., Vice-President for Academic Affairs, and to Professor Wallace B. Nelson, Dean, School of Business Administration, both of The University of Texas at Arlington, as well as to Dean Bruce Thomas and Professor Harold F. Clark, both of Trinity University, San Antonio, Texas. Beyond these persons, I should like to thank Dr. Nettie Lee Benson, Latin-American Collections Librarian of The University of Texas at Austin Library for the

---

(ed.), *Labor in Developing Countries* (Berkeley, 1962); Walter Galenson, *Labor and Economic Development* (New York, 1959); Felecia J. Deyrup, "Organized Labor and Government in Underdeveloped Countries: Sources of Conflict," *Industrial and Labor Relations Review* (October, 1958), pp. 1011–12.

7. To this effect, see the remark of Howard F. Cline in "Mexico: A Matured Latin-American Revolution, 1910–1960," *The Annals of the American Academy of Political and Social Science* (March, 1961), p. 91.

8. See James Riley Hayes, "The Mexican Labor Movement, 1931–1951" (M.A. thesis, University of California); Mary Margaret Harker, "Organization of Labor in Mexico Since 1910" (Ph.D. dissertation, University of Southern California); Rachel Newborn Hill, "A Sketch of the Mexican Labor Movement" (M.A. thesis, Columbia University); and the recently published Robert Paul Millon, *Mexican Marxist—Vicente Lombardo Toledano* (Chapel Hill, 1966).

9. Miron Burgin, "Research in Latin American Economics and History," *Inter-American Economic Affairs*, 1 (December, 1947), 18–19.

many courtesies extended during the period of research, and Professor Daniel Cosío Villegas, Director, El Colegio de México, for encouraging research into this topic.

For permission to use in this book, as Chapters III and IV, an article entitled "Labor and the Theory of the Mexican Revolution under Lázaro Cárdenas," which appeared in *The Americas*, XX (October, 1963), my thanks are due to its publisher, The Academy of American Franciscan History, and to Mathias C. Kiemen, O.F.M., Editor of *The Americas*.

For faithful and efficient service in preparation of the manuscript my thanks are extended to Mrs. Margaret McGrade. Naturally, none of these persons bears any responsibility for the book's shortcomings.

Sometime ago, Eugene D. Owen suggested that studies devoted to the analysis of social and labor problems of Latin America might "make a real contribution in the movement for hemisphere solidarity and help in the study of these problems for the benefit of the countries concerned."[10] It is hoped that this work is a step in that direction.

San Antonio, Texas
September, 1967

10. Eugene D. Owen, "Sources of Information on Social and Labor Problems in Latin-America" *Inter-American Bibliographical Review*, 1–2 (Summer, 1941).

Contents

*Organized Labor
and the Mexican Revolution
under Lázaro Cárdenas*

"Only organized labor can force me or any other citizen in power to satisfy the needs of the people."

—Lázaro Cárdenas

I. Historical Background

The predominantly agricultural nature of Mexico, the widely scattered Indian groups in poor communication, together with the strength of the established social structures as it had been since the conquest worked to prevent any change in the Indian masses.[1] During the last years of the nineteenth century, however, Díaz turned his attention to industrialization of the country, holding out the inducement of a cheap labor supply to the foreign capitalists. Industrial laborers were frequently conscripted for a nominal wage, sometimes bought and sold; they were completely without rights and could be discharged or punished at the slightest sign of displeasure with their lot or the

1. The following works on the Mexican labor movement prior to 1934 are the source of much of the narrative presented in this chapter: Marjorie R. Clark, "Historical Background of Mexico's Labor Movement," *Mexican Life*, II (November, 1936), 18; Marjorie R. Clark, *Organized Labor in Mexico* (Chapel Hill, 1934); Wilfrid Hardy Callcott, *Liberalism in Mexico, 1857–1929* (Stanford University, 1931); Rosendo Salazar, *Líderes y Sindicatos* (México, 1953), and *Historia de las Luchas Proletarias de México, 1923–1936* (México, 1958); Víctor Alba, *Historia del Movimiento Obrero en América Latina* (México, 1964); Rafael Ramos Pedrueza, *La Lucha de las Clases a Través de la Historia de México* (México, 1934); Jesús Silva Herzog, *Breve Historia de la Revolución Mexicana: La Etapa Constitucionalista y la Lucha de Facciones* (México, 1960); Mary Margaret Harker, "Organization of Labor in Mexico Since 1910" (Ph.D. dissertation, University of Southern California, 1937); Rachel Newborn Hill, "A Sketch of the Mexican Labor Movement" (M.A. thesis, Columbia University, 1946); Vicente Lombardo Toledano, *La Libertad Sindical en México* (México, 1927).

expression of a desire to improve it. "This period marked Mexico's first essay into industrialism, and working conditions were even worse than before the industrial revolution in England or in the early machine age in other industrial countries."[2]

Trade unionism was not important in Mexico in the nineteenth century; nonetheless, "mutual aid societies" occurred among the railwaymen. In 1888, the Supreme Order of Mexican Railway Employees was formed under the leadership of Nicasio Idar, an employee in the express department of the National Railways. He had spent considerable time in the United States, and even the name of the organization is reminiscent of such societies in this country at that time. The society was strictly mutualist and accomplished little, lasting only three years. Several years later, in 1897, the railwaymen formed a second organization, also mutualist—the Confederation of Railway Societies of the Mexican Republic—and the leaders of this organization were instrumental in establishing, in 1904, the Grand League of Railway Workers, on more clearly defined trade union lines. These railroad societies were not the first formed. A mutualist society called the Union and Concord was set up in the Federal District in 1874; and by 1879, a central organization of mutualist societies calling itself the Grand Labor Congress was in existence. The shoemakers, bakers, musicians, and mechanics created mutual societies, as did the pulque workers, who named their organization the Divine Providence. It is important to note that the leaders of these organizations were always persons closely connected with the government, and the movements really represented an attempt on the part of the government to prevent an undirected worker movement, a phenomenon that was to characterize the Mexican labor movement for years to come.

By the beginning of the twentieth century, Socialist doctrine had commenced to filter into the country, much of it by way of exiled Spanish anarchists. The three principal centers of such activity were Mérida in Yucatán, Mexico City, and Guadalajara. In 1899, José Zaldívar, an exile from Spain, attempted to found a Socialist-anarchist newspaper in Yucatán. Somewhat later, José María Piño Suárez actually began the republication of the newspaper in Yucatán, which carried on a vigorous but brief campaign against the practice of slavery and the abuses to which the Indians were subjected on the henequen plantations.

Similar conditions of slavery existed on the haciendas of the central plateau. About this time, in Mexico City, the brothers Ricardo and

2. Frank Kluckhohn, *The Mexican Challenge* (New York, 1939), p. 229.

Enrique Flores Magón were the center of an anti-Díaz, anarchist group whose members devoted their efforts about equally to the promulgation of anarchist doctrine and to a fight against Díaz. The first number of their newspaper, *Regeneración*, appeared in Mexico City in August, 1900. The following year, they were instrumental in calling a meeting of liberal clubs in San Luis Potosí in which the church was made the chief point of attack. This combination of new social thought and opposition to Díaz was common to all the radical thinkers of the time.

In 1904, the Flores Magón brothers were forced to flee to the United States, where, in San Antonio, Texas, they continued to publish *Regeneración*. The following year, they moved to St. Louis and created the Junta Organizadora, or organizing board of the Mexican Liberal party. A general uprising against Díaz was instituted by the Flores Magón brothers from villages in northern Mexico in 1906, followed by several more futile attempts at revolt.[3] The influence of these leaders was felt by only a small portion of the working class, however. Still, following these efforts, the Grand Circle of Workers was organized in 1906, the Grand Labor League in 1908, and the Typographical Confederation in 1911.[4]

In Guadalajara, a third nucleus of labor organization was led by Ramón Morales, Roque Estrada, Juan I. Martínez, José María Loreto, Primitivo R. Valencia, and others. This group also published a newspaper, *El Obrero Socialista*, and their energy, more definitely than that of the other groups, was concentrated on the formation of trade unions. They denied any relationship with the Flores Magón followers.

As industrialization of the country proceeded, the cost of living rose rapidly, while wages remained almost stationary. The already miserable standard of living became still lower, yet any attempts on the part of workers to improve their condition were strictly prohibited by law. In December, 1904, a request of clerks in certain stores in Mexico City that the stores close for a few hours on Sunday afternoon so alarmed and enraged many proprietors that meetings were called at which it was proposed "to throw into the street" all clerks who had signed petitions for the closing. A few months later, the workers of Guadalajara, under the leadership of Ramón Morales, declared a strike to call attention to the condition of the working classes.

The two strikes of outstanding importance, however, in the pre-

3. Ricardo Flores Magón, *Land and Liberty: Mexico's Battle for Economic Freedom and Its Relation to Labor's Worldwide Struggle* (Los Angeles, 1913).
4. W. J. Hammond, "Mexican Labor and World Affairs," Institute of Public Affairs, *Mexico and the United States: Proceedings of the Fifth Annual Conference Institute of Public Affairs Auspices Carnegie Endowment for International Peace, 1938*, pp. 89–90.

revolutionary period of the Mexican labor movement occurred in 1906 and 1907—one in the mines of Cananea, the other in Orizaba. The one in the mines of Cananea, Sonora, took place in June, 1906, and was ostensibly a strike for higher wages for the Mexican workers who claimed they were discriminated against in comparison with Americans employed in the same mines. Actually, a liberal club in Cananea affiliated with the Flores Magón brothers was active in distributing strike propaganda, and the manifestoes issued called for representative government and for the withdrawal of Díaz from the presidency. The movement, the first strike of importance in Mexican labor history, was accompanied by bloodshed and violence. Buildings were burned, stores sacked, and fights between the strikers and the company men resulted in more than twenty killed and as many wounded. Federal troops were sent to restore order, and some American miners were hurried across the border to help suppress the outbreak in which it was alleged American women and children were at the mercy of Mexican miners. The workers were forced to return to work under the same conditions as before, and all the strike leaders not killed were imprisoned.[5]

The next year saw an even more violent outbreak, this time in the textile industry, the most highly developed industry in Mexico in 1907. The Grand Circle of Free Workers had been formed in the textile mills in July of the previous year, and it adopted principles that were outlined in a manifesto issued by the Flores Magón group in St. Louis on July 1, 1906: "War to the death to the tyrant who sells us, to the merchant who robs us, and to the employer who exploits us, war without quarter . . . by reason or by force."[6] At the end of 1906, the textile manufacturers in Puebla and Tlaxcala issued new regulations with which the workers were not in accord; therefore, a strike was declared in December, 1906, in various textile factories in the two states, and it rapidly spread to Veracruz. Some of the leaders of the Guadalajara movement were in Veracruz at the time and had a part in fomenting the strike.

President Díaz was asked by the employers to act as arbiter, and he conceded to the striking workmen permission to send representatives to lay their claims before him—a move that in itself was un-

5. Rafael Carrillo, *Ricardo Flores Magón: Esbozo Biográfico* (México, 1945); León Díaz Cárdenas, *Cananea, Primer Brote del Sindicalismo en México* (México, 1936); Bernardo Cobos D., "El Movimiento Obrero en México," *Revista Mexicana del Trabajo* (November–December, 1956), p. 46.
6. Clark, "Historical Background," p. 20. The Grand Circle boasted of branch organizations in the states of Jalisco, Oaxaca, Tlaxcala, México, Querétaro, Hidalgo, Puebla, Veracruz, and the Federal District.

precedented, since it was unquestionably the first time that labor in Mexico had been permitted to express its demands. (This practice began a pattern that was to reach its height under President Cárdenas, the major difference being that, under the latter, decisions were generally in favor of labor.) On January 5, 1907, Díaz rendered his decision, which was unfavorable to labor on almost every count. Wages were still to be subject to fines, although these were to be used in the establishment of funds for widows and orphans, whereas before they had reverted to the employers; children under the age of seven years were prohibited from working in textile factories except with the permission of their parents (and then they might work only part-time); publications that the workers might wish to distribute were to be supervised by persons named by the political chief of their districts; and strikes were prohibited. The twelve-hour day was established on the basis of the highest wages paid in each industrial district. Most of these provisions had been included in the regulations issued by the textile employers a few months earlier, and they were the immediate cause of the strike. Before the decision was made public, federal troops were stationed in the various strike centers.

The workers in the Orizaba district refused to accept the decision of Díaz. The largest textile factories of the country were located in this district, including those of Río Blanco, Santa Rosa, and Nogales. The workers, in an attempt to get food, attacked the company stores and, meeting resistance, set fire to the buildings. Federal troops suppressed the strikers; most of the actual fighting took place at the factory of Río Blanco, with considerable loss of life. In Mexican labor circles, January 7, 1907, has become the symbol of martyrdom to the labor cause. The prompt and drastic action of the federal government, together with rigid supervision of the workers, destroyed the Grand Circle of Free Workers.

Despite the ruthless suppression of the textile strike, the leaders of the movement attempted another strike in 1908, this time on the railways in Aguascalientes, where the Grand League of Railway Workers was apparently strongly organized. But when Díaz threatened to mobilize the railway workers, the strike was called off. Furthermore, interest in politics was becoming so great that it overshadowed any interest the workers might have had in striking. Díaz's "Creelman interview," in which he stated that he would welcome the emergence of an opposition party, was taken seriously and aroused tremendous interest in political action. Among the working classes, political organizations sprang up with much the same rapidity which, later, labor unions were to exhibit. Madero's book, *The Presidential Succession,* published in 1910, added to the excitement. Several of the newly formed parties included in their programs demands for social and economic reform, such as the breaking up of landed estates, regulation of the right to strike, and general protection of the workers. Practically all workers' organizations formulated a petition to President Díaz to resign his office.

Meanwhile, political and economic dissatisfaction was rapidly bringing on the revolution of 1910, "which political in its inception, soon made social reform its chief issue, but which only had vague and conflicting ideas as to the direction such social reform should take."[7] Mexican workers tried to support Madero, but there was little organized and militant effort like that which was to characterize succeeding uprisings. In his Plan of San Luis Potosí, Madero did pledge himself to return to the original owners the lands of which they had been despoiled; otherwise, he made no mention of the working classes. Still, this pledge attracted to the Madero cause the great landless class, more numerous in 1910 than at any previous period in Mexico's history. There were, however, among the laboring classes two sources of opposition to Madero: one was the group of anarchists headed by Ricardo and Enrique Flores Magón, and the other was formed of agricultural laborers under Emiliano Zapata. It was the Zapata movement, in the state of Morelos, that indicated the direction the revolution was to take.

The Magonistas and Zapatistas joined forces against Madero, seeing in him a member of the rich as opposed to the poor class, who wanted only to put himself in the place occupied by Díaz and who offered the people nothing save the right to vote. But the masses gave Madero an unprecedented welcome when he entered Mexico City. A stampede toward labor organization began; at last it seemed that all need for secrecy or caution had been removed. Every kind of social theory the Mexican workers had ever heard of was embraced. In most cases, the newly created organizations were without definite aims and without any clear understanding of the place they should fill in the new scheme. Leaders were untrained and the masses of workers undisciplined; it was a period of blind drawing together, since the few previously mentioned strikes had had little effect upon the working class as a whole.

Organization in Mexico City progressed at a particularly rapid pace. On May 2, 1911, the Typographical Confederation of Mexico was formed. Under the leadership of Amadeo Ferrés, a Spaniard, it

7. *Ibid.*, p. 46.

became the nucleus of the first fighting organization in the country after the Grand Circle of Workers of 1906 and the Grand League of Railway Workers of 1908. Later it was to become known as the National Confederation of Graphic Arts, one of the most powerful labor organizations of the country. Another Spanish anarchist, Juan Francisco Moncaleano, was active in organizing the stonemasons' union; he also began publication (in the summer of 1912) of *Luz*. After he was expelled, his group established the Biblioteca y Casa del Obrero, called by its leader, Jacinto Huitrón, the "modern school" or "national school." Its ideology was anarchistic.[8] An organization open to all workers—not limited to any industry or trade—the Grand Labor League, was formed, reaching a membership (according to its president) of 1,220; however, it lasted only a little more than a year.

In December, 1911, Madero created a department of labor under control of the secretary of public development, but it accomplished little toward the solution of labor problems. Its most definite contribution was the calling of a textile convention in Mexico City in July, 1912. Although the convention was to be of both employers and employees, it was in reality a meeting of employers only. A contract was drawn up fixing wages in the mills as well as conditions of work. Even though the workers' place in the convention was limited, it was a great step in advance of 1907 when Díaz had issued arbitrary commands in the textile dispute and had enforced them by use of the army. Those factories not conforming to the stipulations of the convention were to be taxed 8 per cent instead of 4 per cent. The labor contract, the first in Mexico which had even a semblance of collective bargaining, seemed at the moment very radical in its provisions. It limited the working day to ten hours; fixed the minimum wage at 1.45 pesos per day, which had to be paid in "effective" money instead of the various types of tokens good only in company stores; abolished the onerous system of fines; and made it compulsory for employers to answer complaints of their workers within a period of ten days after they were made. No real attempt was made, however, to enforce the agreement, and conditions in the industry remained unchanged.

Meantime, other groups of workers were being formed in Veracruz, in Tampico, in Torreón, and in Yucatán, organizing activity being confined almost entirely to urban workers. Agricultural workers were still outside the organization movement, except in such military en-

8. Rosendo Salazar, *Líderes y Sindicatos* (México, 1953), pp. 17–19.

deavors as that led by Zapata. Finally, in 1912, out of this chaos of organization, came the first group to give coherence to the labor movement, the Casa del Obrero Mundial, or the House of the Workers of the World. As in previous labor movements, this unity was achieved largely through the influence of foreigners, such as Juan Francisco Moncaleano. The organization had many I.W.W. delegates from the United States and other countries as members. Some of its unions also followed the methods of organization of the French Syndicalists. As W. J. Hammond mentioned, "Many uninformed writers have stated that the Mexican labor movement was dominated by Sovietism, but it must be remembered that the most radical period in the history of Mexican labor occurred before the Russian Revolution."[9]

Even though Madero opposed its activities because he feared its radicalism and the influence of foreigners, the Casa was the dominant labor organization until 1918. By the time Madero was forced out of the presidency, some of the tendencies that were later to become characteristic of the Mexican labor movement had clearly emerged. One was the tendency of the unions to lean upon the government. The second characteristic was to follow persons rather than convictions, which, in large measure, prevented the development of any real class consciousness among the working groups. And, finally, there was the desire to protect their interests through legislation.

When Carranza followed Madero and retreated to Veracruz to take stock of the situation, he began to woo groups that could help him re-establish his regime. He called upon labor groups for this support and received it in exchange for concessions to labor. On February 17, 1915, Obregón signed, for Carranza, a document that bound him to sponsor progressive labor laws. In exchange, the Casa del Obrero Mundial organized the famous "Red Battalions." To obtain similar support from the agrarians, Carranza had issued a decree on January 6, 1915, providing for restoration of common lands taken from villages in previous regimes.[10] When the constitutional convention met in Querétero in 1917, Mexican labor was fully and fairly represented. Already, in 1915, the Casa del Obrero Mundial had made an agreement with President Carranza to support him against Villa if he, in turn, would guarantee labor full protection in the forthcoming constitution, and he was compelled by a combination of organized labor with the agrarians under Zapata and Soto y Gama, with other liberal forces, to live up to this agreement when the constitution was finally

9. Hammond, "Mexican Labor and World Affairs," p. 90.
10. Clarence Senior, *Mexico in Transition* (New York, 1939), p. 7.

formulated.[11] Among the most prominent orators and decisively influential persons at the constitutional convention were Francisco Múgica (later to be minister of communications and public works) and Felix Palavicini. Some people called Múgica the "Lenin of Mexico," seeing a certain physical and philosophical resemblance between him and the Russian leader. Among the allies of General Múgica in making fundamental changes in the 1857 Constitution and in getting Article 123 included was Heriberto Jara, who had gone into the revolution from the Río Blanco textile mills, having worked there at the time of the strike in which Díaz soldiers fired on the strikers. He was also a leader in educational reform.[12]

Supporting these two reformers was Cándido Aguilar, who, together with the delegation from Yucatán, insisted on an entire article devoted to workers' rights.[13] The result was Article 123—the longest in the Mexican Constitution, and in some ways the most fundamental —which provided for a modern labor program, not only allowing labor to organize, but prescribing in detail the eight-hour day, the protection of women and children in every industry, and most of the modern ideas of labor protection.[14]

According to Inman, Article 123 was written not so much to meet the actual conditions in Mexico as to express an ideal and to strike at the foreign industrialists and Mexican *hacendados* who were indifferent to the laborers' welfare. Professor Stocking commented: "Such a labor code established by constitutional mandate in a country 70% of whose population gains its livelihood in agriculture and allied activities and less than 15% of which is directly engaged in industry, is certainly an anomaly if not a paradox. A country with no organized

11. William E. Walling, *The Mexican Question: Mexico and American-Mexican Relations under Calles and Obregón* (New York, 1927), pp. 94–95.

12. J. H. Plenn, *Mexico Marches* (New York, 1939), pp. 158–59.

13. Secretaría de Gobernación, *Diário de los Debates del Congreso Constituyente de 1916–1917*, I, 684, 701; Alfonso López Aparicio, *El Movimiento Obrero en México: Antecedentes, Desarrollo y Tendencias* (México, 1952), pp. 168–69. In this connection, it is interesting to note that Frank Tannenbaum apparently discounted the work of these men, since he said: "Article 123 could have been written into the Constitution only in a political vacuum, where the interest most affected had neither voice nor representation." Frank Tannenbaum, *Mexico: The Struggle for Peace and Bread* (New York, 1950), p. 114.

14. Samuel Guy Inman, *Latin America: Its Place in World Life* (New York, 1947), p. 264. Specific provisions of this article are discussed at some length in a later chapter. See Alberto Trueba Urbina (ed.), *Constitución Política de los Estados Unidos Mexicanos (Anotada). Textos Vigentes y Sus Limitaciones Durante el Estado de Guerra* (México, 1944); Gudelia Gómez, *El Artículo 123 Constitucional y los Sindicatos* (México, 1954). For an English translation of Article 123, see Gilberto Bosques, *The National Revolutionary Party of Mexico and the Six-Year Plan* (Mexico, 1937), p. 259.

labor class to wage its battles and with no native bourgeoisie to fight enacts the most liberal labor code that has yet made its appearance in organized society."[15]

According to Tannenbaum, the theory upon which the labor law was elaborated may not have been new, but it was foreign to Mexican experience. It was a sudden application of imported doctrine unrelated to Mexican conditions. It was a future aim written into the law. He maintained that the aim of Article 123 projected a national working class to counterbalance a foreign industrialist class; it was an effort to develop new sources of national political power based upon workers' organizations. He continued: "In a sense, a limited syndicalized state was foreshadowed, wherein the union, with the support of the State, would become not merely a protective agency in defense of the workers, but also an instrument of the newly discovered nationalistic policy. The important point to remember, however, is that the union was to be the creature of and subordinate to the State. A partnership between the State and the labor unions has been established in the law, the first being the major partner."[16] As Enrique González Aparicio pointed out, state interest found its legality in the Constitution of 1917.[17]

Carranza was inaugurated constitutional president of Mexico on May 1, 1917. Soon he was to show great hostility to militant union action and to peasant seizure of land they thought was theirs, a hostility that led to a break between him and General Obregón. In the struggle that ensued, General Obregón was successful and was inaugurated president of Mexico on December 1, 1920, after another military contest in which Carranza was killed by a traitorous general. The new regime was supported by the newly organized Confederación Regional Obrera Mexicana (C.R.O.M.), which had organized the Partido Laborista in 1919 that nominated Obregón for president against Carranza. The railway and other unions had greatly aided in the campaign against Carranza by sabotage and by sending the "Red Battalions" again into the field.[18]

A meeting of Mexican labor groups, preliminary to the founding

---

15. George Ward Stocking, "The Mexican Oil Problem," Institute of Public Affairs, *Mexico and the United States: Proceedings of the Fifth Annual Conference Institute of Public Affairs Auspices Carnegie Endowment for International Peace*, p. 56.

16. Tannenbaum, *Mexico: The Struggle for Peace and Bread*, pp. 114–15.

17. Enrique González Aparicio, "New Forms of Industrial Organization in Mexico," *Annals of Collective Economy: International Review in Four Editions* (Geneva, 1939), p. 96.

18. Senior, *Mexico in Transition*, pp. 7–8.

of the C.R.O.M., was held in Saltillo in May, 1918. Its chief purpose was to support the fulfillment of Article 123 and to align itself with revolutionary governments. The first year was absorbed mostly in preliminary motions, and the C.R.O.M. was not definitely organized until its convention at Zacatecas in June, 1919. Within a year of its founding, the C.R.O.M. underwent a very rapid evolution in two directions. First, the ultra-radical elements, which were in considerable force at the first convention and were still more strongly represented at the second (consisting at that time of Communists, the I.W.W., revolutionary Socialists, and radical agrarian elements) all left the C.R.O.M. in 1920—some of them to be reorganized the following year in the Confederación General de Trabajadores (C.G.T.), a labor organization patterned after the French model. Secondly, in 1920, there also took place the foundation of the Partido Laborista, mentioned above, under the leadership of Luis N. Morones, the general secretary and chief founder of the C.R.O.M.[19]

Almost from the beginning, the C.R.O.M. included a large majority of the organized workers of Mexico, although the railway unions remained outside this federation. With the appearance of the C.R.O.M., the labor movement in Mexico became a movement of trade unions patterned after the labor movement of the United States rather than following the syndicalist, Marxian, or Soviet type of socialism. The policies of the C.R.O.M. were generally those of the dominant national political party; however, when the interests of the leaders were ignored by the national president of Mexico, the activities of the labor group could be organized against him. There was a smaller number of men within the C.R.O.M., known as the Grupo Acción, dominated largely by Morones, having eighteen members and remaining about the same size during its entire period of existence.[20]

The American Federation of Labor (A.F. of L.) greatly influenced labor organization in Mexico during the 1920's and in 1924 the president of the C.R.O.M., Juan Rico, said: "I want to take advantage of this opportune moment to say that the organized labor movement in Mexico is proud of its strength because it has achieved what strength it has today through the cooperation, the experience and the advice of Samuel Gompers, and also the cooperation of the various organi-

19. Walling, *The Mexican Question*, pp. 95–96.
20. Hammond, "Mexican Labor and World Affairs," p. 91. Clark, *Organized Labor in Mexico*, pp. 5–6. For a detailed picture of C.R.O.M. and Luis Morones, see Joseph H. Retinger, *Morones de México: Historia del Movimiento Obrero en Ese País* (México, 1927); Anfonso López Aparicio, *El Movimiento Obrero en México*, Ch. XI.

zations that compose the American Federation of Labor."[21] In 1924 there was a meeting in El Paso and Júarez between representatives of the C.R.O.M. and the A.F. of L., whose president went to Mexico City to attend the inauguration of President Calles. Samuel Gompers, though tired and sick, moved from place to place celebrating the triumph of Mexican labor under the leadership of Morones. It was while presiding over the meetings of the Pan-American Federation in Mexico City that Gompers collapsed and, a few days later, on December 13, 1924, died in San Antonio, Texas.

The Constitution of the C.R.O.M. abandoned the anarcho-syndicalist doctrine, accepting the theory of the class conflict and the future abolition of private property, still contemplating, however, both syndicalist and political action.[22] The program of the C.R.O.M. consisted of two parts: the defense and execution of the Constitution of 1917 and economic nationalism. Secretary Treviño of the C.R.O.M. remarked that only by those means would Mexico "be able to rid itself of the constant, overhanging menace from the United States."[23] The Labor party and the C.R.O.M. were influential political forces not because they controlled the government but rather because they so loyally supported it and because they were the backbone of the "revolutionary" or constitutionalist forces. Acting alone, they probably would have had little power, for they did not constitute a majority (or anything like a majority) of the Obregón and Calles elements. They were the most militant forces against every type of reaction. While it was probably true that Obregón and Calles could not have maintained themselves without the aid of the Mexican labor movement, it was equally true that the Mexican labor movement would have amounted to little, and the labor and land clauses, as well as the entire structure of the constitution, would have become a dead letter if the revolutionary forces (held together by Calles and Obregón) had disintegrated or if the government had been overthrown. As we shall see, this same analysis could be made of the Cárdenas regime.

At the beginning of his administration, Obregón fastened his hopes largely on the agrarian movement, since the peasants outnumbered the industrial workers two to one. But they were difficult to mobilize and by far the most successful mobilization turned out to be that undertaken by the leading labor confederation, the C.R.O.M. It claimed in 1927 a million peasant members, two-thirds of its member-

21. Quoted in Hammond, "Mexican Labor and World Affairs," p. 92.
22. Vicente Lombardo Toledano, "The Labor Movement," *The Annals of the American Academy of Political and Social Science*, 208 (March, 1940), 50.
23. Walling, *The Mexican Question*, pp. 105–6.

ship, and a considerable part of the entire peasant population. The C.R.O.M. regarded the peasants as agricultural laborers—a branch of the labor movement—rather than as small landowners. Walling felt that the official estimates of 500,000 industrial workers belonging to the C.R.O.M. was too large; nevertheless by 1927 a majority of the industrial workers of Mexico was organized, and a large majority of these organized workers was affiliated with the C.R.O.M.[24]

The C.R.O.M. was a highly centralized body and within it the Grupo Acción contributed from one-third to four-fifths of the total income. Since most of the members of this small group were government officials or Labor party members of the Senate and House, the donations of this group to the C.R.O.M. became one of the chief bases of the accusation that the confederation was supported by the government.[25] Luis N. Morones, founder and first president of the C.R.O.M., was the first great Mexican labor leader of the revolutionary period, the earlier leaders, from Madero through Carranza, doing very little to aid the cause of organized labor.[26] Other leaders of unions affiliated with the C.R.O.M. included Ricardo Treviño, Eduardo Moneda, Fernando Rodarte, Ezequiel Salcedo, Alfredo Pérez Medina, Salvador Alvarez, Reinaldo Cervantes Torres, Juan Lozano, José López Cortés, Juan B. Fonseca, and José López Dóñez.[27] During Obregón's term, a growing coolness developed between the president and General Plutarco Elias Calles, his chief aid, over Obregón's policies toward foreign capital, trade unions, and the peasants. Still, in 1924, when Calles succeeded Obregón as president, he became known as the first "labor president" of Mexico. Calles finally made Morones secretary of the Department of Industry, Commerce, and Labor in the cabinet. Morones became rich, and the labor leaders, whether heads of national unions or sections (locals) followed his example. Companies slipped money to labor leaders to have strikes called off or arrested. Morones was even made an honorary vice-president of the A.F. of L.[28]

During the administrations of General Obregón (1920–24) and General Plutarco Elias Calles (1924–28), the Mexican labor movement made considerable progress, not only in the number of unions formed, but also in the political power of a united proletariat. But, said Lombardo Toledano, the man who was to lead the movement under Cárdenas:

24. *Ibid.*, p. 98.
25. *Ibid.*, p. 100.
26. Kluckhohn, *The Mexican Challenge*, p. 229.
27. Rosendo Salazar, *Líderes y Sindicatos*, pp. 10–11.
28. Kluckhohn, *The Mexican Challenge*, p. 230.

Nevertheless—and this was to have incalculable consequences for the future—the masses did not develop a consciousness of their historic role. Since the organization leaders did not orient the workers in regard to the theory of the class conflict and the immediate and the ultimate objectives of the proletariat, the false notion was conceived that the presence of several members of the C.R.O.M in the government was a truly revolutionary device which would make it possible to effect the transition from a bourgeois society to a socialistic society without a great crisis.[29]

In characterizing the status of the labor movement during the period from 1910 to 1928, the Mexican economic historian, López Aparicio, wrote that the natural fear of business enterprise toward the organized labor movement, the numerous strikes and conflicts—many times artificial—the corruption of the labor leaders, the political exploitation of the workers in their electoral masquerades, the shameful spectacles of the fights between unions (jurisdictional disputes), and the radical program of the unions strongly hindered the prestige of the movement among the upper classes (generally hostile), the middle classes (generally indifferent), and even spread confusion and distrust among the workers themselves. According to this authority, the entire country developed a feeling of ill will toward the organized worker movement.[30] Francisco Bulnes, in 1926, summarized the situation rather pessimistically when he wrote that "Mexico, like all nations with a proletarian class under the influence of the modern doctrine, is in crisis and is almost certain to have begun a period of disaster under communist and syndicalist indoctrination."[31]

After 1928, the C.R.O.M. lost much strength and in time broke into numerous local groups and centrals, recruiting dissident members from the old C.R.O.M. led by Morones. The C.G.T. (General Confederation of Workers), "unalterable in its anarcho-syndicalist creed," was visibly strengthened. In 1930, three large groups of the labor movement separated from the C.R.O.M.: the Printers Union (la Confederación de Artes Gráficas), the Iron and Metalworkers Union (la Confederación de Ferroviários), and the Textile Workers Union (la Federación de Sindicatos de la Industria Textil). These groups united into the Local Federation of Workers of the Federal District (la Federación Local de Trabajadores del Distrito Federal) and the federa-

29. Lombardo Toledano, "The Labor Movement," p. 50.
30. López Aparicio, *El Movimiento Obrero en México*, p. 211.
31. Francisco Bulnes, *Los Grandes Problemas de México* (México, 1926), p. 5.

tions of Veracruz, Michoacan, Guanajuato, Baja California, and Tamaulipas. All of these organizations affiliated themselves with the C.G.T., whose membership in 1931 included ninety-six unions with eighty thousand individuals. The following year saw the birth of the Chamber of Labor of the Federal District (la Cámara del Trabajo del Distrito Federal), formed also from unions that had deserted the C.R.O.M.[32]

Upon the assassination of Obregón on the eve of his second term of office, Calles placed in the presidential chair, in November, 1928, the first of three puppets, Emilio Portes Gil. Even before this time, Calles and his men had begun to reap the rewards of governmental position, to align themselves with foreign business interests, and to control new industries and *haciendas* in Mexico. The leaders of the revolution had begun to grow tired of labor troubles.[33] Pórtes Gil was followed in the presidency by Pascual Ortíz Rubio, who took office in February, 1930, as the successful candidate of the newly organized National Revolutionary party; but after two years, Calles replaced Ortíz Rubio with General Abelardo Rodríguez, a more forceful but no less obedient office-holder. Lombardo Toledano claims that the terms of all three of these men were characterized by the failure of the government to support either the essential program of the labor movement, the completion of the agrarian reform, or the national struggle of Mexico against the foreign economic forces "that have interfered, sometimes illegally, in its domestic concerns."[34] In the opinion of some writers on this period of the labor movement in Mexico, the government of President Rodríguez was hostile to union organization in order to encourage the investment of capital from the United States. José Mancisidor wrote: ". . . during the administration of Calles, Gil, Rubio, and Rodríguez, the national interests were delivered unto the interests of Yankee imperialism, which accounts for the great number of frauds and persecutions perpetuated against the revolutionary elements which remained firm and without a halt."[35]

Meanwhile, Vicente Lombardo Toledano, after suffering defeat as a candidate for secretary general of the C.R.O.M., had split away with a few followers and organized a number of labor unions into the Confederación General de Obreros y Campesinos de México (the General Confederation of Workers and Peasants of Mexico), known as the

32. López Aparicio, *El Movimiento Obrero en México*, pp. 211–12.
33. Senior, *Mexico in Transition*, p. 24.
34. Lombardo Toledano, "The Labor Movement," pp. 50–51.
35. Quoted in López Aparicio, *El Movimiento Obrero en México*, p. 212.

C.G.O.C.M., an organization "considered superior to the C.R.O.M. both in theoretical foundation and in honesty."[36] The two purposes of the C.G.O.C.M. were, first, to organize all the workers of Mexico, and, second, to instill in them a class consciousness.[37] At the Constituent Congress held October 26 to 31, 1933, the declaration of principles "synthesized the aspirations of all organized labor, taking as the basis the struggle against the capitalist order," using two tactics —revolutionary syndicalism: the strike, boycott, manifesto, publicity of injustices, and the establishment of a school exclusively for the proletariat to the end of developing a class consciousness which "will be a bulwark against imperialist attacks and against the bourgeosie regime"; and second, the development of an ample program for economic revindication.[38]

Before the formation of the C.G.O.C.M., the Mexican working class was divided into various groups, caused in part by the "counter-revolutionary conduct of the leaders of the C.R.O.M."; and the C.G.O.C.M. was the national trade union body that unified the majority of the unions belonging to the C.R.O.M., as well as other important groups of the working class. The C.G.O.C.M. "forced the labor authorities by moral pressure" to hand down decisions of vital importance to the working class of the country; it worked zealously for the unification of the trade-union groups, as the only means by which to achieve a change in the policy of the government with respect to the unsolved problems of the Mexican Revolution, and the renewal of the "struggle of the working masses against native capitalists and foreign imperialism."[39] While this process of the unification of the Mexican working class was well on the way toward realization, General Lázaro Cárdenas became president of the nation and a new era in the history of Mexico and the Mexican labor movement dawned.

36. Henry Bamford Parkes, *A History of Mexico* (Boston, 1950), pp. 398–99. See also Lombardo Toledano, "The Labor Movement," p. 51, and Alberto Morales Jiménez, *Historia de la Revolución Mexicana* (México, 1951), pp. 49–64, 225–27.

37. Antonio Bernal, Jr., "De Como y Porqué se Formo la Confederación General de Obreros y Campesinos de México y su Primer Congreso Ordinario," *Futuro*, II (December, 1934), 3–7.

38. *Ibid.*, p. 5.

39. Confederación de Trabajadores de México, *Informe del Comité Nacional 1936–1937* (México, 1938), pp. 63–64.

II. Cárdenas and Labor:
The First Year

In 1934, General Lázaro Cárdenas was nominated by the National Revolutionary party, and, after an intensive campaign that took him to every part of the country, was elected president of Mexico. His election was followed by the first peaceful revolution in Mexican history. Lázaro Cárdenas was strongly influenced by General Francisco Múgica, leader of the leftist forces at the constitutional convention and responsible for the socialist ideas contained in the 1917 Constitution. Few men have possessed the qualities of a leader of the masses that Cárdenas had.[1]

During the years 1925 to 1928, while he was chief of military operations in the Huasteca region on the gulf coast, center of the greatest oil boom on the continent, Cárdenas began to develop the social ideas that were to be his guide from 1934 to 1940. The Tampico boom had just passed its peak and was declining, and Cárdenas had been a soldier for twelve years; what he saw during his stay in the oil fields left him with no doubts about the path he must follow. He could no longer endure the shame of Mexicans being abused by foreigners. For Cárdenas, as for most Mexicans, there were no differences among men because of the color of their skin or the language

1. Victoriano Anguiano Equihua, *Lázaro Cárdenas: Su Feudo y la Política Nacional* (México, 1951), p. 38.

they spoke; he could not understand why one set of men had neat, comfortable, screened houses up on the hills, while others were dumped on the edge of the jungle swamps in ,miserable shacks. General Cárdenas left the oil fields, his mind made up to enter politics. He already had many ideas, including the belief that soldiers and civilian workers should fraternize instead of remaining apart.[2]

In a speech on June 30, 1934, on the eve of his election, Cárdenas sanctioned all the principles expressed in the Six-Year Plan, basic document of the National Revolutionary party published in 1933, as a governmental program, and urged the grouping of the dispersed elements of labor so that they might effectively participate in government.[3] The president-elect proclaimed that the system of collective labor contracts should be strengthened until it became exclusive; urged the adoption of a "clause of exclusion" (a closed shop), which would eliminate the action of unorganized labor, and the abolition of company unions. He then gave his interpretation of the mandates of the Six-Year Plan by promising that, in accordance with the provisions of the document, he would give all aid to co-operative organization in the republic, which would enable the workers progressively to control the sources of wealth and of productive instruments and which he saw as the ideal of the Socialist doctrine of the revolution. With regard to the direction national economic policy would take, he remarked: "In order for this to succeed, it is indispensable to realize the principles of the Six-Year Plan, which provide for the formation of a national economy directed and regulated by the state, which will free Mexico from the character of a country possessing a colonial economy, a field for exploiting human effort, wherein the only essential inducement which inspires capital is that of obtaining prime materials by the hand of cheap labor."[4]

Future events were to demonstrate that Cárdenas took the Six-Year Plan seriously, as the major portion of his economic policy was, in fact, simply putting into effect the dictates of the plan. Since the labor policy of the Cárdenas administration was based on this official document, it may be well at this point to note a few of the sections pertinent to the worker movement. (A more detailed analysis of the labor theory embodied in the plan is reserved for a subsequent chapter.) Ramón Beteta observed that Mexico's Six-Year Plan had one fundamental aim: to change the economic conditions of the country for

2. J. H. Plenn, *Mexico Marches* (New York, 1939), p. 128.
3. Lázaro Cárdenas, "General Cárdenas' Platform: Address to the Nation on the Eve of His Election by President-Elect Cárdenas, June 30, 1934" (Robert H. Murray, tr.), *Modern Mexico*, V (August, 1934), 9.
4. *Ibid.*, p. 10.

the benefit of its laboring classes, so that they might live in dignity and comfort, a fuller life. He maintained that the Six-Year Plan was more than a political platform used to attract votes but, rather, it implied self-criticism and was a revision of the revolutionary proposals, ideals, and principles.[5]

The plan stated that "Every individual, as a consequence of the obligations society imposes upon him to contribute with his energy to the collective development, has a right to the work which permits him to satisfy his needs and honest pleasures."[6] As Beteta confessed, this statement is merely a beautiful concept, but the next principle provided: "The State will intervene, directly or indirectly to the end that every individual in the Republic be able to exercise his right to work." The third principle stated that the provisions of Articles 24 and 123 of the Federal Constitution of 1917 would be enforced until they "constitute an integral reality in our social affairs. . . ." The fourth point dealt directly with labor policy techniques in that it held, "The collective bargaining of wage earners will be urged, with a tendency toward making it the only, or at least the preponderant, form of established relationship between owners and workers, to which effect it will be imperative to include in the collective contracts of labor the clause by which the owner is obliged not to admit non-syndicalized elements."[7]

Concerning the rights of agricultural labor, the Six-Year Plan called for a minimum wage; free housing, furnished with hygienic comforts indispensable for safeguarding life and health; timber from the timberlands of the farm where they are employed, provided timberlands are there, for repairing or enlarging their dwellings; free medical and pharmaceutical care; land for growing household produce, and for the pasturage of their own livestock; free use of water for their home requirements and for their animals; and all other rights established by the Federal Labor Law, "to the end that the countryside wage-earner may rise to the economic and social position to which he is justly entitled as a factor and as a primary element in the agricultural production of the country."[8]

With regard to the question of small private land holdings or com-

---

5. Ramón Beteta (ed.), *Programa Económico y Social de México (Una Controversia)* (México, 1935), p. 210; Beteta, *The Mexican Revolution: A Defense* (México, 1937), p. 28.
6. See Partido Nacional Revolucionario, *Plan Sexenal del P.N.R.* (México, 1934); Gilberto Bosques, *The National Revolutionary Party of Mexico and the Six-Year Plan* (Mexico, 1937).
7. Beteta, *The Mexican Revolution*, pp. 40–43.
8. Gilberto Bosques, *The National Revolutionary Party*, pp. 146–47.

munal holdings, the plan decided in favor of the former. Ramón Beteta felt that this situation was unfortunate since, in his opinion, it would not solve the agrarian problem; nor was it a "productive system compatible with contemporary agricultural techniques." In Beteta's words, "To stop without the distribution of the land, and not to take advantage of the opportunity for its complete socialization, is not only a weakness, but a danger, the danger that in its agrarian aspect the Revolution, having triumphed, will die through not having been carried to its logical conclusion."[9]

Finally, the plan stated: "Confronting the class struggle inherent in the system of production in which we live, the Party and the Government have the duty of contributing to the strengthening of the syndical organizations of the working classes." Beteta explained:

> It is not, then, the intention of the Six-Year Plan to do away with the class struggle, since that would carry the Government fatally in the direction of facism. On the contrary, it recognizes as essential within the capitalist regime— the existence of which it does not at the moment seem to wish to destroy—the struggle of the two social classes created by the right of private property: those who possess the instruments of production, and the proletariat. In this struggle the Party does not remain neutral, but frankly decides in favor of the workers, implying its desire to do away with, not the class struggle, but the classes themselves, by means of the growth of the proletariat, since to strengthen one of the two contenders logically means to look forward to the weakening and final overthrow of the other.[10]

In spite of these observations, Inman maintained that the plan did not represent a distinct turn toward socialism since a study of the plan seemed to show that, after all, there was much emphasis on the protection of private property.[11] On this theme, Ramón Beteta himself concluded that the plan was not revolutionary in the sense in which the term was used outside Mexico, since it did not pretend to attain a radical change in the economic organization of the country. He emphasized that in respecting private property the plan was far from proposing a socialism analogous to that of Soviet Russia.[12] He

9. Beteta, *The Mexican Revolution*, pp. 37–39.

10. *Ibid.*, p. 44. See also: Mexican Government, *Policies of the Present Administration of Mexico* (Mexico, 1936), pp. 41–45.

11. Samuel Guy Inman, "Spirit of the Mexican Revolution," Institute of Public Affairs, *Mexico and the United States: Proceedings of the Fifth Annual Conference Institute of Public Affairs Auspices Carnegie Endowment for International Peace* (1938), p. 25.

12. Beteta, *The Mexican Revolution*, p. 45.

explained this situation, seemingly contradictory to some students of the Mexican scene, on the ground that the Mexican Revolution had kept an ambition, on the one hand, to bring the country out of an oppressive feudalism into a semi-liberal, bourgeois state and, on the other hand, to direct the future along the way toward scientific socialism. Nonetheless, Narciso Bassols, speaking at a meeting to commemorate the twentieth anniversary of the Russian Revolution, which filled to overflowing the Palace of Fine Arts in Mexico City, took issue with the argument to the effect that the Mexican Revolution is a unique phenomenon in the world, something *sui generis* and having nothing to do with other social movements in other countries. He denounced this view, held by "Mexican conservatives and even by some revolutionary members of the government and the official party (including President Cárdenas)" as "pure camouflage," and "an essentially reactionary attempt to isolate the Mexican masses from the exploited peoples of the rest of the world."[13]

In any case, to make a beginning toward the efforts at worker unification that he had promised, in August, 1934, President Cárdenas called together for a convention the workers and employers of the country in what was to become known as the First Mexican Industrial Congress. The theme of the conference was the discussion of problems of the collective organization of labor, strikes, lockouts, collective contracts, and the nature and function of the boards of conciliation and arbitration, along with the problem of social security. Employers, workers, official representatives of the government, and technical specialists studied these problems. The employer sector presented a united front, voting always as a block. And for the first time in meetings of this sort, the worker sector also presented a united front, avoiding the usual sectional strife.[14]

With regard to the point of trade union organization, the worker representatives proposed a reform to the Federal Labor Law of 1931 making union membership obligatory, with only one union to each business or industry—industrywide collective bargaining. Various proposals were presented toward a more liberal regulation of strikes, and some restrictions on this right were opposed by the workers. At the same time, the workers opposed obligatory arbitration of labor-management conflicts. With regard to lockouts, the worker representatives expressed their desire that the Federal Labor Law be modified

13. Workers University of Mexico, *Mexican Labor News* (November 11, 1937), p. 2.
14. *Memoria del Primer Congreso Mexicano de Derecho Industrial* (México, 1934), p. 7.

to make these more difficult to carry out; they also desired to add to the law provisions for the unions to assume the management of businesses under employer lockouts.[15] Concerning the basic doctrine of the labor movement, the Congress accepted as a conclusion that "labor unity should be the result of the evolution of the working class and not the product or the consequence of an act of authority." None of the themes discussed by this first Congress, however, influenced the modification of the Federal Labor Law or resulted in any substitute legislation for it.

The labor movement did not rush to support Cárdenas; rather, the C.G.O.C.M. continued to organize warily and to wait for results. With Cárdenas barely in office, a rash of strikes broke out. The long-threatened strike against the Canadian-owned Mexican Tramways Co., Ltd., began—the first important strike in Mexico City against a foreign corporation. This company was, in the words of Millan, one of the most arrogant in existence, having come to Mexico in the time of Díaz, who gave it a contract to run streetcars for ninety-nine years. The contract stated that the company did not even have to pave beneath its lines, so it ran its antiquated trams, endangering life and liberty.[16] The strike lasted thirty-eight days and ended in what Millan calls a complete victory for the workers. About this time, the Mexican courts and labor arbitration boards, in which the government representatives had the deciding vote, began to make decisions that consistently favored labor. Formerly, although there was advanced labor law, this was always interpreted against the workers; now, the labor conflicts were decided in their favor.[17]

In Mata Redonda, Veracruz, seven hundred workers of the Huasteca Petroleum Company (Standard Oil of New Jersey subsidiary) returned to work after a four months' strike. The Federal Board of Arbitration and Conciliation based its decision in favor of the workers on a report made by a special investigating committee which proved that the company heads and many important employees—most of them foreigners—lived in luxurious bungalows that were usually pointed out to visitors as the workers' houses. The workers actually lived in huts that had no conveniences whatsoever, eight toilets being shared by 150 families. The labor law required that every company

15. Alfonso López Aparicio, *El Movimiento Obrero en México* (Mexico, 1952), pp. 212–13.

16. Verna C. Millan, *Mexico Reborn* (Boston, 1939), pp. 87–88. See also Virginia Prewett, *Reportage on Mexico* (New York, 1941), pp. 94–95; Maurice Halperin, "Mexico, the Incredible. What's Happening Over the Border and Why They Like It," *Current History*, 45 (November, 1936), 47–52.

17. Enrique González Aparicio, "Actitud del Gobierno ante el Movimiento Obrero," *Revista de Economía*, III (May–August, 1939), 83–84.

furnish a schoolhouse for the children of laborers. There were 135 children in Mata Redonda; the schoolhouse had benches for 60, and the rest were forced to stand all day to hear their lessons. This strike, because of these and similar conditions, received great publicity and awakened an unprecedented demonstration of solidarity among labor organizations.[18]

In Mexico City, the employees of the San Rafael Paper Company (Spanish-French capital) picketed the plant for twenty-four days until they won union recognition, rest-day pay, and other concessions. In Tabasco, completely under control of Governor Tomás Garrido Canabal, five thousand workers walked out on the River Transport Company, operated by an American banana trust. This was the first time in fifteen years that the labor movement had dared defy Garrido Canabal, and the atmosphere was one of intense repression and brutality.[19]

The crowning blow came, however, when the Mexican Telephone and Telegraph Company (American Telephone and Telegraph sister company) was idled for a month because of a strike. Calles had watched with utter silence the events of the first six months—the petroleum workers' strike, the tramway strike, and the San Rafael Paper Company strike. But now, when the strikers touched the sacred subsidiary of the A.T. & T., they committed a crime indeed, because Calles had a large block of shares in the company and naturally rose avengingly to protect them.[20] The employees struck on May 22, 1935, with seven pesos as a reserve fund. After sending telegrams to allied organizations asking support, they allegedly had only seventy-five centavos left on which to begin the strike. The workers made various demands on the company, but their chief complaint centered upon a collective contract and the right to organize freely. The union had originally been a "white" union, controlled by the company; but the workers, through the tactic of boring from within, had finally succeeded in getting control by placing several people of their confidence at its head. This strike had widespread sympathy from the beginning; one organization after another offered its help—both moral and economic. Lombardo Toledano brought the entire C.G.O.C.M. to the fore with the threat of a general strike that would affect not only Mexico City but the entire country as well. The Electricians' Union, one of the most powerful and solidly based in the nation, announced a date for a sympathy strike.[21]

Meantime, Calles waited for President Cárdenas to take some ac-

18. Millan, *Mexico Reborn*, pp. 88–89.
19. *Ibid.*
20. *Ibid.*, p. 90; Prewett, *Reportage on Mexico*, pp. 94–95.
21. Millan, *Mexico Reborn*, pp. 90–91.

tion—to make some pronouncement—which would indicate that the president was still of the same opinion as the former political leader of the country. But Cárdenas bided his time. On June 11, 1935, a group of senators, headed by Ezequiel Padilla, visited Calles' residence in the resort city of Cuernavaca. The following morning, *El Universal* headlined the event with the title, "Calles Makes Sensational Declaration." Perhaps not since the time of Díaz had any leader made quite so firm a defense of foreign capital and, at the same time, condemned so bitterly the struggle of organized labor to defend its rights. Because the statement was to trigger a break between Calles and Cárdenas and to have tremendous consequences for the cause of Mexican economic development, it is quoted at some length:

> For six months the country has been shaken by strikes, many of them entirely unjustified. The workers' organizations in many cases are making themselves examples of ingratitude, for strikes hurt capital much less than they hurt the Government, because they cut off from the State its means of prosperity. Thus the good intentions and the tireless work of the President are constantly obstructed. . . . It is unfair of the workers to cause this damage to a Government headed by such an honest and sincere friend of labor as is General Cárdenas. . . . I know the history of all these organizations since they were created; I know their leaders, both old and new. I know that they do not agree among themselves and that they are torn in opposite directions by Navarrete (of the Labor Chamber) and by Lombardo Toledano (head of C.G.O.C.M.), who are responsible for this confusion. I know of what they are capable, and I can state that in all this agitation there are lively ambitions involved, very dangerous in people and organizations without adequate preparations. They are risking the economic life of the nation, without responding to the President's generosity and definite pro-labor inclinations. . . .
>
> Strikes are declared against a State which oppresses workers and denies their rights; but in a country where the Government protects them, aids them, and surrounds them with guarantees, then to disturb the economic progress of the nation is not merely ingratitude; it is treason.[22]

This declaration by Calles was received jubilantly by the press in general, but the semiofficial government paper, *El Nacional*, waited to see what role Cárdenas would take. Still the president made no statement.

22. *El Universal*, June 11, 1935.

On the same day that the Calles declaration was published, June 12, 1935, the officers of the Mexican Electricians' Union called all other local centrals and independent unions to an emergency meeting. (Only the C.R.O.M. and the C.G.T. were missing, and by then they were of only minor importance.) From the meeting came a unanimous declaration, signed by all the important organized labor groups in the country. The National Committee for Proletarian Defense was organized, and the following day, June 13, the group published an answer to Calles, branding him a traitor of the revolution and an enemy of the Mexican working class. The committee also undertook the task of working for the formation of a new trade union federation, which was to become a reality and was to be the strongest in the history of the Mexican labor movement.[23]

Within forty-eight hours, in the papers of June 14, 1935, appeared the reply of Cárdenas to the Calles statement:

> With regard to the labor difficulties which have risen during the past few months, which have resulted in several strikes, I consider that they are the result of the adjustment of the interests represented by the two factors of production. If they cause some uneasiness, and even temporarily injure the economy of the country, when settled reasonably and with a spirit of equanimity and social justice, they contribute, with time, to making the economic situation more stable, since their rightful solution brings about better conditions for the workers, obtained within the economic possibilities of the capitalist sector.
>
> . . . the Federal Executive is resolved to fulfill the program of the Revolution and to carry out the dictates of the Six-Year Plan without regard for the alarm expressed by representatives of the capitalist class. At the same time, it is my duty to say to workers and employers that both will enjoy all guarantees within the law and all support in the exercise of their rights. But in no case will the President of the Republic permit excesses of any kind or acts that involve transgressions of the law or unnecessary agitations. In the working out of such a program, I have full confidence in the labor and peasant organizations of the country, and I expect that they will know how to act with good will and the patriotism which the legitimate interests they represent demand of them. . . .[24]

23. Confederación de Trabajadores de México, *Informe del Comité Nacional 1936–1937*, p. 65; *Futuro* (July, 1935), pp. 474–75.
24. Quoted in Millan, *Mexico Reborn*, pp. 94–95.

Within the next few hours, President Cárdenas had received thousands of messages pledging the support of labor organizations, peasant leagues, state legislatures, student groups, and other organizations throughout the entire country. The majority group of the House of Deputies voted unanimously to support Cárdenas. In the left wing group of the Senate, sixty-one members signed a congratulatory telegram. Overnight Calles was out and Cárdenas was in.[25] Within a little over a year after taking office, Cárdenas had accomplished what no other political or military leader had been able to do in all the history of Mexico. He had overthrown a firmly entrenched conservative political machine without resorting to military rebellion or political assassination. Moreover, he had set going again the stalled car of the revolution. It must not be forgotten that these accomplishments were not those of Cárdenas alone, for behind him were the tireless efforts of Lombardo Toledano, the other union leaders, the rank and file, the peasant groups—not to mention the minister of education, Narciso Bassols, who began the program of "socialized education" to emancipate Mexican youth from clerical influence by teaching the "scientific truth" as revealed by Karl Marx, in the public schools.[26]

Undoubtedly, the most important result of the crisis of June 12 was the united front of the labor movement, which apparently had needed a Fascist threat to scare it into action. "The threat of General Calles to drive Cárdenas from power if he did not alter his conduct and reduce the working class to impotence, which threat occurred in June 1935, simply accelerated the unification of the working class."[27] For months before the crisis, the left-wing groups, and particularly the Communist party, had tried to get the larger unions to agree on some joint program of action, but without success. The Calles declaration, however, gave the workers a taste of what a Callista dictatorship would really be if his group were allowed to assume power once again. The scare was so great that a joint pact was signed, called temporarily the National Committee for Proletarian Defense, as we have seen.

It will be recalled, however, that two labor groups did not sign the pact—the C.R.O.M. and the C.G.T. When Calles attacked Lombardo and other unionists who were leading strikes, the C.R.O.M., which also regarded Lombardo as a traitor, made common cause with Calles. At the same time, it attempted to retain favor with Cárdenas by attacking Lombardo for calling the government "bourgeois." Also,

25. *Ibid.*, p. 96.
26. Eyler N. Simpson, *The Ejido: Mexico's Way Out* (Chapel Hill, 1937), pp. 285–86.
27. C.T.M., *Informe del Comité Nacional 1936–1937*, pp. 64–65.

the C.R.O.M. could not agree with the statement of the Pact of Solidarity of the Committee for Proletarian Defense that openly stated: "The pacting groups declare that they are against collaboration with the capitalist class and that they will act in accordance with a revolutionary policy and with the principle of the class struggle."[28] In addition, the C.R.O.M. sought favor with Cárdenas on the ground that its fraternal relations with the labor movement of the United States had been of the greatest importance to Obregón. But the day of the C.R.O.M. as the government's labor pillar had passed. The struggle against Calles served greatly both to weaken the C.R.O.M. and to unify the labor movement around Lombardo Toledano.

Smooth sailing for labor was not yet to be, however, because, very soon after the June crisis had died down, Calles and his friends renewed their attacks. Antilabor propaganda spread; antilabor organizations sprang up; there were riots, train wrecks—and in these occurrences many thought they saw the work of the C.R.O.M.[29] Other groups besides the C.R.O.M. devoted themselves to attacking the progressive policies of Cárdenas and the Committee for Proletarian Defense. For instance, the Acción Revolucionaria Mexicana, or the "Gold Shirts," as they were known, splendidly supported, according to left-wing accusations, by General Calles and certain business interests, created disturbances that were used by the newspapers to trump up a Communist scare. Even more effective material for the newspapers were the manifestoes and resolutions issued by the National Alliance of United Workers, a new organization composed of C.G.T., the C.R.O.M., and the more conservative factions of the Cámara del Trabajo, which had refused to follow the majority in forming the Committee for the Defense of the Proletariat. They denounced the committee as Communist and pledged themselves to protect the nation against the "reds."[30] On December 12, 1935, *El Universal* claimed that the alliance was intended to stop the work of agitators with "exotic" schemes who were using the pro-labor policies of Cárdenas merely for their own advantage.[31] During this time, President Cárdenas remained calm and quiet, restraining neither labor nor the "Gold Shirts," who announced that on November 20, 1935 (anniversary of the Mexican Revolution), they would parade in honor of Mexico's glorious history. The C.G.O.C.M., knowing that since organized labor and popular groups would also parade and that a clash would

28. *Lux*, July, 1935, p. 22.
29. *El Universal*, December 22, 24, 25, 28, 1935.
30. *Futuro*, III (February, 1936), 8.
31. *El Universal*, December 12, 1935.

be the likely result, petitioned Cárdenas not to permit the parade of the "Gold Shirts." But Cárdenas still would not interfere. As a result, there was a clash in the square in front of the National Palace during which three persons were killed and at least fifty others injured by stones, bullets, or trampling horses.[32]

At a meeting soon after this event, Lombardo Toledano declared that safety lay only in unity and suggested that by May 1, the first step toward social revolution be taken.[33] Addressing a great protest rally sponsored by the Committee for the Defense of the Proletariat on the night of December 11, 1935, President Cárdenas said:

> The Mexican people know that every reform, every action which affects vested and conservative interests, must meet with serious obstacles. Why, then, is it surprising that the Mexican people are today witnessing an attack of intrigue, trickery and betrayal? Such attacks always come, and not only from conservative elements. They come, too, unfortunately, from elements which are led by bastard ambitions and by the influence or prestige of the exploiters to forget the sufferings of the class to which they belong. They abandon the ranks of the Revolution and join with the Revolution's eternal enemies. . . . It is a lie that the organized workers and peasants are engaged in destructive activities. . . . They know how far we can go; they know that there sometimes is need to wait until this regime, until the Revolution which they themselves created, can realize entirely its program for raising the economic and cultural conditions of the people. . . . I am sorry that these men who once were leaders of the masses, who only yesterday filled positions of great responsibility, are now in disgrace. I am sorry that their names are now used in insulting slogans, that their faces are ridiculed in cartoons. But it is not we who have brought about this situation. It is their own friends, who desired to continue, at any cost, the profitable returns they derived from their positions around these men. . . . But I say to the Mexican people, to the organized groups of Mexico, that there is no reason to decree the expulsion of anyone from the country. . . . General Calles and his friends are not a problem, neither for the government nor for the workers. . . . The moral force of the people has been sufficient to suppress these elements, and they ought to remain in the country so that they may feel the shame and the weight of their historic responsibilities.[34]

32. *Ibid.*, November 21, 1935.
33. *Ibid.*, November 25, 1935.
34. *Ibid.*, December 23, 1935.

Cárdenas and organized labor were now partners. The binding link between them was apparently the desire to realize the promise of the revolution.

The National Committee for the Defense of the Proletariat issued a call for a National Unification Congress to be held from February 26 to 29, 1936, in Mexico City. Before examining the course of events at this congress (which was to lead to the formation of the Confederation of Mexican Workers—C.T.M.), however, let us inquire into the labor theory of the Cárdenas regime that we may better comprehend the structure and program of organized labor from 1936 to 1940.

III. Labor Theory of
the Mexican Revolution
under Cárdenas:
The Leaders

In a public address early in his administration, Cárdenas stated emphatically that organization of workers, like the organization of peasants, was indispensable for enforcement of the laws of Mexico; and he added that a superior force, which could be none other than organized labor, must, of necessity, co-operate to overcome the resistance that unfortunately opposed economic betterment of the Mexican people.[1] Concerning the structure of organized labor and the function of trade unions, he thought that unions were the workers' best weapon and worth far more even than the protection imparted by the laws and the authorities; therefore, he urged that workers unite in unions and leagues, then establish consumer co-operative associations in every village. Once these were functioning successfully, he felt, the worker should set up producer co-operative associations.[2]

1. From a speech by Cárdenas, as quoted in Ministry of Foreign Relations, *The Mexican Government in the Presence of Social and Economic Problems: Tour of the President of the Republic—Monterrey—Tampico—Guadalajara* (Mexico, 1936), pp. 35–36.
2. See Departamento del Trabajo, *Policies of the Present Administration of Mexico* (Mexico, 1936), p. 12.

Interestingly enough, Cárdenas and his chief labor lieutenant, Lombardo Toledano, were never quite able to agree on the question of whether workers should unite to form producer co-operatives, since Lombardo did not believe that this process could lead the Mexican workers into socialism. Apparently, the leadership of the central labor federation leaned toward mixed forms of industrial administration in which the state and the consumers had a voice. As a matter of fact, Cárdenas himself was inconsistent on this point; for during his presidential campaign, he told the people in one speech that he considered it contrary to social justice for productive machinery to be inactive, that this in itself constituted a right for the state to intervene, and that if he were elected president, all those factories which had been closed would be rented by the state and turned over to laborers organized into co-operative associations to operate.[3] He restated this position at Monterrey at the time of the speech containing his Fourteen Points, discussed later, when he asserted the principle that an industry that could only survive on low wages, sweatshop conditions, and evasion of labor laws had no right to live, and suggested the solution of worker co-operatives.[4] On another occasion, Cárdenas held that when a factory refused to obey labor laws or decisions of arbitration boards, or when it ceased operations, it could by law be expropriated and turned over to the workers.[5] Further, he maintained that mills, such as the one at Zacatepec, would be founded for the collective benefit, and the funds of the people would be used in extending credit to aid enterprises owned by the laborers themselves.[6]

And yet, in an address to the workers of Monterrey, the president maintained: "The working classes know that they cannot appropriate factories and other instruments of work because they are not, for the time being, either technically fitted for management, or in a possession of the financial resources needed for success of an undertaking of such magnitude."[7] Soon after the New Year's speech of Cárdenas in 1936, a fresh epidemic of strikes broke out, the focus of trouble being in the largest industrial center of Mexico—Monterrey. Workers at the glass factory had gone on strike, and agitators sent by Lombardo

3. William Cameron Townsend, *Lázaro Cárdenas: Mexican Democrat* (Ann Arbor, 1952), pp. 129–30.
4. Nathaniel and Sylvia Weyl, *The Reconquest of Mexico: The Years of Lázaro Cárdenas* (New York, 1939), p. 254.
5. Hudson Strode, *Timeless Mexico* (New York, 1944), p. 326.
6. From a speech by Cárdenas, as quoted in Townsend, *Lázaro Cárdenas*, p. 108.
7. Ministry of Foreign Relations, *The Mexican Government: Tour of the President*, p. 11.

Toledano were causing trouble to other manufacturers as well. Monterrey had been opposed to Cárdenas and was, as an industrial center, a good place for reactionary sentiment to gain force. On February 6, 1936, Cárdenas asked his minister of labor, Génaro Vásquez, to meet him in that city, and after several days of investigations and interviews with leaders of both labor and capital representatives, Cárdenas presented a plan for settling not only that strike, but defining his position with regard to industry, labor, and worker-employer relations.[8]

The plan was made public on February 11, 1936, and was known as The Fourteen Points; it became famous during the first half of the Cárdenas administration. It was Cárdenas' own labor platform, although it was first attributed to Ramón Beteta.[9] Because they summarize in one place the basic ideas of Cárdenas toward labor in the national economy, these points will be presented at some length. A few are quite general; others are specific. The following numbered points make up a transcript of them as published by the Ministry of Foreign Relations:[10]

1. The government will cooperate with labor and capital in the solution of their problems.

2. A united labor front should be organized, since strife between rival labor organizations themselves is detrimental to the government as well as to the workers and employers.

3. The government is arbiter and regulator of social problems. (Yet Cárdenas later opposed compulsory arbitration of labor disputes.)

4. The demands of labor will be taken into consideration only as they come within the limits of the ability of the various industries to pay.

5. When labor's united front is organized, the government will deal with it to the exclusion of minority groups which might choose to continue.

6. Employers shall have no right to intervene in the affairs of labor organizations.

7. Employers shall have the same right as the workers have to associate themselves into a united front.

8. The government desires the further development of industries within the nation, since it depends upon their prosperity for its income through taxation.

8. Townsend, *Lázaro Cárdenas*, pp. 129–30; Samuel Guy Inman, "Observations on Labor, Politics, and Religion in Northern Mexico," *World Affairs,* XLIX (September, 1936), pp. 177–79.

9. Townsend, *Lázaro Cárdenas*, p. 130.

10. For complete document, see Ministry of Foreign Relations, *The Mexican Government: Tour of the President*, pp. 12 ff.

9. Current labor agitation is not due to the existence of communistic groups, since they are so small they have no real influence in the affairs of the nation. The real cause of labor agitation is the fact that the just needs of the laboring masses have not been met, and the labor laws have not been carried out faithfully.

10. Small groups of communists do exist within the country—as they do in Europe and the United States—but their activities in Mexico do not endanger the stability of our institutions nor do they alarm the government, and they need not alarm the industrialists.

11. [This point is not apropos to this discussion.]

12. The attitude of the employers of Monterrey is duplicated in centers such as La Laguna, Leon, the Federal District, and Yucatán.

13. Capital should be very careful not to continue provoking agitations because these would come to constitute a rallying point for political interests, and this would bring on civil warfare.

14. The industrialists who do not wish to continue to operate because of the demands of the unions can turn over their industries to their laborers or to the government, for it to operate. This would be a patriotic step, but simply to close down the factories would not be.

The principle expressed in Point 1 introduces the state into labor-management relations; Point 2 suggests a united labor federation as a method of avoiding many jurisdictional disputes and, perhaps, a belief that the government could better control such a labor organization; Point 3 illustrates well the contention that the general character of the people of the regime was interventionist, with the state being the final judge of social justice for all the classes in the society; Point 4 was the expression of a principle, to be adopted later, of basing wage increases on the ability of the company to pay; Point 5 emphasized what was to become the paternal relationship between the government and the C.T.M. and demonstrates the philosophy behind the political turn taken at the time by the Mexican labor movement; Point 14 undoubtedly presaged the Expropriation Law of 1936 and was a statement of the principle of outlawing the "shut-down." It is surprising, indeed, to note the similarity between the labor theory of President Perón of Argentina and this program of Cárdenas, expressed ten years before Perón's.[11]

11. For a discussion of Perón's labor philosophy, see Joe C. Ashby, "Labor and the Philosophy of the Argentine Revolution," *Inter-American Economic Affairs* 5 (Summer, 1951), 71–96.

After the issuance of The Fourteen Points, the Department of Labor became an agency for the organization and defense of labor. The labor movement was thus definitely wedded to politics, i.e. the state, and vice versa. The chief executive, in spite of repeated denials that the Mexican program had any relation to communism, in public declarations began to glorify the struggle of the classes, and the secretary of education printed millions of texts praising Marx, Lenin, and Stalin as apostles of a modern religious creed for the salvation of humanity.[12] But simultaneously Cárdenas was assuring the nation that in the Laguna District and in Yucatán unrest was being stirred up to lead the Mexican people to believe in the existence of a communistic movement aiming at overthrowing the social order guaranteed by Mexican institutions, when, in reality, all that labor organizations were working for was enjoyment of conquests already embodied in Mexican legislation and pursued by the government since the rise to power of the revolutionary regime. He added: "The Nation can, therefore, see that what is now being done is neither a novelty, nor improvised, and far less a policy deviating from the paths marked by our institutions."[13]

Shortly after the Monterrey speech on March 11, 1936, a coalition of bankers, manufacturers, and traders addressed a memorial to President Cárdenas protesting some of the principles contained in The Fourteen Points, as well as the new policy of the boards of conciliation and arbitration and the Supreme Court toward organized labor. They suggested compulsory arbitration of labor disputes. His reply was that the modern concept of the nature and function of the state and labor legislation required universal extension of the principle that in cases of doubt the state should intervene in behalf of the weaker party, because to give equal treatment to unequal parties was not to impart justice nor to give equity.[14] He reminded the bankers that when they challenged revolutionary construction of the law they were forgetting that labor legislation was passing through an experimental stage that afforded an opportunity for observing in practice those deficiencies which the legislator was unable to foresee; that labor legis-

12. Alfonso López Aparicio, *El Movimiento Obrero en México: Antecedentes, Desarrollo y Tendencias* (México, 1952), pp. 215–16.
13. Ministry of Foreign Relations, *The Mexican Government: Tour of the President*, pp. 9–10.
14. Departamento Federal del Trabajo, *La Obra Social de la Actual Administración que Preside el G. Lázaro Cárdenas* (México, 1936), p. 33; Ministry of Foreign Relations, *The Mexican Government in the Presence of Social and Economic Problems: The Religious Question—The President's Reply to the Memorial from the Employers—Mexico's Economic Situation Rapidly Improving* (Mexico, 1936), pp. 1–21.

lation in all countries had a tutelary character with respect to workers; and that compulsory arbitration would destroy the constitutional right to strike—a right that was necessary as a means of restoring balance between capital and labor.[15] He told the industrialists that in a wider and more general sense factories, real property, and banking capital made up the structure of the national economy; he also maintained that the interests of society were injured when owners ceased to exercise their functions properly, under cover of "an anachronistic conception of what constitutes property rights."[16] On the other hand, Cárdenas maintained that strikes, if within the law and when their demands did not exceed the economic capacity of the undertakings affected, promoted the interests of society in the sense that they helped to solve Mexico's most serious problem—the misery of her workers. He added that any attempt to shut down manufacturing concerns or to paralyze private credit would simply involve intervention by the state to prevent disturbance of economic life "and the most that could happen would be that certain branches be withdrawn from the sphere of private interest to become social service."[17]

It becomes, then, fairly apparent that President Cárdenas believed in the rights of workers to organize and strike to obtain their share of the social product; he was also prepared to utilize the power of the state to assist the workers in their legitimate efforts. Furthermore, those employers who were unable to reorient their policies in this direction might expect their businesses to be nationalized. It is also clear that the Cárdenas government recognized the existence of a proletarian class whose interests were opposed to those of the employers and, too, that Cárdenas proposed the intervention of the state on behalf of labor as a legitimate technique for achieving "balance among the factors of production." But some questions that arise are: "How, by what methods, did Cárdenas and his more articulate followers propose to aid the workers?" "What was the more detailed labor philosophy of this epoch as expressed in what Cárdenas considered the basic documents of the revolution—the Constitution of 1917, the first Six-Year Plan, the Federal Labor Law of 1931, the declarations of the Partido Nacional Revolucionario (P.N.R.) and the Partido de la Revolución Mexicana (P.R.M.), the Confederación de Trabajadores de México (C.T.M.), and the Confederación de Trabajadores de América Latina (C.T.A.L.), the speeches and writ-

15. Ministry of Foreign Relations, *The Mexican Government: The Religious Question*, pp. 11–15.
16. *Ibid.*, pp. 16–18.
17. *Ibid.*, p. 19.

ings of Cárdenas and his economic advisors, Lombardo Toledano, and the Department of Labor?" "Was there any unity in thought?" "What similarities and what differences, if any, did the Mexican labor theory of this era have with labor theories of other countries?" In short, "What was the nature of the thinking of the Mexican government behind the organization of the working class of Mexico during the period 1934–40?" "What was the role of organized labor in the developing economy of Mexico?"

The revolution stressed tendencies toward nationalism, Indianism, and agrarian reform, with extraordinary emphasis on the labor problem. Among the mandates of the Constitution of 1917, Article 27, which dealt with agrarian problems, and Article 123, which was the basis of the whole of labor legislation, were looked upon as the most essential.[18] Teja Zabre, one of the outstanding historians of the period, found in the revolution the following points aiming progressively at actual consummation: (1) to pass from theoretically equal rights, or equality on paper, to actual, that is, economic equality; and (2) in the field of labor to begin with unionism, so as later to achieve socialization.[19] As we shall note at a later point, the term "socialization" may have been used in a somewhat peculiar sense.

The ideas of a "radical" tendency in the Mexican Revolution, Teja Zabre felt, could be stated as follows:

> I. Civilization and culture are the result of the work of man to bring nature under control.
> II. Labor is the fundamental cause and the closest measure of the value of useful things.

18. Alfonso Teja Zabre, *Guide to the History of Mexico: A Modern Interpretation* (Mexico, 1935), p. 347. See also: Daniel James, *Mexico and the Americans* (New York, 1963); Jesús Silva Herzog, *Trayectoria Ideológica de la Revolución Mexicana, 1910–1917: Del Manifesto del Partido Liberal de 1906 a la Constitución de 1917* (México, 1963); Frank Tannenbaum, "Lázaro Cárdenas," *Historia Mexicana*, X (October–December, 1960), pp. 332–41; Marco Antonio Durán, "Epotismo y Revolución Agraria," *México Agrario*, II (July–September, 1940), pp. 225–29; Manuel González Ramírez, *La Revolución Social de México* (México, 1960); Howard F. Cline, *The United States and Mexico* (rev. ed.; Cambridge, 1963); Rosendo Salazar, *La Corta del Trabajo de la Revolución Mexicana: Fundamentos de una Evolución* (México, 1960); Vicente Lombardo Toledano, *La Evolución de México durante la Primera Mitad del Siglo XX* (México, 1956); Lewis Hanke, *Modern Latin America: Continent in Ferment* (Princeton, 1959), pp. 79 ff.; Jorge Vera Estoñal, *La Revolución Mexicana Orígenes y Resultados* (México, 1957); José Mancisidor, *Historia de la Revolución Mexicana* (México, 1958); Moisés González Navarro, "La Ideología de la Revolución Mexicana," *Historia Mexicana*, X (April–June, 1961), 628–36.

19. Teja Zabre, *Guide to the History of Mexico*, pp. 347–48.

III. The structure of society is based on the organization of labor, that is, the technique of production.

IV. The main historical factor is class war. . . .

V. Direct action in this struggle is aimed at all wealth withdrawn from circulation by concentration and absorption, such as property in mortmain held by religious corporations, owners of great estates and exploiting capitalism.[20]

It was necessary to take into account the need for nationalism and the alignment of classes, and once this latter had been accomplished, the fundamental points of the revolution would become the "insurgency of the proletarian classes seeking economic and actual equality" and the "creation of a new State to realize progressive socialization of the means of production."[21] In an analysis that may shed some light on what appears to be a special use of the term "socialization," mentioned earlier, Teja Zabre held that the formula of the Mexican Revolution was intervention of the state in economic production as an element of control, supervision, and balance, and the formation of the government with participation of all the social classes in a functional, democratic system. He added that the Mexican revolutionary system recognized private property, but with limitations for the public interest, and considered it as a social function. In fact, the state tried to develop small property, small industries, commercial property of indigenous agrarians, the co-operative forms of production and consumption, and the use of credit and technology in agriculture.[22]

It will be seen that in this latter description of the formula for the Mexican Revolution, allowance was made for "some private property" and the actual encouragement of "small private industries," as well as the participation of "all the social classes in a functional democratic system"—apparently a sort of popular front, benevolent state attitude, with overtones of the corporate state of 1930 Italy. This arrangement certainly puts certain qualifications on the "insurgency of the proletarian classes seeking economic and actual equality" and the "creation of a new State to realize progressive socialization of the means of production." Apparently, "socialization," as used here, means nothing more nor less than government regulation of the privately-owned productive property for the good of all the classes in a mixed-ownership society. It will be recognized that this concept of socializa-

20. *Ibid.,* pp. 354–55.
21. *Ibid.,* pp. 355–56.
22. Teja Zabre, "El Marxismo en la Revolución Mexicana: Esbozo de una Interpretación Histórica," *Futuro,* III (January, 1935), 1–14.

tion is not the "orthodox" use of the term, which usually denotes public or collective ownership of productive property—not merely state control and regulation of it.

Another interpreter, Antonio Behamonde, emphasized the tone of nationalism in the revolution when he wrote that the government of General Cárdenas had the honor of initiating the last epoch in the liberation of the country from all foreign influences and consolidating the effective independence of the nation, making it the owner of its riches and the master of its destinies.[23]

In answering charges that he was leagued with Soviet Russia, Cárdenas stated in precise terms his politico-economic philosophy when he denied the charge and explained that his government was democratic and liberal, with a few moderate traces of socialism which affected land ownership, and in the laws that refer to the relationship between capital and labor. He claimed that the revolutionary movement of Mexico was born of the hopes and needs of the country, and he staunchly maintained that it was not proper to attribute to it any similarity with existing social movements in other parts of the world except those whose principles are common to any movement "seeking proletarian justice and the cultural and economic improvement of the oppressed."[24]

In an interview with Senator Ezequiel Padilla, a sympathizer with Calles as opposed to Cárdenas in the June, 1935, split, the president stated that he had always protested his loyalty to the Mexican Constitution and the Six-Year Plan. He maintained also that no one could point to a single phrase of his declaring that communism was his doctrine or the inspiration for his policy.[25]

Concerning any possible connection between Cárdenas and Soviet communism, Strode felt that Cárdenas further disproved such a possibility when he admitted to Mexico in 1937 Stalin's arch-enemy, the exiled Leon Trotsky, and absolutely refused to recognize the government of the U.S.S.R.[26] The general secretary of the Communist party of Mexico, Hernán Laborde, in commenting upon a speech by Cárdenas, noted that the president's pronunciations put him on the side of labor. Laborde added that the Communist party did not accept blindly the program of the Cárdenas government because it realized all too well its faults and indecisions. But at the same time the Mexican

23. Antonio Bahamonde, *México Es Así* (México, 1940), p. 10.
24. From a speech by Cárdenas, quoted in Strode, *Timeless Mexico*, p. 354.
25. "An Interview with President Cárdenas," *Modern Mexico*, VI (May, 1935), 3.
26. Strode, *Timeless Mexico*, p. 354.

Communist party recognized the necessity of supporting, with the aid of a strong, united front, a progressive government such as that of Cárdenas "when it is menaced by Fascism."[27] This line of reasoning was adhered to also by the labor leader, Vicente Lombardo Toledano.

Lázaro Cárdenas was convinced of the political importance of the labor movement when, at the base of his break with Calles, the National Committee for the Defense of the Proletariat lent him its backing and endorsement. This was the moment at which Cárdenas began in earnest his efforts to create a united labor front. The Six-Year Plan attacked the problem with much care—it accepted without reservation the thesis of the class struggle and sought the collaboration of the working class to accomplish its ends. At the same time, the state should intervene when required "to prevent the oppression of the class to be aided by the union."[28] Desiring to make the P.N.R. something similar to a popular front, Cárdenas modified its structure and called it the Partido de la Revolución Mexicana, the party of the Mexican Revolution (P.R.M.). It was composed of four equal sectors: military, labor, peasant, and popular. The popular sector was to include all who were not aligned with one of the other sectors, and it was to be the voice of the middle class, which Cárdenas hoped would be weaned from its friendship toward capitalism. The P.N.R. went out of existence, and the party of the Mexican Revolution (P.R.M.) was born on December 19, 1937.

The declaration of principles and the program of action adopted by the P.R.M. stated that its *most fundamental* task was "the preparation of the people for the establishment of a *workers' democracy* as a step toward socialism."[29] According to Vásquez, head of the Department of Labor, the inclination of President Cárdenas for the laboring classes was such that the party was primarily a protector of the working man.[30] Again, it is imperative to remember that the "step toward socialism" which the revolution under Cárdenas claimed to be taking, may have been used in some special sense, as mentioned previously, or, even that it was used by different people at the same time to mean

27. From a speech by Hernán Laborde, quoted in Verna Carleton Millan, *Mexico Reborn* (Boston, 1939), p. 105.

28. Partido Nacional Revolucionario, *Plan Sexenal, 1934–1940* (México, 1934), p. 46; López Aparicio, *El Movimiento Obrero en México*, p. 147.

29. Partido de la Revolución Mexicana, *Pacto Constitutivo, Declaración de Princípios Programa y Estatutos* (México, 1938); Nathaniel and Sylvia Weyl, *The Reconquest of Mexico*, p. 347.

30. Génaro Vásquez, "Introduction," in *Policies of the Present Administration of Mexico* (Mexico, 1936), p. 5.

a different thing—or, even, used at different times by the same people to mean different things. The mere fact that the government party was pledged to be a "protector of the working masses" is not sufficient to warrant naming it a socialist party.

The brilliant young undersecretary of state for Cárdenas, Ramón Beteta, in whom the president seemed to have unlimited confidence, at one time apparently agreed rather thoroughly with an orthodox interpretation of the statement of the P.R.M., with *socialism* understood to include the collective ownership of productive property, since he said: "We think that we should attempt to industrialize Mexico consciously, intelligently, avoiding the dispensable evils of industrialism, such as urbanism, exploitation of man by man, production for sale instead of production for satisfaction of human needs, economic insecurity, waste, shabby goods and the mechanization of workmen. . . . We are convinced that the evils of capitalism are . . . due to a merely legal question: *who is the owner of the machinery?*" (Emphasis mine.)[31] Here, it would seem that Beteta definitely implied something other than private ownership of productive facilities. He elaborated upon the statement by expressing the belief that Mexico, precisely because she found herself in the precapitalist transition, was in a position favorable to the finding of a more humane and just system of economic relations by means of intelligent *intervention* of a *government* with *working-class interests*, provided that she could avoid a fatal conflict with the capitalist imperialism of other countries. He concluded that he believed that Mexico would be able to evolve toward a society *without classes* which "in our day is the condition nearest to the ideal in the economic relations of man."[32]

This latter statement seems to be significant for our purposes for two reasons: first, the reference to the idea of government intervention in behalf of the working class, and, secondly, because of the expression of a desire for a classless society. It was, of course, not clear whether the government with working-class interests was to be made up of members of the proletariat, some other exclusive group, or a popular front. Nonetheless, the reference to evolution toward a classless society, taken together with "who should own the productive machinery?" has a good deal in common with orthodox socialism. Some further hint of the economic theory of Beteta may be gleaned from the following excerpt of a speech: "Some of us believe, furthermore, that profit-making is not the only incentive of human endeavor,

31. Ramón Beteta (ed.), *Programa Económico y Social de México* (*Una Controvérsia*) (México, 1935), p. 44; Clarence Senior, *Mexico in Transition* (New York, 1939), p. 48.
32. *Ibid.*

but rather a motive that happens to have been chosen and over-developed in the capitalistic regime."[33]

Comparing the Six-Year Plan, as the statement of principle for the Cárdenas administration, with the New Deal, Beteta revealed what he saw as a fundamental difference when he said:

> There is a similarity, it is true, between the New Deal . . . and the Mexican Six-Year Plan . . . as they both are efforts at harmony in planning the economic chaos produced by economic liberty. There are, however, fundamental differences between the American and the Mexican approach to the problem. Thus while the aim of the United States Government, as I understand it, is to increase the price by limiting production and making profits possible, we in Mexico are more concerned with the workers' side of the problem than with the industrialists'. *We recognize the existence of the class struggle as one of the inevitable features of capitalism and we have put our sympathy with the working class.* (Emphasis mine.)[34]

In the last two quotations, we note the denial of the profit motive as the only incentive of human endeavor and the recognition of the class struggle as an inevitable feature of the capitalist system, both ideas Marxist.

What of the general socioeconomic theory of another member of the Cárdenas team, that dynamic personality, Vicente Lombardo Toledano, of whom Millan said, "[He is] the most unusual labor leader any country ever had. . . . Today (1939) he probably has more mass support than any other political personality throughout the Republic with the exception of Cárdenas himself, and I do not make this statement lightly."[35] As general secretary of the C.T.M., Lombardo was to play, with the passing years, a decisive role in Mexican politics, and Millan claimed that he had the best all-around political intelligence in Mexico and that the dramatic impact of his speeches could be attributed precisely to their irrefutable logic.[36] Lombardo was appointed by José Vasconcelos, then minister of education, through the intervention of Antonio Caso, as director of the National Preparatory School. Vasconcelos and Lombardo had serious difficulties from the first—as did, later, Lombardo and his master, Caso. They

33. Sanford A. Mosk, *Industrial Revolution in Mexico* (Berkeley, 1950), p. 58.
34. Beteta, *Programa Económico y Social de México*, p. 95.
35. Millan, *Mexico Reborn*, p. 81.
36. Robert P. Millon, *Mexican Marxist—Vicente Lombardo Toledano* (Chapel Hill, 1966) offers what this writer believes to be the best work in English on the thought of Lombardo Toledano.

split over the question of materialism. Lombardo had come to accept the historical materialism of Marx and now talked openly of class struggle as the essential basis for all attempts toward a genuine unification of the working class. Apparently, he differed with the Communists on matters of tactical rather than ideological nature. It should be noted, however, that his thought, along with that of other leaders of the C.T.M., was variable, capable of shifting as the Mexican environment, in response to the world situation, changed. In the words of López Aparicio, "Lombardo Toledano is the greatest intellectual leader of the Mexican labor movement—his ideological position has been mobile."[37]

If it be true that Lombardo was one of the outstanding revolutionary theorists of Mexico, it may be worthwhile to trace farther the evolution of his general economic and labor philosophy through the changing circumstances of the Cárdenas administration. From 1923 to 1931, while Lombardo was still in the C.R.O.M., he had maintained a strict trade-unionist point of view, holding that the labor unions should function primarily as economic organizations for defense of their rights against employers. This was a position similar to that of Calles, who looked on the syndicalist trade unions as the bulwark of capitalism, and that of Morones before the latter made the C.R.O.M. an adjunct of the Obregón electoral machine in 1920. Following the break with Morones in 1931, and before the formation of the C.T.M., Lombardo had been moving more toward a position in which he considered the role of the trade unions political as well as economic.[38]

At the same time, Lombardo's philosophy had veered from idealism and spiritualist theism toward the positivism and humanism of Auguste Comte and then toward the dialectical, historical materialism of the Marxists. During this period, the young scholar was expelled from the National University for "attempting to bring into it an alternative for the prevailing Bergsonian anti-scientific school and to open the way for the Marxist philosophy." He then founded the Gabino Barreda University, named for Mexico's outstanding proponent of Comte's positivism, with the idea of finding a compromise between idealism and materialism. This school was transformed in 1935 to a "Marxist" institution and its name changed to the Workers' University of Mexico.

For some time liberal educators had looked upon the National University as a nest of opposition to their "socialistic tendencies," and Cárdenas shared in this sentiment. With regard to the matter, he observed, while campaigning for the election:

37. López Aparicio, *El Movimento Obrero en México*, p. 219.
38. J. H. Plenn, *Mexico Marches* (New York, 1939), p. 265.

The member of the laboring class who enters the halls of the university or technical schools does not usually become the leader who returns to take culture and help to his fellows, but rather, is the very one who turns his back upon them and goes over to the bourgeoisie. Under such conditions, each son of a working-man who does go to schools of higher learning is lost as a potential leader to the syndicate or peasant organization and becomes another expert at the service of the wealthy classes. The cream of the proletariat come to be, by virtue of this phenomenon, rich spoil for the purposes of the bourgeoisie.[39]

The Workers' University, an auxiliary of the C.T.M., endowed with the good will of Cárdenas and supported partially by government funds, was converted into a center for the diffusion of the ideas of historical materialism.

One of the earliest bulletins of the university set down the aims of the institution in this manner:

The most important task of this epoch of transition is to develop in the working class a consciousness of their historical mission. This is the purpose of the Workers' University. They must be shown their exact place in life and in the world, based on knowledge confirmed by experience; in addition to concrete knowledge of the life of the country in which they live—its physical, economic, and social structure.

"Without a theory of revolution," said Lenin, "there can be no revolutionary action; but it must be seen that no revolutionary theory of the social struggle can exist if there is no scientific notion of the universe." It is for this purpose that the Workers' University comes to fill a grand purpose for the future of the proletariat. Workers will learn in these walls, in a systematic manner, the origin of the world, the origin of life, the appreciation of man, the principle of human society and its development, the material character of all natural phenomena, and the laws of dialectical materialism.

In possession of this fundamental knowledge of the true culture, the exploited will be able to go out with a firm conviction in their daily struggle against the capitalist class and have a clear vision of the future. . . .[40]

In short, the Workers' University claimed to be an institution dedicated to the study of socialist doctrine, to social problems in general, to the characteristics of the bourgeoisie rule, to the aspects of contemporary

39. Townsend, *Lázaro Cárdenas*, pp. 124–25.
40. *Universidad Obrera de México*, 1936, pp. 4, 5, 6.

capitalism, to those countries without "automatic economics," and to the realities of social Mexico.[41] It is interesting to observe at least a partial listing of the faculty of the school. In addition to the director, Vicente Lombardo Toledano, and the assistant director, Alajandro Carillo, there were Lic. Victor Manuel Villaseñor, Lic. Xavier Icaza, Federico Bach, Gonzalo Mora, Francisco Zamara, Alfonso Teja Zabre, Alfonso Millan, Juan O'Gorman, Antonio Ramírez Laguna, and Agustín Yañez.

The dispute between Lombardo and his former professor, Antonio Caso, in 1933, was the beginning of a polemic that has become among the most famous in Mexico. Caso called his former pupil a renegade and an ingrate. Lombardo replied that he had formerly been completely taken in by the idealist philosophy but that he had come to realize the untenability of that point of view. This debate, which raged for weeks in the newspapers, was sensational because it represented the fundamental division between the two main currents of thought in Mexico. During the debate, Lombardo gave a summation of his philosophical position when he stated: ". . . we believe that man is a product of nature; that the exterior world forms and guides his spirit; that his conscience is principally social and not individual; and that it is not man who makes history according to his will, but that history created human ideas, that liberty does not consist of separating man from nature, attributing divine power to him, but in proceeding rationally within the dialectical process of historic laws. . . ."[42] A further commentary by Lombardo is of especial interest because it demonstrates clearly that at one time his thought, like that of Ramón Beteta, was in harmony with "orthodox" socialism.

> Socialization is reached only when private property disappears as the base and aim of social institutions, so that the collectivity, composed exclusively of workers, can impose on production and distribution the modalities necessary for society, without encountering any legal obstacles. So, as long as there is private property, there can be no socialized property. The two forms cannot exist side by side.
>
> Within the capitalistic regime the turning over of some centers of production to the workers does not necessarily lead to socialism. It is solely an act which may temporarily

41. *Ibid.*, p. 7.

42. Vicente Lombardo Toledano, "Debate en pro," *Futuro*, II (October, 1934), 50-63. Books by Lombardo Toledano that are useful in tracing the evolution of his philosophy are listed in the Bibliography,

See also Enrique Ramírez y Ramírez, *La Obra y la Lucha de Vicente Lombardo Toledano* (México, 1952).

help the workers, to a greater or lesser degree, but the bene-
ficiaries do not thereby free themselves of the consequences
of the capitalist regime.[43]

It would seem quite clear that at this stage Lombardo stood for the
public ownership of *all* productive property in the hands of a government composed *exclusively* of *workers* and that any partial "socialization" of property could be of only temporary benefit to the workers
and should be invoked merely as a matter of expediency. This interpretation would seem to exclude naming the socioeconomic system of
Mexico under Cárdenas either Socialist or Communist, since private
property did not disappear—nor did Cárdenas advocate such a situation; the collectivity was not composed exclusively of workers, and,
as we shall note below, Lombardo himself stated that it should not
be so composed. At the same time, the role of labor in the system
precludes naming it Fascist.

In a floor debate at a labor convention in December, 1934, Lombardo declared: "It is not a question of incorporating workers' representatives into the state, but of recognizing the power of the working
class organized against the state. . . . The root of this controversy is
that the comrades who oppose the motion uphold the anarchist ideology and believe that all power, merely because it is power, corrupts.
I believe the opposite, for I believe that we must arrive at the dictatorship of the proletariat."[44]

This position was taken by Lombardo before Calles threw down
the gauntlet to the Cárdenas regime; but after the former president
and foreign business interests began their drive against organized
labor, the Committee for the Defense of the Proletariat was formed
on the initiative of the powerful Mexico City Electricians' Union, and
the C.T.M. was the institutional expression of the unity achieved in
the struggle against Calles and his followers. At first Lombardo and
associates were skeptical of the Cárdenas promises and were prone
to analyze the Mexican situation in terms of a cycle of revolutions
that would eventually sweep labor into power. But the point of view
of Lombardo and the labor movement he led was to change. Apparently, Cárdenas convinced labor, by his actions, of his revolutionary integrity, while the rise of fascism in Europe compelled a
revolution in labor strategy and tactics on an international scale.[45]

43. Plenn, *Mexico Marches*, p. 360.
44. From an address by Lombardo Toledano to the First Congress of the
General Confederation of Workers and Peasants of Mexico, quoted in Nathaniel
and Sylvia Weyl, *The Reconquest of Mexico*, p. 352.
45. *Ibid.*, p. 237.

Cárdenas knew that the revolutionary program could not be carried out by fiat from above and realized that he needed the backing of a powerful labor movement to smash the conservative opposition. In the words of the Weyls, "If the theory of government as the arbiter of class conflict was appropriate to a society in equilibrium, that of a conscious alliance between the state and the working-class organizations applied to a society in transition toward collectivist forms."[46]

The C.T.M. embraced the majority of the organized workers of Mexico, and therefore it is reasonable to accept the official position of that organization as the point of view of Mexican labor as a whole. Furthermore, Lombardo Toledano was the leading figure in establishing the federation and in shaping its policies during its formative years. He, more than any other person, influenced the thinking of the C.T.M. on economic questions; hence, his point of view can be considered representative of the C.T.M. point of view. The first congress of the organization of the C.T.M. declared: "The C.T.M. is a national labor front for the struggle between the classes at the service of the Mexican workers."[47] It went on to say that the C.T.M. would establish the method of conducting the fight against feudalism, imperialism, and for the economic and political independence of the Mexican nation, guaranteeing in this manner the historical development of the revolution. The attitude of the confederation became one of collaboration with President Cárdenas; it was determined not to clash with the rest of the forces that would organize to back the Cárdenas government and with which the C.T.M. had common interests. Here we note one of the first suggestions of a departure from the earlier labor philosophy of Lombardo toward a sort of popular front, demonstrating his ability to change tactics when the material circumstances changed. Soon Lombardo was to say that the proletariat was not self-sufficient to fight international fascism and reaction but that it was the nerve center of the people, as the class that produced human wealth. Labor was going to create a popular alliance to defend the interests of the Mexican Revolution. He held that being a worker was not enough to guarantee the carrying out of a program of workers as a social class, and this would be the first opportunity for the working class, as a social class, to intervene in the orientation and direction of the country's policies.[48] Apparently, the "external" circumstances of the threat

46. *Ibid.,* p. 240.
47. Confederación de Trabajadores de México, *Informe del Comité Nacional* (México, 1938), pp. 63–65.
48. Lombardo Toledano, as quoted in Plenn, *Mexico Marches,* pp. 298–99.

of German and Italian fascism caused Lombardo to vary his former theory, or at least his tactics, and to adopt a policy that advocated government intervention and the popular front. This decision, of course, coincided with the change in the Communist party line from Moscow; however, this is not to allege that Lombardo did not reach the decision independently, as many writers have done.

The new organized labor policy of seeking government intervention on behalf of the workers was reiterated by the C.T.M. in April, 1937: "The proletariat knows well that under the capitalistic system it is impossible for it to receive all that it produces, but there is the possibility of utilizing the Government to enforce the articles of the Constitution, which would alleviate the situation of the masses of workers."[49]

In 1938, Lombardo could say, addressing the Extraordinary Meeting of the National Council of the C.T.M., "There are two attitudes equally dangerous for the proletariat—that of the extreme right and that of the extreme left. The theory that the working class should be put at the service of ambitious individuals (fascism), along with the theory of the self-sufficiency of the proletariat, of its indestructible force, and that after Cárdenas the dictatorship of the proletariat must be instituted are both theories traitorous to the Mexican people and to the Revolution."[50] Apparently, the Mexican labor leader now thought that the dictatorship of the proletariat, at least for the time being, was not the solution to the Mexican labor problem. At this same meeting, he heaped praise upon the policies of the Cárdenas administration; thus, the C.T.M. and the Cárdenas administration were wedded and were dependent upon each other, perhaps much like the Pope and the Crown of Spain in the fifteenth and sixteenth centuries.

Explaining the broader aims of the C.T.M., Lombardo expounded his views at this conference when he claimed that the program of the C.T.M. from the beginning was not limited to the interests of the proletariat exclusively but to the interests of all the people. For that reason, the C.T.M. carried out alliances with groups other than the proletariat. It was the party of multiple action—not in the limited sense but in the sense of being occupied on the one side by activities purely syndical and on the other by purely electoral activities. There was no social problem of any type which did not interest the C.T.M.

49. Confederación de Trabajadores de México, *La C.T.M. y la Carestía de la Vida* (México, 1937), pp. 19–20.

50. Vicente Lombardo Toledano, "Discurso del Lic. Lombardo Toledano," *América Latina*, I (April 10, 1939), 10.

As a force interested in transforming society, it would participate in electoral activity.[51] Thus, we see the complete departure from the early Lombardo theory of strict economic trade-unionism and the expression of the popular front idea, along with interest in political and social activity.

Expressing the attitude of the government toward a popular front, President Cárdenas told the C.T.M. at its first congress, February 24, 1938, that the collaboration of labor, stimulated by the interest the government had in carrying out the principles of the national constitution, required that the efforts of the proletariat be developed in a consistent and unified form to end internal controversies that had led to exhaustion of its forces, to the great detriment of proletarian unity and national production. He added, significantly, that above all, Mexican leaders should make clear in the mind of the universal proletariat that the elimination of imperialistic wars depended upon the peaceful unity of the workers of the world.[52] As the C.R.O.M. was with respect to Callismo, so was the C.T.M. with regard to Cárdenas. All the means of the Cárdenas regime favored the C.T.M.—grants of money, guarantee of union activity, persecution of the enemies of the C.T.M. On the other hand, the Lombardistas were a decisive factor in the election of governors, mayors, congressmen, favorable to Cárdenas. At times, the entire force of the government seemed to be put at the service of this grand central labor organization.[53]

It was Cárdenas who, in calling a congress to unify the labor movement, stimulated the formation of the C.T.M., and so a new era in the Mexican labor movement was inaugurated, which then assumed a strong political as well as economic position. It was J. Manuel Corro Viña, eminent biographer of Cárdenas, who pointed out that in Mexico the shame of yesterday would not be repeated and that the masses of workers and farmers, united with the army, would be the major guarantee that the revolution would go forward.[54] In the view of Robert Alexander, the aims of Cárdenas were forwarded by the change in the international Communist line; that is, the Comintern had entered the popular front period and this made it possible for the Mexican Communists to join the Cárdenas camp. He felt this

51. *Ibid.*, p. 8.
52. Lázaro Cárdenas, *Address Made before the First National Congress of the Confederation of Mexican Workers, February 24, 1938* (Mexico, 1938), pp. 5, 9.
53. López Aparicio, *El Movimiento Obrero en México*, p. 221.
54. J. Manuel Corro Viña, *El Presidente Cárdenas ¿Nos Lleva Hacía la Dictadura del Proletariado?* (México, 1935), p. 69.

point was significant because the Communists were particularly strong in the Laguna cotton-growing area where they dominated the local peasants' union, of which a young Communist, Dionisio Encina, was the chief. He led the organization in a bitter strike in 1936 which resulted in the Cárdenas agrarian reform in that region.[55] (Cárdenas' handling of the problem of peasant organizations was characteristic of his method of statecraft: never to put all his eggs in one basket. While strengthening the unions through the establishment of the C.T.M., he kept the peasants and government employees' unions out of the C.T.M. and directly under the sponsorship of the official government party.)

What was the attitude of the C.T.M. toward this alliance with the government and other sectors of the national life? Although more will be said on this subject in a later chapter, suffice it to record here that one of the desires of that organization was to organize a popular front similar to that in France during the administration of Leon Blum. The idea was adopted at the conclusion of the Seventh Congress of the Communist International in August, 1935, in Moscow. After this meeting, the C.T.M. called for the principal worker organizations in Mexico to form a popular front. These organizations included the National Confederation of Peasants (C.N.C.), the General Confederation of Workers (C.G.T.), the Regional Confederation of Mexican Workers (C.R.O.M.), as well as the Mexican Communist party and the P.N.R.[56] The political position of the C.T.M. was explained, during the celebration of the Fourth National Congress in April, 1937, in the following terms: the C.T.M. of Mexico was to be a united front of the proletariat; a general front and not a homogeneous organization with a united opinion. Intervention in the political struggle did not mean that it believed in the transition from a bourgeois society to a socialist one through the medium of parliamentary action; rather, it meant that its intervention in the Cárdenas government had as its purpose to fight together against the enemies of the Mexican revolution.[57] It would seem, then, clear that collaboration with the Cárdenas administration was purely a matter of expediency insofar as the leaders of the C.T.M. were concerned and that it did not indicate a change in fundamental revolutionary principles. Lombardo Toledano

55. Robert J. Alexander, *Communism in Latin America* (New Brunswick, 1957), pp. 330–36.
56. López Aparicio, *El Movimiento Obrero en México*, pp. 221–23; Ricardo Treviño, *El Espionaja Comunista y la Evolución Doctrinaria del Movimiento Obrero en México* (México, 1952), p. 33.
57. Confederación de Trabajadores de México, *IV Consejo Nacional* (México, 1937), p. 119.

claimed in January, 1938, that the idea of the popular front and then the idea of the transformation of the P.N.R. was an excellent one, much like that planned by President Cárdenas when he earlier had called for an association of industrial workers, farm laborers, intellectuals, and artisans, the army, and small businessmen and farmers.[58]

From 1938 onward, the P.R.M. had relations with the worker movement through the C.T.M., which was really the worker section of the party. This was true in spite of the fact that the original text of Section I, Article 249, of the Federal Labor Law prohibited expressly the participation of unions in political questions—a fact that was simply overlooked. A law was passed in November, 1940, changing Section I of the article allowing for ample intervention of unions in political questions, however.[59] It would seem quite clear that the Cárdenas administration developed a paternalistic and aggressive attitude toward the labor movement from its earliest days and felt that its role was to act as judge between capital and labor, throwing its weight on the side of labor, at least so long as that class was the weaker of the two. At the same time, Cárdenas promised that "Capital which adjusts itself to the new norms of justice, which guarantees good wages, and recognizes the essential rights of the working classes, merits the most complete guarantee and encouragement of the Government."[60]

In any case, the C.T.M. became one of the bulwarks of the Cárdenas regime. Not only did it bring together once again most of the unions in an organization closely associated with the government, it likewise became an integral part of the government political party when Cárdenas reorganized that group. In addition, though, Cárdenas aided Mexican labor in gaining an important position in the Latin American labor movement, since, in September, 1938, the C.T.M. played host to a congress of Latin American trade unions which established the Confederación de Trabajadores de América Latina (Confederation of Latin American Workers, or the C.T.A.L.). The funds for the meeting were in all likelihood supplied by the Cárdenas gov-

58. *Ibid.*, p. 228.
59. Victor Manuel Varela (ed.), *Ley Federal del Trabajo: Texto Oficial Conteniendo Todas las Reformas y Adiciones Hasta la Fecha—Notas y Concordáncias* (México, 1951), Section I, Article 249, 1951, p. 82; see also *Compendio de Derecho Mexicana—del Trabajo*, 2 vols. (tercera ed.; México, 1940); José de Jesús Castorena, *Manual de Derecho Obrero: Ensayo de Integración de la Doctrina Mexicana del Derecho Obrero* (segunda ed.; México, 1949); Mario de la Cueva, *Derecho Mexicana del Trabajo*, 2 vols. (tercera ed.; México, 1949).
60. Corro Viña, *El Presidente Cárdenas*, p. 97.

ernment, which was eager to rally hemispheric support for the oil crisis.[61] In its declaration of principles, however, nothing was added that differed from the labor theory of the C.T.M.[62] The president of the organization was Lombardo Toledano; vice-presidents were Francisco Pérez Leirós, head of the C.G.T. of Argentina, Bernardo Ibañez of Chile, Guillermo Rodríguez of Colombia, and Lázaro Peña of Cuba.[63] In words closely corresponding to those of Cárdenas, the C.T.A.L. Charter announced that the principal task of the Latin American working class consisted in winning full economic and political autonomy for Latin American nations.[64] In spite of the contention of several students of Latin American affairs that the C.T.A.L. became a "purely Communist organization" after 1947,[65] it is pertinent to record, as Millon has done, that its leader, Lombardo Toledano, has been original and brilliant in his application of Marxist ideas to an interpretation of Mexican needs and the formulation of tactical policies. Certainly, the independence of Lombardo Toledano from Soviet communism in this respect was indicated especially by his criticism of the Mexican Communist party and by his formation of a separate Socialist party in 1947—the Partido Popular Socialista.[66]

By 1941, in a speech on January 29 before the Economic Congress of the C.T.M., Lombardo again illustrated his belief in variable tactics as circumstances change when he admitted that the worker movement would change its conduct every time experience advised it to do so— especially when the facts from outside are transformed and indicate the necessity for a new tactic. "The rigid forms—the permanent forms . . . are against the nature of things—are against scientific truth, and

61. Robert J. Alexander, *Prophets of the Revolution: Profiles of Latin American Leaders* (New York, 1962), p. 34.

62. See *Declaration of Principles of the C.T.A.L.*, as quoted in F. Pérez Leirós, *El Movimiento Sindical de América Latina* (Buenos Aires, 1941), pp. 59–61.

63. Stephen Naft, *Labor in Latin America* (New York, 1947), p. 2.

64. *Time* (September 19, 1938), p. 22.

65. Alexander, *Prophets of the Revolution*, p. 41.

66. Millon, *Mexican Marxist—Vicente Lombardo Toledano*. For the point of view that the Mexican labor movement was not Marxist, see Ricardo Treviño, *El Movimiento Obrero en México su Evolución Ideológica* (México, 1948) and *El Movimiento Obrero de México no es Marxista* (México, 1937). See also Vicente Lombardo Toledano, *La Revolución Rusa—La Revolución Mexicana: Pasado, Presente y Porvenir* (México, 1943), in which this labor leader maintains that Marxist principles were simply applied to the particular Mexican environment, and Professor Paul Nathan, "México en la Época de Cárdenas," *Problemas Agrícolas e Industriales de México*, VII (July-September, 1955), 147, in which he insists that it was a "Cardenista" labor movement.

consequently against revolutionary interests," he said.[67] Some specific proposals of the congress which throw light upon the "tactic" of the time were: (1) greater and more direct intervention of the state in the direction of the national economy—this intervention taking fundamentally the form of nationalization of principal sources of production and the administration of them by the state itself through organizations of a decentralized type; (2) organization of the workers in syndical form in these industries solely for the purpose of criticizing and watching the actions of the management (shades of the Webb's labor theory!); (3) strict vigilance of the state over worker co-operatives of independent production to the end of assuring their benefit for workers; (4) co-operation of the state in companies managed by workers for the purpose of lending them direct technical and financial aid; and (5) greater vigilance of the state over private companies to see that necessary reinvestments are made and to keep them from being abandoned.[68] Here may be noted a recommendation for nationalization of "principal sources of production" and the organization of workers into unions for the sole purpose of "criticizing and watching the actions of the management," together with the suggestion of state supervision of private investment.

Lending considerable evidence to the thesis that Lombardo intended to vary the tactics of the worker movement only and that he did not change his basic socioeconomic outlook during the 1930's was his statement during the same meeting to the effect that intervention of workers in the national economy was not revolutionary in the exact sense of the term because it was not in that manner that Mexico would pass from a capitalist regime to a socialist one. On this point, he was emphatic: "No, the historic change has to be a revolutionary change; not a juridical change."[69] Indicating that he looked forward some day to the "real revolution of the proletariat," Lombardo went on to say that in due time a popular revolution would be achieved just as the democratic bourgeoisie revolution had been achieved—a revolution that would make Mexico independent as an autonomous nation.[70] But because of the world situation existing at that time, Lombardo decided that it was more expedient merely to have the

67. Vicente Lombardo Toledano, "Discurso pronunciado en la Sesión Inaugural del Congreso Económico de la C.T.M., Reunido del 29 al 31 de Enero de 1941 en el Palacio de Bellas Artes," en *Importantes Resoluciones al Congreso Económico de la Confederación de Trabajadores de México* (México, 1941), n.p.
    68. *Ibid.*
    69. *Ibid.*
    70. *Ibid.*

unions press for the intervention of the state in the national production rather than have actual worker administration of the sources of production. This position he made abundantly clear in the early 1940's in a speech on the "fifth column" in Mexico, when he insisted that labor did not want a dictatorship of the proletariat or a Communist regime in Mexico; rather, it wanted national unity, popular government —not a workers' government, not a government of faction.[71] With regard to his being a Communist, Lombardo stoutly maintained that he never had been, nor was he then, a member of the Communist party; that he had never made commitments of any kind to the Communist International; and that on many occasions he had disagreed with the Communists.[72]

We have reviewed at some length the labor theories (and, indeed, the theories of statecraft) of several leaders of the Mexican Revolution during the 1934–40 era. Before attempting a summary statement of the predominant philosophy, however, we may find it worthwhile to record the view of President Cárdenas, as well as that of the chief Mexican economist of the time (Jesús Silva Herzog) on the capitalist system. Cárdenas felt strongly that the formation of a Mexican national economy would free the country from a certain kind of capitalism, "the incentive behind which is none other than to obtain raw materials by means of cheap labor; a capitalism that becomes a menace to nationality in troublous times and that only leaves behind it, in the last event, exhausted lands, a depleted subsoil, starvation wages and unrest foreboding disturbance of order."[73] Jesús Silva Herzog also gave his opinion concerning capitalism and what Mexico did *not* want but, like Cárdenas and other Mexican leaders, did not give a systematic blue-print theory for a program of action save in the most general terms. Silva Herzog held that history was the story of people trying to improve their well-being, even though by different methods, but in the process they forgot man and made him the victim of the system. He would not deny that capitalism had been a creative system; the material progress realized in England and some other countries at the end of the eighteenth century, and a little later, was magnificent, but only in the sense of science and technology—not in that which is essential to the most intimate life of man. He felt that since the end of the nineteenth-century capitalism had ceased to be the instigator of progress because of its internal contradictions: the periodic crises, the

71. Vicente Lombardo Toledano, *5th Column in Mexico* (New York, n.d.), p. 17.
72. *Ibid.*
73. Departamento del Trabajo, *Policies of the Present Administration of Mexico*, p. 15.

increasing conflict between workers and employers, and the international rivalry among the great economic units of the most powerful
empires—all of which had resulted in dire consequences for the individual and society. He continued by stating that at no time in history
has there been produced such profound pain and sorrow as in our days
and that this had occurred while we could still hear the echo of the
voices of the superficial optimists of the years 1927, 1928, and a good
part of 1929, which claimed that at last capitalist society had found
the formula for perpetual human well-being. At the same time, Silva
Herzog rejected the theories of fascism and Soviet communism as the
solution (along with classical liberalism), when he observed:

> And now several solutions offer themselves—Fascism; the
> system of Marx and Engels with its many successes, but at
> heavy costs, cruelty, and inevitable errors, and it is a long
> way from final victory; and finally a third system, founded
> on the ancient principles of political democracy and political
> liberty also—a system which has been until now for the
> benefit of the minorities, which has the odor of an old thing,
> worm-eaten by the implacable work of time. We would have
> no objection if it were a new democracy and a new liberty—
> a liberty of economic democracy as well as political and social
> democracy—a democracy and a liberty without subterfuge,
> which embraces all horizons of culture.[74]

As an alternative, he implied support for the Cárdenas approach to
Mexico's problems.

But what, in summary, was this approach? What can be said with
regard to the socioeconomic theory of the Mexican Revolution under
Cárdenas and especially with regard to the role of labor in Mexico's
"fourth position"? It seems to me that Samuel Guy Inman came very
near to the best answer possible when he wrote that the aims of the
Mexican Revolution were in some respects self-contradictory—to
socialize all life and at the same time to develop private industry. But
the *via media* agreed upon by the devotees both of revolution and
private initiative was half socialism, half capitalism (pseudo-socialism,
the radical calls it; bolshevism crises, the conservative). In any case,
the aim was to improve upon the system of Soviet Russia and also to
permit Mexico to keep on fairly good terms with its powerful capitalistic neighbor of the North.[75]

74. Jesús Silva Herzog, "Lo Humano, Problema Esencial," *Cuadernos Americanos*, I (January-February, 1941), 9–16.
75. Samuel Guy Inman, *Latin America: Its Place in World Life* (New York,
rev. ed., 1947), p. 278.

IV. Labor Theory of
the Mexican Revolution
under Cárdenas:
The Documents

Behind Cárdenas, the official government party, Lombardo Toledano, and the administration advisers in formulating their labor philosophy lay Article 123 of the Constitution of 1917, as well as the Federal Labor Law of 1931. Since both Cárdenas and the P.N.R. constantly insisted that they were merely carrying out the provisions of these two basic documents, it is necessary to examine at least pertinent sections of them. This approach would seem particularly valid when analyzing labor theory of any Latin American country, since the labor movements in those countries have always depended to a much greater extent than their United States counterparts on protective social legislation rather than on collective bargaining with employers. That is to say, they have been much more *politically* oriented than *economically* oriented. Indeed, recent studies reveal that this phenomenon is characteristic of labor movements in underdeveloped and developing countries.[1]

1. For ample support of this thesis, see W. E. Moore, *Industrialization and Labor: Social Aspects of Economic Development* (Ithaca, N.Y., 1951); Walter

The P.N.R., in its original declaration of principles, pledged itself to follow the provisions set out in Article 123 of the constitution.[2] When the convention was called at Querétaro in 1917 to write a new constitution, Carranza, in charge of the executive power, submitted a draft largely based on the political document of 1857. But the progressive social forces swept the politically minded delegates before them, and the document that was finally approved, with the famous Articles 3, 27, and 123, became one of the most radical constitutions adopted by any state up to that time.[3] The longest article in the Mexican Constitution, and in some respects, the most radical, is Article 123, which provides for a modern labor program that not only allows labor to organize but prescribes in detail the eight-hour day, the protection of women and children in every industry, and most of the modern ideas of labor protection. It prescribed that for each six days of work there should be one day of rest and that women, during the three months before childbirth, should not do heavy work and should have one month off from work following childbirth at full salary, employment being kept open for their return. It further stated that the minimum wage should be "that considered sufficient, according to the conditions in each region, to satisfy the normal necessities of life of the worker . . . and the workers should have the right to participate in the regulatory boards."[4]

The principle of equal pay for equal work, regardless of sex or nationality, was established; double pay for any work over eight hours was set, and in no case could overtime exceed three hours per day for more than three consecutive days—with women and men under sixteen being prohibited from working overtime. In all agricultural, industrial, and mining industries, or whatever other class of work, the employers were obligated to furnish workers with comfortable and clean houses, and rent could not exceed 0.5 per cent per month of the

Galenson (ed.), *Labor in Developing Countries* (Berkeley, 1962); Walter Galenson (ed.), *Labor and Economic Development* (New York, 1959); Bruce H. Millen, *The Political Role of Labor in Developing Countries* (Washington, D.C., 1963); George I. Blanksten, "Latin America," in Gabriel A. Almond and James S. Coleman (eds.), *The Politics of Developing Areas* (Princeton, 1960).

2. Partido Nacional Revolucionario, *Constitución del P.N.R.* (México, 1934), p. 12; Alfonso López Aparicio, *El Movimiento Obrero en México: Antecedentes, Desarrollo, y Tendencias* (México, 1952), p. 247.

3. Samuel Guy Inman, *Latin America: Its Place in World Life* (rev. ed.; New York, 1947), p. 261. See also Alberto Trueba Urbina (ed.), *Constitución Política de los Estados Unidos Mexicanos* (México, 1944); Rosendo Salazar, *La Carta del Trabajo de la Revolución Mexicana: Fundamentos de una Evolución* (México, 1960). For other references, see the Bibliography.

4. Trueba Urbina, *Constitución Política de los Estados Unidos Mexicana*, Sections IV–VI.

taxable value of the property. They were also obligated to establish schools, hospitals, and other services necessary for the community.[5]

Employers were made responsible for accidents at work and for professional illnesses of the workers suffered in line of duty. In addition, a death benefit payment of a certain amount was required. Like the workers, the employers were permitted to join together in professional associations. The right to strike and the shut-down were recognized. Article 18 stated that strikes were legal when they had as their object "the establishment of equilibrium between the diverse factors of production, harmonizing the rights of labor with those of capital." Article 123 went on to provide that, in the case of public utilities, the strikers had to give ten days' notice to the Federal Board of Conciliation and Arbitration and that the strike would be considered illegal if the majority of the strikers exercised violence against persons or property, or in the case of war industries. The shut-down was to be considered legal when an "excess of production makes it necessary to suspend work in order to maintain an income equal to the cost of production," provided the approval of the board had been received.[6]

The constitution provided that the differences or conflicts between capital and labor were subject to the decision of a board of conciliation and arbitration formed by an equal number of representatives of the employer and the laborers and one government representative.[7] (It will be noted that this arrangement gave the government the deciding vote on any issue brought before the board.) The arbitration and conciliation were not compulsory; consequently the government could not decide on the issue involved in a strike unless both parties agreed to it. If one of them did not accept arbitration, the strike continued until one of the adversaries gave in. If the employer refused to negotiate his differences by means of arbitration, however, or to accept the award of the board, he had to terminate the work contract and was obligated to pay the worker the equivalent of three months' salary.[8] An employer who discharged an employee without justification, or for having taken part in a trade union organization or a legal strike, was obligated, at the election of the worker, to rehire him or to pay him three months' salary. Transportation to and from the place of work was to be free to workers.[9] On August 21, 1929, the Federal

5. *Ibid.*, Sections XI, XII.
6. *Ibid.*, Sections XIV, XVI–XVIII, Article 19.
7. *Ibid.*, Article 20.
8. *Ibid.*, Article 21.
9. *Ibid.*, Articles 22, 25.

Congress was given authority to enforce these provisions rather than the various states, and the Federal Labor Law of 1931 was born of this act.

Felix Palavicini, in the prologue to Trueba's work on Article 123 of the constitution, commented that until 1917 no constitution in the world included such far-reaching social guarantees; and Trueba Urbina, with careful documentation, shows that the Constitution of Querétaro was the forerunner, in structure, of modern constitutions.[10] (The next constitution to do so was the Weimar Constitution of 1919, in Germany.) This event marked the beginning of the end of the doctrine of *laissez faire* and the inception of the belief in state intervention in the economic process for the good of the community. Without much question, the supreme law of 1917 broke the classical molds when it included such precise requirements as those contained in Chapter VI, Article 123, on labor and social welfare. Article 123 was designed to guarantee the aspirations of the working classes in Mexico, victims of a prolonged era of injustice. Trueba maintained that the 1917 Constitution expressed the significance of Mexico's freedom movement—a change of the judicial system and the economic and social system for a new one—by offering a minimum amount of protection to the workers against any who tried to use human labor illegitimately.[11]

But López Aparicio held that different philosophies contained in the document contradicted each other so that, ever since 1917, deadly opposites had been able to swear by the highest law of the land, and common adherence to the constitution had never guaranteed common action in Mexico. On the one hand, for example, Article 4 asserted the liberty of the individual to pursue his own privately chosen way of life and business, just as in 1857; on the other hand, the famous Articles 27 and 123 definitely limited that right. Article 27 referred to land, but by restricting the freedom of property in land, argued López Aparicio, it indirectly restricted the freedom of the property owner—for, instead of belonging directly and only to the owner, land is considered, under Article 27, as belonging primarily to the state. Private persons hold it only through permission of the state, explicitly or tacitly granted. On this basis, the state has the right, under this article, to expropriate private property and to redistribute national resources whenever the public good so requires.[12]

10. Felix F. Palavicini, in Alberto Trueba Urbina, *El Artículo 123* (México, 1943), p. 13.
11. *Ibid.*, pp. 23, 27–28.
12. López Aparicio, *El Movimiento Obrero en México*, p. 28.

It is significant that Article 123 was not included in the 1917 Constitution at the suggestion of Carranza. In fact, the original project of the constitution contained no codification of the rights of workers. The delegation from Veracruz, headed by Cándido Aguilar, together with the delegation from Yucatán, insisted on an entire article devoted to the workers' rights.[13]

The principles of Article 123 relating to the rights of labor were embodied in the Federal Labor Law of 1931. This statute legalized collective bargaining, prohibited lockouts, made the closed shop legal but not obligatory, restricted the right of employers to suspend operations or discharge workers, provided for dismissal wages for employees discharged without just cause, and provided for the establishment of government boards of conciliation and arbitration.[14] The law has been amended from time to time. A law of February 19, 1936, required payment for the weekly rest day, thus increasing wages by approximately 17 per cent, according to a report of the United States Tariff Commission. The principle of "profit sharing" was incorporated in the settlement of a strike in the electrical industry in July, 1936.[15]

Trade unions were not only permitted, but required; employers, when requested to do so, had to enter into a collective contract with the union. The right of the worker to his job was assured until the Board of Arbitration had determined otherwise, and if discharged unjustly, the worker was entitled to three months' salary from the employer. Once a strike had been declared legal by the Labor Board, the employer had to pay the worker for the time lost during it. The Federal Labor Law put no particular prohibition on the ideology of the labor movement in its effort to defend the common interests of the workers. It was so general that all the theories of the labor movement could be included, although the fourth section of Article 249 implied that revolutionary syndicalist tactics were prohibited. Fomenting violent action against persons or property was a prohibition imposed upon the unions.

Cárdenas held that collective bargaining with workers would be strengthened until it should prevail to the exclusion of all other forms of contract.[16] Further, the collective contract in Mexico and that in

13. Secretaría de Gobernación, *Diário de los Debates del Congreso Constituyente de 1916–1917*, I, 684, 701.
14. Victor Manuel Varela (ed.), *Ley Federal del Trabajo: Texto Oficial Continendo Todas las Reformas y Adiciones Hasta la Fecha—Notas y Concordancias* (México, 1951).
15. United States Tariff Commission, *Economic Controls and Commercial Policy in Mexico* (Washington, D.C., 1946), p. 18.
16. Departamento del Trabajo, *Policies of the Present Administration of Mexico* (México, 1936), p. 12.

Europe and the United States were viewed somewhat differently by students of Mexican labor jurisprudence. In the European collective contract, the parties are the employer and each worker considered individually. In the Mexican contract, the parties are the employer and the union. The unions not only determine the conditions of labor for all their members, but they intervene to protect their members individually, stipulating provisions expressly in the collective contract. It can be affirmed that the collective contract in Europe fixes general rules or norms with which the individual contracts must be harmonized but that the collective contract in Mexico is a contract to be executed itself, absorbing the contents of all the individual contracts and displacing them entirely.[17]

On January 18, 1935, because of the lack of legislation in some states, Congress amended the constitution to give the federal government power to issue laws on labor in accord with Article 123 of the 1917 Constitution for all the republic and, also in that year, the Federal Board of Conciliation and Arbitration was established.[18]

The rights of organized laborers were covered by the general statement that the right to work could not be interfered with except when the rights of third parties or of society were involved, as defined by law. When a strike was declared legal and a minority of the strikers attempted to resume work against the will of the majority, the rights of society were offended, and the state could prohibit the return of the minority to work. Also, when a strike was declared legal, the employer could not replace the workers before a ruling by the Board of Conciliation and Arbitration, in accordance with the law.[19] Article 260 prescribed the objectives for a legal strike by stating that strikes were legal if they had the following for their object: to insure equilibrium among the diverse factors of production, thus harmonizing the rights of labor with those of capital; to obtain fulfillment of a contract or to enforce revision of an expired contract; to support a strike that has been declared legal. Strike activity had to be limited to the single act of suspension of work, and the strike was illegal if the majority of the strikers carried out violence against persons or property.[20]

Some students of Mexico have contended that Mexican law did not regard the strike as a test of force between employer and worker, for such a view would contradict the underlying theory of the role of law in conflicts between parties of unequal power. In answer to the ques-

17. Roberto G. Amoros, *Derecho de Clase 2* (México, n.d.), p. 25; Mario de la Cueva, *Derecho Mexicano del Trabajo* (México, 1938), Vol. I.
18. Varela, *Ley Federal del Trabajo*, p. 8.
19. *Ibid.*, Section VI, Article 1, p. 12, Section VIII, Article 1, pp. 12–13.
20. *Ibid.*, Articles 260, 262, 263.

tion "Is there a place for the strike within the framework of Mexican industrial jurisprudence?" the Weyls claimed that if the strike is defined as a method of bettering labor standards by means of economic coercion, the answer must be negative. They reasoned that if the stoppage were declared legal, the workers would rely on the police force of the state, while if it were outlawed, labor would almost invariably be defeated by governmental action. They concluded that it might therefore be argued that Mexico had effective compulsory arbitration without its accompanying advantages of uninterrupted production and at least superficial industrial peace.[21] It should be noted, however, that the increasing stake of Mexican labor in the economic life of the nation was making the traditional combat philosophy of the trade unions inapplicable and obsolete because the classic theory of trade-unionism was part and parcel of the competitive capitalist ideology of enlightened self-interest; and when organized labor is given partial responsibility for the management and ownership of industry, it acquires broad concomitant duties that spring from the dual position of employees and employers. Cárdenas hinted at this view in his message to the convention of the Mexican Oil Workers' Union on July 1, 1939, when, reprimanding a minority group for acts of sabotage, he told them, ". . . the workers must be made to understand that the position of the Oil Workers Union cannot be that of fighting against the State, which in this case, is neither a capitalist unit nor a profit organization, for an improvement in the condition of oil production will necessarily be reflected in larger incomes for the workers and for the peoples as a whole."[22]

In a matter of collective conflicts attributable to "economic order" related to the establishment of new conditions of labor, suspensions or stoppages of work, which by their special nature could not be resolved under terms set up in Chapter IV of the Federal Labor Law, disputes were to be handled under the terms of Chapter VII of Title IX, which provided that a collective contract might be changed before its term had expired. This procedure might become necessary if, during the life of a contract, conditions so changed that it became undesirable to continue it in force. In such a situation, a procedure called "eco-

21. Nathaniel and Sylvia Weyl, *The Reconquest of Mexico: The Years of Lázaro Cárdenas* (New York, 1939), pp. 241–44.
22. Ramón Beteta (ed.), *Programa Económico y Social de México* (México, 1935), pp. 175–77; for a further discussion of the strike in Mexican law, see Venustiaro Rodríguez Meza, "La Limitación del Derecho de Paro General o Lock-Out en la Legislación Mexicana de Trabajo," *Revista del Trabajo*, 31 (March, 1948), 71–90; Alfonso Estandia Cano, *La Reglamentación de la Huelga* (México, n.d.); Alberto Trueba Urbina, *Evolución de la Huelga* (México, 1950).

nomic conflict" could be entered before the Board of Conciliation and Arbitration. In this event, the board ordered the maintenance of the *status quo* and an investigation by three experts, whom it appointed, aided by two commissions—one of workers and one of employers— equal in number. After both parties had had the opportunity to object to the findings of the experts, the board rendered its decision, based on the status of the company or industry with regard to its ability to pay. It could change the terms of the contract to accord with its findings.[23] The decision of the board had the binding force of a judicial decision, and some students of the problem felt that this section of the code was less favorable than the ordinary procedure, since capacity to pay rather than contractural right was the dominant consideration. Generally, a conflict became "economic" when the employer maintained that he was unable to meet labor's demands, but there was apparently no precise boundary between conflicts of this nature and other disputes. In the oil dispute, discussed at some length in the following chapters, the *union* brought the suit of "conflict of economic order" on the grounds that prices had risen and the companies' ability-to-pay had increased; hence, terms of the collective contract ought to be changed.

Another interesting and specific provision of the labor law was the power of the government to establish "contract law." When the collective contract had been entered into by two-thirds of the employers and workers belonging to unions in a definite region, it could be made obligatory on all employers and workers in the same branch of the industry in the region indicated if the president of the country so decreed.[24] (This possibility seems quite similar to the procedure made available in the United States under the National Industrial Recovery Act of 1933.)

The boards of conciliation and arbitration in Mexico were, under the Law of 1931, composed of an equal number of representatives of capital and labor and of a government representative who, of course, held the balance of power. The particular party that the boards, the courts, and the government would support obviously could (and did) change from time to time; for example, as between the time of Cárdenas and the later administration of Alemán. The general philosophy embodied in the 1931 Labor Law was interpreted by Supreme Court Justice Xavier Icaza, in a pamphlet for workers, in much the same way in which Cárdenas understood it when the former explained that man-

---

23. Varela, *Ley Federal del Trabajo*, Chapter VII, Article 576; Wendell C. Gordon, *The Economy of Latin America* (New York, 1950), pp. 152–56.
24. Gordon, *The Economy of Latin America*, p. 153.

kind was divided into only two categories—those who work and those who do not work, or those who are useful to the society into which they are born and the parasites whose sole occupation is to appropriate and enjoy the creative labor of their brothers. He then added that two unequal parties must be judged in terms of their inequality with an attitude of protection toward the weaker side.[25] And, as López Aparicio saw it, the Labor Law was in direct contrast with the idea of individualism, which puts man above the group, in that it put the interest of the group above that of any individual. Yet, any person was free to join, not to join, or to withdraw from a union.[26]

In the observations that follow, the intent is to point up what appear to have been the major currents of thought on the role of government and organized labor in a changing Mexico to the end of furthering the understanding of the whole culture of the nation and, particularly, of its economic policy; for, as Mosk said, "what went on during the time of Cárdenas has had an indirect effect on the subsequent industrial development."[27] In a report of the Confederación de Cámaras Nacionales de Comercio e Industria, a statement was made to the effect that the intellectuals who, in this epoch, directed the revolution were, in the main, Marxists, and it noted that their fundamental postulate was an equitable distribution of the national wealth.[28] While it is undoubtedly true that this was an important principle of the revolutionary thinkers of the time, it is doubtful that in itself it is sufficient evidence to classify them as Marxists. Truly, almost without exception, the spokesmen of the government during this period accepted the postulate of the class struggle—a doctrine traditionally attributed to Marx and Engels. They accused private capital of using its powerful economic position to dominate the political and economic life of the proletariat; but they felt, at the same time, that in the world condition existing at the time private capital was necessary. They simply desired to strip it of its impersonal influence and place it at the service of the people who were responsible for production—the workers. In the words of the above-mentioned report, ". . . the strategy of the revolutionary intellectuals was not to destroy private capital, but to regulate it so that it would be the servant of the workers."[29] It is possible to argue, of

25. Xavier Icaza, *El Nuevo Derecho Obrero Mexicano* (México, 1936), p. 3. See also Nathaniel and Sylvia Weyl, *The Reconquest of Mexico*, p. 240.

26. López Aparicio, *El Movimiento Obrero en México*, pp. 196–98.

27. Sanford A. Mosk, *Industrial Revolution in Mexico* (Berkeley and Los Angeles, 1950), p. 59.

28. Confederación de Cámaras Nacionales de Comercio e Industria de los Estados Unidos Mexicanos, *Análisis Económico Nacional 1934–1940* (n.p., 1940), p. 43.

29. *Ibid.*

course, that the principle of private ownership with state regulation is much more akin to the economics of fascism than to that of Marxism, except that under fascism the system might not be made the servant of the workers, since free trade unions are not a branch of the political machinery.

Time and time again, President Cárdenas stressed the fact that united labor organizations and the government should work together, under the guidance of the government, in a united front for the betterment of all classes of the society, toward the glory of a greater Mexico —all of this to be achieved, in the main, under state regulation of privately owned productive property. Outstanding evidence of such a philosophy, which smacks of popular-front, benevolent fascism—even to the glorification of a particular race—was given in a farewell address by Cárdenas to his beloved organized labor movement:

> Now that my term of office is drawing to a close, and with the authority derived from my being a friend to you workers, I wish to beg you to spare no effort toward the elimination of personal animosities. Terminate your quarrels no matter how deep-seated they may be. Do not let your efforts cease until you have attained the complete unification of the proletariat of Mexico. Until this unification is attained, the cause of nationalism cannot advance. . . . As the Revolution desires the maximum of happiness for all Mexicans, it is logical and just that as fast as laborers obtain for themselves greater economic, cultural, and political power, their responsibility to themselves and to the nation is likewise increased. The turning over to them of sources and means of production should carry with it in like degree the obligation to do their part to increase production so that all the inhabitants of Mexico may live better and do away with the wretched conditions that as a millstone have hindered the forward surge of our land. Every worker with an opportunity to produce, who does not throw all his effort and capacity into his work, or who gives himself over to vice or parasitic practices, is evading his responsibility. He is a traitor to his class and an enemy of Mexico's revindicating movement.[30]

In this speech may be noted the tone of nationalism, usually considered an element of fascism; but, at the same time, the statement is made that the means of production will be turned over to the laborers and that they must prepare themselves for this responsibility—a principle that is definitely socialist. On other occasions, the pronouncements

30. William C. Townsend, *Lázaro Cárdenas: Mexican Democrat* (Ann Arbor, 1952), p. 346.

of Cárdenas, as well as of officials of his administration—and even of Lombardo Toledano—indicate their belief, as we have seen, that the Mexican workers were not yet capable of running by themselves either industrial production or the government and that the aim of the revolution *at that stage* was to encourage private capital ownership, merely regulated by the state in favor of the workers, as well as all classes of the society. It may be that Cárdenas favored turning land and agricultural productive facilities over to the workers—as he, in fact, actually did—and, as Strode thought, did not really intend to nationalize *industrial* productive property until he felt circumstances forced him to do so. Although privately owned farms increased in numbers 44 per cent between 1930 and 1940, it should be noted that much agricultural enterprise was turned over to private owners, but in a semi-collectivized framework, differing under various circumstances. Also, several statements of Cárdenas indicated a general belief in moving in the direction of "socialization of the means of production" as a *general principle*, with no reference to accomplishing such a change only when private capital forced the issue. It is evident that there were fundamental contradictions in the economic philosophy of the president—some principles bearing a relationship to fascism at times and to socialism at others. Millan was undoubtedly correct when she lamented that Cárdenas' conduct was often marked by exasperating inconsistencies, "contradictions that are inevitable, indeed, in any leader whose ideological position does not rest upon a firm, solid theoretical basis."[31]

It is pertinent that not only was the general politico-economic thought of Cárdenas and his administrative officers somewhat contradictory and ever-changing but also that the philosophy of Lombardo Toledano—the legitimate spokesman for the organized labor movement during the period—was most variable. It shifted from the position that workers organized into trade unions were for the sole purpose of opposing the government and establishing a dictatorship of the proletariat, with the complete socialization of property, to the position that the goal of Mexican workers was nothing more than to co-operate with a progressive administration to achieve the passage and enforcement of legislation favorable to the working class, as well as all other sectors of the society. He claimed that Mexican workers were not capable of, and did not want, a government exclusively of themselves. It would seem, however, that Lombardo's variability could better be explained in terms of changing tactics to meet what he saw as a world-wide Fascist threat than as a change of basic philosophy

31. Verna C. Millan, *Mexico Reborn* (Boston, 1939), p. 79.

other than "orthodox" Marxism during the period.

One of the most consistent theorists of the Cárdenas administration was Ramón Beteta, who was convinced that the evils of capitalism were attributable primarily to the legal question of who owned the productive machinery. He desired the intervention of government with working-class interests toward the end of establishing a society without classes "which in our day is the condition nearest to the ideal in the economic relations of man."

The main principle of the Cárdenas labor theory seems to have been that the function of the modern state was primarily that of arbiter in the conflicts between capital and labor, lending its support to the working class. This philosophy of labor-employer relationships presupposes the existence of a private employer class; therefore, the president may not have had in mind a Socialist society in the traditional sense. This posture may indeed be referred to as a "fourth position," quite similar to that to be adopted in a later era in Argentina, which cannot properly be termed Fascist, Socialist, or Communist, but which contains certain elements of all three.

To facilitate the functioning of this paternalistic government-labor relationship, the administration felt that the workers should belong to unions, joined in a united front organization, closely aligned with the government, with which the government would deal exclusively to the slight of all other worker groups. While arbitration by government boards was not compulsory, it should be noted that if the strike accompanying a dispute had been declared legal by the government board, the employer was responsible for the wages of the workers for the time lost while on strike. Therefore, as long as the boards were favorably inclined toward labor, the employer had little choice but to settle. The alternative was to close down and to turn the establishment over to the government to be run for the laborers.

The inclusion in the nation's constitution of an elaborate article outlining minimum requirements for the protection of human labor reflected the denial of the individualistic philosophy of *laissez faire* and accepted the doctrine that the state should assume the responsibility for protecting workers from the vagaries of the "free market" economy. The Federal Labor Law of 1931 indicated the general belief in state intervention to protect workers, as set forth in the constitution. It further encouraged associations of both workers and employers for purposes of collective bargaining, but with the state as mediator in individual disputes.

Millan saw the same apparent contradiction at which we have been hinting and claimed that the greatest flaw in every plan of the Mexican government had been that, on the one side, it approved "Socialist" education, co-operative farming, and other measures that, if carried out fully, would inevitably effect a complete transformation of the entire social system; yet, on the other hand, it protected private, domestically owned property, while opposing only certain kinds of foreign capital.[32] Mexicans themselves could not agree on the precise philosophy of the reform movement called "the Revolution." For example, Bahamonde claimed that any objective analysis of the problem would show that Mexico did *not* imitate anybody in her work for the national well-being; rather, her doctrine, found basically in the Constitution of 1917, was going little by little toward a *particular brand* of socialism, adjusted to the social needs of the people which, it was clear, had a completely domestic and local aspect, absolutely different from all other countries. He felt that the approach did somewhat resemble Italian fascism in that Mexico respected private property but imposed upon it determined limitations, especially on mineral and agricultural property, and the state did mediate between labor and capital. But he maintained that fascism, communism, or classical liberalism did not adequately describe the system and thought that the solution Mexico sought was distinct in that she had taken the doctrines of liberalism, socialism, syndicalism, and communism and recognized in all of them some indisputable realities, proportions of which contributed to progress.[33]

A quite different viewpoint was expressed by Narciso Bassols, former ambassador to Great Britain, delegate to the League of Nations, and minister of education during the early part of the Cárdenas administration. He maintained that the Mexican Revolution was not a unique phenomenon in the world, something "*sui generis* and having nothing to do with other social movements in other countries." He denounced this view as "pure camouflage, and an essentially reactionary attempt to isolate the Mexican masses from the exploited peoples of the rest of the world."[34]

There is little doubt that the "socialism" toward which Cárdenas claimed to be taking the nation differed considerably from the communism of Soviet Russia. He admired greatly the social democracies of Scandinavia, but he studied the needs of his people in relation to their temperaments and potentialities and Mexico's resources and *mores*, and he used common sense as well as humanitarian principles to

32. *Ibid.*, p. 73.
33. Antonio Bahamonde, *México Es Así* (México, 1940), p. 65. Supporting this view, among others, was Charles A. Thomson, "Land for Peons. . . . Agrarian Reform in Mexico," *Southwest Review*, 18 (January, 1938), 148–66.
34. *Mexican Labor News*, November 11, 1937.

motivate his reform.[35] In spite of the fact that such talented economists as Dr. Federico Bach, Moisés de la Peña, Enrique González Aparicio, Dr. Jesús Silva Herzog, Lic. Ramón Beteta, and Ricardo Zavada were available, the economic leadership of the Cárdenas regime lagged behind the political leadership and hampered the nation's progress by a rather traditional approach. The Cárdenas state was an ally of the workers and peasants in the peaceful transformation into socialism of a *special kind* from a hybrid feudalism and capitalism. His approach differed from European social democratic theory in that the state became the conscious organizer of trade unions, the guide of the people in the class struggle, and the custodian of an educational procedure that trained the new generation for the specific tasks of the long period of social revolutionary change. But in its emphasis on the intrinsic values of democracy, cultural multiformity, and the right of the individual to dissent, the Cárdenas viewpoint differed markedly from that of Soviet Russia. These were perhaps the chief contributions of Cárdenas to the strategy of a directed social evolution.[36] One point remains clear: it was never made explicit how the co-operation of the propertied classes in the gradual take-over of their assets was to be successfully accomplished. Is it possible for all social classes to participate in the formation of a democratically functioning government, while, at the same time, fomenting the uprising of the working class so that they may seize full political power and eventually socialize property?

All serious students of the Mexican Revolution seem to be correct in holding that the general aim of the Cárdenas administration was the improvement of the position and influence of the working masses, particularly the Indian, through state intervention of one sort or another, as circumstances demanded, on their behalf. Although it was announced that this goal was to be achieved through progressive "socialization" of the means of production, it must be remembered that what was meant by "socialization" varied from nationalization to co-operative ownership to private ownership with government regulation in favor of the workers.

The labor theory actually evolved during the Cárdenas administration was one of having a unified, organized labor movement, under the influence of the administration, joined with other sectors of the society into a popular front, with the government acting as arbiter between capital and labor, favoring the working class. Other gains for labor were to be achieved through favorable legislation and limitations upon the use of private property. This sort of give-and-take be-

---

35. Hudson Strode, *Timeless Mexico* (New York, 1944), p. 311.
36. Nathaniel and Sylvia Weyl, *Reconquest of Mexico*, pp. 377, 381–82.

tween the state and organized labor has apparently come to be a characteristic facet of statecraft in developing countries. Nonetheless, it is difficult to understand just how private owners are expected to remain interested in this sort of arrangement during the transitional phase to some form of worker-dominated society. It may well be, however, that a system of "countervailing power" can be evolved during the course of development which may become a permanent fixture of the developed, or mature, economy.

It seems apparent that the Cárdenas administration accepted the Marxian analysis of the economic crisis of capitalism but often sought to apply a native remedy—shaped largely by outside forces—which cannot properly be classified under any of the existing "isms." This fundamental lack of theoretical unity, or consistency, referred to above and pointed up especially well by Simpson,[37] may go far in explaining the different approaches to reform in the national economic policy of the Cárdenas regime, as evidenced by government-labor policy in the Laguna region, in the railroad problem, and in the oil controversy. To examine the structure of the labor movement, as well as labor policy in connection with these questions, is the purpose of the remainder of this book.

37. Eyler N. Simpson, *The Ejido: Mexico's Way Out* (Chapel Hill, 1937), Chapters 18, 19.

V. Structure, Program, and Leadership of the Labor Movement

Close on the heels of the Monterrey episode, on February 26, 1936, an assembly of unification, called by the National Committee for the Defense of the Proletariat, convened in Mexico City. In attendance were more than two thousand delegates of industrial workers' organizations, intellectuals, federal employees, and peasants, "joined together by their own efforts and, in many cases, at the cost of genuine sacrifices," to create a central labor organization. The C.G.O.C.M., as well as other centrals, was liquidated in this congress of unification, and the Confederación de Trabajadores de México (C.T.M.), or the Confederation of Mexican Workers, was born.[1]

This central federation was characterized as a national labor front, within the class struggle, at the service of the Mexican workers, pledged to fight at the time, not for the transformation of the system of private property and the establishment of the dictatorship of the proletariat, but simply for the fulfillment of the provisions of the laws resulting from the Mexican Revolution.[2] Chapter I of the statutes of the C.T.M.,

1. Confederación de Trabajadores de México, *Informe del Comité Nacional 1936–1937* (México, 1938), p. 65; see also by the C.T.M., *C.T.M. 1936–1941*, p. 31 ff.
2. *Ibid.*, pp. 31, 33.

containing the declaration of principles, purpose, and tactics of the organization stated:

> The program of the labor movement must be formed with full recognition of the structure and historic evolution of society, in order that labor may act, with the greatest possible success, as a conscious and decisive factor in opposition to the prevailing system of exploitation. . . . In Mexico, the liberal tradition still persists as the ideal of an essentially individualist population. But the reality of this regime of free enterprise has been continual disorder and the rule of various native oligarchies, always under the economic and political domination of the imperialist powers, principally the United States. . . .
>
> The working class of Mexico must never forget that *the final aim of its struggles is the abolition of the capitalist regime*. Nevertheless, since Mexico is subject to imperialist domination, before arriving at that final aim it is first necessary to achieve the political and economic freedom of the country.[3] [Emphasis mine.]

The statutes also pledged that the C.T.M. would lead the continuing fight for shorter hours, for higher real wages, for uniform conditions of work, for education and technical training, for sports and recreation, for protection of working women and young people, and for improved labor legislation. In addition, the C.T.M. would oppose any infringement upon the right to strike or to organize, was against any restrictions of the right to meet and speak freely, opposed unemployment, was against the use of technological advances without corresponding benefits for the workers, and, above all, was against any effort on the part of government, employers, or other groups to curtail the rights of labor or subject the labor movement to control.[4] The Congress of Unification of the C.T.M. in addition proposed a program for the agricultural as well as for the urban workers, a program considerably in advance of existing agrarian legislation. It urged ample credit for peasant farming and the abolition of rent payments for land. Large landed estates, which had been immune to distribution, were to be expropriated and divided among the still landless peasant communities, to be worked collectively.[5]

3. "Estatutos de la Confederación de Trabajadores de México," *C.T.M. 1936–1941*, pp. 67–68. For evidence that this early spirit of the C.T.M. was altered appreciably during the 1950's, see Moisés Poblete Troncoso, *The Rise of the Latin American Labor Movement* (New York, 1960), pp. 102–7; Rosendo Salazar, *La C.T.M., Su Historia, Su Significado* (México, 1956).
4. C.T.M., *C.T.M. 1936–1941*, pp. 67–68.
5. *Ibid.*, pp. 48–49.

Tactically, the C.T.M. declared that it would employ all the weapons of revolutionary syndicalism, which consist in direct action of the workers in their economic disputes with the capitalist class, and took a stand in *opposition to all collaboration*, to prevent subjection to organs of the state which might limit the possibilities of economic and social elevation. The statutes declared that direct action was intended to suppress the use of intermediaries between workers and owners. While there was to be no collaboration with organs of the state, alliances could be made with groups promoting similar aims, so long as there was no compromising with labor's essential aims.[6] Lombardo Toledano declared in an address at the Congress of Unification that the C.T.M. had received money from no one, nor had it asked for any, adding that the organization was free, positively independent and autonomous, but that it would "assure aid to the government of Cárdenas in all its revolutionary actions and in all its endeavors to favor the exploited masses of Mexico."[7] It is interesting to observe that in spite of these declarations, there was to be a great deal of collaboration with the state and, further, Labor Department officials were to act as intermediaries in disputes between capital and labor more often than not. This latter situation may be accounted for by the fact that labor department officials in the Cárdenas regime, as well as boards of conciliation and arbitration, turned out to be more favorable toward labor than had been anticipated. Furthermore, the ideology of the C.T.M. varied from time to time as the circumstances within and without Mexico changed and was not always definite. The Calles position and the later oil crisis were events that inevitably were to bring the C.T.M. into politics. As the Mexico City electricians declared in October of 1939: "All events in the life of a community are political in nature. For any organization to proclaim itself apolitical, and especially for any organization of workers to do so, is to deny the basic principles of its existence. . . . All important functions of workers' organizations, such as work stoppages, the general strike, etc., are profoundly political and often more significant than any parliamentary proceedings."[8] In addition, the threat of spreading world fascism prompted labor to take the lead in organizing a popular front—an activity to be discussed in the next chapter.

Structurally, the C.T.M. was composed of national industrial unions

6. *Ibid.*, p. 69.
7. Vicente Lombardo Toledano, "Discurso de Clausura," C.T.M., *C.T.M. 1936–1941*, p. 63.
8. *Lux*, XII (October, 1939), 7.

and local federations of unions in all the economically important regions of the country. In other words, according to its leader, Lombardo Toledano, "its organization is both horizontal and vertical, and in this respect it corresponds to the realities of Mexican economic life, which embraces at one extreme such survivals of the colonial period as the household manufactures, and at the other extreme, large factories of the most modern type."[9] As would be expected in a semi-colonial country with large tropical regions, the principal enterprises of Mexico were the raw-material industries and the public services necessary to the commercial interchange on which, in part, its economic life depended—mining, oil, the electrical industry, railroads, automobile transport, the cultivation of tropical fruits, and other products typical of the soil. The increasingly well-defined and determined purpose of the revolution to provide a greater measure of economic independence of the country resulted during this period in a pronounced development of domestic manufacturing, to which were added the so-called "montage" industries, which import raw or semi-finished materials from the most important industrial countries to meet the demand of the Mexican worker. The major industries of this class were textiles, shoes, prepared foods, chemicals, and automobile assembly plants.

In accordance with the Constitution of the C.T.M., the national federations were required to transform themselves into national unions of the corresponding branch of industry, made up of as many sections (local unions) as there were centers of work controlled by the members of the organization. This structure was considered more efficient in defending the interests of the workers than the old form of independent unions associated in a national federation, particularly since the Federal Labor Law empowered plant or industrial unions to conclude collective contracts with their employers, whereas the federations of unions did not enjoy the right. United under the C.T.M. from the beginning were the C.G.O.C.M., which dated from 1933, the Confederación Sindical Unitaria de México, the Cámara Nacional del Trabajo, the Sindicato de Trabajadores Ferrocarrileros, the Sindicato de Trabajadores Mineros y Metalúrgicos de la República Mexicana, the Sindicato Mexicano de Electricistas, the Alianza de Uniones y Sindicatos de Artes Gráficas, the Alianza de Obreros y Empleados de la Compañía de Tranvias, and many other federations and unions

---

9. Vicente Lombardo Toledano, "The Labor Movement," *The Annals of the American Academy of Political and Social Science*, 208 (March, 1940), 52.

of the states.[10] There was not, however, even at the birth of the C.T.M., complete unification of the labor movement. Remaining outside this central were the old C.R.O.M. unions, the C.G.T., which continued under the banner of anarcho-syndicalism, and many other groups, unions, and federations of different ideologies. Nonetheless, powerful from the beginning, the C.T.M. gathered extraordinary strength. In all ways, the government favored this grand central—donating money, giving complete guarantees for union activity, persecution of the enemies of the C.T.M., etc. As we have seen, both Lombardo and President Cárdenas denied this type of government aid to the C.T.M. Whatever the exact truth may be in this respect, it cannot be denied that the C.T.M. leaders obtained seats in the Senate and the House of Deputies, and the weight of this organization, in union with the National Peasants' Confederation (C.N.C.) was a decisive factor in the election for governors, municipal presidents, city councils, and representatives of the Congress of the Union of the States.[11] In spite of the disproportionate aid given to the C.T.M. by the government, the Cárdenas regime was one of intense struggle among unions, and many times resulted in bloodshed, as among the textile workers in the zone of Atlixco and several factories in the State of Veracruz.

Internally, the permanent authority of the C.T.M. was vested in the National Executive Committee, made up of seven secretaries: the secretary general, secretary of labor and conflicts, secretary of organization and propaganda, secretary of peasant action, secretary of education and cultural problems, secretary of social welfare and technical matters, and secretary of statistics and finance.[12] Serving in these respective positions, as of August, 1938, were Vicente Lombardo Toledano, Juan Gutiérrez, Fidel Velázquez, Mariano Padilla, Professor David Vilches, Manuel Gutiérrez B., and Salvador Lobato.[13] Other

10. For a complete list of affiliated national unions, as well as state and local federations, see "Informe del Comité Nacional de la C.T.M., Al Segundo Congreso General Ordinario de la Misma Institución," *C.T.M. 1936–1941*, pp. 1105–10, and Departamento Federal del Trabajo, *Directório de Agrupaciones Obreras y Patronales de Jurisdicción Federal y Local* (México, 1939). See also Departamento Federal del Trabajo, *Prontuario de Organizaciones Sindical* (México, 1937); Juan de Dios Bojórquez, *Directório de Associaciones Sindicales de la República* (México, 1936); Confederación de Trabajadores de México, *5 Años de Vida de la C.T.M.* (México, n.d.).

11. Alfonso López Aparicio, *El Movimiento Obrero en México: Antecedentes, Desarrollo y Tendencias* (México, 1952), pp. 211, 219.

12. "Estatutos de la Confederación de Trabajadores de México," *C.T.M. 1936–1941*, p. 71.

13. Confederación de Trabajadores de México and Confederación Campesina Mexicana, *A Todos Los Trabajadores de la República* (México, 1938), p. 8.

important leaders were Fernando Amilpa, Alfonso Sánchez Mado-
riaga, Jesús Yurén, Luis Quintero, Enrique Rangel, Leonardo Flores,
Pedro Téllez Vargas, and Vidal Díaz Muñoz.[14]

As in the case of the C.R.O.M., the characteristics of this new confederation were linked closely to those of its leader, Vicente Lombardo
Toledano. He was the brain, the organizer of the C.T.M., who had
begun as a figure in the social struggles of Mexico as a leader in the
C.R.O.M., whence he came to occupy a place of prime importance in
the labor movement of Mexico. Few figures have been the object
of more discussion in Mexico than Lombardo, who did not come
from the factory or office, but from the halls of the universities.
"Gifted with an uncommon intelligence, provided with great theoretical preparation on social questions, and with a vast experience in
trade union matters, Lombardo is, furthermore, a brilliant speaker
and an untiring fighter. . . ."[15] Cárdenas, Lombardo, and Lenin were
born the same year. Lombardo was the son of the owner of the
Teziutlan Copper Company, and at the age of fifteen he was sent
to Mexico City as a boarding student in the Internado Nacional, a
preparatory school that was the favorite of provincial families who
could afford to pay tuition and board for their sons. The dwindling
of his family's fortune brought the young law student, as in the case
of other young men, to look deeper into the revolutionary convulsions
that had begun to shake the nation. As a young lawyer he turned to
politics as the most promising field for his talents, and politics at
that time—the period of Obregón's rise—was developing a definitely
laborist trend. In the thesis for his law degree, Lombardo defended the
idealist philosophy as opposed to materialism in a manner brilliantly
becoming one whom Caso regarded as his star pupil, protegé, and
possible successor.[16]

In 1918, Lombardo Toledano was named secretary of the Popular
University, a cultural center that arranged lecture courses of a popular
nature. Here, the future labor leader first rubbed elbows with the city
proletariat. In his lectures at this time, Lombardo showed decided
traces of Carlyle's influence. Two years later, already a professor at
twenty-five, he took a combined professional and vacation trip to

14. Rosendo Salazar, *Líderes y Sindicatos* (México, 1953) p. 110.
15. López Aparicio, *El Movimiento Obrero en México*, p. 219.
16. J. H. Plenn, *Mexico Marches* (New York, 1939), p. 262. See also: Enrique Ramírez y Ramírez, "Vicente Lombardo Toledano, Un Militante de la
Clase Obrera de México," *Futuro*, VI (March, 1941), 35–42; *La Obra y la
Lucha de Vicente Lombardo Toledano* (México, 1952). For a scholarly discussion of the evolution of Lombardo's ideology, see Robert Paul Millon, *Mexican
Marxist—Vicente Lombardo Toledano* (Chapel Hill, 1966).

the State of Guerrero. The semibarbarous living conditions of many natives, their complete neglect in the face of devastating malaria and leprous skin diseases, and the heartbreaking poverty of these people left a permanent mark on the young professor. "His brain was already churning with attempts to reconcile these things, the situation of the city workingman, the retreat of the Puebla Indians to the hills, with the idealist philosophy in which was inherent the notion that there is a Divinity that shapes our ends."[17] After José Vasconcelos was appointed minister of education following the fall of Carranza, he named Lombardo director of the National Preparatory School—a post regarded as highly important in Mexican cultural life—and formerly reserved as a mark of honor for mature men who had achieved fame and distinction. During this period, Lombardo moved closer to trade-union circles, as did many others under the frankly laborist tendency of the Obregón administration. He was soon in the C.R.O.M. as head of the Educational Committee, where he became a collaborator with Luis Morones, whose social trajectory was the reverse of Lombardo's. The young Lombardo continued in the C.R.O.M. at the side of Morones until 1931, when the former, with a group of followers, rebelled and formed a C.R.O.M. of its own, later to become the C.G.O.C.M., which, in turn, was to be the nucleus of the C.T.M.

Probably the second most influential figure in the C.T.M. was Juan Gutiérrez, secretary of labor and conflicts, and the head of the powerful and conservative Railway Workers' Union. He was regarded by some as having fully as much authority in the C.T.M. as Lombardo. While this is probably an exaggeration, the point was that Lombardo had no one union back of him and that primary power in the C.T.M., as in any labor confederation, was wielded by the direct representatives of the unions. In Plenn's view, those who argued in this fashion forgot that back of Lombardo, even before the C.T.M. came into existence, was the strong C.G.O.C.M. and its various constituent regional federations of workers and peasants, formed by Lombardo's group after the split from Morones.[18]

According to the registry of the secretary of industry, commerce, and labor, at the end of the administration of President Cárdenas there were 2,781 registered unions, 51 federations, and 9 confederations of federal jurisdiction.[19] At its first National Congress, in February, 1938, Lombardo Toledano reported a membership in the C.T.M. of 945,913 individuals in 3,594 affiliated organizations, national, regional, state,

17. Plenn, *Mexico Marches*, pp. 263–64.
18. *Ibid.*, p. 277.
19. López Aparicio, *El Movimiento Obrero en México*, p. 213.

and local. Included were 76,000 railroad workers, 50,000 sugar workers, 25,000 textile workers, and 12,000 oil workers.[20] The 945,000 estimate was probably too high, since there were at the time only about 1,100,000 workers in mining, trade, communications, transportation, and government in all of Mexico and since, in addition to the C.T.M. membership there was the Miners' Federation, which claimed 100,000 members, along with the Electricians' Union, both of which had left the C.T.M. as a result of the Communist split of April, 1937. Moreover, there were an estimated 50,000 members in the C.R.O.M. led by Júlio Ramírez and 30,000 in the C.G.T., led by Francisco Ramírez Escamilla, both outside the C.T.M. There were also, outside the C.T.M., the newly formed Union of Federal Employees, which, "in deference to the government's wishes," the C.T.M. announced it would not seek to make an affiliate. Then the peasants, many of whom once belonged to the C.R.O.M., were organized, at the time these statistics were released, into the government-sponsored National Peasants' Federation.[21] Apparently, however, the C.T.M. membership figures included at least the peasants who had received land in the form of *ejidos*.[22] At any rate, López Aparicio held that at the end of the six-year Cárdenas regime, the C.T.M. counted in its files more than a million workers.[23]

Concerning membership figures for Mexican trade unions, Sanford Mosk noted that since the founding of the C.T.M. in 1936, they have tended to be erratic because factional disputes have often led to temporary withdrawals of component unions, therefore sizable fluctuations have occurred with little warning. In addition, at any one time the status of some of the member unions was apt to be unclear, and the claim of the C.T.M. regarding affiliations sometimes conflicted with statements coming from other sources, including leaders of the unions in question. Still, Mosk continued, it could not be doubted that the C.T.M., even as late as 1949, embraced the majority of the organized workers of Mexico.[24]

20. C.T.M., *Informe del Comité Nacional 1936–1937*, p. 67; Clarence Senior, *Mexico in Transition* (New York, 1939), p. 26; Poblete Troncoso, *The Rise of Latin American Labor Movements*, p. 103.
21. Senior, *Mexico in Transition*, p. 26.
22. C.T.M., *Informe del Comité Nacional 1936–1937*, p. 67.
23. López Aparicio, *El Movimiento Obrero en México*, p. 219.
24. Sanford A. Mosk, *Industrial Revolution in Mexico* (Berkeley and Los Angeles, 1950), p. 100. For a discussion of the difficulties involved in obtaining membership figures in Mexican trade unions, as well as for estimated membership as late as 1953, see Horace B. Davis, "Numerical Strength of Mexican Unions," *Southwestern Social Science Quarterly*, 35 (June, 1954), 45–55; "Workers' Organizations in Mexico," *Monthly Labor Review*, 57 (September, 1943), 535, 536.

A very peculiar and very significant aspect of the labor movement during the Cárdenas administration was the fact that the peasants, who constituted the largest, and in many ways the most important, economic sector in the country, could not freely join with industrial labor because the major peasant organizations were controlled by the National Revolutionary party; apparently this prohibited the C.T.M. from taking over the organization of this segment of agricultural labor. Cárdenas probably did not intend that too much power should be concentrated in the hands of Lombardo Toledano; therefore, he opposed the aspirations of the C.T.M. toward control of the peasants.[25] Whether this is a fact that was the key to government rather than C.T.M. sponsorship of the peasant organizations is difficult to determine. Virginia Prewett reported that as early as 1936 Cárdenas had attempted to create a counterbalance to the C.T.M., but the treachery of Portes Gil scuttled it.[26]

At any rate, it is certain that upon his return to the capital from the Monterrey trip in mid-February, 1936, Cárdenas, in a report to the press, when asked what he thought about the intention of the C.T.M. to call a congress for peasant unity in opposition to a similar plan of the P.N.R., replied that he had approved the holding of the workers' congress and looked upon it as the initial step resolutely taken toward complete organization of the industrial proletariat. He added, however, that the C.T.M. must refrain from calling a peasant congress, since "due to the special situation of the latter, the Government sprung from the Revolution has always looked upon itself and still does so, as obliged to espouse their organization."[27] He stated further that the P.N.R., in sponsoring the peasant assemblies then meeting in the various states of the country, had simply obeyed an order "made by the Executive under my charge. . . . Consequently, should the Confederation of Mexican Workers or any other similar organization, in competition with Government action, attempt to organize rural workers for its own account, far from succeeding in this, it would only incubate the germs of dissolution, by introducing among the peasantry internal conflicts, which have given such fatal results in the case of the industrial proletariat."[28]

In July, 1935, President Cárdenas had given an order to the National Executive Committee of the P.N.R. This stated that the lack

25. Henry Bamford Parkes, *A History of Mexico* (Boston, 1950), pp. 402–3.
26. Virginia Prewett, *Reportage on Mexico* (New York, 1941), p. 62.
27. Ministry of Foreign Relations, *The Mexican Government in the Presence of Social and Economic Problems: Tour of the President of the Republic—Monterrey—Tampico—Guadalajara* (México, 1936), p. 31.
28. *Ibid.*

of organization in most units of the country had led to conflicts and to delay in the granting of lands. Unscrupulous officials had sometimes combined with owners and had been an obstacle to the economic liberation of the peasants. Since it would aid in carrying out the agrarian legislation now in force and that yet to be passed and would raise the living standards of the peasants, the P.N.R. was, according to Cárdenas, the proper agency for the unification of all peasants. Therefore, its Executive Committee should proceed to formulate a plan of action for organization of the peasants upon being given land by the government. The order specified that the committee should call conventions in every state of the union for the purpose of having but one League of Agrarian Communities in each unit of the nation, each *ejido* to have two elected delegates to the convention of unification. After the league had been organized in the states, the National Executive Committee of the P.N.R. was to call a great convention to organize the Mexican Peasant Confederation, which was to be the central organ in the scheme. And, finally, the order stated that the Executive Committee of the party should proceed to formulate drafts for laws on peasant life insurance, insurance against agricultural sickness and accidents, insurance against loss of crops, and all other laws tending to insure the social and economic well-being of the members of the National Peasant Confederation. After the order was given, the P.N.R. and the Secretariat of Agrarian Action and Peasant Organization accomplished the unification of Leagues of Agrarian Communities in the Federal District and several states, including 8,203 local groups with a total membership of 1,094,260 family heads, representing a population of 5,471,300 peasants, undoubtedly the largest workers' organization in the country.[29]

Announcement was made on August 9, 1938, of the completed plans for the celebration, beginning August 28, of the National Congress for Peasant Unification, to be held under the auspices of the P.R.M. for the purpose of constituting a national peasant confederation, known as Confederación Nacional de Campesinas, or C.N.C. The C.N.C. included all the *ejidatarios*, as well as many other small farmers and agricultural workers. *Mexican Labor News* commented, however, that the bulk of the landless rural population would still be without representation in the federation because of the lack of local organization and that this group remained the most important sector of

---

29. Gilberto Bosques, *The National Revolutionary Party of Mexico and the Six-Year Plan* (México, 1937), pp. 311–14. For a list of peasant groups organized by states, including number of peasants and number of villages represented, see Appendix B.

Mexico's working class still to be organized.[30] This paper, the semi-official organ of the C.T.M., held that although the process of organizing the peasants had undoubtedly suffered from the fact that in a good many instances the organizers had been professional politicians of the old P.N.R. instead of genuine peasant leaders, it was expected that in the constituent congress of the new national body the rank and file would make itself heard strongly enough to place several of its own people on the governing body. It continued by predicting that the close association with the labor movement within the P.R.M., as well as the increasingly good relations between the peasant organizations and the C.T.M., would undoubtedly, within a short time, give the National Peasant Confederation a more genuinely popular and less official character.[31]

The C.T.M. protested the loss of control over its peasant unions in the commercialized agricultural industries, and a compromise was worked out wherein it was agreed that those peasant unions already formed should go into the C.N.C. with the understanding that they would be permitted to "consult with the C.T.M."[32] The policy of the C.T.M. with regard to the new C.N.C. was to urge all its own rural members and affiliated unions to cooperate closely with the national peasant body, and in some cases it advised them to enter the C.N.C.[33]

The Executive Committee of the C.N.C., as of April 8, 1940, was composed as follows: secretary general, Professor Graciano Sánchez; secretary of education, health, and special services, Isaías Suárez; secretary of agrarian and syndical affairs, Augustín Olvera; secretary of organization and statistics, Eduardo F. Arellano; secretary of press and propaganda, Ricardo Altamirano; secretary of feminine action, Josefina Vicens; secretary of juvenile action, Fibronio Choperena; secretary of finance, Sacramento Joffre; and chief clerk, Manuel Castaño B.[34]

Not only was the C.T.M. hampered in its activity by being prohibited from organizing the peasants, but it was torn from within, temporarily at least, by an internal schism occurring in the spring of 1937, when members of the Communist party who were also C.T.M. union leaders headed a revolt on questions of tactics and of authority. Subsurface animosities had been growing since the Third National Council meeting, held in Veracruz in October, 1936. At the Fourth

30. Workers University of Mexico, *Mexican Labor News*, August 11 and 18, 1938.

31. *Ibid.*

32. Prewett, *Reportage on Mexico*, p. 162.

33. *Mexican Labor News*, September 1, 1938.

34. Partido de la Revolución Mexicana, *En Defensa de la Soberanía Nacional, 18 de Marzo* (México, n.d.), p. 26.

National Council meeting in Mexico City on April 28, 1937, a serious split occurred which, it was feared, would cause the C.T.M. to lose a quarter of its membership. The Communist party withdrew, charging that the council was illegally constituted; it was followed by the railroad workers and the electrical workers of the Federal District. Three secretaries of the National Committee, Juan Gutiérrez, of the railroad union, Miguel Velasco and Pedro Morales, both of the Communist party, also withdrew, declaring that they could not be a party to the "illegal resolutions or actions taken by the Fourth Council."[35]

In his speech at the closing session of the council, Lombardo made a strong plea for the return of the bolting organization and officials, pointing out that of the total membership of the C.T.M., 3,183 organizations, with 599,641 individual members, had remained within the council, thus giving a substantial majority over the 141,000 members whose delegates had voted to abstain. He maintained that all the acts of the council were thus legal, since they had been approved by a majority of the membership in accordance with the organization's constitution and by-laws. He went on to analyze the attitude of the Communist party toward the C.T.M., charging that the party had imposed its own discipline on its elements within the trade union organization, to the detriment and at the expense of the larger discipline of the C.T.M. He condemned in the strongest terms the action of the party in precipitating a break in labor's ranks on the very eve of the first of May. For their part, the Communist party and the various non-Communist organizations that left the council accused Lombardo and his closest associates of attempting to establish a bureaucratic, personalist control over the C.T.M. to the exclusion of all those elements unwilling to submit themselves to such dictatorship. They claimed that bona fide delegates to the council were excluded because of partisan motives and that in various state congresses and organizations the ruling clique in the C.T.M. had attempted to impose its own unconditional supporters on the membership, over-riding the will of the rank and file. *Mexican Labor News* commented, "Unquestionably, the dispute has been a severe blow to the Mexican labor movement. Not only may it deprive the C.T.M. of a substantial bloc of its membership, but it removes such powerful and influential unions as the electricians and perhaps the railroad workers, together with various state organizations of considerable importance."[36]

35. *Mexican Labor News*, May 5, 1937. For a more detailed discussion of this schism in the C.T.M., see Confederación de Trabajadores de México, C.T.M., *C.T.M., 1936–1941*; L. O. Pendergast, "Growing Pains of Mexican Labor," *The Nation*, 144 (June 12, 1937), 671–74.
36. *Mexican Labor News*, May 5, 1937.

The specific cause of the break seems to have been a dispute over the organization of the teachers' union at the Querétaro congress for teacher unification and over the Federation of Workers of the State of Nuevo León, where the Communists apparently made an attempt to capture the local leadership. It was the exclusion of the Nuevo León delegation from the council as having been improperly constituted which precipitated the walk-out. The veteran leaders of unions and state federations within the C.T.M. were up in arms against the recent tactics of the Communist party in attempting to seize the leadership of old and new organizations by purely mechanical means, without making a genuine appeal to the membership. This, they claimed, was particularly true of the way in which the Communists captured control of the Querétaro teachers' congress and of the Mexican Federation of Educational Workers resulting from it. The refusal of the C.T.M. to admit the teachers' union into the organization of the C.T.M. was one of the principal reasons advanced by the dissidents, particularly the railroad workers, for leaving the council.[37]

The more general cause—and perhaps the most accurate—of the split was explained by *Mexican Labor News* as follows: "On the whole, it may be said that the present break and the disputes leading up to it must be charged to the general immaturity of the Mexican labor movement and the extreme difficulties under which it has developed. It has never been a truly independent movement and due to the peculiar circumstances of the revolution and the governments emanating from it, there has always been far too great an intervention of government officials in the movement for its own soundness and health."[38] It is significant indeed to note the voice of Mexican labor making the same observations for which Mexicans severely criticize observers from the United States for making; that is, the undue influence of government in the trade-union movement. The paper went on to say that there appeared to be good reason for supposing that a large part of the current difficulties was at least indirectly because of maneuvers and intrigues fomented by certain members of the government attempting to use sections of the trade-union movement for their own political purposes. Leaders on both sides of the dispute had, apparently, willingly allowed themselves to be made the tools of selfish interests alien, if not actually hostile, to labor. The report concluded by noting that, from an objective point of view it would appear that the Communist party must bear the chief responsibility for the break

37. *Ibid.*
38. *Ibid.*

because of attempting to set too rapid a pace for the mass of the labor movement to maintain. "What the Communists and their present supporters appear to have ignored is that Lombardo Toledano has had to work with the conditions and the personalities he found, and that neither could be changed overnight. . . ."[39]

The Fourth National Council of the C.T.M. resolved to fix a period within which the dissident organizations would have to accept the validity of its decisions and empowered the National Committee to suspend those organizations which did not obey the ruling. It issued a call to the Communist workers, as members of the C.T.M., to submit unconditionally to the decisions of the directive organs of the trade-union institutions in preference to their party commitments, for the purpose not only of maintaining the unity of the C.T.M. but also to make possible the fulfillment of the vast program that the confederation had laid out in relation to national and international problems.[40]

The Plenum of the Central Committee of the Communist party of Mexico held from June 26 to 30, 1937, resolved that the decisions of the Fourth National Council of the C.T.M. should be obeyed.[41] The party revised its tactics of struggle and assured the C.T.M. of its loyal co-operation to strengthen the internal unity of the confederation and to insure that the decisions of its representative body and institutions were respected. Shortly after the plenum, the dissident organizations returned to the C.T.M., and it was once again in a position to direct its attention to other problems of the Mexican workers. Only the Federal District's Mexican Union of Electrical Workers, some two thousand strong, maintained its former position and refused to join in the peace move. The returning unions publicly acknowledged their error in having abandoned the Fourth Council. Of the three secretaries of the National Committee who led the dissident movement, two resigned, while the third—Juan Gutiérrez, general secretary of the Railroad Union—was restored to his position on the committee.[42]

One of the major problems with which the C.T.M. was forced to cope —even before it had achieved complete internal unity—was the question of organized labor's participation in a popular front. In the ensuing struggle over this matter, there was revealed once again the dominant role of the government in the labor movement, as well as the re-impact of the labor movement on the government. Obviously,

39. *Ibid.*
40. C.T.M., *Informe del Comité Nacional 1936–1937*, p. 69; C.T.M., *C.T.M., 1936–1941*, pp. 256–67.
41. *Ibid.*, pp. 69–70; Prewett, *Reportage on Mexico*, p. 16.
42. *Mexican Labor News*, August 4, 1937.

two embarrassing points involved in achieving such a front were the fact that the statutes of the C.T.M., as we have seen, opposed any alliance with the government. At the same time, the P.N.R. probably did not relish the idea of risking its organized peasants to the influence of the C.T.M. These obstacles were removed, at least in large measure, by the resignation from the P.N.R. of Portes Gil and other important Calles supporters and by Lombardo's belief that a popular front was necessary, and immediately so—not to mention the fact that President Cárdenas felt that all the popular elements should be bound together to defend the revolution.

The C.T.M. had been formed shortly before the Spanish Civil War broke out, and as that conflict progressed, Lombardo and his followers espoused the loyalist cause and the popular front idea with enthusiasm. Since the C.T.M.'s growth was sometimes hampered by Cárdenas' action in sponsoring independent peasant and government employee unions, its leaders championed a popular front plan even more fervently.[43] In the view of López Aparicio, Lombardo's wish to sponsor a popular front similar to that organized in France during the regime of Leon Blum in function was simply further proof of the Marxist-Leninist line of the C.T.M., since the idea of the formation of popular fronts in all countries was developed at the end of the Seventh International Congress of Communists held in August, 1935, in Moscow, along with the idea that industrial workers should enter into an alliance with the rural workers and small business groups in the cities.[44] With this latter interpretation it is difficult to agree entirely, since in many countries of the Western world there was collaboration between farmers, workers, and small businessmen, entirely independent of any decision of Communists in Moscow.

In September, 1936, the P.N.R. had issued a manifesto to labor calling for a type of popular front within the party:

> The new democracy to which the P.N.R. aspires is conceived in terms of an increasing influence of organized workers and peasants in the political and economic direction of the community. The fictitious equality, which in the past has only been used to justify . . . the oppression exercised by the propertied minorities and their allies over the producing majorities, no longer can serve as a standard for a region which tends towards true democracy, because of the people —whose will is expressed through the opinion of the majority

43. Prewett, *Reportage on Mexico*, p. 163.
44. López Aparicio, *El Movimiento Obrero en México*, p. 222. Also see Víctor Alba, *Historia del Frente Popular: Análisis de una Táctica Política* (México, 1959); *El Frente Único en México* (Habana, 1938).

—is composed preponderantly of workers. Therefore the National Executive Committee of the Party realizes the importance which the participation of members of revolutionary unions and ejidal groups has for the Party. And the Committee does not think of this participation in order to control it, but rather to aid these elements in achieving their aim as a class.[45]

At the Second National Council of the C.T.M., in October, 1936, the question was debated, and the decision was made to participate in a front with the P.N.R.[46] In January, 1937, *Mexican Labor News* reported that according to an announcement just made by Lombardo Toledano, Mexico would soon be the third country in the world to complete the organization of a popular front of all the progressive forces of the nation, since after three months of negotiations with the various organizations involved, the C.T.M. could state that an agreement in principle had been reached and the formal pact of union would be signed within a short time. Further, it was stated that the popular front would be made up of the Mexican Peasant Confederation (C.N.C.), the P.N.R., the C.T.M., and the Communist party of Mexico. It was, however, stated that the Mexican body would differ from the popular fronts already in existence in Spain and France in that it would *not* be a political party contending in national or local elections. It would instead function as a united front organization of all progressive forces and elements in the country in defense of the interests of the peasants, the working classes, the lower middle class, and, in general, the interests of the nation as a whole against the aggressions and encroachments of foreign imperialism.[47] It is somewhat ironic that the popular front turned out to be exactly what Lombardo claimed it would not be—a political party!

To the charges leveled against it that it had been completely collaborationist and was being made an adjunct of Cardenismo as the C.R.O.M. had been an adjunct of Obregonismo, the C.T.M. claimed that as long as there was a progressive government running the country, the C.T.M. would lend its support, maintaining its autonomy and freedom of action, because the proletariat had historic ends to fulfill which were different from the functions of government. Until the state of semifeudalism disappeared from Mexico and the country lost its characteristics as a colony for outside economic forces, as long as there was the menace of fascism or any other form that the decadent

45. *El Nacional*, September 6, 1936.
46. C.T.M., *C.T.M., 1936–1941*, pp. 215, 223.
47. *Mexican Labor News*, January 27, 1937.

big bourgeoisie could use against the interests of the people, and as long as these things constituted an obstacle to the inevitable transformation of the capitalist system, the Mexican proletariat would not only maintain the alliance that existed between it and other exploited sectors of the population, but it would fight staunchly to keep the government as a faithful representative of the people's interests and loyal executor of the revolution.[48]

The C.T.M. invited the peasants, the Communist party, and the P.N.R. to join it in a popular front, and the invitation was accepted. According to an American journalist, Joseph Freiman, Cárdenas approved and stated that he hoped his successor would be chosen by a popular front. But Prewett held that Lombardo's popular front never came into being because of receiving two checks—one indirect, the other direct and final. First, there was the difficulty caused when General Múgica and Diego Rivera were successful in compelling Cárdenas to admit Leon Trotsky into Mexico.[49] The C.T.M. protested and lost. The storm of the discussion resulted in widespread publication of Lombardo's alleged relations with the Communists and Stalin and thus widened the division between the conservative elements of the P.N.R. and the C.T.M. leadership. The ultra-left segment began to group itself around General Múgica, who opposed—as did Trotsky —a popular front.[50]

The final blow to Lombardo's conception of a popular front came when President Cárdenas announced in a speech on December 19, 1937, his plans for the complete reorganization of the forces of the Revolution into a new official party to replace the P.N.R. In his 1938 New Year's Message to the nation, Cárdenas gave the details of the new party discussed previously.[51]

The reformed official party may not have been exactly what the C.T.M. would have desired; nonetheless, in a speech on January 5, 1938, Lombardo Toledano declared that the idea of the popular front and now the idea of the transformation of the P.N.R. was an excellent one on the part of President Cárdenas, with which he agreed, "because the workers are not treated as an exclusive class, but are treated as in association with the workers of the field, intellectual workers, artisans, and small enterprisers, and all sectors of the middle class and the army."[52] He claimed that the new political party was not a popular front in name, but in fact it would fill that function, as it

48. Plenn, *Mexico Marches*, pp. 272–73.
49. Prewett, *Reportage on Mexico*, pp. 63, 166.
50. *Ibid.*
51. Lázaro Cárdenas, *Mensaje de Año Nuevo, 1938* (México, n.d.), pp. 16–17.
52. López Aparicio, *El Movimiento Obrero en México*, p. 223.

would unite in a single political organism the labor movement, the organized peasants, the army, and the progressive sections of the middle class. His comment on the failure of the popular front first suggested by the C.T.M. was: "Various circumstances have prevented the formation of the Popular Front in the form projected earlier by the C.T.M.; nevertheless, the agreement between the P.N.R. and the C.T.M. of last spring for the creation of a temporary "Popular Electoral Front" resulted in the election of numerous direct labor representatives to the new Congress, although inadequate control and lack of experience allowed professional machine politicians in many regions of the country to cheat the people's vote."[53]

He added that after nearly three years of constant agitation, the C.T.M.'s campaign for a popular front was at last being realized in the president's proposal for the new party. Lombardo pointed out that the party would not be a "leftist" or sectarian group, which, if that were the purpose of the labor movement, "it could easily create by itself without the necessity of inviting the collaboration of other sectors." Rather, the proposed party would be a genuine political organism of the whole people, and he asked the National Council of the C.T.M. to discuss the proposal and to decide on the basis and conditions of labor's participation. A commission was named to study the question and to submit a report the following day for the council's approval. On January 6, 1938, the committee submitted a draft resolution that contained essentially the following principal points: (1) the organism created by the popular sectors which form part of the P.N.R. will conserve their autonomy and liberty of action for the fulfillment of their own special ends; (2) the labor unions, agrarian communities, units of the army, and other groups representative of the popular sectors whose individual members enter the P.N.R. will not form part of that institution as such groups but will create political bodies to represent them and which will constitute the base of the structure of the party; (3) the designation of the officials of the party's executive organ shall be made from among the representatives of the most important organized popular groups. The resolutions were unanimously approved by the council and the C.T.M.'s National Committee was empowered to conduct all negotiations looking toward the co-operation of the labor movement in the formation of the new party on the basis outlined above.[54]

In the constituent congress of the new party, the voice of the C.T.M. was represented, and on March 30, 1938, the pact creating the Partido

53. *Mexican Labor News,* January 13, 1938.
54. *Ibid.*

de la Revolución Mexicana (P.R.M.), or the party of the Mexican Revolution, was signed. It claimed, at its inception, over 4,000,000 members, distributed as follows: labor, 1,250,000; peasants, 2,500,000; soldiers, 55,000; and popular sector, 500,000, consisting primarily of government employees.[55] It served as a clearing house for the C.T.M., the C.N.C., the army, politicians, and government employees, and it also provided a method through which government officials could neatly balance army against labor, labor against peasant, and fill in with bureaucratic strength wherever there were gaps. Prewett commented that the new front presupposed that all of the labor movement, the peasants, and the middle class were happy with the Cárdenas revolution which, unfortunately for official hopes, was not true. It was for this reason, she held, that the formation of the new party did not bridge differences between Lombardistas and Portesgilistas.[56]

López Aparicio was in agreement with Prewett when he wrote, "The internal dissensions, the inter-union struggles, and the inevitable clash of ideologies, caused the program of the popular front in Mexico to fail."[57] An example of inter-union struggle occurred when the C.R.O.M. was split by the internal jockeying for leadership between the old Morones groups and the leaders of the majority of the organization's membership. The ostensible reason for the dispute was the question of C.R.O.M.'s participation in the new political party, the P.R.M. The Morones-controlled elements attempted at all costs to prevent the organization from cooperating politically with the government. As this group was in control of the Central Committee and apparatus of the C.R.O.M., the split took the form of the expulsion of the "anti-Moronistas" by the Executive Council. Nevertheless, the opposition to Morones' group formed the great majority of the organization and included important C.R.O.M. groups of the states of Zacatecas, Veracruz, Nuevo León, Lower California, and other regions. The prominent C.R.O.M. leaders affected by the expulsion were Ricardo Treviño, Eduardo Moneda, José López Cortés, and Juan Lozano Padilla. The majority of the C.R.O.M. was represented in the convention of the new political party and signed the constituent pact together with the C.T.M., the C.G.T., and the other labor groups. As a result of this action, Morones, although he remained theoretically in control of a reduced number of the C.R.O.M. members, was practically excluded

55. Partido de la Revolución Mexicana, *Partido de la Revolución Mexicana* (México, 1938), p. 97.
56. Prewett, *Reportage on Mexico*, pp. 168–69.
57. López Aparicio, *El Movimiento Obrero en México*, p. 223.

from the labor body he formed in 1918, which at one time was the strongest force in the Mexican trade-union movement.[58]

Largely as a result of the oil crisis, discussed in some detail in following chapters, the C.T.M. and the Peasants' Confederation issued, in August, 1938, a joint manifesto calling on the workers to show their "tranquillity and patriotism" and appealed to the employing class to do likewise. Some observers interpreted this move as a plea for a truce in the class struggle, and the Employers' Center hastened to announce that it would be only too delighted to call a halt, since it had always believed in class collaboration, anyhow. On August 6, 1938, *Hoy* summed up the employers' contention for a "real unity between Mexican capital and Mexican labor." But these efforts toward harmony and co-operation were transformed into mockery in the face of actual fact, for one week after the editorial in *Hoy* appeared, Mexico was shocked by one of the most brutal, cold-blooded massacres in all labor history: the wholesale slaughter of union workers—twenty-six at one time—on the lumber hacienda of El Chaparro, in the State of Michoacán.[59]

In October, 1938, at the direct order of President Cárdenas, the government moved to expropriate the sawmill of the hacienda El Chaparro and stated that similar action would be taken on any hacienda on which peasants were murdered by "white guards"—company police.[60] Still, the employer sector, or at least a part of it, was in no mood actually to co-operate with organized labor. Employers of Mexico were organized into groups for the purpose of bargaining collectively with labor. On June 30, 1938, there were 265 such employer associations, with a total membership of 7,589 persons registered with the Ministry of National Economy. The stronghold of the Employers' Center was the important industrial city of Monterrey, and it was from that place, on July 29, 1938, that a United Press dispatch reported that the Fascist and anti-Semitic Gold Shirts—who had theoretically been disbanded by an order from President Cárdenas—had clashed with the C.T.M. during a strike at the National Coal Factory. The dispatch quoted the C.T.M. as stating that "Nationalists and Gold Shirts assaulted the strikers" and that the Monterrey police and other public authorities were supporting the strike-breakers. At this time, there appeared an anti-C.T.M. publication that headlined the proph-

---

58. *Mexican Labor News*, March 31, 1938.
59. *Ibid.*, p. 279. An excellent account of the El Chaparro tragedy is given in Plenn, *Mexico Marches*, pp. 278–82.
60. *Mexican Labor News*, October 13, 1938.

ecy: "Monterrey will be the tomb of the C.T.M."[61] Late in 1938 the fight continued unabated. Monterrey employers announced their intention of putting a stop to further union organization. Their control of many public officials, they believed, would help them in their drive. In September, 1938, the Employers' Center asked Cárdenas to intervene in the Monterrey situation, and a similar request was made to the state governor. The new crisis arose over the arrest of Ramón Contreras, a C.T.M. organizer, on a charge of "frustrated homicide." His arrest led to threats of a general strike in Monterrey, which the employers laughed off, asserting that the "C.T.M. does not represent the proletariat of Monterrey." Then the electric light plant was shut down, buses stopped running, there was no telephone service, the roundhouse came to a standstill, the smelter and foundry furnaces cooled. This impasse did not last very long, but the judge who had ordered him jailed found that, after all, there really had been no legal basis for arresting Contreras and set him free. The stoppage ended quickly.[62] It would appear that the oil controversy was not, as Prewett and López Aparicio claimed, a sufficient crisis to bring about real collaboration between capital and labor in Mexico.

In addition to the C.T.M. and the C.N.C., there was yet another organization that, although not exclusively Mexican, was important in the Mexican labor scene—the Confederación de Trabajadores de América Latina (the Latin American Labor Confederation), known as the C.T.A.L.[63] The four-million-worker body, established at an international convention of the large majority of national trade-unions of Latin America in Mexico City in September, 1938, was a moving force behind the rapid development of South American trade-unionism.[64] In the words of Vicente Lombardo Toledano, its president, it was founded "just when Fascism ceased being merely a menace for certain individual countries and became an international danger for all mankind."[65]

The primary policies, outlined at the inaugural convention in Mexico

61. Plenn, *Mexico Marches*, pp. 274, 275.
62. *Ibid.*, p. 276.
63. For details of the activities of this organization, 1942 through May, 1946, see Confederación de Trabajadores de América Latina, *Por Un Mundo Mejor: Diário de Una Organización Obrera Durante La Segunda Guerra Mundial* (México, 1948). The general philosophy of the C.T.A.L. was discussed in a previous chapter.
64. John Horner, *Labour's Struggle in Latin America* (London, 1945), p. 6.
65. *Ibid.*, p. 6. For further information on the founding of the C.T.A.L., see the speech by a labor lawyer in New Jersey, Abraham J. Issermann, "El Trabajo en México," *Revista del Trabajo* (January, 1939), 75, 87. See also Francisco Pérez Leirós, *El Movimiento Sindical en América Latina* (Buenos Aires, 1941).

City, were the "complete economic emancipation of Latin America" and "the defense of democratic forms of Government nationally and internationally."[66] The preamble to the Constitution of the C.T.A.L. stated:

> The workers of hand and brain of Latin America declare that the social regime at the present prevailing in the majority of countries of the world should be substituted by a regime of justice, based on the abolition of the exploitation of man by man, on the democratic system as the means of governing the interests of the human community, on respect for the economic and political independence of all nations, and on the solidarity of all peoples of the world, proscribing forever armed aggression as an instrument for solving international disputes and condemning wars of conquest as contrary to the interests of civilization.[67]

The trade-unions of Latin America frankly acknowledged that advantages won by them for their members had so far been small; the reason for this was the backward economy resulting not only from the feudal past but also from the stranglehold exercised by foreign monopoly. Unification of the labor movement in each of the affiliated countries figured largely among the objectives of the C.T.A.L.'s original program, and one of the earliest and most signal successes in the campaign for unity was the establishment of a united labor organization in Cuba. The leadership of the C.T.A.L. endeavored to link the labor movements of North and South America in a Hemisphere International, and the "Good Neighbor Policy" of President Roosevelt immeasurably assisted the C.T.A.L. in this respect. Soon after its formation, a meeting was held in Mexico, with representatives of the C.I.O., where Lombardo met John L. Lewis. After the election of Philip Murray to the presidency of the C.I.O., that body established a standing Committee on Latin-American Affairs to strengthen the bonds with the C.T.A.L. and to work toward the extension of Pan-American trade-unity.[68]

Addressing the inaugural session, John L. Lewis said that in recent years, two great statesmen had appeared on the North American continent. "They have extended a helping hand to labor. In the United

66. Horner, *Labour's Struggle in Latin America*, p. 6.
67. *Mexican Labor News*, September 15, 1938. A copy of the Constitution of the C.T.A.L. is reproduced on pp. 3–8 of this issue. See also *Congreso Obrero Latino Americano, Ciudad de México, 5 al 8 de Septiembre de 1938* (México, 1938).
68. Horner, *Labour's Struggle in Latin America*, pp. 6–9.

States, President Roosevelt is that man; in Mexico, President Cárdenas is that man."[69] At the International Congress Against War and Fascism, Lewis declared, on September 11, 1938:

> Between us and fascism there can be no peace. In the United States the reactionary corporate employers have always opposed the right of workers to organize and to take concerted action in their own behalf. These reactionary elements have not yet resorted to fascism, but we can expect that they will turn to fascism when it is convenient and necessary to do so. . . . When employers use spies, provocateurs, form company unions, spread lies and false propaganda, form "law and order" and vigilante committees against workers, and corrupt public officials to use the forces of the State against workers, then they are using the weapons of fascism. We know that in the United States there are groups, agents of certain foreign countries and of our own "super-patriots," which seek to consolidate these forces and practices into the brutal system of fascism.[70]

William Green and other officials of the A.F. of L. were invited to the congress establishing the C.T.A.L. but refused to attend. Green condemned the congress as an attempt to spread Communist doctrine among the labor movements of Latin America. The president of the A.F. of L. threatened to make an effort to revive the long-dead Pan-American Labor Federation, founded by Samuel Gompers, as a countermove against the C.T.A.L.[71]

At the end of the Cárdenas administration, Lombardo increasingly devoted his organizing gifts to building the C.T.A.L. He consistently warned the United States of the danger of the new fifth column tactics in Latin America, with its spurious claims of "Hispanidad." At the Cali Conference, Colombia, December, 1944, Lombardo stated, "We are living in the age of the Industrial Revolution in Latin America. We have not reached the age of socialism here. This must be the hour of real, genuine democracy, not the formal democracy of the last century, empty of true human significance."[72]

At the time of this congress, Lombardo and O. A. Knight, of the Oil Workers' Union in the United States, agreed upon the need for

69. Quoted in *Mexican Labor News*, September 8, 1938.
70. *Ibid.*, September 15, 1938.
71. *Ibid.*, August 11, 18, 1928. Later, the A.F. of L. was to aid in the establishment of a rival organization.
72. Horner, *Labour's Struggle in Latin America*, p. 13. See Vicente Lombardo Toledano, *The C.T.A.L., The War and the Postwar* (México, 1945); Confederación de Trabajadores de América Latina. *Segundo Congreso General de la Confederación de Trabajadores de América Latina, Cali, Colombia, Diciembre de 1944* (México, 1945).

affiliation with the World Trade-Union Conference.[73] Lombardo, presiding as president of the organization, declared that the industrialization of Latin America should not be left to the uncontrolled initiative of private capital, national or foreign, with private profit as the sole consideration; rather, the investment of capital should take place under a series of guarantees and controls set up to guard the basic interests of the economy.[74] Labor and management were later to sign a pact pledged to the industrialization of Mexico.[75] As early as 1941, Lombardo maintained that the time for national solutions had passed and that the Latin-American labor movement was designed to unite with, not to separate from, the rest of the world.[76] By 1945, he was to emphasize this point by insisting that one of the most important lessons of the war was that the economic and social problems facing the different countries of the world could not be learned on a national level. He held that "if the monopoly powers of finance capitalism were left to operate freely there would be another war" and urged workers to participate in political activity to keep this from happening.[77]

But with the end of World War II, and the beginning of Mexico's "turn to the right" under Alemán, charges of communism began to shake the president of the C.T.A.L. from his dominant position as a labor leader in South and Central America.[78] At Lima, Peru, in January, 1948, a trade-union conference was held which saw the establishment of a new anti-Communist Latin American labor federation, the Inter-American Confederation of Workers.[79]

To a charge of being bought by Moscow, Lombardo replied, "Only people who are in the habit of selling themselves assume that oppo-

73. "Second General Congress of the Confederation of Latin American Workers," *International Labour Review*, 51 (February, 1945), 236–43.
74. *Ibid.*, p. 242. For further information on the aims and policies of the C.T.A.L. at this time, see David Efrón, "Latin American Labor Comes of Age," *Annals of the American Academy of Political and Social Science*, 240 (July, 1945), 116–30; Confederación de Trabajadores de América Latina, *Estatutos* (México, 1938); *Presente y Futuro de la América Latina* (Cali, 1944).
75. "La Alianza Patriótica entre los Industriales y los Obreros," *El Popular*, April 9, 1945.
76. Vicente Lombardo Toledano, "Informe Rendido por el . . . Presidente de la Confederación de Trabajadores de América Latina al Congreso General de la Propia C.T.A.L. el Día 22 de Noviembre de 1941," *México Agrario*, III (October–December, 1941), 387–433.
77. "Congress Extraordinary of the Confederation of Latin American Workers, Meeting in Paris on 10–12 October, 1945," *International Labour Review*, 52 (November, 1945), 557–60.
78. "Toledano Faces Labor Revolt," *World Report*, December 31, 1946, 30; Serafino Romualdi, "Labor and Democracy in Latin America," *Foreign Affairs*, 25 (April, 1947), 477–89.
79. "Inter-American Confederation of Workers," *International Labour Review*, 58 (December, 1948), 795–98.

nents can be bought. I was not bought by Moscow, but no Trade Union leader can be an enemy of the Soviet Union today."[80] Certainly Horner was correct in writing, "Whatever the ultimate degree of importance Toledano may have in American politics his leadership of the C.T.A.L. has unquestionably not only quickened but has initiated many major progressive trends in Latin America during the last decade."[81]

In any case, as the term of President Cárdenas drew near its end, the C.T.M., in its capacity as the most important part of the structure of the Mexican labor movement, played an active role in the selection of Cárdenas' successor. At a special national council, attended by five hundred delegates from all the affiliated national, state, and local organizations, the C.T.M. endorsed the candidacy of General Manuel Ávila Camacho to succeed Lázaro Cárdenas as president of Mexico in 1940. Ávila Camacho had won the endorsement over his two announced rivals—General Francisco Múgica and Rafael Sánchez Tapia.[82] A peasant convention also, on February 24, 1939, endorsed the candidacy of Ávila Camacho; he appeared before the convention the next day to accept the endorsement, making a short speech that marked his first public action in the campaign.[83] Lombardo Toledano declared to the Tenth National Council of the C.T.M., meeting in July, 1939, that the workers could not confine labor action merely to the economic aspect of trade-union struggles and problems, "for their very existence as an organized labor movement is now threatened by the possibility of the victory of a reactionary government in the next elections, which would destroy all the advances registered in recent years."[84] In a speech to business leaders in Saltillo, capital of the State of Coahuila, on October 21, 1939, Lombardo assured the group that it was not true that the Mexican working class wished to suppress private property; nor was it true that at the present stage of the revolution labor had attempted to obtain any gains not stipulated by existing legislation.[85]

The National Committee of the C.T.M. issued, on September 4, 1939, a circular to all its affiliated organizations defining its position on the European war and making recommendations to all labor unions for guidance in their activities in the immediate future. It said, in part:

80. Horner, *Labour's Struggle in Latin America*, p. 7.
81. *Ibid.*, p. 7.
82. *Mexican Labor News*, February 23, 1939.
83. *Ibid.*, March 1, 1939.
84. *Ibid.*, July 20, 1939.
85. *Ibid.*, October 26, 1939.

What it is possible to affirm is that no country in the world will be neutral in this struggle, either because it is contributing economically, politically, or morally to the victory of one of the two sides. From this view of the problem—and there is no other way of looking at it—it is logical to expect that sooner or later all the countries of America will participate in the conflict, either directly or indirectly and that, therefore, Mexico will likewise be involved, an event which will be no more than the natural result of its entire international position as a defender of democracy and peace. . . .

All organizations of the C.T.M. shall declare that, notwithstanding the inter-imperialist character of the new war, the principal enemy of the working class, of civilization, and of culture, is fascism and that, consequently, the moral and material aid of the workers of all countries should be given to the people fighting against fascism, for the purpose of exterminating this system of government. . . .[86]

It becomes apparent, then, that insofar as the organized labor movement of Mexico was concerned, collaboration with other sectors of the economic society in a popular front was viewed as a temporary expedient, designed to thwart the threat of national and international fascism. The ultimate goal of a fundamental change in the economic structure to socialism was not abandoned. Nor should the resignation of Lombardo from the presidency of the C.T.M. at its second congress (February 25 to March 1, 1941) in Mexico City be allowed to detract from the role he played during the years of the Cárdenas administration—the subject of the remainder of this study.[87]

86. *Ibid.*, September 7, 1939.
87. "The Trade Union Movement in Mexico," *International Labour Review*, 53 (April, 1941), 463–64.

VI. Major Labor-Capital Conflicts, 1936–1940

Undoubtedly the most important labor-capital conflicts of the Cárdenas administration were those involving the National Railways, the land question in the Laguna district, and the foreign-owned petroleum industry. Because of their far-reaching implications, both nationally and internationally, these disputes are treated in separate, later chapters. In addition to these labor conflicts, however, there were other strike movements of considerable significance in the history of the Mexican labor movement under Cárdenas. Some of the primary ones not mentioned in Chapter II will be discussed in the present chapter.

As the National Committee of the C.T.M. explained, in Mexico the working class concluded that the unification represented by that organization, on the one hand, and the advent of General Cárdenas to the presidency of the republic, on the other, "offered wide perspectives for the masses; therefore it proceeded at once to demand the fulfillment of its undeniable rights which had not been fulfilled by the State." The principal aims of the labor demands were the increase of wages and of social services, the standardization of working conditions in the various branches of industry, and the increase of the number of compulsory collective contracts of a regional and national character.[1]

1. Confederación de Trabajadores de México, *Informe del Comité Nacional 1936–1937* (México, 1938), pp. 72–73.

Toward the end of the government of Carranza (1920), there were only 173 strikes in the republic; in the first year of Obregón's administration (1921), which had promised the working class to defend its interests, the number of strikes increased to 310 but rapidly declined. At the beginning of the government of General Calles (December, 1924), there were 136 strikes, but the following year they diminished to 51; in 1926, they dropped to 23; in 1927, to 16; and in the last year of the Calles regime, they were reduced to 7. At the beginning of the provisional presidency of Emilio Portes Gil (1929), strikes increased again to 14. Under President Ortíz Rubio (1930), almost the same number was maintained, dropping again in 1931 to 11. When the government of General Aberlardo Rodríguez began in 1932, strikes increased to 56, only to fall once more to 13 in the following year. As a result of the work of the C.G.O.C.M., as well as the new political atmosphere accompanying the presidential campaign of General Cárdenas in 1934, strikes increased to 202. In 1935, the first year of the Cárdenas administration, there were 642 strikes, and in 1936, there were 659.[2] In 1937, there were 833 strikes registered, the number falling again in 1938 to 794.[3] After the oil expropriations, the number decreased until the end of the Cárdenas regime.

In February, 1937, the Industrial Union of Miners and Metal Workers announced its intention of resorting to a series of strikes on a national scale in an effort to force a collective labor contract with the American Smelting and Refining Company, the corporation that, with its many plants throughout the country, dominated the Mexican mining industry. The union charged that after six months of discussion, it was still impossible to induce the company to retreat from its intransigent attitude. So no recourse but the strike weapon was open to it to obtain the contract demanded in the company's San Luis Potosí plant. It announced that it would call three strikes, one of one hour, one of eight hours, and one of twenty-four hours, in all the "Asarco" mills and plants at dates to be determined later. Moreover, if these measures proved insufficient to bring the company to an agreement, it would begin a nationwide general strike in the mining and metals industries which would last until its demands had been granted. At the same time, an interview with President Cárdenas was requested so the union might lay before him the facts of the case "to demonstrate that the workers are not resorting to extreme measures of their own wish but because of the company's attitude leaving them

2. *Ibid.*, pp. 73–74.
3. Alfonso López Aparicio, *El Movimiento Obrero en México: Antecedentes, Desarrollo y Tendencias* (México, 1952), p. 216.

with no other alternative."[4]

Not until October, 1937, did President Cárdenas announce that he would personally intervene in the mining conflict in an effort to avert the threatened general strike, which would have tied up the major portion of the industry. A proposal by the Labor Department for a month's discussion by a mixed commission of workers and employers was turned down by the company, with the result that the union was determined to call out seventeen thousand employees of "Asarco" in a nationwide strike. Cárdenas summoned representatives of both sides to Mexico City. Meantime, preparations for a strike were pushed—a strike fund of more than one million pesos had been collected by the workers. The C.T.M. announced also that it would give full support to the strikers, even though the miners had withdrawn from that organization more than a year earlier. The railroad workers also pledged solidarity with the miners.[5] In the middle of December, 1937, the company, presumably at the request of President Cárdenas, agreed to enter into discussion of the proposed collective contract and to draw up its definite terms within a two-month period. These discussions were predicated upon the supposition, understood in advance by both sides, that wage increases would be granted and that the contract would establish identical wage scales and working conditions in all the plants of "Asarco" throughout Mexico. According to labor sources, the company yielded only after several months' threat of a general strike. Frequent one-hour sitdown strikes in every shift throughout the company's units also softened the company's doggedness.[6] As the end of the period within which "Asarco" had agreed to sign a new contract drew near, there were no indications that an agreement would be concluded; therefore, the possibility of a general strike in the industry again loomed. Principal demands made by the union were for an upward revision of wage scales and for standardization of wage rates and working conditions in all the mines, refineries, and smelters operated by the American company in Mexico.

Explaining its support of the miners, the C.T.M. claimed that the conflict was very similar to that provoked by the foreign oil companies, which had always looked on Mexico as a weak, cheap-labor country easily subjected to the demands of their imperialist, economic, and political power. For that reason, the National Committee of the C.T.M. decided to furnish the widest possible support to the Union of Mining and Metallurgical Workers in their struggle against the

4. *Mexican Labor News*, February 10, 1937.
5. *Ibid.*, October 14, 1937.
6. *Ibid.*, December 19, 1937.

American Smelting and Refining Company.[7] In March, authorities of the Labor Department summoned representatives of the company and the workers to a new series of discussions, while an official of the company from New York went to investigate the situation. At the same time, the unions decreed a new series of one-hour sitdown strikes, which the company protested on the ground that such movements violated the existing labor contracts. The union replied that the company still refused to sign a general collective contract covering workers in all its plants; therefore, its actions were justified.[8]

On April 5, 1938, as a result of an agreement signed by both parties, the outstanding difficulties came to a temporary halt. Largely because of the oil crisis, the miners postponed strike action and endeavored to reach a partial agreement until "general Mexican conditions" were again normal. Meantime, according to union statements, the company had taken advantage of the existing situation to close several of its plants and to discharge some three thousand workers. By the terms of the truce, all the discharged workers were immediately to be reinstated and the closed plants at Monterrey and in the State of Chihuahua reopened. The company agreed to resume negotiations with the union for the proposed general collective contract. Apparently, the Miners' Union decided to abandon the strike at the request of the National Committee of the C.T.M. and the Labor Department,[9] no doubt because of the oil crisis.

In April, 1937, a strike movement voted by the convention of the Postal Workers' Union for increased wages and improved working conditions, after repeated petitions to the Post Office Department, the Ministry of Communications, and the president had failed to obtain any satisfaction, received a serious set-back when Cárdenas announced that a strike would not be tolerated by the government. He maintained that federal employees were not accorded the right to strike under the Labor Law and that any walkout would therefore be illegal. The position of government employees with respect to the Labor Law had never been satisfactorily determined. According to the constitutional article on which the labor legislation was based, government employees were forbidden to strike "in time of war or national emergency," but nothing was said of any general prohibition of this right. Until the question could be cleared, Cárdenas promised the post office workers a wage increase, beginning in January, 1938.[10]

7. *Ibid.*, February 24, 1938.
8. *Ibid.*, March 10, 1938; March 11, 1938.
9. *Ibid.*, April 14, 1938.
10. *Ibid.*, April 28, 1937.

Meantime, Cárdenas submitted a Civil Service Bill to Congress which was designed to govern labor relations between the *executive branch* of the government and its employees. This measure included the rights to organize and to strike. Certain limitations, however, were placed on the exercise of these rights. Strikes for redressing just grievances, such as nonpayment of wages or failure on the part of higher officials to observe the requirements of the law, were to be legal if they were supported by a majority of the employees in the department involved and were peacefully carried out. In the preamble to the bill, it was pointed out that it was fallacious to consider a strike of federal employees as a strike against the state, as such, since in all cases they were movements directed against abuses for which individuals, not the state, were responsible.[11]

Only the police and members of the army were excluded from the terms of the bill. All other government employees were divided into categories, and only those termed "basic" were affected by the bill. This excluded also "confidential employees"—those holding executive and responsible positions. Still, the most serious grievances and injustices under which government employees had traditionally suffered were corrected. The provision of the Labor Law calling for three months' pay as compensation for unjust discharge was absent from the Civil Service Bill, as well as payment for the seventh day of the week. Among the important provisions of the measure were annual vacations of twenty days for all employees after six months' service; a minimum wage not inferior to that in force in private industry in each economic zone of the country; an eight-hour day; one month's leave with pay for women before and after childbirth, with special rest periods for feeding nursing infants; a six-day week; strict limitation on the amount of overtime work and all overtime to be paid double; wage rates for each category of work to be fixed each year in consultation with the workers' representatives; and, perhaps most important of all, the non-removability of "basic employees" in the event of changes in the administrative personnel. Labor circles stated that on the whole the bill was received among government workers with great enthusiasm, and it was generally felt that the president had achieved one of the most notable accomplishments of his administration with the project.[12] Special tribunals and boards were provided with jurisdiction over disputes involving government employees covered by the bill.[13]

11. *Ibid.*, July 7, 1937.
12. *Ibid.*
13. *Ibid.*, July 14, 1937.

During the early months of 1940, organized labor and government officials dealt at great length with the operation of the civil service statute and proposals for its amendment. As a result of a series of incidents, the federal government had modified the right to strike which the measure gave government employees, prohibiting demonstrations by employees in government offices. The decree declared that it was the exclusive prerogative of the executive power to fix hours of work, subject to a limited right of appeal before administrative officers. This order, issued in December, 1939, by which the personnel of the frontier customs service were placed on a military footing, thus deprived certain classes of customs employees the seniority rights granted under the civil service statute. On petition of ten thousand federal employees in the capital, the Treasury Department suspended the February decree, pointing out, however, that the administrative deficiencies that had led to the militarization of the customs service would have to be corrected. The corrective measures were drafted and submitted by the Union of Government Employees shortly afterward; the incident served to throw open to discussion the operation of the civil service law in all its aspects.[14]

Establishment of a forty-hour week was accomplished when a telephone strike, scheduled to begin at noon on November 12, 1937, was averted by a last-minute settlement granting the workers practically all of their original demands. This marked the first formal establishment of the forty-hour week in the country. In addition, the new contract arrived at provided for retirement pensions; a minimum of fifteen days' vacation each year; five additional compulsory rest days; a workers' saving fund; and the reduction of the number of "confidential employees" to an insignificant minimum. A considerable increase in wages, as well as higher wage rates for those working in tropical and unhealthy zones was also secured. The total benefits won by the union came to approximately 500,000 pesos a year.[15]

Earlier in the year, the field and factory workers in the great sugar plantation and mill at El Mante, Tamaulipas, called a strike after discussions for a new collective contract for workers of the plant broke down. The National Sugar Workers' Union announced that although very few clauses of the contract remained to be settled, the strike had become unavoidable because of the company's refusal to make important economic concessions to its employees—the principal point of dispute being over payment of back pay due the workers from 1931

14. Pan American Union, *Labor Trends and Social Welfare in Latin America: 1939–1940* (Washington, D. C., 1941), p. 53.
15. *Mexican Labor News*, November 18, 1937.

to 1935 for unpaid overtime. During that period, the working day was illegally increased to twelve hours instead of the eight stipulated by the law. The union claimed that for years the Mante plant was operated in defiance of the Labor Law because of the special influence its owners enjoyed under the Calles regime, the plantation and mill having been established by the inner ring close to General Calles. Calles himself had an interest in the business. It was reported that hours were shorter and wages higher in foreign-owned sugar plants than in this one operated by former revolutionary leaders.[16] In September, 1937, it was announced that the Agrarian Code had at last been applied to the sugar district of El Mante, although only a part of the total area was affected by the ruling. Over 9,000 hectares (about 23,000 acres) of sown, irrigated, irrigable, semiarid, and uncleared land was distributed to 721 heads of families.[17]

In Los Mochis, Sinaloa, the United Sugar Company threatened in July, 1937, to abandon the year's sugar harvest as a means of ridding itself of its existing working force, a measure that would have affected four thousand workers.[18] There had been a previous maneuver by the company to break the existing collective contract, but such action had been stopped by the authorities of the Labor Department. The C.T.M. appealed to the labor authorities, the president of Mexico, and to the governor of the state to make an immediate investigation of the conflict in Los Mochis and to prevent the company's action, since it would have brought disaster to the entire region, almost wholly dependent upon the sugar industry. Troubles in the plant at Los Mochis had been frequent throughout the previous two-year period. The union was a militant one, and the company was American owned, had a dominant position in the sugar monopoly and was frankly antilabor. The present company move stemmed from a protest strike carried out by the union against local municipal authorities who, in addition to favoring the company, were claimed to have been systematically looting the town treasury. Labor troubles continued until December, 1938, when the government applied the Agrarian Code, much as it had done in the Mante region, distributing large tracts of land, mainly planted in sugar cane, to the inhabitants of the villages in various parts of the State of Sinaloa. Although the United Sugar Company plant was not touched, large tracts of land in the area were affected when 564,000 acres were granted to 94 villages with a population of 44,046; 9,025 heads of families received plots.[19]

16. *Ibid.*, March 10, 1937.
17. *Ibid.*, September 1, 1937.
18. *Ibid.*, July 21, 1937.
19. *Ibid.*, December 15, 1928.

With regard to the sugar industry, President Cárdenas took steps to revive, reorganize, and stimulate the refining part of the industry as well as the growing of sugar cane. One of the most important projects was in the valley of Morelos, where sugar production had been reduced to negligible amounts during the various revolutions succeeding the Díaz regime. The soil and climate are ideal for sugar cane, and for some years there had been consistent pressure on the government to make it possible for the local small farmers to sell such sugar cane as they might wish to plant. As a result of this pressure, the Land Bank was ordered to survey and to arrange for the installation of a sugar factory to be bought by the government, which would purchase from farmers their crops of sugar cane. The plans were to put the entire zone of Zacatepec in sugar cane, with crop loans to be paid back by the farmers from the sale of sugar cane to the factory during the crop season.[20] Cárdenas built a large, completely modern sugar refinery at Zacatepec, and the mill, completed in 1938, was made a co-operative venture in which both refinery workers and peasants participated. The peasants who raised the sugar cane were organized into a number of co-operatives; then, as a group, they participated in the management of the mill, co-operating with the refining employees.[21]

Labor activity in the sugar industry continued unabated when it was announced that discussions to seek ways and means of averting a general strike in the industry were begun on February 15, 1939, among various government officials and the representatives of the workers at which Lombardo Toledano represented the workers. The Sugar Workers' Union asked for wage increases, medical service throughout the industry, and a tuberculosis sanitorium. A general collective contract, binding on the entire industry, had been in force for three years and had been recently renewed by presidential decree for an additional year. Nevertheless, the workers were pressing for new wage scales in view of the sharp increase in the cost of living and for badly needed medical services to maintain the health of the industry's employees, the majority of whom worked under extremely unhealthy conditions in the tropical regions of the country.[22]

20. F. E. O'Neil, "Mexico Has a New Deal," *Modern Mexico*, 8 (February, 1937), 6.

21. Sanford A. Mosk, *Industrial Revolution in Mexico* (Berkeley and Los Angeles, 1950), p. 57.

22. *Mexican Labor News*, February 15, 1939. Under Mexican labor law, such a "collective contract of general application" becomes binding on all workers and employers in a given industry when it has been accepted and signed by a majority of them and is therefore elevated to the category of a "contract-law" by government action.

To avoid a walkout, the government authorized a tax of one centavo on each kilo of sugar, the proceeds to be used for meeting the demands of the workers which had been turned down by the employers. A delay in the payment of benefits derived from this tax again brought about the threat of a strike—in March, 1940, when the government assumed responsibility for the benefit payments to start immediately, in the amount of 2,000,000 pesos a year.[23] The National Union of Sugar Workers, composed both of the workers who grow the cane and of those who refine it in factories, inaugurated an important National Council on January 28, 1940. They had been organized in an industrial union for only a relatively short time, and the union included 45,000 members, with the membership divided into 102 sections. A large number of members worked on *ejidos*, and in several of these there were sugar refineries operated co-operatively by the workers. The majority of the union members, however, worked for private employers, and a uniform collective contract determined their conditions of labor. The strike, scheduled to begin on March 25, was called off when a three-way agreement was reached among the owners, the government, and the union. Still, all the workers' demands were not fulfilled, although their most pressing requirements were satisfied, as noted above. The wage increases asked by the union were not conceded.[24]

Of all the labor conflicts during the Cárdenas administration, perhaps none was more bitter than those occurring in the textile industry, largely because many of them involved inter-union disputes among the affiliates of the C.R.O.M. and the C.T.M. During the absence of President Cárdenas from Mexico City, when, in September of 1936, he visited the Laguna region, trouble between the two federations came to a head in the mill town of Atlixco. The C.R.O.M. had been supreme there for a number of years, but agitators from the C.T.M. had been able to make some gains. The competition resulted in occasional killings on both sides. These events were apparently not altogether the fault of the laborers, for judges were said to have been accepting handsome bribes for lenient treatment of the killers. In late September, 1936, Cárdenas visited Atlixco and called together the leaders from both labor organizations, making it plain that rivalry and bloodshed would have to cease. He obtained a promise from them to accept his personal arbitration. His decision stipulated that the two groups should work together for one year under the direction of a unification committee. At the end of the year, the laborers were to be permitted to

23. Pan American Union, *Labor Trends and Social Welfare*, p. 50.
24. *Mexican Labor News*, March 28, 1940.

vote on whether to join permanently the C.T.M. or the C.R.O.M. Meanwhile, the ten most irreconcilable leaders of each group were to be ordered to leave the zone. If a laborer belonging to the C.T.M. were murdered, the C.R.O.M. would have to indemnify his family, and vice versa.[25]

But by February, 1937, the war between the two organizations throughout the textile region was apparently as far as ever from being settled, despite efforts toward a solution on the part of Cárdenas and the governor of the State of Veracruz. Clashes between members of the C.T.M. and the C.R.O.M. occurred almost daily, and the toll of dead and wounded was mounting. Most of the disturbances now took place in Orizaba rather than Atlixco. In mid-February, a delegation from the Veracruz Federation of Workers arrived in Mexico City to confer with the National Committee of the C.T.M. on the situation and to obtain an interview with President Cárdenas in order to lay the case before him once again. The Veracruz delegation threatened to carry out a resolution adopted at the Third National Council of the C.T.M. to call a statewide general strike in protest against the existing conditions.[26] The C.T.M. itself appealed to the governor of Veracruz to fulfill his promises of immediate action and addressed a petition to the federal government to assume the policing of the city of Orizaba, using federal troops, "as the local police authorities are notoriously sympathetic to the C.R.O.M. organizations."[27]

In mid-April, 1937, a battle among members of the F.R.O.C. (Regional Federation of Workers and Peasants), belonging to the C.T.M. and the C.R.O.M. in the textile factory at San Martín Texmelucan, Puebla, resulted in three workers killed and eighteen wounded. Relations between the two groups had been strained for some time in this factory where, according to the C.T.M., it had a clear majority among the workers. Order was restored by federal troops, and 146 members of the F.R.O.C. (C.T.M.) were arrested. The C.T.M. charged that the C.R.O.M. was the aggressor; that it set fire to the F.R.O.C. headquarters in San Martín, in addition to committing outrages at the factory itself; and that in spite of these facts the local police arrested only F.R.O.C. members. The C.T.M. sent a message of protest to President Cárdenas, inviting his personal intervention to end the serious conditions existing in the region.[28]

25. William Cameron Townsend, *Lázaro Cárdenas: Mexican Democrat* (Ann Arbor, 1952), pp. 172–73.
26. *Mexican Labor News*, February 17, 1937.
27. *Ibid.*, March 4, 1937.
28. *Ibid.*, April 14, 1937.

In late April there was another outbreak of violence in the Veracruz textile region when a fight among workers of both organizations took place in a factory in Orizaba; three persons were killed and four were wounded. The C.R.O.M. declared a general strike of all its elements throughout the state; this closed two electric plants, halted service on the Veracruz railway for several hours, and closed all textile factories as well as several other mills. Immediate intervention on the part of the federal government and state authorities ended the strike movement after three days, and Orizaba was patrolled by federal troops to prevent fresh outbreaks. The C.T.M. claimed that the difficulty arose because the C.R.O.M., in an effort to prevent an increasing number of its former adherents from joining the C.T.M., had resorted to open terrorist methods in which it had been aided by local municipal authorities under its influence, as well as by the mill owners who were equally desirous of preventing their workers from entering the militant C.T.M. organization.[29]

The C.T.M. charged further that the fact that most of the collective contracts in the textile region were with the C.R.O.M. was due chiefly to a maneuver carried out in agreement with the Industrial Company of Orizaba, the largest mill operator of the state. A fake strike of C.R.O.M. elements was simulated, with a series of fabricated demands, to provide the company with a pretext for signing a new contract with the C.R.O.M., giving it control of certain factories where the C.T.M. had a strong representation. Consequently, in the C.T.M. version, the C.R.O.M. had, in practice, been playing the part of a company union to prevent the workers of the region from following their own inclinations to enter the C.T.M. The frequent aggressions and acts of violence, for the most part instituted by the local C.R.O.M. leadership, had been fomented in order to keep alive and to increase the hostility between the two organizations and thus prevent affiliation. The C.T.M. claimed that it had made little effort to organize in the region and that all those workers who had affiliated with it were for a time operating as independent unions after having left the C.R.O.M. They joined the C.T.M. chiefly because they sought protection against the terrorist tactics of the C.R.O.M. leaders.[30]

President Cárdenas announced that he would personally intervene to impose a compromise solution within a week. When he rendered his executive resolution, which, as far as its legal effects were concerned, was only an expression of opinion, the daily press hailed it as a decision that would bring to an immediate end the long-standing

29. *Ibid.*, April 21, 1937.
30. *Ibid.*

inter-union dispute in the Veracruz textile factories. Actually, as viewed by the C.T.M., the resolution did no more than establish the basis on which the executive organs of the government would probably proceed in future situations of similar nature. It hinted at the necessity of introducing important reforms in Mexico's labor legislation at the next regular session of Congress. The presidential resolution, which directed the recognition of the C.R.O.M. union in the Cocolapan factory and a recount of the workers to determine the majority group in the Mirafuentes plant, was apparently made public before the president was informed that the entire conflict was being studied by the Labor Chamber of the Supreme Court, whose verdict was expected within a few days. The resolution indicated the executive preference for recognizing the majority organization in any given plant as the titular contracting agency for collective bargaining. In the textile industry, however, the C.T.M. maintained, the special labor relations law that had become effective some time previously, gave this right to the union established in the plant, even though the ownership might change hands. The Cocolapan workers (C.T.M.), although in a temporary minority, carried their injunction suit against the decision of the Labor Department to the Supreme Court, seeking a clarification of their special situation. The C.T.M. declared that, aside from the narrowest C.R.O.M. circles, the president's opinion in the Orizaba case was met with a certain coolness and that the internal disputes of the working class should be settled by the working class itself without outside interference.[31] The C.T.M., while making no public statement on the matter, planned to censure the head of the Federal Labor Department whose bungling of the case throughout the last year, it claimed, had been in large part responsible for the tragic outbreaks both in Veracruz and Puebla.

In early May, 1937, the Supreme Court handed down a decision which, in effect, nullified President Cárdenas' resolution. The president had given the right to administer the collective contract in the Cocolapan factory to the C.R.O.M. union which claimed the majority within the plant. The C.T.M. union, which now existed in the plant, was composed of former members of the C.R.O.M. When, approximately a year previously, they had decided to leave the C.R.O.M. and form an independent union, they claimed the right, as the majority group, to continue in possession of the collective contract with the company. Later their independent union affiliated itself with the

31. *Ibid.*, April 28, 1937. It is interesting to note, however, that on occasions when they stood to benefit, these "militant unions" were only too eager to invite "outside interference."

C.T.M. Under this version, now upheld by the Supreme Court of Mexico, the C.R.O.M. workers simulated a strike in connivance with the company, forming a new union and obtaining a new collective contract, under the closed-shop terms of which the former workers were barred from their jobs. It was this situation which gave rise to the previously discussed conflict battle in Orizaba. The local Labor Disputes Board to which the case was presented decided in favor of the C.R.O.M. union, and the C.T.M. organization then carried its injunction against the decision to the Supreme Court. It was on this injunction suit that the Supreme Court now acted, deciding in favor of the original C.T.M. union and stating that it never lost its rights to the administration of the collective contract because of the special sections of the legislation governing labor relations in the textile industry which relates to such cases. Contracts in this industry, by the law established shortly after the textile convention approximately ten years earlier, were made not with the owners but with the plant and would continue in force even should the ownership of the mill change hands, as was apparently true in this case.[32]

As late as September 1, 1937, the Cocolapan factory was still shut down, and eighteen thousand men were idle in the Veracruz textile zone, despite the Supreme Court's decision favoring the C.T.M. which should have brought the conflict to an end. The C.T.M. appealed to the Labor Department to reverse its earlier decision and reopen the plant.[33] In the early part of September, the Industrial Company of Orizaba, operator of the Cocolapan mill, requested the C.T.M. union to furnish personnel to overhaul the machinery and prepare the mill for reopening, and on September 17, work was resumed. In spite of this, however, reports from Orizaba indicated that the labor difficulties had not been entirely overcome, since the C.R.O.M., frankly dissatisfied with the outcome of the conflict, was said to be preparing a new attack by which it still hoped to regain control in Cocolapan.[34]

In a decision reached under the auspices of the Federal Labor Department on December 11, 1937, between representatives of the C.R.O.M., the C.T.M., and the Industrial Company of Orizaba—a decision that had the approval of President Cárdenas—it was agreed that twenty-three C.R.O.M. workers then employed in Cocolapan would be transferred to the Mirafuentes mill, operated by the same company, in which the C.R.O.M. had a majority, while twenty-three

32. *Ibid.*, May 12, 1937.
33. "Comments on the Economic Situation," *Modern Mexico*, IX (August, 1937), 13; *Mexican Labor News*, September 15, 1937.
34. *Mexican Labor News*, September 22, 1937.

C.T.M. workers from Mirafuentes would be brought to Cocolapan. The remainder of the workers belonging to the minority group in each factory would not be re-employed, and the respective trade-union organizations were charged with the duty of finding them employment in the plants which they controlled.[35] In spite of this mutual agreement, however, to which it was a party, the C.R.O.M. brought an injunction suit against the order of the Labor Department, claiming that there were no C.T.M. workers in Mirafuentes to exchange.[36] On Monday, January 17, 1938, there occurred a bloody battle growing out of a general strike throughout the State of Veracruz, which had been called by the local Federation of Workers to protest against the court delays in deciding the dispute. Twelve workers were killed and many injured, the majority of casualties being C.T.M. members. President Cárdenas journeyed to Orizaba for the purpose of supervising the re-establishment of order and proposed the following terms of settlement, which were immediately accepted by the C.T.M.: (1) to set aside the decision of the Labor Department of December 11, 1937, and proposing the exchange of C.T.M. and C.R.O.M. workers; (2) to notify the Industrial Company of Orizaba to proceed with the repair of the sluice gates controlling the water power of the Cocolapan plant within the period of twenty-four hours; (3) to allow the C.R.O.M. workers to repair the water system which was damaged and not to delay goods sent to the Río Blanco plant for final treatment; (4) the company would resume operations and rehire all workers hired there before April 22, 1937; (5) the administration of the collective contract for the Cocolapan mill would be given to the C.T.M. union in the plant, in accordance with the Supreme Court decision of September 7, 1937; (6) both the C.R.O.M. and the C.T.M. unions in all the "Cidosa" plants would assume the solemn obligation to respect each other's rights and to refrain from all such actions as might produce friction, interrupt the normal course of work, or provoke conflicts or violence. Both organizations were also (7) to assume the obligation and to admit into their membership any workers who from the date of resumption of operations in Cocolapan expressed a desire to change their union allegiance; (8) the rights of C.T.M. workers in the Mirafuentes plant who were working there up to the month of April, 1937, were to be safeguarded; and (9) the workers were to be replaced in their jobs without delay.[37] Both the C.T.M. and the C.R.O.M. accepted the president's solution.

35. *Ibid.*, December 19, 1937.
36. *Ibid.*, January 13, 1938.
37. *Ibid.*, January 20, 1938; January 27, 1938.

Then, on February 11, 1938, in one of the few joint actions ever undertaken by the three national labor organizations in Mexico, the C.T.M., the C.R.O.M., and the C.G.T., all cotton thread and textile mills in the nation were shut down for two hours in a general protest strike against the companies. A mixed convention of workers and employers was holding a textile meeting to draw up a revised compulsory collective contract for the entire industry. As a result of greatly increased living costs throughout the country, the three labor organizations demanded immediate provisional wage increases to relieve the situation of the workers. The employers refused to grant the temporary increases, and the strike was voted by all the groups as a protest against their attitude. Originally planned as a twenty-four-hour movement, it was later agreed to limit the shutdown to two hours.[38]

When, by the following October, no agreement had been reached, all the cotton textile mills in Mexico were closed on Friday, the seventh, and thousands of operators belonging to all three of the trade union centers joined in another protest strike that lasted until Saturday morning. In spite of notice served on the labor organization the previous day by the Federal Labor Department that the stoppage would be deemed illegal, the union officials decided to proceed with the movement in answer to the demand from the rank and file of the unions for vigorous action to obtain improved conditions in the industry. The mixed commission had been in session for several months in an effort to draw up a new contract which, when agreed upon, would have the effect of law in the cotton branch of the textile industry. The existing contract had been written by a similar convention in 1927, had stabilized labor conditions to a great extent, and was one of the first general collective agreements to be raised to the status of "contract law."[39] Toward the end of the employer-worker convention in the cotton textile industry, a tendency to establish wage differentials in various parts of the country and between certain different types of cotton textile mills had been suggested, whereupon President Cárdenas issued a warning to the employers that he would refuse to ratify any agreement reached which contained such differentials. He believed that the constitutional principle of equal pay for equal work should be the basis of any contract finally drawn up.[40]

A compulsory collective contract was approved for the industry. But the refusal of the Industrial Company in Orizaba to establish the wage scales and working conditions contained in this contract

38. *Ibid.*, February 17, 1938.
39. *Ibid.*, October 13, 1938.
40. *Ibid.*, December 30, 1938.

threatened to provoke a new period of industrial unrest in June, 1939. The division of the workers in the company's plants between the C.T.M. and the C.R.O.M. prevented a completely united front on the issue, but the C.R.O.M. announced that, although it would not join a strike should such a movement develop, it would likewise not obstruct it in any way. Other unions of the C.T.M. in the State of Veracruz, however, considered a general sympathy strike in support of the textile workers of the Río Blanco and Cocolapan mills.[41] The problem was discussed between company representatives and the officials of the National Textile Federation (C.T.M.) before mediators of the Federal Labor Department, but no progress toward an agreement was made by June 6, the date on which all the cotton textile mills of Mexico were shut down for one hour in a general sympathy strike called to demonstrate the support of the nation's textile workers for the strike against the Industrial Company of Orizaba which began on June 3. The C.T.M. workers struck the Cocolapan mill of the "Cidosa" and also paralyzed the company's power plant. The Río Blanco mill was struck by workers belonging to the wing of the C.R.O.M. led by Francisco Ramírez Escamilla, the dissident majority of the organization that had broken away from the leadership of the Morones-controlled central committee. Although the presidential decree making the contract law throughout the country had not yet been issued, the workers insisted that its terms should be immediately put into force, as the "Cidosa" signed the agreement in common with the other textile operators of the country, who had already established the new conditions of work. The C.T.M. maintained that the company provoked the strike movement in the hope that the enmity between the C.T.M. and the company-controlled C.R.O.M. units in the Orizaba region would insure its failure and thus present the possibility of undermining the terms of the new general contract even before it became effective.[42] The strike movement was declared legal by the Federal Board of Conciliation and Arbitration, and on June 14 the Federation of Workers of the State of Veracruz voted a general strike in sympathy with the textile strikers of Orizaba, scheduled to begin on June 27, 1939. The strikers voluntarily agreed to submit to arbitration by the Federal Labor Board, the C.T.M. having vetoed proposals for an unlimited general strike on the grounds that it would have unjustly penalized employers already operating under the new collective contract and who were not responsible for the attitude taken by the "Cidosa." Meantime, the strike in Orizaba was maintained in

41. *Ibid.*, June 1, 1939.
42. *Ibid.*, June 8, 1939.

full force.[43] On July 11, after the Federal Labor Board handed down an arbitration award upholding the workers in their grievances against the owners, the strike was lifted. The award ordered the company to put the general collective contract into immediate effect and found the causes of the strike were imputable to the employers, which meant that the company was required to pay full wages to its employees throughout the entire period of the strike, as well as the differences between the old wage scales and the new levels established by the compulsory contract. It was estimated that the payment of back wages alone would exceed half a million pesos. Of the award, Lombardo Toledano said, "The National Committee of the C.T.M. is satisfied with the award handed down by the Board because it not only recognizes that the workers were in the right but also establishes an extremely important precedent for the future in connection with compulsory collective labor contracts."[44]

But the question was not to be settled that easily, for the company refused to abide by the decision of the board and instituted injunction proceedings in the federal courts seeking a restraining order against execution of the decision. Meantime, the contract was raised to the status of "contract law" by publication in the Official Gazette.[45] The contract, applicable to the entire country, was to be in effect for two years and covered spinning, weaving, printing, dyeing, and finishing of cotton, as well as of all fibers mixed with cotton. Under the contract, only workers whose names appeared on union lists could be employed by the mills; union representatives could intervene directly in the application of the legal and technical aspects of the contract. Promotion was determined in accordance with seniority as certified by the union lists, as well as by competence in the job; every worker was entitled to twelve days' vacation with pay each year, or to proportionate leave for services of less than a year. A minimum wage of 2.80 pesos a day was to prevail uniformly throughout the industry, wages being payable once a week and payment to be made during working hours; second and third shifts were allowed wage increases of 12.5 per cent and 17.5 per cent over the uniform rate. All claims presented by the union were to be settled within six days, an extension of time being allowable through mutual consent; death benefits were to be paid at the rate of 835 days' pay in addition to 45 days' pay for funeral costs; permanent and total disability payments were to be equivalent to 1,095 days' wages; temporary disability benefits were

43. *Ibid.*, June 29, 1939.
44. *Ibid.*, July 13, 1939.
45. *Ibid.*, August 3, 1939.

payable at full wage rates, beginning with the third day of such disability. A deduction of 2.75 per cent of wages was to be made by the employer and turned over to the union for welfare work and related benefits, unless such benefits were administered jointly by the union and the employer, or unless the latter provided such services by consent of the union. Financial aid on account of non-occupational illness was to be extended to all workers, and maternity leaves of forty-five days were granted. Employers could not interfere in union affairs, any agent of the employer found guilty of such interference being subject to dismissal. Apprentices were to be paid a minimum wage of 1.50 pesos during the first six months and were to be chosen exclusively from union lists.[46]

The companies obtained an injunction against the Cárdenas decree of January, 1940, extending the collective contract for another two years. Workers opposed company efforts to lower wages, and in the Río Blanco mill the workers began a sitdown strike on Saturday, March 16, 1940, when the American-owned Industrial Company of Orizaba attempted to pay them the wages prevailing before the establishment of the new collective contract. Representatives of the Department of Labor rushed to Orizaba to conciliate the dispute; a tentative settlement was reached, and the workers abandoned the factory. They expressed their willingness to submit to the decree of the Supreme Court on the question, since an appeal against the injunction granted by the lower courts had already been sent there, and the officials of the textile unions were confident that the company would not be permitted to pay wages less than those stipulated in the contract. Once the workers had left the factory, however, the company claimed that their recourse to a strike while the conflict was still being considered by judicial authorities was illegal; therefore, the company had the right to break its labor contract with them altogether. That is, they were fired. In reply, the workers immediately took possession of the mill again, and the Labor Department and federal troops appeared in Orizaba. Since two of the company's power plants were also in possession of the workers, the current for two other mills was stopped and the workers there were likewise obliged to join in the strike. The union controlling these two mills, however, was an affiliate of the C.R.O.M., under the leadership of Morones, while the Río Blanco union belonged to anti-Morones C.R.O.M. men. Consequently the Morones union did not wish to co-operate with the Río

46. Pan American Union, *Labor Trends and Social Welfare*, p. 51; "National Agreement in Cotton-Textile Industry in Mexico, 1939," *Monthly Labor Review*, L (May, 1940), 1140–46.

Blanco workers, although the C.T.M. unions in other mills had been aiding them in every possible way. Danger of another inter-union conflict, as well as an employer-labor conflict, was therefore looming.[47]

But in early April, 1940, the Supreme Court ruled that the injunction granted by a lower court to the several textile companies violated the law and constitutional precepts which no judge ought to have forgotten. Thus the appeal of the textile workers against the injunction was upheld, and it was stated that the companies must pay the wages stipulated in the collective contract of 1938–39, which had recently been extended by presidential decree for an additional two-year term. In addition, the decision established the constitutionality of the "contract law." In only one of the mills involved in the controversy was there any remaining difficulty. The workers of the Río Blanco mill struck to defend their wages when the Industrial Company of Orizaba began to make reductions. The "Cidosa," on the other hand, declared its contract with the strikers broken and announced that it would rehire only disciplined workers whom it did not consider responsible for the strike. Consequently, when the Supreme Court announced its decision, the Río Blanco men could not return to work because their terms with the company were still unsettled. With the intervention of the Department of Labor, however, a partial agreement was reached, and the mill was reopened on April 4, 1940. According to the agreement, all the workers employed before the strike were to be taken back; the difference between the higher wages due the workers and those they received until the date on which they struck was to be paid; the company was to continue to pay the higher wages in compliance with the Supreme Court's decision. All other points at issue, such as determination of the party responsible for the strike, the payment of wages accrued during the strike, and any penalties incurred by either party, were to be settled by arbitration of the Labor Department. At any rate, the workers gained their primary objective, since the wages for which they fought were established both by the Supreme Court and the Labor Department.[48] In this manner came to an end, at least temporarily, one of the longest and most bitterly fought conflicts in the history of Mexican labor, complicated by the claims of rival union groups, the activities of an anti-union company, and rather involved intervention of government authorities. Certainly, the fact that President Cárdenas did not treat with the C.T.M. unions exclusively in the struggle was evidence to refute claims made by some writers, noted earlier, that he refused to deal with any but unions

47. *Mexican Labor News,* March 21, 1940.
48. *Ibid.,* April 4, 1940.

affiliated with that central. Further, the textile case illustrated that labor disputes were not used as an excuse to expropriate foreign-owned industries, provided that such enterprises were willing to abide by decisions of Mexican courts, as was true with the textile companies, and was not true with respect to the oil companies.

Meanwhile, in April, 1937, a protest strike against the high price level was partially carried out by the National Federation of Electrical Workers. The eight-hour stoppage, which partially paralyzed twenty-two states of the republic, was originally scheduled to last a full twenty-four hours. Its duration was, however, reduced by the workers themselves in order to inflict as small a degree of discomfort as possible upon the general public, consistent with making an effective protest. A request from the Federal Labor Department to call off the strike was received after telegraphic orders for its commencement had already been sent from the headquarters of the federation in Mexico City to all its local bodies throughout the country. The movement was 100 per cent observed by the local bodies in the country—electric light and power were completely cut off for the eight hours during which the protest lasted.

The union complained that no concrete action or measures tending to bring about a reduction of prevailing food prices had been taken by the government; nor had there been any official notice taken of the study of the problem and recommendations for its solution presented on April 2 by the C.T.M. Furthermore, there had been an official authorization for another increase in the price of sugar, although the sugar industry had already once raised the price only a month earlier. Meantime, various organizations, such as the Lawyers' Socialist Front, many individual unions, and the Communist party of Mexico, had publicly declared their approval of the C.T.M. analysis and called for the adoption of the measures it proposed. Insofar as the C.T.M. was concerned, the problem of prices continued to be the greatest question facing the Mexican government in the spring of 1937, "for unless drastic action is soon taken, the most serious economic and social consequences may be expected."[49]

Nonetheless, the strike movement of the National Federation of Electrical Workers protesting the high prices received a strong rebuke from President Cárdenas because the federal government was taking measures to repress any abuses connected with the rise in prices and the independent action by labor organizations would interfere with, rather than aid, the government's efforts. This official view was in

49. *Ibid.*, April 14, 1937.

marked contrast to opinions the president had issued a year earlier, when he had upheld such labor action by saying that only by means of strikes could "economic equilibrium" be achieved and maintained. It would appear that executive coolness toward further strikes was motivated by a desire to avoid any widespread agitation which might jeopardize the economic boom Mexico was undoubtedly enjoying. It seemed doubtful, however, that even the president's expressed disapproval would suffice to prevent continued popular action against the high cost of living, since the position of workers and peasants in many parts of the country was growing extremely precarious, and, further, since such measures as the government had already taken had produced few results. Independent action on the part of organized sections of the poorer population was felt to be the only hope for early relief. Among the slogans issued by the C.T.M. to all its affiliated organizations for the May Day, 1937, demonstrations, the struggle against high prices occupied the most prominent place.[50]

The bakery workers of the Federal District began a strike on January 3, 1938, which lasted until the seventh, to force the baking companies to recognize, as the sole representative of their interests, the unified organization which had merged a multitude of formerly existing small plant and craft unions, as well as to obtain a collective contract for the entire baking industry.[51] The strike was postponed once on the promise that the employers would enter into discussions, but they failed to do so. Five hundred bakeries were tied up by the movement.[52] After the strike, the workers won a small, immediate increase in wages, 50 per cent of their wages during the strike, and a formal agreement from the employers that a collective contract would be signed by all the bakeries involved within a period not to exceed thirty days. On August 31, 1939, President Cárdenas signed the executive decree raising a collective contract, which had been accomplished, to the status of law.[53]

In May, 1938, the National Committee of the C.T.M. sent a message to Cárdenas in which it announced that the self-imposed ban on strikes would be lifted unless the government took measures to restrain employer action looking toward wage cuts and dismissals. The truce in strike action on the part of labor was adopted as a temporary measure of co-operation with the government in the oil crisis, and the C.T.M. charged that many industrialists, chiefly in the electric

50. *Ibid.*, April 21, 1937.
51. C.T.M., *Informe del Comité Nacional 1936–1937*, p. 76.
52. *Mexican Labor News*, January 6, 1938.
53. *Ibid.*, August 31, 1939.

power and cotton textile industries, were attempting to take advantage of labor's restraint to impose wage reductions and readjustments of personnel. Since such a policy would increase the economic difficulties by further reducing mass purchasing power, the C.T.M. warned that it would resort to the strike weapon if necessary to defeat such maneuvers by employers.[54]

The British-owned transit company which operated the Mexico City streetcar system entered an economic suit before the Federal Board of Conciliation and Arbitration in September, 1939. Its purpose was to obtain authorization for a series of wage cuts and layoffs among the workers on the lines. The company pleaded financial inability to maintain operations at the existing wage scales, whereupon the Alliance of Street Car Employees charged that the suit was merely a maneuver to split the union and to institute a counter-offensive to prevent revision of the collective contract, discussions for which had been in progress because the existing contract was to expire in another month. The workers had asked for wage increases and new regulations on pensions, vacations, medical attention, and other social welfare benefits in the new contract.[55] On November 1, 1939, the workers of the company struck, after discussions were broken off on October 31, when last-minute efforts to reach an agreement failed. Final offers and demands of the union included postponement of the strike for forty-five days; discussion during the first thirty days of all the economic clauses of the collective contract, with the provision that all points not agreed upon within that time be decided by a previously designated arbitrator; appointment of a mixed commission to investigate the technical, administrative, and financial condition of the company; discussion during the final fifteen days of the new wage scales; withdrawal by the company of its economic suit which was pending before the Labor Board; payment by the company of the fees of experts consulted in the investigation, as well as of wages of the worker delegates in the discussion of the contract; payment by the company of 5,000 pesos for strike expenses incurred by the union; and, finally, the obligation to make the economic clauses of the contract retroactive to October 21.[56] After two weeks on strike, the workers returned to their jobs on November 15, since mediation by the Federal Labor Department, acting on direct instructions from President Cárdenas, was successful in bringing both sides to a temporary settlement. Both the company and the workers agreed to submit the

54. *Ibid.*, May 11, 1938.
55. *Ibid.*, September 28, 1939.
56. *Ibid.*, October 12, 1939.

main question at issue—the financial capacity of the company—to the arbitration of the head of the Labor Department, and both bound themselves not to seek any recourse whatever, legal or otherwise, against the decision of the arbitrator. The company agreed to pay the wages of the worker delegates to the commission that was to investigate its financial condition, as well as the fees of whatever experts were called for the investigation. The commission, composed of company, worker, and government representatives, was to make a thorough study within sixty days of the company's real financial condition. On the basis of its findings, the arbitrator was to hand down his award. The company agreed to withdraw its economic suit for permission to make wage cuts and dismissals.[57]

On March 1, 1940, the expert commission gave notice of its conclusions, which favored the demands of the workers. The commission found that the company was in a position to increase salaries and other payments to its workers up to the amount of 2,159,000 pesos, and could, in addition, make economies in other directions, so that its final profit would be increased rather than diminished. The commission suggested the use of this profit for the repairing of equipment, which had not been renewed for many years.[58] The arbiter awarded wage increases of 2,000,000 pesos a year, or an average daily increase of 1 peso per worker.[59]

On April 5, 1940, twelve hundred copper miners struck against the Cananea Consolidated Copper Company, owned by American capital. Ever since January, negotiations between the company and Section 65 of the Miners' Industrial Union had been proceeding under the guidance of a special commission appointed by the Federal Labor Department, because the revised contract presented by the union for the company's approval contained some six hundred clauses and required a long time for consideration. The company refused the most important demands of the workers, such as wage increases, indemnities for workers incapacitated by their labor, a longer vacation period each year, and reinstatement of various workers whom the union considered to have been unnecessarily discharged.[60] The conflict had a special significance for labor, since it was at Cananea, in the very same copper mines, that workers struck in 1906 in one of the first uprisings of labor against the Díaz regime. At that time, the Mexican miners demanded the same wages and the same treatment that the

57. *Ibid.*, November 16, 1939.
58. *Ibid.*, March 7, 1940.
59. Pan American Union, *Labor Trends and Social Welfare*, p. 52.
60. *Mexican Labor News*, April 11, 1940.

American miners, imported by the company into Cananea, received. In 1906, it was practically hopeless for workers to strike; the outcome was inevitable—bloody suppression of the movement and no improvement in conditions. It was in Cananea in 1906 that the workers were shot down for their audacity. The April, 1940, dispute was ended on September 11 of the same year, when the Mine Workers' Union announced a complete victory for the workers. The final solution was reached through the intervention of the C.T.M. in the dispute; its force, combined with that of the mine workers, finally persuaded the Cananea Company to come to terms. The settlement provided for a 60-centavo increase in the daily wage, the payment of approximately 600,000 pesos in back wages, the construction of a medical clinic, and a revision of the life insurance system to the benefit of the miners. The relationship between the Mine Workers' Union and the C.T.M. was reported to have been greatly strengthened as a result of the active support given by the central during the strike.[61]

A study of the labor-capital conflicts surveyed in this chapter shows that the pattern developed for their settlement was one of government intervention at the request of one or both parties (usually labor), after a strike had been declared, with the result a decision by arbitration—generally granting at least part of labor's demands through the medium of a new collective contract. The three disputes of outstanding significance for the national economy of Mexico during the Cárdenas administration are treated in some detail in the following chapters. They illustrate clearly that whenever foreign-owned companies failed to abide by the decision of Labor Department authorities and the courts, expropriation was the course taken by the Mexican government, with strong support of the organized labor movement.

61. *Ibid.*, September 14, 1940.

VII. Labor
and the National Railways

A few minutes after the strike of railroad workers against the National Railways of Mexico, Inc., had begun—at five o'clock in the evening of May 18, 1936—the Federal Board of Conciliation and Arbitration declared it illegal. Upon learning the board's decision, the Union of Railroad Workers ordered the return to work of the strikers. The strike had been called because of the company's refusal to revise the collective labor contract, to pay the wages of the seventh day of the week (the compulsory day of rest) to its office employees, and to accept other trade-union and economic demands. The strike and the decision of the Labor Board resulted in a cohesion in the ranks of the railroad workers which secured the payment of their demands a few weeks later. This cohesion also effected the nationalization of the National Railways, which soon afterward were to be turned over to the Union of Railroad Workers to be managed by it.[1]

Because of the importance of the board's decision in declaring the strike movement illegal, the National Committee of the C.T.M. convoked representatives of its diverse organizations for the First National

1. Confederación de Trabajadores de México, *Informe del Comité Nacional 1936–1937*, p. 76; *C.T.M. 1936–1941*, pp. 1111–12. See also Rodrigo García Treviño, "Los Sindicatos en la Administraicón de las Indústrias," *Revista de Economía*, III (January–April, 1934), 33–45.

Council of the C.T.M., which met during the first several days of June, 1936. The council resolved that on June 18, 1936, there would be held an hour protest strike against the decision of the federal board in all the activities of the country whose workers were affiliated with C.T.M. unions, with work to be stopped thirty minutes during the morning and during the evening. Another purpose of the protest strike was to demonstrate the right of workers to strike—a right guaranteed by the constitution. This decision by the board, the C.T.M. claimed, also illustrated the fact that every time there was a strike movement against an enterprise dominated by foreign capital, the rights of the workers were denied, since foreign influence governed the acts of the public administration.[2] The protest strike occurred as planned throughout the country, and in Mexico City various sections of the population cooperated in paralyzing all transportation. The National Committee of the C.T.M. maintained that the award of the board was made even before the strike began, that the board did not listen to the points of view of the workers, and of the employers, as was required by Article 270 of the Federal Labor Law, and that the decision would establish a precedent which would be used not only to prevent the exercise of the right to strike in public utility industries but would be amplified to interfere with that right in all types of business enterprises.[3] Out of the dispute arose a demand for nationalization of the National Railways.

At the time of Cárdenas' election to the presidency, the National Railways were in a deplorable condition: between 1911 and 1936 ton-kilometers of freight carried had increased 90 per cent, but the number of freight cars had declined from 20,389 to 14,621. Locomotives, on the average, were twenty years old, and in seven years only twelve had been purchased. Meanwhile, accrued interest on the railroad bonds had increased to a point such that it exceeded the face value of the obligations, while peso depreciation had multiplied the burden of dollar indebtedness.[4] Railway connections among the several parts of Mexico were almost completely neglected—a defect still felt in Mexican economic life. As one of Mexico's leading economists, Alejandro Carrillo, pointed out, the threat of bankruptcy faced by the railways of Mexico at the beginning of the twentieth century was

2. C.T.M., *C.T.M. 1936–1941*, pp. 90–91. Although the Mexican government owned the majority of stock in the National Railways, they were operated primarily for the benefit of foreign bondholders. Henry Bamford Parkes, *A History of Mexico* (2nd ed.: Boston, 1950), p. 407.

3. C.T.M., *C.T.M. 1936–1941*, pp. 91–92, 102–03.

4. Nathaniel and Sylvia Weyl, *The Reconquest of Mexico: The Years of Lázaro Cárdenas* (New York, 1939), p. 270.

due partly to the fact that they received silver money for their services and had to meet their obligations to foreign creditors in gold, while silver was continually decreasing in value.[5]

In 1929, according to the First Industrial Census of 1930, the length of kilometers of all railways lines constructed in the republic was 23,777.5. Of these lines, 523.3 kilometers were street railways, and 405.6 kilometers were unexploited. The major part of the lines included in this figure consisted of lines built during the thirty-six years of the Díaz dictatorship; these had been built at tremendous cost to the nation in the way of concessions and subsidies granted in cash obtained through overseas loans contracted primarily in Europe. As was mentioned above, the construction of these lines, in which the state held a majority stock interest, was haphazard, serving private rather than national interests, varying in gauge and forming no real system of trunk lines and, therefore, following no sound plan for nationwide development.[6] The National Railways constituted about 66.9 percent of all Mexican railway lines; no improvements were made on them between 1926 and 1937, while the cost of keeping the old and inadequate equipment repaired was exorbitant.[7] A year before the Madero revolution broke out, measures were taken toward reorganization, and the lines in which the state had an interest were consolidated. According to Bosques, however, this measure was so disastrously accomplished that the capital represented by the various consolidated companies rose from 509,085,727 pesos to 1,230,000,000 pesos "by the usual juggling and legerdemain customary under the capitalistic system whenever such transactions are effected."[8] This huge sum was represented mainly by mortgage bonds drawing $33,050,000 interest per annum. The first years of the consolidated administration of the National Railways yielded an income of $61,-483,147, more than half of which would have been absorbed by the mortgage interest service. When the revolution began, the railways were for a time seized by the revolutionary authorities and the debt service was suspended; since then, the railways have been a "thorn in the side of every revolutionary Government."[9] In the view of an-

5. Alejandro Carrillo, *Mexico's Resources for Livelihood* (The Hague, 1938), p. 23.

6. Gilberto Bosques, *The National Revolutionary Party of Mexico and the Six-Year Plan* (Mexico, 1937), p. 324. See also: Moisés T. de la Peña, "La Administración Obrera de los Ferrocarriles Nacionales de México," *Revista de Economía*, II (September–December, 1938), 684–85.

7. Moisés T. de la Peña, "La Administración," p. 689.

8. Bosques, *The National Revolutionary Party*, pp. 324–25.

9. *Ibid.*, p. 325.

other eminent Mexican economist, tariff rates discriminated against the small producer, and the National Railways "figured as the most determined upholder of the middle-man, making it impossible for small producers to get access to the markets. . . ."[10]

The railroads needed large numbers of men for construction and "purchased" them from the big haciendas. Once construction was completed, these workers flocked into the towns to swell the reserves of the industrial proletariat. Contact with the outer world allowed these men to communicate with the syndicalist organizations then existing in the United States, and they began to organize themselves in similar fashion. It was, in fact, the railwaymen who first began to organize themselves toward the end of the last century. As a result of the events of the revolution, the railway workers had attained the position of being the best-paid workers in the country and were in no mood to renounce this apparently preferred position. The first attempt to reorganize the railroads and make them profitable was made by reducing personnel and wages, which met the opposition of the workers,[11] as it was to do under Cárdenas.

Against this background, President Cárdenas, on June 23, 1937, issued a decree expropriating the National Railways of Mexico and establishing instead an official department to handle the system. With regard to this historic move, Cárdenas and Lombardo Toledano were in seemingly complete accord. In August, 1937, the management of the railways was promised to the workers, and on April 21, 1938, the Mexican Senate approved the bill to turn them over to the worker administration.[12] This move by President Cárdenas was the first large-scale application of the Expropriation Law of November, 1936, under which the government was authorized to expropriate, "for the benefit of the public any private properties that might be opposed to the collective interests, or whose operation was not being carried on in conformity with collective interests."[13] The decree stated in part:

> The Federal Government will assume direct responsibility for the proper functioning of railroads and will endeavor to develop them in accordance with the economic and social needs of the country.

10. Federico Bach, "The Nationalization of the Mexican Railroads," *Annals of Collective Economy: International Review of Four Editions*, XV (1939), 74–75.

11. *Ibid.*, pp. 77–78, 84.

12. Hudson Strode, *Timeless Mexico* (New York, 1944), p. 328.

13. Bach, "The Nationalization of the Mexican Railroads," p. 70. For a complete copy of the Expropriation Law, see Bosques, *The National Revolutionary Party*, p. 250.

The railways will henceforth belong to the Nation, so that a definite orientation of public service may be given to them, suppressing profit as the fundamental motive, and correcting the deficiencies that have traditionally existed in the National Railways of Mexico, and which have been a serious obstacle to their technical development and financial stability.[14]

The motives for expropriation were given in the Decree of June 23 as follows:

The better organization and functioning of the railroads must constitute a high place in the consideration of the public power since the system of communications is a factor of greatest importance to the economic and social progress of a country the state of which is a good index of the general state of the nation. In our country the business called National Railways of Mexico is organized on a capitalistic basis, and it has come to create vice and deficiencies in the management of the system, which has slowed the rhythm of technical progress of the lines.[15]

In short, it was felt by the Cárdenas administration that expropriation of the most important railroad network in the republic was the best way to utilize the railroads toward the end of public service.[16] Or, as it was expressed by De la Peña, "Any business whatever that is able to exist solely on the basis of the public misery, has no right to exist, and that has been the case of the National Railways of Mexico."[17] Not all writers agreed, however, on the motives for expropriation. Correa, in maintaining that the Expropriation Law itself was unconstitutional, claimed that "In all the expropriations Cárdenas was not guided by the collective interest of the nation, but by 'particularism' in favor of a determined social class."[18] He held that the real reason for expropriation was that the C.T.M. needed to acquire prestige among the worker elements, so that it could become more powerful than the older labor groups; therefore, Cárdenas took over

14. Quoted in Carrillo, *Mexico's Resources for Livelihood*, p. 24. For a copy of the Expropriation Decree of June 23, 1937, see C.T.M., *C.T.M. 1936–1941*, pp. 273–75.

15. Quoted in Confederación de Cámaras Nacionales de Comercio e Industria de los Estados Unidos Mexicanos, *Análisis Económico Nacional 1934–1940*, (2nd ed.; México, 1940), p. 55.

16. Armando de María y Campos, *Múgica: Crónica Biográfica* (México, 1939), p. 284.

17. Moisés T. de la Peña, "La Expropiación de los Ferrocarriles Nacionales de México," *El Trimestre Económico*, IV (1937), 217.

18. Eduardo J. Correa, *El Balance del Cardenismo* (México, 1941), p. 139.

the railroads to demonstrate his favoritism for that particular worker group.[19] While it was no secret that the entire Cárdenas program favored the working class, there is no conclusive evidence that the railroad expropriation favored the C.T.M. over any other segment of the working class, as Correa asserted; his opinion was apparently a minority one.

According to most sources, the decree of expropriation came as a surprise, but, at the same time, it was hailed by all groups in Mexico for both its courage and its soundness.[20] Even *El Universal*, conservative organ of the Mexican press, claimed it was necessary to nationalize the railways. "The imperative logic of economic and social facts demands that the State should take over the railways. What was lacking was a government capable of undertaking that task and carrying it through. Praise for this has been won by President Cárdenas."[21] *Mexican Labor News* noted that "Even in conservative and reactionary circles, where all measures even hinting at 'expropriation' are immediately condemned as rank communism, it has been recognized that the best interests of Mexico have here been splendidly served. All social classes, from the extreme right to the extreme left, have signified their approval of President Cárdenas's action."[22] The C.T.M. sent a congratulatory telegram to Cárdenas, and the Railroad Workers' Union expressed its complete approval and support; the president of the Third General Convention of the union, Eutimio Rodríguez, declared at the time that the workers would not be affected by the labor law applying to state employees, but would retain all their rights under the Federal Labor Law. Further, he stated that discussion for a new collective contract would not be interrupted, but would be carried on with the new Autonomous Railroad Department.[23]

Perhaps the Expropriation Decree should not have been too surprising in view of the fact that in his eve-of-election speech Cárdenas had said: "The necessities of the country demand the construction of new railway lines and the improvement of those now in existence. My impression is that the railway system demands a general reorganization, as much to facilitate the construction of other lines as to bring about a lowering of freight rates, to contribute to the development of agriculture and industry."[24]

19. *Ibid.*, p. 142.
20. "Comments on the Economic Situation," *Modern Mexico*, IX (August, 1937), 13; *Mexican Labor News*, June 20, 1937.
21. Bosques, *The National Revolutionary Party*, p. 325.
22. *Mexican Labor News*, June 20, 1937.
23. C.T.M., *C.T.M. 1936–1941*, pp. 276–77.
24. Lázaro Cárdenas, "Address to the Nation on the Eve of His Election by President-Elect Cárdenas, June 30, 1934," *Modern Mexico*, V (August, 1934), 10.

The decree stated that the minority stockholders would be reimbursed, but no reference was made to the various international obligations, amounting roughly to $250,000,000, and to accrued interest of $275,000,000.[25] The Law of Expropriation of 1936 provided for experts to fix the value of any expropriated properties within sixty days, payments to begin in accordance with the law. In November, 1940, however, the Confederación de Cámaras Nacionales de Comercio e Industria reported that not only had the experts rendered no opinion as to the value of the properties, but they had not even been designated, nor had an inventory been made of all the properties expropriated, nor had the quantity of indemnity been determined.[26] In view of these circumstances, particularly, it is interesting to speculate, as Gordon did, as to why the action gave rise to comparatively little objection or reaction among either the bodies primarily concerned or the general public, especially considering that it preceded the oil expropriations and that almost as large a foreign investment was involved.[27] Perhaps the answer lies in the fact that in the oil case the industry was very prosperous and paid regular income to the owners, whereas in the case of the railroads the industry had been in a state of economic distress for some time and was furnishing no such income either to the owners or to the creditors. Under these circumstances, it could have been that the private interests felt that through nationalization they might receive at least partial reimbursement.

The day after expropriation, the government created an Autonomous Railway Department, separate from the Ministry of Communications and Public Works, to manage the system.[28] Cárdenas announced that while the state reserved for itself the ownership of the expropriated lines and of those under construction, he would place their administration in the hands of the union and would select from the union's ranks the officials for the newly created Railways Department.[29] The bonded debt of the system was consolidated with the general debt of the federal government, thus depriving the foreign creditors of the right to intervene in the management of the lines.[30] The alternatives considered available to the government at the time

25. "Comments on the Economic Situation," *Modern Mexico*, IX (August, 1937), 13.

26. Confederación de Cámaras Nacionales de Comercio e Industria de los Estados Unidos Mexicanos, *Análisis Económico Nacional 1934–1940*, pp. 58–59.

27. Wendell C. Gordon, *The Expropriation of Foreign-Owned Property in Mexico* (Washington, D.C., 1941), p. 136.

28. "Comments on the Economic Situation," *Modern Mexico*, IX (August, 1937), 13.

29. Bosques, *The National Revolutionary Party*, pp. 325–26. Lines entirely owned by private interests were not nationalized.

30. Nathaniel and Sylvia Weyl, *The Reconquest of Mexico*, pp. 270–71.

of expropriation were either to give the roads to the Railroad Workers' Union to administer as a co-operative, or to maintain ownership of the lines in the state and allow the workers to manage them for five years. If at the end of that period, the experiment were not considered successful, a new form of administration was to be tried. The second of these alternatives was decided upon, and on June 29, 1937, the Directive Board of the National Railways met and officially accepted the transfer.[31]

For a year, the newly created government railroad department struggled to make the properties pay. Its problems were not alleviated by the fact that the Cárdenas government had concentrated on building showy trunk highways parallel to the railroad lines, which served to increase truck and bus competition. Furthermore, the economic crisis in the United States had serious repercussions on Mexico, and throughout the latter part of 1937 freight revenues were on the decline. The ratio of operating costs to gross revenues on the National Railways increased from 83 per cent in 1936 to 109 per cent in December, 1937.[32]

One disturbing question under this administrative system was that relating to the status of the railroad workers under the Federal Labor Law. Immediately after the nationalization, President Cárdenas had announced that the existing collective contracts with the union and all the trade-union conquests of the organization acquired during its years of struggle to achieve its relatively favored conditions would be fully respected. Nevertheless, the actual relations to be established between the union and the new government department administering the roads were not specified, although an official was at work drafting the bill which would govern such details after its adoption by Congress. Pastor Súarez Hurtado, member of the Railroad Workers' Union and labor representative of one of the Federal Boards of Conciliation and Arbitration, appealed to his union, asking support for the thesis that the Federal Labor Law be so reformed that railroad workers would be specifically excluded from the category of government employees.[33] In January, 1938, it was reported that the controversial question had been settled by a ruling issued on the instructions of President Cárdenas in response to a direct question raised by the Railroad Workers' Union. On January 14, a communication was sent to the head of the Autonomous Railroad Department and to Juan Gutiérrez, general secretary of the Railroad Workers' Union, to the effect that for all

31. De la Peña, "La Expropiación," pp. 217, 224–25 "Comments on the Economic Situation," *Modern Mexico*, IX (August, 1937), 13.
32. Nathaniel and Sylvia Weyl, *The Reconquest of Mexico*, p. 271.
33. *Mexican Labor News*, October 21, 1937.

legal purposes coming within the scope of the Federal Labor Law, the new Railroad Department would be considered the successor of the private company, "National Railways of Mexico," so that the department was thus responsible for the fulfillment of the collective labor contract which existed between the extinct company and the union, and all the trade-union rights of the workers guaranteed by that contract remained in force.[34]

On April 23, 1938, there was created a body separate from the federal government, called The National Worker Administration of the Railroads; its character was that of a public corporation, to be directed by an Executive Council composed of seven members named by the Railroad Workers' Union. Two comptrollers, representing the federal government, were to aid the council.[35] With regard to this move, Bosques stated, "In giving the administration of the nationalized lines to the railway workers union, President Cárdenas has acted strictly in compliance with the National Revolutionary party's policy of placing the means of production and distribution of wealth in the hands of organized workers, a policy correctly defining Mexican Socialism."[36] This procedure was not consistently followed, however, since the expropriated oil properties were not managed by the Oil Workers' Union exclusively. The Executive Council members of the worker administration were given a two-year term of office, with the right of re-election, but were subject to recall at any time. The council elected its president, who was placed in charge of administration. President of the council, or board, and general manager was Salvador J. Romero, said to have a magnetic charm not surpassed by that of President Roosevelt.[37] From head of personnel in Guadalajara, he climbed to the presidency of the Office Workers' Union, and later, to

---

34. *Ibid.*, January 20, 1938; *ibid.*, January 27, 1938. For a copy of the collective contract as of August 31, 1936, which contained 81 clauses, see "Contrato Colectivo de Trabajo Celebrado entre los Ferrocarriles Nacionales de México, S.A., y Líneas Administradas y el Sindicato de Trabajadores Ferrocarrileros de la República Mexicana," *Revista Mexicana del Trabajo*, VII (September–October, 1936), 185–228. For the revised contract, in force from April 1, 1937, see "Contrato Colectivo de Trabajo Celebrado entre los Ferrocarriles Nacionales de México, S.A., y Líneas Administradas y el Sindicato de Trabajadores Ferrocarrileros de la República Mexicana, en Vigor desde el día 1º de Abril de 1937," *ibid.*, VIII (April–May, 1937), 262–316.

35. Andrés Ortíz, "Los Ferrocarriles Nacionales de México," *Investigación Económica, Tercer Trimestre*, IV (1944), 256. For a copy of the law creating the corporation, see "Administración Obrera de los Ferrocarriles Nacionales de México," *Revista Mexicana del Trabajo*, X (April–May, 1938), 316–19; *Mexican Labor News*, April 21, 1938.

36. Bosques, *The National Revolutionary Party*, p. 326.

37. "The Workers Run the Railroads," *Modern Mexico*, X (December, 1938), 7.

head of personnel of the entire railway system. Another member of the council was Elías Terán Gómez, general secretary of the Railroad Workers' Union, formerly office manager of a department. Other members included Jesús Zertuche, an accountant; F. Aguilar; David del Arco, a conductor; Rafael Martínez, superintendent of a division; and Santos Fierro, master mechanic.[38]

Restrictions were established against the sale, mortgage, or entailment of the properties without the express permission of the federal executive; nor could the worker administration contract loans without the government's concurrence.[39] Rates were to be fixed by the worker administration of the National Railways, subject to the approval of the federal government. Any funds obtained from the sale of property had to be used to improve capital equipment. Certain obligations were imposed by the law upon the new administration, and it had to keep operating expenses below 85 per cent of gross revenues: (1) 5.36 per cent of gross revenue was required to be invested annually in improvements and materials; (2) when the gross revenue exceeded 125,000,000 pesos, the administration was required to pay the government a share in such revenues amounting to 5.64 per cent, and it had to pay the government 3.64 per cent of gross revenues when they were less than 125,000,000 pesos; (3) it was required to dispose of additional revenue obtained by reduction in operating expenses by paying 25 per cent to increase the government's share, 25 per cent to the special insurance fund of the railroad workers, 25 per cent to the fund for improvements of the lines and 25 per cent for reserves against poor years. The administration was also required to pay taxes.[40] The labor relations of the workers under the new administration were to continue to be governed by the Federal Labor Law and the existing labor contract, the worker administration becoming the new signatory to the contract with the Railroad Workers' Union, thus dissipating entirely the fear of the workers that they might be converted into government employees.[41]

In the view of some observers, the Executive Council of the worker administration attacked the many problems confronting it with energy and decision. Forty-five unneeded engineers and all political employees were discharged, their duties being assumed by the department heads (all trade-unionists), and younger men were placed in the leading positions. Within a few months, three hundred railroad cars which

38. *Ibid.*
39. *Mexican Labor News*, April 21, 1938.
40. Nathaniel and Sylvia Weyl, *The Reconquest of Mexico*, p. 272; *Mexican Labor News*, April 21, 1938.
41. *Mexican Labor News*, April 21, 1938.

had been damaged during the revolution and left in the yards, were repaired and placed in service. About 25,000,000 pesos of short-term debt, much of it incurred as a result of equipment purchases and rental of rolling stock from the United States, was paid. During the eight months of labor administration—to the end of 1938—operating costs were reduced to 87.17 per cent of gross income, as compared with 92.39 per cent in the equivalent 1937 period. Gross income and freight revenue remained approximately the same in the two periods, but the worker administration increased net returns from 7,442,381 pesos to 12,523,825 pesos by stringent economies. It repaired more track than its predecessor, maintained a higher proportion of its locomotives in operation, and increased average train speeds. The Weyls pointed out that "Mexican businessmen who gloat over the precarious state of the National Railways tend to forget that trade-union management cannot be held responsible for economic difficulties that have their counterpart in countries where the roads are under private or state control. Thus, in 1934, the Mexican expenditure was 73 per cent of gross income as against 105 per cent in Germany, 110 per cent in Italy, 113 per cent in Great Britain, and 123 per cent in Austria. The National Railways is probably still earning a larger rate of return than the European systems."[42] These writers held further that American tourists who ascribed their transportation difficulties to the evils of trade-union management forgot that speed on the Mexican railroads was severely limited by the fact that few of the lines were double-tracked, gradients over mountain passes were necessarily steep, and neither the wealth of the area serviced nor the indicated future revenue of the lines warranted the sort of ambitious modernization program instituted by the American companies.[43] According to another source, 1,000,000 pesos was saved by cutting off the payroll those persons hired because "my friend needs a job," and by pensioning those persons who deserved it. Freight loadings were rushed, and care was taken to fill each car to capacity in order to decrease the number of cars in service. Heavier rails were laid to replace those worn out or found to be too light, and, said the report, trains were arriving on time; ". . . and what is more remarkable, eight million pesos was paid within the first three months of this new administration on the current debt."[44] Not all observers were so enthusiastic with regard to the success of worker administration.

42. Nathaniel and Sylvia Weyl, *The Reconquest of Mexico*, p. 273.
43. *Ibid.*, pp. 273–74.
44. "The Workers Run the Railroads," *Modern Mexico*, X (December, 1938), 8.

One of the most serious economic, as well as controversial, problems experienced by the railroads was the expenditure—held by some to be disproportionate—on wages and salaries.[45] In 1920, at a time when revenues were declining, President Obregón authorized an increase in railroad personnel from 33,597 to 47,486, and an increase in wages and salaries from 33,000,000 to 61,000,000 pesos. While by 1939 the total number of workers employed by the national lines had been reduced to some 44,000, wages and salaries still absorbed a share of total expenditure that was excessive when compared with the situation in other countries. The fact that the average annual wage was only 1,849 pesos in 1937 was somewhat misleading, since that figure included thousands of unskilled workers who earned the minimum wage prescribed by state legislation.[46] Professor Jesús Silva Herzog declared that labor costs on the National Railways were excessive, citing statistics showing that machinists, conductors, and train dispatchers earned more in Mexico than in the United States, despite the enormous differences in living standards and costs.[47] The Weyls reported that the proportion of labor costs to total expenses jumped from 63.2 per cent in 1937 to 66.1 per cent in 1938; these figures compared with 47.9 per cent in the United States, 44.6 per cent in Great Britain, and 39.0 per cent in Italy. They added that the Mexican ratio left little room for modernization of lines, reinforcement of roadbeds, and renovation of equipment.[48] At the same time, Moisés T. de la Peña maintained that an argument much exploited was that railroad salaries in Mexico were too high when, in fact, railroad workers were paid about the same wages as those paid in other industries of the country. He added that the bad conditions of the railroads could not be attributed to incapacity of the workers, excessive personnel, or high salaries. To substantiate his position, De la Peña produced figures giving comparable data for 1934 (see the following table). He maintained that freight rates were too high, considering the price of the raw materials shipped, such as corn, and that salaries were too low.[49] With regard to salaries of the railroad workers, President

45. De la Peña, "La Administración," pp. 691–93.
46. Nathaniel and Sylvia Weyl, *The Reconquest of Mexico*, p. 274.
47. *Ibid.*
48. *Ibid.*, p. 274. See also: A. B. Cuéllar, "Railroad Problems of Mexico," *Annals of the American Academy of Political and Social Science*, 187 (September, 1936), 193–206.
49. De la Peña, "La Administración," p. 685; see also: Moisés T. de la Peña and Alfredo Navarrete, "Reorganización de los Ferrocarriles Nationales," *El Trimestre Económico*, (January–March, 1941), 616–34; "El Grave Problema de los Ferrocarriles Mexicanos," *Acción Social*, 2 (April, 1941), 9–11, 20.

Cárdenas had stated that the wages of the workers on the railroads were low, "inferior to the average salary in the other great industries of the country, despite the fact that 55 per cent of the gross receipts went to the payment of salaries."[50] On the other hand, *Mexican Labor News* commented, "It is true that in comparison with most Mexican industrial workers, the railroad workers are well paid, which is not to say that their wages are absolutely very high."[51] Apparently, the analysis of De la Peña is as accurate as any to be found.

Industry	No. Workers	Total Income (pesos)	Average Annual Salary per Worker (pesos)
Beer	2,629	3,978,232.00	1,512.00
Iron and Steel	4,908	5,655,601.00	1,153.00
Light and Power	7,527	11,783,295.00	1,565.00
Petroleum (field)	8,070	16,910,051.00	2,095.00
Refineries (oil)	7,081	12,284,976.00	1,735.00
Cement	1,196	1,370,765.00	1,149.00
Metal plants	13,898	14,351,185.00	1,026.00
Cigars	3,671	3,739,819.00	1,019.00
National Railways	35,518	52,584,929.00	1,481.00

Moisés T. de la Peña, "La Administración Obrera de los Ferrocarriles Nacionales de México," *Revista de Economía*, II (September–December, 1938), 693.

Besides the salary, debt, lack of equipment, and declining freight revenue problems, there were other difficulties to be faced by the worker administration. Not the least of these, closely connected with the salary question, was the inter-union unrest growing out of the vast differences between the income of the unskilled worker (who earned barely enough to keep alive) and the skilled worker, the aristocrat of the working class. Indicative of the dangers inherent in this situation was the fact that one convention of the Railroad Workers' Union fled Mexico City to escape angry demonstrations of common labor elements for wage increases. When the roads were turned over to the Railroad Workers' Union for management, the trade union decided to retain the old employer-employee relationship and to keep the collective contract intact. The right to strike was maintained; dues were collected, as before, through the check-off system; the union was empowered to designate all company officials,

50. Gordon, *The Expropriation of Foreign-Owned Property in Mexico*, p. 139.
51. *Mexican Labor News*, June 30, 1937.

to control hiring and firing, and to insist upon advancement strictly by seniority. Expulsion from the union, which had to be ratified by the membership, deprived a worker of the right to remain in the employ of the National Railways. Thus, an anomalous situation had been created in which the union acquired the dual relationship of employer and employee which, in some cases, may have caused discipline to break down, since the authority of officials was vitiated by the fact that they themselves were subject to recall by the trade-union members. In addition, from the outside, the worker administration was flayed by the conservative press for its imagined sins. Revolts of the rank and file against a supposedly Communist leadership in the union were invented or magnified; and the golden opportunity of the reaction arose with the unprecedented series of train wrecks in late 1938 and early 1939.[52] Salvador J. Romero, general manager of the lines, declared that enemies of the labor administration of the lines were responsible for the outrages, in an effort to discredit the worker management and indirectly to bring the Cárdenas administration into disrepute. He called attention to the fact that most of the accidents had occurred on the principal trunk lines to the United States and invariably to passenger and the special tourist trains, whereas freight trains and passenger trains on other, less important, routes had suffered no similar mishaps. He denied that the accidents were caused either by incompetent personnel or by faulty materials and noted that in the case of the derailment of the Laredo train, the American passengers took up a voluntary collection for the engineer as a token of gratitude for his expert handling of the locomotive; his action prevented a disaster of major proportions.[53] A climax to the series of accidents occurred on April 13, 1939, with the wrecking of the Laredo–Mexico City train and the loss of forty lives. The general manager again charged sabotage; however, an investigation disclosed that the Laredo train crew had slackened speed to repair a defective air hose without placing the necessary warning signals on the track. As a result, the Guadalajara express had collided with the train. Members of the crew were immediately arrested on homicide charges, and the entire worker administration, including the department heads, placed their resignations before the convention of the Railroad Workers' Union.[54] New men were elected; Manager Romero was retained in his old position. Drastic reorganization of the structure of

52. Nathaniel and Sylvia Weyl, *The Reconquest of Mexico*, p. 275.
53. *Mexican Labor News*, March 30, 1939.
54. Nathaniel and Sylvia Weyl, *The Reconquest of Mexico*, pp. 275–76; *Mexican Labor News*, April 6, 13, 20, 1939.

worker control to eliminate the dual role of the trade-union was forecast. In a circular to the workers, Salvador Romero expressed "plain
and unpalatable truths":

> Lack of cars, negligence and perhaps even bad faith, re-
> luctance to obey orders and to comply with the most ele-
> mentary obligations, even to safeguard life, have been the
> causes of these disasters which have also damaged the finest
> rolling stock in the country and cost millions of pesos. . . .
> If we should again meet with indolence, disobedience of
> orders or bad faith on the part of selfish and incorrigible
> groups, the labor administration . . . will act with the severity
> that each case warrants and exact full responsibility from
> chiefs and executive personnel who tolerate actions that merit
> punishment.[55]

Romero pointed out that the National Railroads were the property of the nation, which the government had entrusted to the workers
with the purpose of rendering a secure and efficient public service,
and that it was the workers' duty to conserve and enlarge this source
of wealth and of individual and collective well-being through the
maximum efforts of all. He mentioned that the administration was
studying the details of a new system of rewards and promotions for
all railroad workers who distinguished themselves for conspicuous
fulfillment of duty and maintenance of the necessary discipline and
morale to ensure the safe operation of the lines at a high level of
efficiency.[56]

Despite the efforts of the worker administration to prevent further
accidents and to improve rail service, two wrecks in early 1940 resulted in the appointment by the Executive Committee of the Railroad
Workers' Union of a new Executive Board to direct the worker administration of the National Railways. It was reported that Salvador
Romero felt that unanimous resignation was indispensable under the
circumstances, and that in the emergency the union should appoint
new men who would be able to restore public confidence. The new
general manager was Juan Gutiérrez, one of the outstanding figures
in the Railroad Workers' Union and secretary of labor disputes of
the C.T.M. It was stated that Romero and his associates were not
considered personally responsible for the two accidents that had occurred in the previous month under their administration, but that
the change of management was simply a gesture on the part of the
workers to show that they would make every effort to provide safe
and competent transportation service to the Mexican people. The

55. Nathaniel and Sylvia Weyl, *The Reconquest of Mexico*, p. 276.
56. *Mexican Labor News*, May 4, 1939; *ibid.*, March 14, 1940.

new council published another circular addressed to all workers of the roads, calling upon them for greater care and responsibility. Not only machinists and conductors, but all members of the train crews and all workers, even when traveling as passengers, were made responsible for the safe and efficient functioning of the lines. It was feared that the carrying out of these instructions might be hindered by the dissatisfaction which certain locals of the Railroad Workers' Union showed with the change in council membership, but apparently an explanation by the council itself and by the Executive Committee of the Union of Sections 15, 16, 17, and 18 and of the reasons for the change, resulted in the withdrawal of their protests and brought forth a vote to support the new council.[57] In July, however, after only a brief term in office, the council resigned in a body. This move cleared the way for an attempted complete reorganization of the system.[58]

In August, 1940, the Railroad Workers' Union presented a plan of reorganization to President Cárdenas in the hope of putting the roads on a paying basis without taking many benefits from the workers themselves. The first point of the plan called for a separation of the worker administration of the railroads from the officials of the Railroad Workers' Union itself which, it was felt, would make for greater efficiency, and would also enable union officials to occupy themselves exclusively with the problems of the union members, leaving the question of railroad management to distinct officials.[59] The remainder of the plan requested economic co-operation from the government for the purpose of paying off the inherited debt without reducing salaries. President Cárdenas announced his agreement with the greater part of the plan, and stated that after further study, he would call the union committee for further discussion and final arrangements. *Mexican Labor News* commented: "The Railroads have been a white elephant in the hands of the Union since management was first taken over, and considerable dissatisfaction has been shown in the Union over the fact that the need for paying off tremendous debts has prevented necessary wage increases."[60] Cárdenas offered to remove the government's 10 per cent on the railway's income in return for the union's agreement to a thorough reorganization, which would have meant an additional income of some 18,000,000 pesos a year for the

57. *Ibid.*, March 21, 1940; *ibid.*, April 4, 1940.
58. Pan American Union, *Labor Trends and Social Welfare in Latin America: 1939–1940* (Washington, D.C., 1941), p. 53.
59. *Mexican Labor News*, August 23, 1940. This arrangement would be somewhat similar to the administration-union relationship in the nationalized oil enterprise.
60. *Ibid.*, August 23, 1940.

railways. Still, there was a great deal of opposition from certain union quarters, since reorganization would have meant a considerable number of dismissals, especially of upper-level personnel.[61] Finally, the government agreed to advance sufficient credit to the National Railways to enable them to purchase new rolling stock and equipment from the United States, together with the announcement that the federal railway tax of some 5 per cent (previously reported as 10 per cent) of total income would be temporarily held in abeyance. The new economy measures being put into effect were calculated to save the railroads approximately 8,000,000 pesos annually, which, added to the 7,000,000 in taxes that the roads could now keep, and in addition to the government's offer of credit, could be expected to go far in placing the National Railways in good financial condition.[62] Early in the administration of Ávila Camacho, substitution of the worker administration of the National Railways by an executive committee representative of government and labor, similar to that which governed the national petroleum industry, was predicted[63] and was soon to come about.

With regard to an evaluation of the success of labor management of the National Railways, as well as to the sources of difficulties encountered, opinions vary greatly, ranging all the way from that of Professor Gordon: "Seldom has the operation of any enterprise been so roundly condemned, and with such manifest justice, as the handling of the railroads by the workers,"[64] to the conclusion of the Weyls that worker management was successful.[65] Even greater disagreement exists over the question, granting that worker management was not successful, as to the source of difficulties encountered. It is probably in regard to this latter point that further analysis is most useful. According to De la Peña, the railroad union, in accepting the management of the lines under the conditions laid down by the government, knew that it would gain no material benefits and that it was making a great sacrifice for the collectivity.[66] On May 1, 1938, when the worker administration took over, the business was in a desperate state. The total debt, including interest, was 1,025,309,526 pesos, against a probable value of 993,062,703 pesos. De la Peña claimed, however, that this value

61. *Ibid.*, October 11, 1940.
62. *Ibid.*, October 19, 1940.
63. *Ibid.*, December 20, 1940; De la Peña and Navarrate, "Reorganización de los Ferrocarriles Nacionales," *El Trimestre Económico*, VII (1940–1941), 616–34.
64. Gordon, *The Expropriation of Foreign-Owned Property in Mexico*, p. 141; Strode and Parkes came to similar conclusions in *Timeless Mexico*, p. 238; and *A History of Mexico*, p. 407.
65. Nathaniel and Sylvia Weyl, *The Reconquest of Mexico*, p. 273.
66. De la Peña, "La Administración," p. 699.

was not real because the real value was actually around 450,000,000 pesos. In the months from May to June, 1938, the debt was reduced both in the United States and in Mexico. Another difficulty was that the poor road beds and an insufficient number of repair shops made service both poor and slow.[67] The Weyls maintained that the impact of unfavorable economic conditions was accentuated by a "cycle of appalling administrative blunders."[68] In the spring of 1938, a delegation from the Railroad Workers' Union surveyed the lines, terminals, and repair shops and prepared a blistering report on the incompetence of the autonomous government department which had been in charge of management since expropriation. They found that in the large Aguascalientes repair shops, 90 per cent of the most essential tools and repair parts could not be found. As a result, locomotives and freight cars were kept idle needlessly while workers waited for replacement parts. The government railroad administration had decided to buy Mikado locomotives from the United States at 150,000 pesos apiece, rather than modernize 119 engines in the Aguascalientes shop at a per-unit cost of 30,000 pesos. Although freight and passenger cars could be built more inexpensively in Mexico, the government railroad department preferred to import them. One-half million dollars was spent in 1936 in the rental of American cars. Millions of pesos were squandered, according to the trade-union delegation, in planting eucalyptus trees along the roalroad lines at a time when track laid down a a quarter of a century before was in urgent need of reinforcement.[69] In spite of these adverse factors, by August, 1938, the renting of foreign cars had almost disappeared—almost 6,000 such cars had been rented in April of the same year at a cost of 32,910 pesos a day. On August 13, there were only 812 rented cars, saving nearly 28,240 pesos daily—or 847,200 pesos a month. The rotation of cars was stepped up by 9 per cent, which was one of the major reasons why fewer cars had to be rented.[70]

As a result of the oil controversy and the drop in the value of the peso, gross income fell. Tons carried and freight income increased in 1937 and 1938 over 1935 and 1936; therefore, according to De la Peña, the decrease in income must have been because of a drop in passenger income. This economist concluded that "The worker administration, in the first three months of operation, in spite of the

67. *Ibid.*, pp. 694–95, 699. According to *Mexican Labor News*, the railroad debt was to form a part of the national debt; thus, the railroads would not be directly responsible for its liquidation (June 30, 1937).
68. Nathaniel and Sylvia Weyl, *The Reconquest of Mexico*, p. 271.
69. *Ibid.*
70. De la Peña, "La Administración," p. 700.

unfavorable conditions under which they took over the lines, have done better than was done in the past twelve years of semi-capitalist operations."[71] De la Peña was of the opinion, in the fall of 1938, that if the economic progress enjoyed by the nation between 1934 and 1938 returned, the worker administration would be able to improve the railroads. If the economic crisis caused by the oil expropriations continued, however, the new management was bound to end in failure.[72] But note that any possible failure would be due to "external" circumstances—not to worker management of the lines.

In the spring of 1940, when Cárdenas suggested a drastic reorganization and the reduction of labor costs, the workers protested. They also disclaimed any responsibility for the shortage of capital investment and blamed, this time, the worker administration for incompetence. The labor administration countercharged the workers with incompetence and even sabotage. As we have already seen, the second labor administration resigned under fire in July, 1940,[73] after the workers refused to accept the revocation of salary increases granted by the former council. In a report presented by the auditors of the railroads it was said that in the two years of worker administration the sums set aside for wages and salaries had increased by 8,000,000 pesos.[74]

The Weyls contended that Cárdenas' tendency toward anarcho-syndicalism expressed itself in the formation of pure types of worker control, such as the National Railways, and rendered the judgment that "The justice of turning over a vast enterprise to its workers, disregarding the interests of the consumers (in this case, the industries, farms, and people of Mexico) is extremely dubious."[75] The suggestion by certain observers in the United States (Tannenbaum, among others) that the program of the Cárdenas government might shatter the power of the Mexican middle class, is strange, indeed, considering the fact that the announced goal of the P.N.R. and the P.R.M. was, in effect, to do just that! As the Weyls suggested, "Through publicly controlled enterprises, the State is in a position to channelize the reinvestment of a portion of industrial profits and to regulate private industry by means of governmental competition. This factor seems of vital im-

71. *Ibid.*, pp. 700–2. Although this statement was made late in 1938, it is interesting to compare the evaluation of worker management of the lines with that made by Gordon, mentioned above.

72. *Ibid.*, p. 698.

73. Virginia Prewett, *Reportage on Mexico* (New York, 1941), p. 215.

74. "Railroads," Banco Nacional de México, S.A., *Review of the Economic Situation of Mexico*, August 31, 1940, p. 17.

75. Nathaniel and Sylvia Weyl, *The Reconquest of Mexico*, p. 277.

portance in view of the gigantic economic problems confronting the country and the scant resources available for their solution."[76]

The critics of the worker administration of the National Railways, in charging that profits were not utilized for improving roadbeds and equipment, that service was poor, and that trains often did not arrive on time, seem to forget that these same charges could have been—and were—equally valid against the privately owned and operated railroad systems of other countries during the same period, particularly in the United States. They seem to forget that it was only with the outbreak of World War II that the railroads of the United States, for example, were able to meet their bond obligations and to show a moderate return to stockholders. And, above all, it was only during the postwar period that new equipment began to appear on the North American lines. Therefore, to conclude that the shortcomings of the National Railways of Mexico during the latter half of the Cárdenas administration were attributable to worker management appears to involve extremely dubious reasoning. Rather, the evidence appears to indicate that, under the circumstances, the worker administration was at least as satisfactory as any other, if not a considerable improvement.

With reference to the question of whether worker administration merited the support of the "revolutionary proletariat," or whether it would have been preferable to support nationalization of industry administered by the state, Sr. García Treviño concluded that orthodox Marxism and Leninism would say worker administration, regardless of the mistakes made; but that the Stalinists would prefer state ownership and worker support.[77]

76. *Ibid.*, p. 278.
77. Rodrigo García Treviño, "Los Sindicatos en la Administración de las Industrias," *Revista de Economía, III* (January–February–March–April, 1939), 41–45.

VIII. Labor and the Laguna Experiment

Historically, Mexico has been a country of vast estates. "Land monopoly by the few has gone hand in hand with landlessness for the many. The hacienda has steadily encroached upon and swallowed up the *ejidos*, the communal lands of the villages."[1] Agrarian reform commenced in 1915, with the Decree of January 6, from Carranza's Plan de Veracruz, later embodied in Article 27 of the 1917 Constitution. The decree was not, however, definite as to the method of property ownership, since it provided that a regulatory law should determine the condition in which the lands restored or adjudged in behalf of pueblos should remain and the manner and time in which they should be distributed among the inhabitants who, in the meantime, were to enjoy their possession in common. Emphasis was apparently upon the individual; not upon the village in its corporate capacity.[2] Apparently, Article 27 of the Constitution of 1917 added nothing to the Decree of 1915 concerning property rights, since it postponed the question again for some future date by stating that all villages of what-

1. Charles A. Thomson, "Agrarian Reform in Mexico," Institute of Public Affairs, *Mexico and the United States: Proceedings of the Fifth Annual Conference Institute of Public Affairs Auspices Carnegie Endowment for International Peace*, 1938, p. 32.
2. Eyler N. Simpson, *The Ejido: Mexico's Way Out* (Chapel Hill, 1937), pp. 56–57, 317.

ever type already in possession of, or yet to receive, lands should have the right to enjoy them in common until such time as the manner of making the division of lands should be determined. As Simpson pointed out, Article 27, in the extremely wide powers it granted to the nation to impose on private property such limitations as the public interest might demand, opened wide the door for the development of almost any conceivable system of landholding. The specific limitations it placed upon ownership certainly qualified the traditional understanding of privately owned property, but still the article fell far short of the socialization of real property. In Simpson's view, advanced as were the ideas of the authors of Article 27, private property was still the point of departure in their thinking, and private property, even though controlled in the public interest, was their ultimate goal. "In approving the right of villages to hold land collectively, the fathers of the constitution did not set out to establish a form of land tenure in opposition to private property. Rather they thought of themselves as simply recognizing the social necessity of giving legal status to the only kind of property familiar and comprehensible to one rather backward section of the population. The *ejidos* were to be in the nature of temporary expedients, bridges over which certain groups were eventually to pass to private property."[3] The ideas of the constitutional convention came from several scattered sources, but, according to General Múgica, the soldiers wanted to socialize property; yet, they were frightened, especially since they found all the learned men in the convention opposed to them. Therefore, Article 27 was a compromise.[4] Luis Cabrera made it clear that, in his view, the aim of the revolu-

3. *Ibid.*, pp. 317, 73.
4. Frank Tannenbaum, *Peace by Revolution* (New York, 1933), pp. 166–67. The article in question stated in Para. 7 Sec. VI: "Private title to lands and waters is not original but results from an act of the Nation . . . private property shall not be expropriated except for reasons of public utility and by means of indemnification. . . . the Federal and State laws shall determine within their respective jurisdictions those cases in which the occupation of private property shall be considered of public utility; and in accordance with the said laws the administrative authorities shall make the corresponding declaration. . . . Properties held in common by co-owners, settlements, towns, congregations, tribes and other bodies of population which, as a matter of fact or law, conserve their communal character, shall have legal capacity to enjoy in common the waters, woods and lands belonging to them, or which may have been or shall be restored to them according to the law of January 6, 1915, until such time as the manner of making the division of the lands shall be determined by law." As quoted in Simpson, *The Ejido*, pp. 66–69. For an English translation of Article 27, see Gilberto Bosques, *The National Revolutionary Party of Mexico and the Six-Year Plan* (Mexico, 1937), p. 328. See also Andrés Molina Enríquez (author of Article 27), "Mexico's Defense: Action in Agrarian Reforms and Expropriation of Oil Lands," *Atlantic Monthly*, 163 (March, 1939), 375–84.

tionaries was the individual ownership of small parcels of land, not the communal system of *ejidal* exploitation.[5] On the other hand, Rosado de la Espada maintained, "The *ejido* is an institution in accord with our tradition; not so small property, which has existed only as an exception. The *ejido* cannot but suffer in competition with small property."[6] The League of Agrarian Socialists stated that the entire agrarian reform was simply an effort to break up the semifeudal *latifundio* system, and that effort happened to coincide with the wishes of industrial and financial capitalism. "The desire was to redistribute the land, and in some instances it was to be collectively held because to divide it into very small individual parcels would lose the advantage of improved technology."[7] This "middle-of-the-road" course was that followed by Cárdenas, since his program provided, as we shall see, for both small, privately owned parcels and the collectively farmed *ejido*. This "straddling-of-the-fence" position was taken also by organized labor under Cárdenas, since, in August, 1938, the C.T.M. and the C.C.M. stated: "We are in accord with the government in believing that all aid should be given to the ownership of small agricultural property; but all the aid of the government and all the force of peasant organization should be toward *ejidatarios* of the country, which constitute the medium and the base of the agricultural economy of Mexico."[8] It would appear that by this date both Cárdenas and labor had changed the "march toward socialism" to a "march against fascism," instituting a popular front to be "all things to all men." Such an observation is not intended as a criticism; it is merely further evidence that an external force—the spread of international fascism—interrupted the march of the Mexican Revolution under Cárdenas toward a Socialist society, thus adding further confusion to an already confused agrarian labor program.

Simpson summarized very well the apparent total effect of the Constitution of 1917 when he said:

> The Constitution of 1917 is a hybrid, begotten partly in an effort to straddle the fence between traditional notions of *laissez faire* and modern functional conceptions and partly in

---

5. Luis Cabrera, *Un Ensayo Comunista en México,* (México, 1937), pp. 80–82.
6. Diego Rosado de la Espada, "El Ejido y la Pequeña Propriedad," *México Agrario* (July–August, 1939), pp. 22–23.
7. Liga de Agrónomos Socialistas, *El Colectivismo Agrario en México: La Comarca Lagunera* (México, 1940), pp. 2–6.
8. Confederación de Trabajadores de México and Confederación Campesina Mexicana, *A Todos los Trabajadores de la República* (México, 1938), p. 7.

an attempt to be realistic and give legal sanction to the great variety of property concepts coexisting in Mexico and at the same time leave the way open for the development of new and presumably more "socialistic" forms of land tenure. It is this fact which gives the Constitution the appearance of a patchwork quilt—a background of rugged individualism on which there have been sewn here and there bright red scraps of collectivistic principles.[9]

The next milepost in the course of Mexican land reform came when Obregón signed, on December 28, 1920, the Ley de Ejidos, or the first Law of Ejidos. This measure was annulled on December 10, 1921, and another, the Agrarian Regulatory Law of April 10, 1922, took its place. It would seem that this second law was more definite, answering such questions as which villages were to receive land, how, and how much. Pressure of circumstances forced the National Agrarian Commission to assume the powers of regulating the *ejidos*. Circular 51, issued October 11, 1922, set forth a plan of "Simple Collectivism," which opened with a statement of basic principles, declaring that the distribution of land to villages was only the first step in the work of the National Agrarian Commission and that in addition it should assume the responsibility for regulating the development of the *ejidos* and directing their progress. Then there was introduced the idea that

9. Simpson, *The Ejido*, p. 486. The following summary of land reforms to the time of Cárdenas is based on Simpson's great book. In addition, these works on Mexican agrarian reform were useful: Lucio Mendieta y Núñez, "The Balance of Agrarian Reform," *Annals of the American Academy of Political and Social Science*, 208 (March, 1940), 121–31; Gonzalo Blanco Macias, "The Ejido At Work down Mexico Way," *Land Policy Review*, 3 (November, 1937), 18–22; Emilio López Zamora, "El Parcelamiento Ejidal. Promesa del Nuevo Gobierno," *Revista de Economía*, 4 (January, 1941), 20–30; Antonio Vargas MacDonald, "Agrarian Reform in Mexico," *Annals of Collective Economy: International Review in Four Editions*, 15 (January–April, 1939), 120–41; Clarence Senior, "Reforma Agraria y Democracia en La Comarca Lagunera," *Problemas Agrícolas e Industriales de México*, 8 (April–May–June, 1956), 3–174; E. Munguía, "Agrarian Problems in Mexico," *International Labour Review*, 36, (1937), 49–85, 200–38; Manuel Gámio, "An Analysis of Social Processes and the Obstacles to Agricultural Progress in Mexico," *Rural Sociology*, 2 (1937), 143–47; H. Adams, "Agrarian System of Mexico," *American Review*, 7 (1936), 409–21; José Reyes Pimental (ed.), *Despertar Lagunero. Libro que Relata la Lucha y Triumfo de la Revolución en la Comarca Lagunera* (México, 1937); Manuel Moreno-Sánchez *et al.*, *Político Ejidal* (México, 1960); Dirección General de Estadística, *La Reforma Agraria en México* (México, 1937); Lucio Mendieta y Núñez, *El Problema Agrario de México* (4th ed.: México, 1937); Marte R. Gómez (Secretary of Agriculture and Development under Ávila Camacho), *La Región Lagunera* (México, 1941); Francisco Frola, "Los Ejidos Colectivos en México," *América*, 1, (July, 1943), 39–41. For an unfavorable report on the *ejido* system, see Manuel A. Hernández, "The 'ejido' Is Not Mexico's Way Out," *Mexican-American Review*, 9 (March 1, 1941), 12–14, 56.

the existing state of technology dictated the abolition of small agriculture and its replacement by organized, co-operative, and communal efforts.

Even if the original revolutionaries did not intend collectivism, the Agrarian Commission of 1922 did! Moreover, the philosophy expressed in this plan is in accord with that held by Ramón Beteta in the 1930's, as was noted in an earlier chapter. The circular continued to outline in detail the method of government of each *ejido,* land use under the system, as well as a method of profit distribution. Suffice it to say that with the promulgation of Circular 51, *ejido* lands were to be held and worked in common—all for one and one for all—and economic and social control of *ejidos* was to be vested immediately in *ejido* administration committees; and this situation continued for three years.

Calles, following Obregón, was pledged to carry out agrarian reforms, but he was a firm believer in the idea that the salvation of Mexico lay in the creation of a large body of small landholders—the *ejido* being simply one step in this direction. The final goal was to be private property. This idea found expression in a law passed on December 19, 1925, known as the law of Ejido Patrimony, which, in the minds of its supporters, would make the *ejido* simply a training school from which the *ejidatarios* were eventually to graduate into the status of peasant proprietors. The major innovation of the new law was that of providing for the division of the crop lands of the *ejidos* into parcels and the vesting of title to these parcels not only in the village in its corporate capacity, but in the individual *ejidatarios,* as well. In the minds of its framers, the purpose of the law was to curtail the power of the village agrarian authorities and to take the first step in converting the *ejidatarios* from members of a commune into proprietors of individually owned and independent private properties. In preparing the way for this new law, it had been charged in the Chamber of Deputies that hardly an *ejido* in the country was working the land communally, anyway. Rather, the regular procedure was for a village, just as soon as it got its lands, to allot them in severalty; therefore, *ejidatarios,* by this very action, had clearly demonstrated their lack of faith in the communal method. There was some opposition in congress, and Senator Monzón attempted to prove that many *ejidos* were operating with the greatest success on purely communistic principles, reading letters from peasants which held that the proposed Law of Ejido Patrimony was an attempt to "strangle the agrarian reform."

Nonetheless, the law passed by an overwhelming majority; it was revised on several occasions, but almost entirely with regard to procedure and detail rather than basic principles, and was embodied in the Agrarian Code of March 22, 1934. The National Bank of Agricultural Credit and the Agrarian Department were charged with the social and economic organization of the *ejidatarios* in the zones where the bank operated, and crop land granted to the village was to be apportioned among the individual *ejidatarios*, property rights in the separate *ejido* parcels of crop land vested in the individual *ejidatario* to be imprescriptible and so not subject to alienation or lien. Clearly, Calles and his followers believed that the goal of agricultural reform was private property—more justly distributed, but private property just the same; to his opponents this end was a betrayal of the ideals of the revolution. As Simpson saw it, the Law of Ejido Patrimony was the first sign of a rift in the "revolutionary lute."[10]

In the view of the Mexican Peasants' Confederation, expressed in September, 1934, the lack of success in *ejidal* areas between 1924 and 1934, was attributable to the lack of economic means for carrying out their program, as well as a failure to "consolidate a system and to organize the human element not only as a factor in production but as an integral part in society. . . ."[11] In Simpson's opinion, the lack of success was due chiefly to the failure to agree upon the fundamental question of the collectivistic *vs.* the individualistic conception of the *ejido*, the Law of Ejido Patrimony being a compromise and "as it stands it is obviously neither fish nor fowl."[12]

We have seen that there was always a division of opinion between Mexican revolutionary leaders concerning the direction agricultural reform should take. By mid-1933, these two groups were called the *veteranos* and the *agraristas*. The *veteranos*, led by former President Calles, believed that *ejido* distribution of land should be ended and that emphasis should be placed on the creation of a large number of middle-class independent farmers. The *agraristas*, on the other hand, while criticising agrarian policies of the past, demanded that complete socialization of land should be the goal for the future. The *ejido* should be recognized not as a transitory but as a permanent feature of the Mexican agricultural system.[13] As mentioned previously, President Cárdenas apparently felt that there was a place for both individual and collective farming, depending upon the economic circumstances in each case. It is because the Laguna experiment repre-

10. Simpson, *The Ejido*, p. 334.
11. *Ibid.*, p. 339.
12. *Ibid.*, p. 340.
13. Thomson, "Agrarian Reform in Mexico," p. 34.

sents the major effort under Cárdenas toward revitalizing the communal *ejido,* together with the fact that organized labor played a prominent role in the events, that this project has been chosen for special treatment here.[14]

Upon entering office, President Cárdenas apparently cast his lot with the *agraristas* in the case of land in the Laguna area. This was indicated in a speech at Torreón, November 30, 1936:

> In the early stages of the Revolution there may possibly have been some people in whose mind the ejido was but a mere supplement to the wage-earning system and insufficient in itself to guarantee the land laborer the economic independence that is the foundation of every civil liberty. But this view exerts no influence whatsoever on the fulfillment of the duties of the Government today. Groups of peasants were in the past given worthless bits of land, and lacked farming implements, equipment, credit and organization. . . . But the nation's conception of the ejido has been in reality far other. . . . As an institution it shoulders a double responsibility; as a social system it must make the country worker free from the exploitation to which he was subject under the feudal as well as under the individualistic system; and as a system of agricultural production it must render such a yield as to provide the country at large with food. . . .[15]

In 1938, César Garizurieta wrote that the two important groups in the social struggle were the *ejido* and the trade union, the latter a product of the city, the former of the country. But the problem was one of how to break up the great estates sown with cotton and henequen, which were cultivated with complicated techniques requiring expensive equipment that the poor *ejidatarios* could not purchase. In an effort to answer this question, it became necessary to modernize the concept of the *ejido,* "bringing it into the present economic concepts, rather than leaving it as thought of in colonial times. In a word it

14. Similar collective experiments were carried on in Yucatán, Lombárdia, Mexicali, and other places, but none was as important as the Laguna event. The pattern followed in these instances was essentially that of Laguna. For brief descriptions of the Yucatán procedure, see Alfonso Cortina, "The Agrarian Problem in Yucatán," *Annals of Collective Economy: International Review in Four Editions,* XV (January–April, 1939), 70–93; Enrique González Aparício, "El Problema Ejidal en Yucatán," Sociedad Agronómica de México, *Primer Ciclo de Conferencias (de Octubre a Noviembre de 1937)* (México, 1938), pp. 85–96; John Vavasour Noel, "Yucatán Resurgent," *Mexican Life* XV (February, 1939), 22, 24. For the theme that the Laguna reform was largely the work of organized labor, see Dorothy W. Douglas, "Land and Labor in Mexico," *Science and Society,* 4 (Spring, 1940), 127–52.

15. Quoted in Thomson, "Agrarian Reform in Mexico," pp. 34 ff.

became necessary to transform the familiar system of existence into a productive economic system."[16] This necessity brought about the reform of Article 139 of the Agrarian Code, formulated by Lázaro Cárdenas in the city of Mérida, Yucatán. The article stated: "In the ejidos that require cultivation by the industrial process for the sale of their products and for that reason must have investments greater than the economic capacity of the individual *ejidatario*, exploitation is organized in collective form without having to adopt this system in all cases in which another system would be more convenient for the better economic development of the country."[17]

It is evident that this article did not provide for the universal establishment of collective *ejidos*; therefore, Cárdenas could not be classed absolutely with the *agraristas*. Even in those *ejidos* where farming was communal, Garizurieta maintained that the *ejido* was a capitalistic economy at the service of the organized peasants.[18] Similarly, Hernán Laborde noted that the partial redistribution of land was not a socialist movement, but a universal bourgeoisie reform, saying, "The *ejidatario* in general, even on the more 'collectivized' lands, is subject to capitalist exploitation, both in the market and in the form of credit."[19] Therefore, it can be surmised that the method of land distribution in the Laguna area was conditioned by special circumstances that obtained in only a few other instances.

Perhaps at no place in Mexico, outside of Yucatán, was the concentration of land in a few hands more patently obvious than in the Laguna region.[20] This area was a sort of privileged inland empire, where foreign interests and certain influential Mexican generals continued to own and maintain large farms in a manner savoring very much of the old colonial system. Wages were extremely low; the people lived in hovels, without schools and with no chance of bettering their miserable state.[21] In the colonial period, forced labor in the mines of the nearby mountains, forced work for the missions, encroachments on native lands, and the usual relations between colonial adventurers and natives led finally to Indian revolts. According to Senior, tens of thousands of Indians perished before the superior

---

16. César Garizurieta, *Realidad del Ejido* (México, 1938), p. 83.
17. *Ibid.*
18. *Ibid.*, p. 85.
19. Hernán Laborde, "Cárdenas, Reformador Agraria," *Problemas Agrícolas e Industriales de México*, IV (January–March, 1952), 60.
20. Verna C. Millan, "La Laguna: An Experiment in Communal Farming," *Mexican Life*, XV (September, 1939), 15.
21. William Cameron Townsend, *Lázaro Cárdenas: Mexican Democrat* (Ann Arbor, 1952), p. 170.

force and cunning of the invaders. As early as 1690, some revolts were settled by restoration of lands. There was a great deal of rivalry between Franciscan and Jesuit orders for the privilege of saving the souls of the Indians, as well as for collecting tithes and living in comfort in churches and homes the Indians built for them. The first irrigation canals in the area were built for the benefit of the Spanish landowners around Parras; these were built by the Jesuit converts, who were expelled in 1646. A favorite of the Spanish king, Francisco de Urdinola, was owner of almost 3,000 000 hectares (7,410 000 acres) within twenty years after his arrival from Spain; through marrying Urdinola's granddaughter, the Marques de Aguayo, became the lord of this vast domain. In 1719, one of his descendants, who held the same title, was named governor of Coahuila and Texas; he gave up politics three years later to devote himself to enlarging his possessions. For 250 pesos and "half one year's income," the Marques purchased most of what is now known as the Laguna region from the Crown of Spain. More royal grants brought his total holdings to well over 8 000 000 acres. Military measures, plagues, droughts, and famine all but obliterated the indigenous population of the area, so that few of the present inhabitants are direct successors of the Indians who lived in the region when the conquerors came.[22]

Soon after the republic was definitely established in the 1820's, a later Marques de Aguayo sold his properties in Durango and Coahuila to the already rich heir of a priest of Monclova, Don Melchor Sánchez Navarro, who bequeathed it to his heirs. They accepted the responsibility for paying a debt of 30,000 pesos to the descendants of the Marques who lived in Spain. Payment was demanded in 1848, and, to obtain the sum, part of the land was sold—more than two-thirds of the region going to Don Leonardo Zuloaga and Don Juan Ignacio Jiménez for 80,000 pesos. The following year, the two owners began construction of dams to divert the waters of the Nazas to their lands. They promptly came into conflict with another landowner over water rights, a source of constant trouble in the region from that time on. Zuloaga was faced with unceasing revolts, most of them originating around Matamoros, a village many years old, which claimed that the lands worked by the villagers had been theirs for generations. State government troops suppressed the rebellions, but when the village was host to President Júarez during the French intervention, he decreed the restitution of land claimed by Matamoros. Because her husband had supported the French, the properties of Zuloaga's widow were

22. Clarence Senior, *Democracy Comes to a Cotton Kingdom: The Story of Mexico's La Laguna* (Mexico, 1940), pp. 9–11.

ordered confiscated by the State of Coahuila after the fall of Maximilian. The widow was able to obtain federal intervention, however, and maintained the estate intact until she decided to sell the land to liquidate certain debts. The new owners, British and German in large part, were connected with commercial firms, and some of the large estates were sold to smaller owners. At the time of the expropriation of the lands in 1936, 70 per cent of the land was foreign owned—40 per cent by two British companies.[23] With few exceptions, the area presented the usual picture of a plantation economy—absentee landlords, hired superintendents, company stores, company currency, credit extended in a manner that enslaved the peons, utter lack of sanitation, paucity of education, and other detrimental human relations, even to beatings of recalcitrant workers. In 1895, the Tlahualilo Land Company imported seven hundred Caribbean Negroes, but the entire lot died of smallpox soon after their arrival in Torreón.[24]

The Revolution of 1910 divided the region clearly along class lines —the landowners and the businessmen who depended on them supported the old regime and became Huertistas after Victoriano Huerta, who was instrumental in the death of Francisco I. Madero. The peasants followed "Pancho" Villa, whose troops captured Torreón three times. Many of his lieutenants had been leaders in labor troubles on the haciendas, the first outbreak of which had occurred in 1894.[25] The triumph of the constitutionalist forces and the return of peace to the Laguna brought a suppression of the groups that had seized land during Villista days. From 1927 to 1933, working conditions in the Laguna became increasingly difficult. The development of capitalism in the region, the intervention of corporations with international backing to replace the former wealthy families, and the modernization of working methods by the use of tractors and other farm machinery created widespread unemployment. Thousands of workers who had drifted in from other regions each year—migratory cotton-pickers— found themselves without means of livelihood. Those peasants who had lived on the land for years merely knew that the amount of their work was greatly reduced and that they were badly paid. At the same time, the landowners took a drastic resolution that increased the general unrest: they decided to expel from the region all those peasants who had no fixed means of livelihood. This decision vitally affected some fifteen thousand families who were faced with ultimate starvation or the alternative of returning to a migratory existence. Strikes

23. *Ibid.*, p. 12.
24. *Ibid.*
25. *Ibid.*

broke out, "those spontaneous unorganized strikes, often without any definite goal—nevertheless serving to foment social unrest." In 1935 alone, 104 strikes were declared in isolated fields without any coordinated action.[26]

Nothing important was done about land distribution in the area until 1934, when, to siphon off their discontented peons, the *hacendados* raised 2,500,000 pesos, purchased marginal land on the outskirts of the region, and invited President Abelardo Rodríguez to give it to the peasants who wanted land; this was done in two presidential decrees on October 15, 1934.[27] This action on the part of the *hacendados* and President Rodríguez was preceded by a study made of the Laguna situation in 1928 by the secretary of agriculture; this study recommended breaking up the land monopoly and putting the land into many hands. For the nonsalaried farm laborers who remained, they recommended the following privileges:

1. Absolute liberty to organize into syndicates under the law.
2. Guaranteed annual work, with a minimum salary of 1 peso per day.
3. A small plot of land on which to build a house and have a few domestic animals.
4. A small bit of land on which each man can produce for himself—a minimum of 1 hectare.
5. A place to pasture team and to sow a bit of seed.
6. Permanent medical services, and in case of death expenses for funeral, indemnity for accidents in accordance with the law.
7. Schools for each population center with more than 15 families.[28]

It was felt that these concessions would end hostilities among the owners and the agricultural workers. The owners were of course hostile to the report. As the condition of the peasants grew worse in 1930, much discontent was manifest throughout the Laguna area, and the landowners organized to attempt to solve the problem. They conceived the idea of forming a series of districts, known as *ejidal* districts, which would accommodate the peasants. The districts were to remain outside the principal cultivatable areas of the Laguna region. The major points in the plan of the owners, represented by the Cámara

26. Millan, "La Laguna," pp. 3–16.
27. Senior, *Democracy Comes to a Cotton Kingdom*, pp. 12–13. See also: MacDonald, "Agrarian Reform in Mexico," pp. 120–41; Liga de Agrónomos Socialistas, *El Colectivismo Agrario en México*.
28. Liga de Agrónomos Socialistas, *El Colectivismo Agrario en México*, pp. 33–34.

Agrícola Nacional de la Comarca Lagunera, were:

1. That the Laguna region be considered as one agricultural unit, to embrace all the lands improved by the Nazas and Aguanaval Rivers.

2. That a mixed commission take a minute census to determine which inhabitants were entitled to *ejidal* rights and which were not.

3. At the end of the census, a common agreement to be reached between the Secretary of Agriculture, the owners, and the people with *ejidal* rights and proceed to grant them as follows:

    a. Determine the extent of the land granted to date which was not yet improved.

    b. Use the unimproved land to grant to the people as determined by the new census.

    c. If this land were not sufficient to satisfy all the *ejidatarios*, the Secretary, with the owners, would find other lands to complete the grants, the cost to be covered pro rata by all the owners of the region in proportion to the tax value of their lands.

    d. Quick fulfillment of this plan and the refusal to hear further petitions for grants in the Laguna District.[29]

An agreement was reached with the secretary of agriculture, and the National Agrarian Commission found that up to that date only eleven *ejidos* had been established, containing 2,318 *ejidatarios* and embracing 21,640 hectares—only 5,600 of which were cultivatable. Of these, only Ciudad Lerdo could be considered in the principal zone of Laguna—the remainder were on the edges, far from markets and with completely inadequate water supply. The commission found it necessary to establish eighteen new villages, located outside the limits of the haciendas, and this plan only separated the workers of the area, rather than unifying them. During this period, the influence of the owners over the federal government was so strong that the agrarian laws were not enforced. In 1934, as we have seen, President Rodríguez created two *ejidal* districts—one in Durango and the other in Coahuila —and no more petitions for *ejidos* were to be entertained. Very soon it was evident that the problem had not been solved, and discontent and agitation among the workers on the haciendas did not diminish.[30]

The Agrarian Regulatory Law of 1922 specifically prescribed that only localities having "political status" should have the right to petition for land. Ordinarily, political status was achieved only after the vil-

29. *Ibid.*, p. 35.
30. *Ibid.*, p. 37.

lage had attained considerable size. This requirement led to attempts by laborers to locate in clusters of sufficient size to request political status, as well as to attempts by the *hacendados* to prevent the formation of permanent groups large enough to qualify for such status. In a few instances, complaints were made to the effect that landowners burned to the ground the huts of villagers who refused to scatter into small clusters or to move off the landowner's property.[31] Exploitation was typically capitalistic—each business was an economic agricultural unit, utilizing irrigation and the latest techniques and machinery. The workers were salaried peons, paid, for the most part, by the week. It was customary for the owners to have contracts with farmers who had sufficient capital for them to organize and run the farms. But the situation differed from that in other parts of the country since the peasants of the Laguna could not cultivate small plots of land for themselves. Their only source of income was the weekly pay check. This arrangement made the Laguna agricultural worker very similar to the city worker. The houses of the peasants were of adobe or reed or in caves. In 1935, wages ranged between 0.50 and 1.0 peso per day, and usually the peons did not work every day of the week. Goods had to be bought in stores owned by the *hacendados* and Spaniards. Sometimes bonuses were paid for each kilo of cotton picked so that a worker could make two or three pesos a day, but this occurred only during about two months of the year. By contrast, the average annual income of the *hacendados* was more like 20 000,000 pesos, an income that was spent in the cities of Europe, the United States, and Mexico. The treatment of the peasants by the foreman—often a Spaniard—was a constant source of irritation. The foreman, on horseback and with pistol, constantly pushed the peons to work harder. This produced discontent among the peasants which gathered momentum, but their efforts to organize and protest were always opposed by the local authorities and police, who were placed in charge by the owners. Although the Revolution of 1910 originated in this area, the Federal Labor Law did not apply here; the agrarian laws were mocked. The municipal authorities, kept in power by the *hacendados*, were always oppressive of the workers' efforts to improve their condition.[32]

Most of the peasants were incorporated into the League of Agrarian Communities, which had a weak, somewhat diffuse, program of action tending to separate and provoke distinctions between the peasants and the industrial workers. The C.G.T. was still strong here, but it thrived under government protection, and, as such, was often converted into

31. Nathan L. Whetten, *Rural Mexico* (Chicago, 1948), p. 217.
32. Liga de Agrónomos Socialistas, *El Colectivismo Agrario en México*, pp. 37–38.

a political weapon against the workers' interests. But by 1936, the C.T.M had come into existence, and in the Laguna it began an immediate campaign of unification. Most of the old C.G.T. elements were won over and incorporated in the C.T.M.; simultaneously the Agrarian League came to realize the necessity for a popular front among the workers in order to support their demands.[33]

Protest strikes became more numerous—there were 104 in 1935—with the object of obtaining a minimum wage of 1.50 pesos a day. In August, 1936, there was a general strike to gain a collective contract affecting some 28,000 agricultural workers.[34] As Saint Albans queried, "Who could foresee that General Cárdenas would strain all his own faculties and those of the country to see that the underdog was given a boost upward whether he wanted it or not? Or that a new labor leader, Licenciado Lombardo Toledano, would come to power to initiate a period of nation-wide strikes?"[35] Lombardo encouraged organization and demands for better houses, more schools, medical attention, and finally, their own *ejidos*. Sporadic strikes were launched, and two thousand strike-breakers were imported by alarmed *hacendados*. Agitation and hostilities mounted.[36]

In 1935, a few months after Cárdenas had become president of Mexico, the movement for trade-union organization in the cities achieved considerable success. In Torreón, a group of workers, albeit small, was able to organize and to unite some of the most revolutionary unions of that city, with some experience in the labor struggle. This group was known as the Federación Sindical Revolucionaria de la Comarca Lagunera (The Federation of Revolutionary Unions of the Laguna Region). On June 30, 1935, it joined with the Sindicato Metalúrgico, el de Mecánicos, el de la Fábrica de Hilados y Tejidos de La Fé (Union of Metal Workers, Mechanics, and Textile Workers of the Faith), formed exclusively by city workers prior to that time. Together they instructed the agricultural workers and inspired them with enthusiasm.[37] There also existed other labor groups in Torreón, including peasants, such as the C.G.T., La Liga Socialista (The Socialist League), all with moderate tendencies. In the city of Gómez

33. Millan, "La Laguna," p. 16. See also: Sanford A. Mosk, *Industrial Revolution in Mexico* (Berkeley and Los Angeles, 1950), p. 56; Miguel Othon de Mendizabel, "The Agrarian Problem of La Laguna," *Annals of Collective Economy: International Review in Four Editions*, XV (Geneva, 1939), 163–208.

34. De Mendizabel, "The Agrarian Problem of La Laguna," pp. 186–87; Hudson Strode, *Timeless Mexico* (New York, 1944), p. 321.

35. Mary Saint Albans, "What about the Laguna?" *Modern Mexico*, XI (June, 1939), 11.

36. *Ibid.*

37. *Ibid.*

Palacio, Durango, there was formed another group similar to the Sindical Revolucionario de Torreón (The Revolutionary Union of Torreón) called Federación de Sindicatos de Obreros y Campesinos de la Comarca Lagunera (The Federation of Worker and Peasant Unions of the Laguna Region). After the Committee for the Defense of the Proletariat was formed in Mexico City, it set up a regional committee in the Laguna area which included both city workers and peasants. The group carried on active organization of the peasants and also aided in the formation of collective contracts on the haciendas.[38]

In response to the organizing efforts of the peasants, the owners began to organize peasants into syndicates of their own, so that in a short time nearly all the agricultural workers in the Laguna area belonged to unions. Those unions affiliated with the revolutionary organizations were known as "reds," while those formed by the owners were known as the "whites." The owners themselves organized into the Sindicato Patronal de Agricultores de la Comarca Lagunera (Owners' Union of Farm Workers of the Laguna Region). Two strike movements of great importance occurred simultaneously: one was in the town of San Pedro and the other in Matamoros, and both were against most powerful owners. The one in San Pedro was begun by a union organized by the owners which turned to the cause of the peasants. The strikes were declared illegal, but, even so, they continued. Then the subsecretary of state intervened and declared against the strikers; the strikes ended with a manifestation of protest by the workers of the city of Torreón. In April, 1936, President Cárdenas journeyed to the north of the country and visited the Laguna region. He was dined in Torreón by the Federación Sindical Revolucionaria and the Comité Regional de Defensa Proletaria, and these groups explained to him the difficulties they were having in the organization. The president urged them to attempt to prevent strikes, saying that, in return, he would study the possibilities of applying agrarian legislation in the Laguna area during 1937. But the state of agitation among the workers' unions and the *hacendados* continued, and the latter began to dismiss workers of the "red" unions—especially the leaders—and to replace them with members of the "white" unions. The result was a series of strikes which had for their purpose the reinstatement of the dismissed workers. At times the struggle was bloody and reached major proportions. Taking their cue from the Sindicato Patronal, the workers conceived the idea of forming a single Sindicato de Obreros Agrícolas to combat the Patronal association. They presented the

38. *Ibid.*, p. 40.

owners with a collective contract covering all the workers in the entire area and threatened a general strike which was to begin on May 26, 1936.[39]

Demands did not seem excessive. The workers asked for the minimum wage paid to all workers throughout the region in accordance with the Federal Labor Law—at that time, 1.75 pesos a day. They wanted payment for the "seventh day," also provided by the law; a humane working day—that is to say, hours of work that would not be abusive—although the workers themselves realized that in farm work it was impossible to place precise limits on time because of many outside factors. They wanted new houses to replace the primitive and unsanitary huts in which they lived; effective medical service to curtail chronic dysentery, malaria, and typhoid, which were rampant; and, last of all, the schools required by law to be built in every working center. In reality, they asked nothing except enforcement of the Labor Law in the area. The federal government was up against a serious crisis because the issue was clear-cut and defined. The whole future of national cotton production was at stake. The workers were asking for nothing except that which was authorized by the national Labor Code; yet, many students of the problem thought that, if the board decided in favor of the workers, the landowners would have been bankrupt in no time, and this, in turn, would have injured the workers still more.[40] In the words of de Mendizabel, "Faced with this grave crisis, provoked by organized labor, the Federal Government had only two courses open to it; that is, naturally, only two courses that came within the lofty social ideals that inspired it. First, it might solve the problem by application of the Labor Code, compelling the *hacendados* to provide permanent work, with Sunday pay, and giving the proletarianized peasant all the advantages to which he would have a right under the code. Secondly, it might solve the problem by grants of *ejidos*." The first plan would likely have very quickly brought about the complete ruin of the *hacendados* of the Laguna, without any lasting benefit for the workers.[41]

Before the day of the strike arrived, the federal government intervened and called representatives of both sides to Mexico City for talks in the Department of Labor. At the outset, it was agreed that the owners would reinstate the suspended workers if the unions would postpone the strike for twenty days. In the meantime, a worker-employer commission, presided over by the chief of the Labor De-

39. *Ibid.*, pp. 40–42.
40. Millan, "La Laguna," p. 16.
41. De Mendizabel, "The Agrarian Problem of La Laguna," p. 187.

partment, discussed the petitions of the workers. The labor organizations which began the strike movement were the Federación Sindical Revolucionaria de la Comarca Lagunera, the Federación de Sindicatos Obreros y Campesinos de Gómez Palacio, and the Cámara del Trabajo de Torreón, assisted by the C.T.M. Ten days after the beginning of the discussions, the owners had not agreed on the method of reinstating the ousted workers. The owners threatened to break off the talks and even to remove themselves and their businesses from the country. A day before the twenty days had expired, no agreement had been reached on the fundamental demands, but there was a new agreement to postpone the strike for another forty-five days. In the meantime, a committee of experts was appointed by the government to study the possibility of the companies' ability to meet the demands of the workers. The owners maintained they were operating their businesses at a loss; the peasants asked for higher salaries, sufficient to sustain their families. Meanwhile, the owners instituted a propaganda campaign in the press and over the radio against the "red" unions and began to hire strikebreakers to initiate a counterrevolution, importing them from neighboring states and paying them salaries of six to seven pesos a day.[42]

The owners had in their favor the fact that the leaders of the Liga de Comunidades Agrarias y Sindicatos Campesinos de Coahuila and the Federación Municipal de Torreón, and those of the Liga Socialista, did not sympathize with the strike movement and were more preoccupied with inter-union disputes than with the struggle of the workers against the owners. Nevertheless, the workers of these three centrals pressed their leaders to agree on a general strike with the other organization. When the commission of experts rendered its decision, favorable to the workers, the owners would not accept it. Three months' discussion had ended in nothing. There had been hardly any agreement even on the secondary issues, much less on the primary ones. At the end of the forty-five days, the workers felt there was no course other than to declare the general strike; this was done on August 11, 1936, and the strike was to begin on August 18. The strike was arranged solely by the Federación Sindical Revolutionaria de Torreón, the Federación de Sindicatos Obreros y Campesinos de Gómez Palacio, and the Cámara del Trabajo de Torreón, the latter led by the Communist party.[43] The movement comprised 104 unions,

42. Liga de Agrónomos Socialistas, *El Colectivismo Agrario en México*, pp. 42–43.
43. *Ibid.*, pp. 43–44. See also Pimental (ed.), *Despertar Lagunero: Libro que Relata la Lucha y Triunfo de la Revolución en la Comarca Lagunera* (México, 1937), pp. 73 ff.

with approximately 20,000 agricultural workers. The boards of conciliation and arbitration of Torreón and Gómez Palacio, reflecting the attitude of their governments, declared the strike "nonexistent." Soldiers from the Sixth Military Zone sided with the owners, and there was some bloodshed between the strikers and the soldiers. The leaders of the movement were jailed. The strikers asked for an injunction against the board's decision, and the federal district judge granted it.[44]

Eight days after the strike broke out, the president called to Mexico City a strike committee for the purpose of discussing ways of solving the grave problem. Cárdenas offered, as we have seen, to apply the Agrarian Law toward the end of October in return for the lifting of the state of strike; the workers accepted, but made it clear they would renew the strike if the land were not divided during the month of October. By September 3, 1936, the strike had ended. The owners used every means to express their dissatisfaction with the president's decision. They offered to listen to the demands of the workers and to come to an agreement with them. They attempted to get the most influential people in the country to convince Cárdenas that the move would be a failure. They even began a subversive movement with the "gold shirts" at its head. The owners, who, during the conflict with the workers, had threatened to go to other countries, now tried by every means to save their haciendas; but all was useless. Possibly, the energetic attitude of the workers influenced Cárdenas to apply the Agrarian Law. By the middle of September, a delegation of engineers and representatives from the Agricultural Department in the region did the preliminary census work and formulated a plan for dividing the land and water.[45] Gabino Vásquez, chief of the Agrarian Department, flew to the region with six hundred workers following him.[46]

A conference between President Cárdenas and the delegates of the National Federation of Workers of the Laguna Sectors resulted in the following general resolutions concerning the distribution of land in the Laguna district:

1. Land to be distributed to workers of the region without their having to make application.
2. The first distribution shall take place, at the latest, on October 1 of the year 1936.
3. The Government, besides distributing land, will provide the necessary financing to work it.

44. Liga de Agrónomos Socialistas, *El Colectivismo Agrario en México*, p. 44.
45. *Ibid.*, pp. 44–45.
46. Saint Albans, "What about the Laguna?" pp. 11–12.

4. Demands for wage payments during the strike will be continued in the courts.

5. All owners who let out their land on a partnership basis will leave the area as soon as possible.

6. Employers shall respect collective contracts and shall employ only union labor.

7. If some of the employers do not wish to gather crops, the Government will step in until the land is distributed.

8. In case of workers who become destitute, the Federal Government will provide food until the land and the necessary financing are made available.

9. The Commission appointed by the President to initiate the work at Laguna shall have the power to see that the waters of the Nazas River are used by the landholders to protect the next crops, and our sympathizers should co-operate with the members of the Commission, as it is certain that the landowners, in refusing to irrigate the lands, do so with the object in view that when the lands are passed on to the peasants the next crops will fail.

10. A few days before the distribution of the first large estate takes place, General Cárdenas will go in person to the Laguna area to address all the peasants of that region and point out to them the importance of the distribution of the land and to reiterate his stand on enforcing the law.

11. The President decided that Attorney José Cantú Estrada, the General Secretary of the Labor Department, would immediately pass on the matter of reinstating the workers dismissed in the area.[47]

These resolutions indicate that the government and the labor groups desired a change in the property system then prevailing in the Laguna area; the system had continued to exist in spite of the agrarian laws in effect.

The position of the government was made clear: "The defeat of individualism will be a conclusive feature in this district since it is a system that cannot prove its efficiency in the frame of the *ejido* scheme."[48] Mosk summarized the reasons for the government's attitude in the Laguna case very well when he said that the decision to organize collective *ejidos* was based on three conditions: the erratic nature of the irrigation supply; existence of a network of canals available for large units; and economies to be realized through the use of

47. "Comments on the Economic Situation," *Modern Mexico*, VIII (November, 1936), 9.

48. Mexican Government, *The Mexican Government and the Solution of the Agrarian Problem in La Laguna District* (Mexico, n.d.), p. 21.

modern farm equipment, already developed in the area, would have been sacrificed to a certain extent by individual operation of small holdings.[49]

The C.T.M. insisted that the division of land in the Laguna signified not only a change in the title to the land, but also an absolute transformation of the methods of work, of the system in general, of the production, of the organized intervention of the peasants in the policies and organization of this zone toward achieving a working model for the revolution.[50] Engineer Marte R. Gómez, in an article in *El Nacional* in February, 1941, said that it was to remedy a grave economic crisis, not to create it, that the government applied such radical measures in the Laguna area.[51] Laborde maintained, however, that this analysis was only partly true in that the reform was as much a result of the struggle of the workers and their request for a collective contract and an increase in daily wages. "The general strike of August 1936, which paralyzed all of the area, was also a decisive argument in favor of the reform." He felt that the change in the property system in the Laguna region was more than a revindication for the Laguna worker; it was a necessity for the national economy in that the decree divided the land and yet preserved agricultural and industrial production in the area. He took the opportunity to emphasize that ". . . the Mexican Revolution is a democratic-bourgeoisie Revolution, not a socialist one."[52]

In defending his action in the Laguna crisis and explaining its necessity to the nation, President Cárdenas pointed out that out of an apparent prosperity enjoyed by the landowning class, there grew apace the discontent of the numerous labor class, organized for the class struggle, "conscious of the fact that it was being cheated in its rights, and awaiting the opportunity to demand what it was legally entitled to have."[53] He stated that the steps in the development of the Laguna region envisaged the organization of communal *ejidos* and the establishment of credit machinery adequate for the social banking service given by the state to *ejidatarios* and to small landholders. And, finally, the change from one system of land ownership to another system afforded an opportunity for the reorganization of urban, educational, rural-hygiene and other services. "With regard to the economic and

49. Mosk, *Industrial Revolution in Mexico*, pp. 56–57.
50. Confederación de Trabajadores de México, *El Problema de la Laguna: Antecedentes, Soluciones* (México, 1937), p. 7.
51. Quoted in Hernán Laborde, "Cárdenas, Reformador Agraria," p. 68.
52. *Ibid.*, pp. 68–70.
53. Lázaro Cárdenas, *A Message to the Mexican Nation on the Solution of the Agrarian Problem of La Laguna* (Mexico, 1937), p. 15.

social aspects of the *ejido*," he continued, "the State's intervention in its behalf makes for the improvement of the nation's economy and is a function of public order."[54] In the social realm, the duty of the state was seen to be to guarantee the economic self-sufficiency of the peasant groups that were given land, and in the economic aspect its duty was said to be to insure that agricultural production throughout the country did not decrease and injure domestic consumption and foreign trade. Cárdenas emphasized that it was of the utmost importance that the schools in the *ejidos* "keep faith with the socialist doctrine of education, abiding by the exact prescriptions of Article 3 of the Constitution. This mandate entrusts to the State the task of creating in the mind of young children a consciousness of their social and economic responsibility toward the environment where their lives are to be lived, and the further task of molding a robust lot of able workers in order that Mexico may depend on a well organized population that can efficiently contribute to the development and the advancement of the country."[55] He concluded by insisting that the federal government intervened in Laguna to keep any "untoward situation from coming up, which would have affected the economy of the entire nation."[56] It will be noted that in the case of both the land and oil expropriations, Cárdenas attributed the government's action to the necessity of preventing economic chaos brought about by the activities of organized labor.

As early as June, 1935, Lombardo Toledano had insisted that, to increase output, wages, and to achieve better living conditions for the people in the area, the following steps should be taken in the Laguna area: (1) Landed estates should be so divided that the maximum size would be two hundred hectares; (2) the prohibition of direct or indirect exploitation of more than one or two units by the same person should be made; exploitation by foreigners should be prohibited; (3) distribution of the land should be made to agrarian communities; (4) a decree calling for a single collective contract among all the owners and peasants within the Laguna area (with a salary of three pesos per day as a minimum, as well as fundamental obligations for social provisions, such as houses, schools, pure water, hospitals, etc.) should be expedited; (5) technical control of production according to a prior plan should be introduced; (6) taxes should be unified and simplified; (7) all indirect taxes should be abolished; (8) the electrical energy plant then existing should be expropriated as a public

54. *Ibid.*, p. 10.
55. *Ibid.*, p. 16.
56. *Ibid.*, p. 11.

utility and the service it furnished should be socialized; (9) the workers should participate in the collective profit of the industries of the region; and (10) there should be absolute respect for the vote of the masses of workers and peasants of the region in the election of authorities who represented them.[57] It is interesting to observe that several of these suggestions were incorporated in the final solution of the problem in the Laguna region. It is to the nature of this solution that we now turn to grasp the role which organized labor may play in the agricultural organization of a developing country.

Complying with the promise made to the workers if they would end the general strike of August, 1936, President Cárdenas issued, on October 6, a presidential decree giving lands and water to all the rural villages which presented their *ejidal* petitions to the competent authorities. All irrigated areas under cultivation not exceeding 150 hectares (375 acres) were to be respected as small private holdings. It was considered by many that the decree instituted a new epoch in the land reform of Mexico, even though it represented simply the enforcement of laws already in effect.[58] Deprived of their vast estates, the *hacendados* did not retire gracefully from the scene. Acts of sabotage were frequent—active sabotage, such as the dynamiting of water pumps and irrigation locks, and passive sabotage which consisted of sowing mistrust in the peasants' minds against the banks and the government.[59]

The decree stated that the *ejido* districts established previously had failed to solve the agrarian problem; hence it was necessary to invoke the provisions of the current Agrarian Code and apply them to the Laguna region. The National Commission of Irrigation was to pay the *hacendados* for whatever irrigation wells were included with the expropriated land. The National Ejido Bank was to furnish credit in sufficient amounts to prevent serious interruption of commercial production in the area. The new use of waters was adjusted for the primary use of the *ejidos* instead of the small, private owners, as the case had been previously. This measure was very important for agrarian reform, since it was established simultaneously with the *ejidal* credit

57. Vicente Lombardo Toledano, "La Comarca de La Laguna en Cifras," *El Problema de la Laguna: Antecedentes, Soluciones* (México, 1937), pp. 15–16.
58. For a copy of the Decree, see Ministry of Foreign Relations, *The Mexican Government in the Presence of Social and Economic Problems: Presidential Plan for Incorporation of Federal Territories—Ideology and Work of National Revolutionary Party—Mexico and Spain and the League of Nations—The Agrarian Problem in the Laguna Region* (Mexico, 1936), pp. 23–28; Liga de Agrónomos Socialistas, *El Colectivismo Agrario en México*, pp. 45 *et seq.*
59. Millan, "La Laguna," pp. 17, 218–19.

organizations that would prevent the paralysis of agricultural production in the country. The National Bank of Agricultural Credit was
to provide capital to the small landowner. The Socialist Agrarian
League held that the distribution of land in the area completed one
of the obligations of the Mexican Revolution to the working class,
even though the decree "contained the same major defect that all the
agrarian reform had contained . . . that is it distributed the land among
the men, when, under the circumstances, it would have been better to
have distributed the men among the land."[60] The league felt also that
it was a mistake to allow the small property owner (of 150 hectares)
to remain between the *ejidos*, thus breaking the unity of cultivation.
Each owner was allowed to retain 370 acres of land of his choice;
hence, most of them chose land surrounding their homes and barns,
adding to the interruption of unified cultivation by the communal
ejidos.[61] The owners were offered forty-year agrarian bonds, which
some refused. The value of the land was determined by consulting
the records of what the owners themselves had said the land was worth
when the tax assessor asked them, then 10 per cent was added. In
less than two months, the 221 property owners of the area who had
an average of 6,800 hectares each were reduced to a maximum of 150
hectares of irrigated land apiece. According to the National Confederation of Commerce and Industry, not one cent of the tax value
of 55,000,000 pesos for the land had been paid as indemnity by 1940;
nor had there been any payment for the system of irrigation works,
valued at 35,000,000 pesos.[62] The Association of American Owners
of Land in Mexico contended that the entire process of establishing
the Constitution of 1917 was in violation of the Constitution of 1857,
and that "Any settlement to be made with the Mexican Government
should concretely bind the government of Mexico, to derogate and
annul Article 27 of the Constitution of 1917 and all laws and decrees
proceedings taken thereunder."[63] Apparently, the association did not
comprehend the meaning of the term *revolution*! Of the 191,268
hectares of irrigated land in the region, 114,814 were expropriated;

60. Liga de Agrónomos Socialistas, *El Colectivismo Agrario en México*, pp.
51–54.
61. Senior, *Democracy Comes to a Cotton Kingdom*, p. 15.
62. Confederación de Cámaras Nacionales de Comercio e Industria de los
Estados Unidos Mexicanos, *Análisis Económico Nacional 1934–1940* (2nd ed.:
n.p., 1940), pp. 51–52.
63. Association of American Owners of Land in Mexico, *Mexico's Agrarian
Laws: How the Titles to Lands Owned by Americans Are Affected and Their
Right to Acquire Lands Restricted—Expropriation Authorized* (n.p., n.d.),
pp. 5, 22.

of the 1,314,224 hectares of nonirrigated but usable (as pasture) land, 127,272 were turned over to the peasants.[64] The area divided represented about two-thirds of the cultivatable portion of the region; the other third remained in the hands of the former owners. Since members of this latter group had been permitted to select the lands they would keep, the result was that their one-third was reported to contain about two-thirds of the artesian wells. Undoubtedly, this situation had a great deal to do with the fact that production per acre on the privately held properties was sometimes greater than that on the collective holdings. It is well to remember, too, that the Laguna region represented not a completely collectivized system of agriculture but a mixed system in which both *ejidos* and individual properties operated side by side.[65]

President Cárdenas himself spent forty days in the Laguna region working out the system under which the new region would function. By December 1, 1936, ninety-one communal *ejidos* had been organized in the State of Durango, benefiting 10,019 peasant family heads and covering 100,011 hectares (247,027.17 acres), of which 39,678 hectares (97,004.66 acres) were irrigable land. In the State of Coahuila, 159 *ejidos* were organized, benefiting 23,782 peasant families and covering 188,247 hectares (464,960.09 acres), including 94,640 hectares (233,760.80 acres) of irrigable land. Altogether, 250 communal land holdings, held by 33,801 family heads with over 125,000 dependents and covering 288,258 hectares (711,987.26 acres) were created. Prior to this government action, the areas had been held mainly by 12 corporations, two-thirds of which were foreign-owned.[66] Of interest, however, is the fact that even after the land distribution in the Laguna fewer than 10 per cent of the *ejido* farmers of Mexico worked on the collective basis established there.[67]

According to the Secretaría de Gobernación, in 1940, *ejidatarios* (both collective and individual) had received 34 per cent of irrigated lands and 42 per cent of the "temporal" (nonirrigated, but cultivatable) lands in the country. In his last message to Congress (September, 1940), Cárdenas gave the total figures on his agrarian works. His predecessors had made 4,349 grants of 6,972,293 hectares to 422,301 peasants. From December 1, 1934 to August 31, 1940,

64. Senior, *Democracy Comes to a Cotton Kingdom*, p. 15.
65. Thomson, "Agrarian Reform in Mexico," pp. 38–39.
66. Cárdenas, *A Message to the Mexican Nation on the Solution of the Agrarian Problem of La Laguna*, p. 2.
67. Townsend, *Lázaro Cárdenas*, p. 171.

Cárdenas made 10,651 grants of 18,352,275 hectares for 1,020,594 peasants. Of these, 15,000 went to *ejidos*, 25,324,568 hectares to 1,442,895 *ejidatarios*.[68]

The C.T.M. commented that if the Laguna experiment failed and if production fell, it would be a strong argument for the reactionaries against the principles of the Mexican Revolution. If, however, the trial were successful, it would have the possibility of changing the entire social structure of Mexico.[69] The success or failure of the Laguna experiment cannot be judged on the basis of production figures alone, nor even upon the basis of wages and cost of living statistics. Nonetheless, estimates of these economic facts are useful in evaluating the new system of economic activity in the area. They must be considered, however, in relation to the respective figures before and after expropriation, together with the various other circumstances, both internal and external, which affected the course of events in the area. Then these figures, together with a consideration of the more "subjective," intangible results of the action, may serve as a basis for individual evaluations, which could scarcely be expected to be in complete harmony. Production and income statistics are available in various accounts of the project.[70]

In addition to the wages paid by the Ejidal Bank, many *ejidatarios* accepted work off the *ejido* at a higher wage, often at a time when their services were badly needed on the *ejido*, even though this situation was, under the Agrarian Code, illegal. Some *ejidatarios* rented a part of their own lands to *hacendados* and worked for them as peons.

68. Laborde, "Cárdenas, Reformador Agraria," pp. 61–62.
69. C.T.M., *El Problema de la Laguna*, p. 5.
70. See, for example, Lombardo Toledano, "La Comarca de La Laguna en Cifras," Confederación de Trabajadores de México, *El Problema de la Laguna*; Mexican Government, *The Mexican Government and the Solution of the Agrarian Problem in La Laguna District*, p. 8; Laborde, "Cárdenas, Reformador Agraria"; Liga de Agrónomos Socialistas, *El Colectivismo Agrario en México*, p. 288; Moisés T. de la Peña, "El Crédito Agrícola en la Económica Mexicana," *El Trimestre Económico*, 7 (April–June, 1940), 96–115; Ramón Fernández y Fernández, "El Comercio del Trigo en la Comarca Lagunera," *México Agrario*, 2 (January–March, 1940), 19–54; José Reyes Pimental, *La Casecha* (México, n.d.); Comisión Nacional de Irrigación, *La Obra de la Comisión Nacional de Irrigación durante el Régimen del Sr. gral. de división Lázaro Cárdenas, 1939–1940* (México, n.d.); Julián Rodríguez Adame, "El Banco Nacional de Crédito Ejidal S.A., y la Reforma Agraria," *Agricultura*, 2 (May–June, 1949), 3–7; Banco Nacional de Crédito Ejidal, *Breves Informaciones Sobre la Organización, Funcionamiento y Resultados de los Sociedades Locales Colectivos de Crédito Ejidal en la Comarca Lagunera* (México, n.d.); Ramón Fernández y Fernández, *El Problema Creado por la Reforma Agraria de México* (México, n.d.); Renato Molina Enríquez, "La Evolución Histórica del Ejido y sus Transformaciones," *Revista Banco Obrero*, 11–12 (October–November, 1938), 1–3.

By 1943, eight *ejidal* societies (24.2 per cent) in the Laguna region made a profit; 226 (68.3 per cent) broke even; and 25 (7.5 per cent) were failures.[71] Whetten concluded that all observers seem to agree that the *ejido* program in this area was accompanied by the development of certain social services enjoyed by the population as a whole which were not available before. They also agree that, with regard to medical services, distribution of purchasing power, and individual freedom, the standards of living for the peasants of the area were improved.[72] Medical services were provided by organizing a group called the Peasant Co-operative for Ejidal Medical Services in the Laguna district, into which was paid 2.85 pesos per hectare of land cultivated, or an average of 0.94 pesos a month for each family head, which secured medical services for all members of the family. The district was divided into nineteen medical units, under a chief in the city of Torreón, where the main hospital was founded in 1936.[73]

From the beginning of the collective experiment in the area, the problem of internal organization was a difficult one. A particularly knotty aspect was the question of representation of the *ejidatarios* before the Banco Ejidal, or Bank of Ejidal Credit. Various groups competed for leadership of the peasants, and three or four different trade-union organizations attempted to obtain the right to represent the *ejidatarios*. Ambitious politicians saw their chance to climb into power on misunderstandings that were certain to arise in an undertaking of the character and size of the Laguna endeavor. The result was chaotic meetings in many *ejidos*, with conflicting claims of authority presented to the bank officials. Some of the serious administrative problems were solved by the creation of an inclusive organization of the peasants, the Central Consultive Committee of Ejidatarios. It afforded a mechanism for better communication between the bank and the *ejidos* and gave the farm workers an organization over which they had control and in which they had confidence. Senior noted that under the system devised, "strikingly reminiscent of the organization of the ancient Mexicans as described by Bandelier," each zone elected six "delegates," charged with general oversight of either education, administration, health, credit, grievances, or agricultural matters. In addition, a region-wide assembly elected eight delegates to represent the *ejidatarios* of all thirteen zones, six corresponding to the six in each zone, and two handling commercial matters and region-wide services, such as irrigation. The work of the zone delegates was to check upon

71. Whetten, *Rural Mexico*, pp. 230–33.
72. *Ibid.*, pp. 238–39.
73. Liga de Agrónomos Socialistas, *El Colectivismo Agrario en México*, p. 368.

the functions of the community which came within his field and to initiate activities about which he learned through his special outside contacts. The regional delegate dealt with zone delegates to increase inter-*ejido* communication and social competition, and in cases of dispute, he alone, or the full committee, presented the peasant case to the Bank. The Central Committee soon built itself inseparably into the regional organization, thus enabling the bank to spend less time bolstering the *ejidos* or trying to straighten out inter-organization disputes, and more time on its economic and agronomic functions. This arrangement allowed the workers to feel that possible future changes in Mexican politics which might endanger the new Laguna organization could be contemplated with far less fear than before the Central Consultive Committee of Ejidatarios was created. Both bank and peasants found the committee so useful that they recommended to President Cárdenas that such a device be made legally necessary in all collectivized ejidal zones in the country, and in December, 1939, Congress so amended the national Agrarian Code. The new organization became known as Unions of Ejidal Credit Societies and had broader economic functions than those formerly exercised by the consultive committees. The regional organization was known as the Central Union of Ejidal Credit Societies and in 1939 consisted of delegates from all sixteen zones, in addition to a representative of the Ejidal Bank. The number of divisions of work was reduced to five: credit, commercial and insurance, agriculture, machinery, and social services. The latter delegates attended to most of the matters formerly handled by the education, health, and administration delegates. In addition, there was a vigilance committee with auditing and supervisory functions.[74]

In the spring of 1937, an executive order signed by President Cárdenas and the minister of finance invited all organized peasant co-operatives throughout Mexico to name delegates to local assemblies at which the policies and methods of the National Bank of Ejidal Credit were to be freely discussed. The bank had been founded a year previously in accordance with provisions of the Six-Year Plan to make ample credit available to the *ejidos*. The order had as its purpose a general review of the activities of the bank and of the results of its effort to realize its dual purpose, and the collaboration of the peasants themselves in the discussions was asked that the many charges of abuses of power on the part of local agencies of the bank might be investigated and its future operations be made more effective.[75] In the

74. Senior, *Democracy Comes to a Cotton Kingdom*, pp. 18–21.
75. *Mexican Labor News*, March 4, 1937.

Bank of Ejidal Credit, the government owned Class A and Class B shares; *ejidos* owned Class C shares.[76] Eventually, the *ejidos* were to control the bank, which was a combination of banker, agricultural expert, family doctor, school teacher, lawyer, and personal advisor. Financially, the bank functioned to advance two forms of credit; seasonal loans for seed, advanced to members and to be used in preparing the annual crop, with repayment within eighteen months, and five-year loans, the proceeds of which were to be used to finance the purchase of tools and machinery, animals, and fruit trees or crops that could not be planted, harvested, and sold within the same season. It also helped procure twenty-year loans for wells and other long-range investments from another government bank. The bank had no security except the sound functioning of the societies, since *ejido* land could not be alienated for any purpose, either by individuals or the group. Eight per cent interest was charged—about one-third as low as the commercial farm interest rate in Mexico, and crop loans were made up to 70 per cent of the probable value of the crops.[77]

On the old hacienda of Santa Teresa, the bank and the federal agricultural authorities founded an Ejidal Agricultural School, where some fifty students, selected from promising young peasants in the *ejidos* of the region by the bank's zone chiefs and the Central Union, attended for eighteen months. The school was run as an *ejido* so that the students gained practical experience as well as the advice of the agronomists on the faculty. Jointly with the peasant organizations and with branches of the federal government, the bank sponsored the organization of women, anti-alcohol campaigns, a socialized medical service, and a forceful campaign of education for young and old. It owned fourteen warehouses for the storage of crops until they could be shipped or until markets had improved. It helped the peasant groups choose the best machinery, tested and reported on seeds, sold the cotton and wheat crops, combatted plagues and pests, furnished veterinary service, made soil analyses, supervised the ginning and classification of cotton, advised as to the best use for land, and ran contests to choose young peasants to be sent to school or to factories in the United States for practical experience and training. It organized wheat crop insurance against hail, fire, rain and plagues, and planned a similar system for cotton. Blueprints for inexpensive modern houses were furnished the *ejidatarios* and community building of houses was

76. Lázaro Cárdenas, *Condiciones Económicos de México* (México, 1937), pp. 10–11.
77. Senior, *Democracy Comes to a Cotton Kingdom*, pp. 21–22.

financed, the bank recording 1,159 new farm homes built.[78]

In spite of many difficulties, the bank reported that 40 per cent of the *ejidos* repaid their loans and made a profit the first year; however, the bank failed to recover more than 5,000,000 pesos of the amount it advanced for the first year's crops, which was 34,143,009.67 pesos. The second year, there was an investment of 28,839,676.39 pesos and a gross profit of 1,981,051.53 pesos. The bank continued to carry the account of the societies that were not able to pay back either the first or second year advances, although the number of groups making net profits increased to about half the total. By the third year, the new organizations showed a gross profit of 7,850,549.78 pesos, with an investment of 24,730,987.86 pesos. Almost 5,000,000 pesos were repaid to the bank; 60 per cent of the *ejidos* showed profits. Estimated gross profits for the 1939–40 season were 10,500,000 pesos.[79] The method of profit distribution of the bank had three aspects, worked out during Cárdenas' stay in the region. The first was based on daily work and on skill, the member receiving each week an advance which took the place of his former wage. The field laborer got 1.50 or 2.00 pesos a day; tractor mechanics, well-tenders, and others who were skilled or semi-skilled, received from 3.0 to 5.0 pesos. The work-chief got 3.0 or 4.0 pesos. Secondly, during the cotton picking season, piece rates were paid; and third, when the crops had been sold for the *ejido* by the Ejidal Bank, the seasonal loan and one-fifth of the five-year loan paid, and other deductions (such as interest on loans, purchases of Class C stock by the *ejido*, seasonal loans and interest, taxes—3 per cent of value of crop; social fund for local community betterment—5 per cent of crop value; medical service contribution; irrigation fee—5.0 pesos per hectare) made, the profits of the community endeavor were distributed among the members—not on the basis of their daily rate, but according to the number of man-hours contributed to the community fund of work during the season. Senior found that, over the region, the average income had been raised from around 75 centavos or a peso a day to 2.25 pesos in 1938 and to 3.04 pesos in 1939. Beyond this nominal wage and the various

78. *Ibid.*, pp. 25–26.

79. *Ibid.*, p. 23; Banco Nacional de Crédito Ejidal, S.A., *Informe que Rinde el Consejo de Administración del Banco Nacional de Crédito Ejidal, S.A., a la Tercera Asamblea General de Accionistas, Por el Ejercicio de 1938* (México, 1939). See also the bank's reports for 1939 and 1940. For further information on the operation of the Ejidal Bank, see Ramón Fernández y Fernández "La Reforma Agraria Mexicana," *Revista de Economía* (September–December, 1938), 703–15; Roberto Hinojosa, *El Tren Olivo en Marcha* (México, 1937), pp. 23–38.

services previously mentioned, in most cases the peasant had animals and the produce of a community garden plot, which he had not enjoyed under the former system.[80]

By 1940, the centralization of many of the aspects of the life of the region in the hands of the Ejidal Bank, necessary at the beginning of such a widespread social reform, had been whittled down by the development of the peasants' own instrumentalities for control. The organization of the Central Consultive Committee of Ejidatarios lifted from the bank a load of work which the peasants could carry through their own representatives. In the *ejidos* themselves, the former peons ran their own affairs with increasing self-confidence and skill in villages which never before had even a vestige of self-government, and the number of complaints concerning internal affairs in the *ejidos* had steadily decreased.[81] For the purpose of economic operation, the cultivatable part of the Laguna region was divided into twenty-four zones, each headed by a zone chief, who was directly responsible to the federal government. Each chief had from ten to twenty *ejidos* under his supervision in matters of taxation, consumers' associations, finances, education, hygiene, and sports. Directly responsible to the zone chief was the labor (or work) chief of each *ejido*, elected by popular vote of his community.[82] The work chief instructed the *ejidatarios* in cultivation, organization, construction, and social activities. He was assisted by a representative of the National Bank of Ejidal Credit. The work chief had duties analogous to the "riding boss," whip in hand, gun on hip, of the Southern cotton plantation—the difference being, as Senior viewed it, that the work chief was elected by and from among the peasants on the basis of their own knowledge and experience with him as a man and as a worker. Few such officers had to be changed by 1940 before their terms of twelve months expired, and in the first three years of the new system only 409 work chiefs were elected. Each week, the work chief met with the administrative committee, the vigilance committee, and a representative of the Ejidal Bank to map out the work program for the week. He made a detailed distribution of work to each member, keeping account of what was assigned and what was accomplished. Each *ejidal* member carried a work card which showed, at the end of the week, exactly what he had done and to what weekly compensation he was entitled.

80. Senior, *Democracy Comes to a Cotton Kingdom*, pp. 23–24. For a summary of *ejidal* funds spent on works of "Collective benefit," see Appendix C.
81. Senior, *Democracy Comes to a Cotton Kingdom*, pp. 42–43.
82. Jack Starr-Hunt, "Mexico's Collective Farms Show Profit," *Modern Mexico*, IX (November, 1937), 15.

A duplicate card was kept by the *ejido* office as a check and in case the original should be lost. The work chief also kept a detailed daily record of the use of the society's machinery, animals, feed, fuels, and other resources. Weekly, the bank representative sent a summary of the work to the bank headquarters, where records were compared with past performance and with those of other *ejidos*.[83]

The Ejidal Society was the unit of credit, and, since the previous minimum wage in the district was 1.50 pesos per day, the Ejidal Bank advanced this sum to each *ejidatario* for his maintenance until the crop was harvested and sold by the government. After deductions from each man's share of the amount of money advanced to him for maintenance, plus approximately 20 per cent to cover cost of seeds, machinery, and livestock provided by the government, as explained above, the remainder of the profit was divided among the *ejidatarios* according to the work that each had done as recorded on his weekly work chart by the work chief. In this manner, the formerly irresponsible peon was supposed to share directly in the responsibility for cultivation of his land and in the profits. Starr-Hunt pointed out that the peasant was paid according to his actual work, as was shown by the fact that in the division of profits from two *ejidos*, the rate of compensation varied from 1,450 pesos ($391.50) paid to the best worker to 278 ($85.00) paid to the poorest.[84] In 1940, only about half of the Collective Ejidal Credit Societies worked under a set of model rules for self-government drafted by the bank in consultation with peasant groups. Approval of the rules was required by 51 per cent of the members in a regular assembly, and the rules set forth the foundation of whatever discipline was deemed necessary. Attendance at the monthly general assemblies of the *ejidos* was obligatory—lack of attendance without excuse being punishable by denial of work for one day for the first occurrence, three days for the second, and up to fifteen days for each ensuing absence. Members were required to be ready for work at 7 A.M., or lose their right to work for the day if they were late without reason. They were obligated to accept the decisions of the work chief they elected, and could be denied work for three days if they refused to abide by his instructions. Continued lack of willingness to work under the direction of the elected authorities could lead to expulsion from the *ejido*, a step seldom taken.[85]

Despite the best efforts of the labor organizations, the government, and the Bank of Ejidal Credit, there were many difficulties to be over-

83. Senior, *Democracy Comes to a Cotton Kingdom*, pp. 16–17.
84. Starr-Hunt, "Mexico's Collective Farms Show Profit," p. 16.
85. Senior, *Democracy Comes to a Cotton Kingdom*, p. 17.

come in the Laguna area. Could the political boss in the local *ejido* be prevented from becoming a worse tyrant than the former land-owner? Could the extension of agricultural credit by the central government be so controlled that national credit agencies would not become organs of absentee domination, exploiting the peasants to the advantage of the political groups in power at the capital? Could the collective *ejido* system overcome the tendency of the Mexican peasant to grow only enough food for his own needs? Perhaps these questions could not be answered with exactness; but it is apparent that the local political boss was, under the new system, at least elected by his fellow workers and could be removed at the end of his term. Furthermore, central credit agencies could scarcely exercise more domination than the foreign owners and the private sources of credit prior to expropriation. With regard to the tendency of the Mexican peasant to raise only enough food for his own needs—if that was a general tendency in Mexico—then, surely, the organized efforts of labor and the government to overcome it could have been as effective as were the efforts of the former private owners. Most students of the experiment agreed that lack of discipline among the laborers was one of the most serious problems confronting the collective *ejidos*, since, even though a competent work chief might be chosen, he had little authority to enforce the program and had to rely largely on the power of persuasion for the simple reason that he could be removed from office at any time by vote of the general assembly. The bank had some authority to enforce certain regulations through the withholding of credit, but generally it preferred to follow a policy of free persuasion rather than to impose sanctions.[86] This situation was a far cry from the tyranny which existed under the *hacienda* system, and would not seem to indicate that the Ejidal Bank had become a new master in place of the old, as was charged by some critics of the Laguna experiment.[87]

Among the more serious problems of the Laguna region was the fact that, after expropriation, there were more workers than were necessary for the efficient cultivation of the land. The population was much smaller before the reform than after; in 1939, the number of workers in permanent houses was sixteen thousand; those not permanent, but nomadic in character, numbered ten thousand; hence, there were twenty-six thousand workers. During the harvest, some fifteen

86. Whetten, *Rural Mexico*, pp. 226–27.
87. For an example of such criticism, see Frank L. Kluckhohn, *The Mexican Challenge* (New York, 1939), p. 193; Luis Cabrera, *Un Ensayo Comunista en México*, pp. 19–20. This harsh judgment against the Laguna experiment seems to lack solid foundation.

thousand *bonanceros* were added, bringing the total number of adult workers to about forty-one thousand. Under the old hacienda system, it was considered that the average number necessary for one hundred hectares of cotton was twenty workers; after the reform, the average number of workers per hundred hectares was thirty-one, eleven more persons on the same amount of land. Therefore, the shortage of labor on the *ejidos* was not the problem; rather, it was an over-supply. In 1940, the labor force was classified into four types: (1) the organized *ejidatarios* in the Local Credit Societies; (2) the *ejidatarios* not organized in the societies; (3) free peons, and (4) peasants not *ejidatarios*, but members of the societies—the small landowners. As we have seen, in some cases the worker's income was supplemented by work outside the *ejido*, depending upon the time of year and the area in which the *ejido* was located. The League of Agrarian Socialists contended that this situation was made necessary because of the poor distribution of the land when the *ejidos* were created and the fact that there was some competition for hand labor between the collective farms and the small, private proprietors. The league held that the reason for the decrease in productivity per man hour after the reform was due to the reduction in the number of work hours per day, as well as to the increased number of workers in the area. In addition, the *ejidos* were not created on economic principles, but on the grounds of political expediency.[88] The new agrarian units were often carved out of lands of inferior quality, with poor communications, bridges, roads, and canals.[89] Above all, the entire pattern of production was interrupted by the 150-hectare plots of the small properties, including the best lands nearest sources of water. Many of the wells were sabotaged by the owners, pumps were removed, and the wells filled with cement. The Ejidal Bank furnished new pumps, valued at from 10,000 to 25,000 pesos, and 492 new wells were dug, valued at approximately 7,500,000 pesos.[90]

Added to these obstacles was the fact that the illiteracy rate in the region was 73 per cent, most of the peasants never having gone beyond the third grade. Company credit, company stores, saloons, and gambling establishments near the pay office, and complete lack of sanitation and medical care marked most of the *haciendas*. Accompanying these circumstances, the Mexican heritage of superstition further complicated the social scene; the disease rate was high; witch-doctors (*curanderos*) indiscriminately sold herbs and incantations for

88. Liga de Agrónomos Socialistas, *El Colectivismo Agrario en México*, pp. 203–06.
89. *Ibid.*, p. 61.
90. *Ibid.*, pp. 67–68.

smallpox, measles, whooping cough, diphtheria, tuberculosis, dysentery, and venereal disease. Lack of adequate and safe drinking water in 1938 still accounted for 45 per cent of all illness and 10 per cent of all deaths in the region. By 1939, these figures had dropped to 25 per cent and 6 per cent, respectively. Although new wells were being sunk rapidly, 65 per cent of all *ejidos* still lacked a safe and dependable source of drinking water in 1938. In the schools, in some cases, there were both toilets and shower baths, and an attempt was made to supply rational explanation for day-to-day events which, in many instances, was still explained in family circles in supernatural terms.[91]

Against these almost insuperable odds, what conclusions can be drawn with regard to the success or failure of the new order of work in the Laguna region? Insofar as the peasants themselves are concerned, the attitudes expressed toward the new system depended largely upon those held before expropriation—that is, there were those who felt that the general strike of workers won the distribution, that they forced the government's hand, those who were thankful that Cárdenas intervened in their behalf; and there were those who were loyal to the owners and wanted to become small owners. Most of the latter group became either small owners or loyal *ejidatarios*. Each worker continued to specialize in his own type of work, just as he had when he worked on the hacienda—the only difference being that the decision as to each worker's job was despotic before; now it was made by his own *ejidal* companions. The majority of criticism leveled at the National Bank of Ejidal Credit was not well-founded, and the bank was the most important instrument for making the *ejidos* a success, since credit for them would otherwise have been so expensive that the reform would have failed miserably. Even so, in the view of the League of Agrarian Socialists, it was possibly a mistake to utilize the personnel of the old banks, since they were generally in sympathy with the *hacendados*.[92] In this regard, a "purification" of bank personnel in the Laguna was begun in 1937, and an effort was made to use the local credit societies more fully, as we have seen.

President Cárdenas, speaking before more than thirty thousand farmers at the Convention of Co-operative farmers of the Laguna District, near the City of Torreón, in June, 1940, declared that the co-operative farmers had been important fighters in the struggle of the Mexican Revolution against the obstacle of a backward system of social injustice. He added that labor had been the farmers' staunchest

91. Senior, *Democracy Comes to a Cotton Kingdom*, pp. 28–29.
92. Liga de Agrónomos Socialistas, *El Colectivismo Agrario en México*, pp. 71–75.

ally and expressed his belief that a continuation of the program would result in the agrarian ideal: "The unification of the working class is a fundamental step towards the achievement by farmers and workers of their historic destiny. The new agrarian organization in the Laguna district marks the beginning of the second period of the transformation which the Mexican revolution is bringing about. The first began with the distribution of the lands; the second has begun with the organization of production."[93]

With respect to the condition of workers in the Laguna region, Ramón Beteta stated that the most superficial observation showed there had been improvement; but even if that were not true, "the change in the people's psychology, from one of well-defined servility to that of the independent land worker, is an achievement not to be denied."[94] Roberto Guerra Cepeda wrote that experience in Mexico had shown the failure of the individually worked *ejido* and that the collective *ejido* was the solution to great exploitation and a "remedy to the social injustices of the latifundia system."[95] As early as August, 1938, Dr. Louis Gottschalk, head of the History Department of the University of Chicago, having visited Russia and grown skeptical of the agrarian reform there and having announced his skepticism of Mexico's efforts, enthusiastically wrote, after a thorough consideration of matters in the Laguna region, "I came, I saw, I was conquered."[96]

When Cárdenas left office, it was absurd to deny the economic betterment of the peons who received land. As Strode wrote, "The most superficial observer, if not blind with prejudice, would see improvement in the houses, the clothes, and the daily food. But from Cárdenas' viewpoint, more significant was the change in the people's psychology from servility to independent worker."[97]

Even some sources outside Mexican labor, government officials, and intellectuals in both Mexico and the United States, felt that the new system in Laguna was an improvement. James Byington, U.S. acting consul, declared that business in Torreón had improved to a surprising extent; that, as a class, Laguna workers financially, educationally, and hygienically were better off than before.[98] And from the leading local daily of Torreón comes this comment:

93. Quoted in *Mexican Labor News*, June 27, 1940.
94. Ramón Beteta, *The Mexican Revolution: A Defense* (Mexico, 1937), p. 30.
95. Roberto Guerra Cepeda, *El Ejido Colectivizado en la Comarca Lagunera* (México, 1939), p. 183.
96. Quoted in Senior, *Democracy Comes to a Cotton Kingdom*, p. 44.
97. Strode, *Timeless Mexico*, pp. 320–21.
98. Quoted in Saint Albans, "What about the Laguna?" pp. 9–10.

1938 was a Good Commercial Year . . . the level of sales rose considerably above previous years and held up to the end. . . . Especially in clothing, shoes, hats, hardware, drugs, etc. there was considerable movement with consequent profit. . . . The increase in business was due to various causes, among others being the better distribution of money as a result of the *ejido* work. The distribution of profits by the Banco Ejidal, even though not great, always starts waves of buying which become noticeable immediately after the distribution. . . . With the increased purchase of shoes in place of old huaraches; hats of better quality for huicholes; better clothing for women and children; beds and other furniture; tableware and kitchen utensils, the desire of the peasant for material improvement has been demonstrated.[99]

The peasants were eating more of their basic foods—corn, wheat, and beans. Corn consumption increased from 64,520 tons in 1936 to 84,896 in 1938. Wheat rose from 18,341 tons in the former year to 22,803 in the latter, and consumption of beans went up from 3,585 tons to 8,079 tons in the same period.[100]

And, finally, Professor Simpson concluded:

In my opinion, any and all attempts to curtail the ejido program or to distort the collectivistic conception of the ejido cannot be regarded otherwise than as efforts to weaken and eventually and inevitably to destroy the only truly revolutionary thing the Mexican agrarian movement has produced. For it should be obvious that there is nothing revolutionary about an undertaking merely to redistribute landholdings.

The Revolution will have fulfilled itself if and when Mexico has been transformed from a land of privately-owned, individualistic haciendas and *ranchos* into a land of socialized ejidos, and not before.

Eventually all agricultural real property in Mexico, except such areas as the federal government may for the good of the whole country see fit to hold in trust as national forests, parks, and agricultural reserves, must be held collectively and be exploited cooperatively by agrarian communities.

The responsibility for the carrying out of the ejido land distribution program must rest in the first instance with the federal government and the basis of operations must be

99. Quoted in Senior, *Democracy Comes to a Cotton Kingdom*, pp. 34–35.
100. *Ibid.*, p. 35. For a later evaluation of the Laguna program, see Clarence Senior, *Land Reform and Democracy* (Gainesville: University of Florida Press), 1958.

agricultural regions rather than individual agrarian communities.[101]

It is undoubtedly true that with the government of Lázaro Cárdenas came freedom to form trade-unions, and with them the possibility for the peasants to struggle for their own interests. The struggle of the peasants for conquest of the land failed so long as they did not form a united front with the industrial workers against the economic-political front of the banker-owners in the protection of their own interests. "It was the coalition of the masses of workers and peasants which created the situation which made it possible for the Government to feel obligated to distribute the land."[102] It should not be forgotten that coupled with the pro-labor administration of Cárdenas was the genius of one of the greatest intellectual labor leaders of the Western Hemisphere, Vicente Lombardo Toledano.

In the opinion of some observers, the process at Laguna represented an extension of state socialism.[103] In the view of others, the *ejido* was a capitalistic institution "at the service of the organized peasants."[104] Some alarmists saw in the reform a principle of communism and claimed that the government had socialized the land. Garizurieta took the stand that such a position was false, since the collective *ejidal* system of the Laguna and Yucatán were capitalistic organizations that were established to achieve a commercial position in the world economy. He maintained that the system was not Socialist because it was established toward the end of profit; it was also an organization that complied with the rules of demand, as under capitalism, and production was neither directed nor controlled by the state. Garizurieta concluded, "I think that the present form of the *ejido* prepares a strong and healthy proletariat that will achieve the final assault against capitalism."[105] Whatever name may be given by this or that writer to the system instituted in the Laguna region, it is certain that the goal of the government and the Labor leaders was to improve the life of the peasants in the district through the destruction of the privately owned hacienda system and the substitution of some type of collective production more in harmony with modern technology. The method used for achieving the end-in-view was the unique use by the state of a labor movement that it had created for the purpose. This role of labor in a developing country may have become a pattern for others to emulate.

101. Simpson, *The Ejido: Mexico's Way Out*, pp. 512–13, 518.
102. Liga de Agrónomos Socialistas, *El Colectivismo Agrario en México*, p. 476.
103. Thomson, "Agrarian Reform in Mexico," p. 37.
104. Garizurieta, *Realidad del Ejido*, p. 86.
105. *Ibid.*, p. 87.

IX. Labor and the Oil Expropriations: Part I

It has been said that upon expropriating the properties of the foreign-owned oil companies in Mexico on March 18, 1938, President Cárdenas "telescoped Mexican history into two significant epochs: before expropriation and after."[1] If it is admitted that this approach is oversimplified, it is nonetheless tenable in any attempt to understand Mexico as a modern nation. Closely interwoven in the oil controversy were the activities of the organized labor movement. What was the role of this force during this particular era of the Mexican Revolution?

In the National Palace on March 18, 1938, several men perused a telegram to President Cárdenas from the offices of the Oil Workers' Union: "In spite of our good will, our earnest desire to comply with your wishes in the present case, we find it impossible any longer to maintain an attitude of patience, since the decorum of the nation demands putting an end to a situation which it is no longer possible to tolerate. . . ."[2] There were other messages from peasants' organizations, teachers' unions, trade-unions in both Mexico and the United

1. J. H. Plenn, *Mexico Marches* (New York, 1939), p. 11.
2. *Ibid.*, pp. 17–18.

States. All urged the Mexican government not to let the workers down.

News of the meeting in the National Palace had spread. Outside the room in the palace had gathered labor leaders, congressmen, bankers, editors, lawyers, newspaper reporters—all still remembering the echoes of the husky voice of Cárdenas as he told the American ambassador, Josephus Daniels, through a spokesman, earlier in the day how he felt about the pressure that had been exerted on behalf of the oil companies: "Respectfully inform His Excellency, the Ambassador, that if the richest oil fields in the world stood in the way of maintaining our national dignity, became an insuperable obstacle to maintenance of that honor which we prize so highly, we would burn the oil fields to the ground rather than sacrifice our honor."[3]

Just before 10 o'clock in the evening of March 18, 1938, radio listeners heard an announcement that the current program would be interrupted for a vital message from the president of the nation. There followed a moving broadcast to the world by an underdog nation; it said, in part:

> In refusing to comply with the mandates of the Nation's judicial institutions which, through the Supreme Court, condemned them on every count to pay their workers the judgment in the economic suit which they themselves brought before the judicial tribunals by reason of their inconformity with the resolutions of the Labor Tribunals, the oil companies have adopted a position which obliges the Executive of the Union to seek among the recourses of our legislation an efficacious means of definitely preventing, now and in the future, the annulment or the attempted annulment of judicial decisions at the simple will of one or both of the parties to a dispute by means of a declaration of insolvency, as is being attempted in the present case, with the result that the dispute is brought back to the very question that has already been judicially decided. It must be realized that such action would destroy the social norms governing the equilibrium of all the inhabitants of a nation. . . .
>
> This is a clear and evident case obliging the Government to apply the existing Expropriation Act, not merely for the purpose of bringing the oil companies to obedience and submission, but because, in view of the rupture of the contracts between the companies and their workers pursuant to a decision of the labor authorities, an immediate paralysis of the

3. *Ibid.*, p. 19. For a review of the recalcitrance of the oil companies in the labor dispute, see E. David Cronon, *Josephus Daniels in Mexico* (Madison, 1960), pp. 286 ff.

oil industry is imminent, implying incalculable damage to all other industry and to the general economy of the country.

In each and every one of the various attempts of the Executive to arrive at a final solution of the conflict within conciliatory limits, and which include the periods prior to and following the *amparo* action which has produced the present situation, the intransigence of the companies was clearly demonstrated.

Their attitude was therefore premeditated and their position deliberately taken, so that the Government, in defense of its own dignity, had to resort to application of the Expropriation Act, as there were no means less drastic or decision less severe that might bring about a solution of the problem.

The oil companies' support to strong rebel factions against the constituted government in the Huasteca region of Veracruz and in the Isthmus of Tehuantepec during the years 1917 to 1920 is no longer a matter for discussion by anyone. Nor is anyone ignorant of the fact that in later periods and even at the present time, the oil companies have almost openly encouraged the ambitions of elements discontented with the country's government, every time their interests were affected either by taxation or by the modification of their privileges or the withdrawal of the customary tolerance. They have had money, arms, and munitions for rebellion, money for the antipatriotic press which defends them, money with which to enrich their unconditional defenders. But for the progress of the country, for establishing an economic equilibrium with their workers through a just compensation of labor, for maintaining hygienic conditions in the districts where they themselves operate, or for conserving the vast riches of the natural petroleum gases from destruction, they have neither money, nor financial possibilities, nor the desire to subtract the necessary funds from the volume of their profits. . . .

It has been repeated to the point of weariness that the oil industry has brought large capital for the development and progress of the country. This assertion is an exaggeration. For many years, throughout the major period of their existence, the oil companies have enjoyed great privileges for development and expansion, including customs and tax exemptions and innumerable prerogatives; it is these factors of special privilege, together with the prodigious productivity of the oil deposits granted them by the Nation, often against public will and law, that represent almost the total amount of this so-called capital.

Potential wealth of the Nation; miserable wages to native

labor; tax exemptions; economic privileges; governmental tolerance—these are the elements of the rise of the oil industry in Mexico.

Let us examine the social contributions of the companies. In how many of the villages bordering the oil fields is there a hospital, or school, or social center, or a sanitary water works, or an athletic field, or even a light plant to utilize the millions of cubic meters of gas allowed to go to waste?

What center of oil production, on the other hand, does not have its private police force for the protection of private, selfish, and often illegal interests? These organizations, whether authorized by the Government or not, are guilty of innumerable outrages, abuses, and murders, always on behalf of the companies that employ them.

Who is not aware of the irritating difference between the housing facilities in the company fields? Comfort for the foreign personnel; misery, drabness, and insalubrity for the Mexicans. Refrigeration and protection against tropical insects for the former; indifference and neglect, and always grudgingly given medical service and drugs for the latter; lower wages and harder, more exhausting labor for our people.[4]

Many persons recalled the two sentences uttered most often by Cárdenas during his electoral campaign: "I pledge my honor to the promise of fulfilling my obligations to the working class if I am placed in power. . . . My only hope is that some day you can say that Lázaro Cárdenas fulfilled the promises he made as a soldier and citizen of the Revolution."[5]

At one in the morning of March 19, 1938, Cárdenas was still at the palace; among his visitors at that hour were cabinet members Súarez, Buenrostro, Villalobos, and Santillán, and labor leaders Lombardo Toledano and Juan Gray.[6] These men were but a few among the many destined to play leading parts in the struggle of the Mexican

4. Cárdenas' Expropriation Message to the Nation, March 18, 1938, in Government of Mexico, *Mexico's Oil: A Compilation of Official Documents in the Conflict of Economic Order in the Petroleum Industry, with an Introduction Summarizing Its Causes and Consequences* (Mexico City, 1940), pp. 877–79, referred to hereafter as Government of Mexico, *Mexico's Oil.* For the Spanish language edition of this work, see Gobierno de México, *El Petróleo de México: Recopilación de Documentos Oficiales del Conflicto de Orden Económico de la Industria Petrolera, con Una Introducción Que Resume Sus Motivos y Consecuencias* (México, 1940). See also Cárdenas' Expropriation Message to the Nation, March 18, in Workers' University of Mexico, *The Oil Conflict in Mexico* (Mexico City, 1938), pp. 91–92.

5. Plenn, *Mexico Marches,* p. 21.

6. *Ibid.,* p. 25.

Revolution under President Cárdenas against the forces of economic imperialism.

The oil controversy was a major—if not *the* major—episode in that continuing historic battle. The controversy cannot be separated from the labor problem which was at its source and ran as a swelling current through the stream of the Cárdenas administration. In the words of George W. Stocking, speaking of the expropriation,

> This action not only brought to a dramatic close a labor controversy which had disturbed the oil industry and the national economy since the strike of the oil workers in May, 1937, but it also sounded the knell of economic imperialism in Mexico and marked an epoch in the Mexican Revolution which had begun so ostentatiously under Madero's leadership in 1910. . . .
>
> It is interesting to note that the Mexican goal of the nationalization of oil was eventually achieved not through Article 27, which directly provides for it, but through the instrumentality of Article 123, which ostensibly is nothing more than a liberal labor code.[7]

Or, as Alejandro Carrillo said in an address delivered at the Institute of Public Affairs at the University of Virginia on Friday, July 8, 1938:

> The oil conflict in Mexico is a rather complex problem which can be best understood if its two fundamental periods or aspects are analyzed separately.
>
> The first . . . is the conflict between the oil companies and their workers, or what is perhaps truer, the struggle of the oil trusts and the labor movement. The second is the effort of the Mexican people and their Government to defend the sovereignty and the dignity of their nation, so dangerously menaced by the arrogant, rebellious attitude of the Standard Oil and the Royal Dutch Shell, including, of course, their subsidiary and associate companies.[8]

Prior attempts at exploitation having been unsuccessful, the Mexican petroleum industry really began in 1901 with the enactment by the Mexican government in December of a law highly favorable to the interests of foreign investors. This legislation was an expression of the policy of the Díaz regime to broaden and strengthen the national economy by inducing foreign capital to invest in mining, petroleum,

7. George W. Stocking, "The Mexican Oil Problem," in *International Conciliation*, 345 (December, 1938), 45–46. See also Henry B. Parkes, *A History of Mexico* (Boston, 1950), p. 407.

8. Alejandro Carrillo, *The Mexican People and the Oil Companies* (Mexico City, 1938), p. 8.

and other enterprises. The socio-economic philosophy of the Díaz administration favored a corporate individualism similar to that which had come to characterize Anglo-Saxon nations—the building of national strength by granting special privileges to enterprises that displayed boldness and vigor in their undertakings. As a by-product, the government itself could, through taxation, gain increased strength from such new enterprises. The Mining Law of 1884—there were then no special petroleum laws—made petroleum, among other items, the exclusive property of the owner of the land, who might exploit and utilize it without formal declaration of intention, subject only to police regulation. The Mining Law of 1892 was more conservatively phrased: without referring to ownership of subsoil resources, it gave the owner of the soil the right to exploit freely certain underlying mineral substances, including mineral oils. The Mining Law of 1909 returned to the wording of the 1884 Law and, after enumerating certain substances that are of the direct ownership of the nation, named other substances, including mineral fuels in their various forms and varieties, as of the exclusive ownership of the owner of the soil.[9]

The Petroleum Law of 1901 was concerned especially with concessions for exploration and exploitation and with special privileges for developers, rather than with ownership, the nature of which continued to be provided for in the mining laws. This law decreed that the federal executive was authorized to grant permits for the exploration of the subsoil of the national lands, lakes, lagoons, and salt-water inlets of federal jurisdiction for the purpose of discovering sources of petroleum or gas and that discoverers of petroleum and gas who had obtained patents in accordance with the law should enjoy certain exemptions. The exemptions of 1901 were aspects that accounted in large measure for the rapid development of the oil industry. Among them were (1) exportation, duty free, of the natural, refined, or finished products resulting from their exploitation; (2) importation, duty free, of the initial lot of requisite materials and machinery for any new well, pipeline, or refinery; (3) exemption of invested capital and capital goods of exploitation for two years from all federal duties, excepting the stamp tax; (4) and continued enjoyment of the provisions of Article 4 of the Mining Law relative to free exploitation without the need of special concessions.[10]

As Person suggested, a branch of modern capitalism was thus grafted on a semifeudal trunk. The foreign companies considered it

9. Harlowe S. Person, *Mexican Oil: Symbol of Recent Trends in International Relations* (New York, 1942), pp. 35–36.
10. *Ibid.*, pp. 36–37.

necessary to maintain a police force of their own, or they paid bandit leaders for protection. The principal concern of the companies was procurement of titles or leases from landowners and keeping wages and taxes as low as possible. "Gradually, under pressure wages were increased and became among the highest in Mexican industry; but the companies never caught up with the development and ramifications of the labor problem, and in the end it became their Nemesis."[11]

One of the most revealing first-hand descriptions of living conditions in the oil centers was given by Verna Carleton Millan:

> . . . Tampico and the oil fields are eloquent testimonies of the lives the worker lived there. It is possible to doctor statistics and hire publicists, but no one can wipe out twenty thousand shacks overnight, and those shacks are still there, for anyone to see. I have seen poverty in the United States, particularly among the Negroes and poor whites of the South, that sickened me. because there is a level beneath which life cannot descend and remain life at all, but rather fevered, apathetic clinging to existence. In Tampico and the oil fields I saw this poverty again.[12]

In addition to the bad living conditions of the oil workers, more allegations against the oil companies were forthcoming. The Mexican leaders charged that the manner in which the fields were exploited violated the principal purpose of the concessions—prudent use; that Mexico was drained of hundreds of millions of dollars of exhaustible assets without one permanent benefit; that desolation was the only monument to the nation's hospitality. Operations in the oil fields, not being immediately affected by the Revolution of 1911 and the expulsion of Díaz—possibly since the producing areas were located on the tropical coast and with inferior transportation ties—remained outside the orbit of upsetting revolutionary attention. Eventually, however, the impact of the idealism and radicalism of the revolution by degrees made itself felt throughout the industry. In 1912, registration of oil companies was required, and a decree was issued imposing a tax on crude oil. For the first time, the government felt the taste of revenue from this source. The fall of the Madero government in 1913 retarded the development of any program of regulation of the industry, however. During the presidency of Carranza, renewed attention was given to the industry, and the "bar dues" on exports, and

11. *Ibid.*
12. Verna C. Millan, *Mexico Reborn* (Boston, 1939), pp. 214–20. For a further description of living conditions in the oil fields prior to 1938, see Introduction to Government of Mexico, *Mexico's Oil*, pp. 50–51. See also Elvira Vargas, *Lo Que Vi en la Tierra del Petróleo* (México, 1938).

decrees affecting royalties, rentals, and special taxes were proclaimed. Carranza had extensive plans relating to the oil industry, other industries, and agriculture, but because of political distractions, these ceased for a time to command separate attention. Eventually they merged into a general program of basic constitutional reconstruction. From May 1, 1917, the effective date of the new constitution, the petroleum issue became a phase of the problem of implementing the document.[13]

The Constitution of 1917 restated fundamental Mexican law and declared that the legal ownership of petroleum and hydro-carbons—solid, liquid, or gaseous—was vested in the nation; that only Mexicans and Mexican companies had the right to acquire ownership and resources or to obtain concessions to develop them, although foreigners could acquire such concessions under limited conditions; that private property should not be expropriated except for reasons of public welfare; that there should be indemnification for expropriated property; and that the amount of indemnification should be based on the sum at which the property was valued for purposes of taxation plus 10 per cent. The 10 per cent was later eliminated by amendment. The Expropriation Law of November 1936 merely provided for the execution of this clause of the constitution, but with a different method for establishing and carrying out indemnity payments.[14]

Besides her own legal traditions in these matters, Mexico had the precedent of the United States congressional action during Taft's administration, separating subsoil from the surface rights on public lands. There were also the British oil laws of 1917, in which the Crown was given exclusive rights to drill for oil in the United Kingdom. Mexican legislators pointed to the British government's direct participation in the capital of oil companies and to the legal prohibition regarding transfer of oil company stock to other than British citizens.[15]

In addition to Article 27, the Constitution of 1917, through Article

13. Person, *Mexican Oil*, pp. 36–40.
14. *Ibid.*, pp. 39–40; *The Mexican Constitution of 1917 Compared with the Constitution of 1857*, translated and arranged by H. N. Branch (Philadelphia, 1917), pp. 15–18; Alejandro Carrillo, *Mexico's Resources for Livelihood* (The Hague, 1938), p. 13. See also Herbert I. Priestly, "The Contemporary Program of Nationalization in Mexico," *Pacific Historical Review*, 8 (1939), 59–80; J. Richard Powell, *The Mexican Petroleum Industry, 1938–1950* (Berkeley, 1956); "Expropriation in Mexico," *The Economist*, CXXX (March 26, 1938), 678–79; Departamento de Petróleo, *Legislación Petrolera: Leyes, Decretos, y Disposiciones Administrativos Referentes a la Industria del Petróleo* (México, 1938); Juan Botella Asensi, *La Expropiación en el Derecho Mexicano: El Caso del Petróleo* (México, n.d.).
15. Plenn, *Mexico Marches*, p. 37.

123, gave Mexican labor a charter as liberal as any nation had at that time. "In this document Mexican labor obtained at a single stroke, and with relatively little effort on its part, the legal benefits for which labor had been struggling desperately and often fruitlessly in many more advanced countries."[16] Lombardo Toledano, commenting on the significance of the 1917 Constitution for labor, remarked that it established the right of association, the right to strike, the reduction of working hours, a minimum wage, the protection of expectant mothers, and other provisions of equal importance. Further, he maintained, the constitution established the principle that the nation possessed the original title not only to the land but also to the subsoil, and as a corollary, it established the idea that the state had the right to impose on private property such restrictions as might be required in the public interest.[17]

While this constitution was hailed as the most advanced of national charters by those identified with "leftist" views throughout the world, it was deplored by "conservatives" as a symbol of a dangerous trend. Any objective analysis must conclude that it reflected the deep-seated feelings of the Mexican people and that Mexican military and political leaders were influenced by the implicit social philosophy for the very reason that it reflected such feelings. These leaders sought followers, and to obtain them they wasted no time with doctrines to which the mass of Mexican citizens was not already sensitive. Although the substance of the constitution may have expressed the will of a sovereign people, it created consternation among several strong group interests—landowners, church, and foreign capitalists. Two of these groups were domestic—the landowners and the church. To proprietors of haciendas it threatened a ruin similar to that which had come to the landed gentry of the southern states of the United States during the Civil War. To the Catholic church, still a substantial landholder, it threatened some impairment of its revenues and especially of its hold on the people through a clergy then largely Spanish. The third group was not domestic, and adjustment involved a conflict in foreign relations, since the special privileges acquired during the Díaz regime were threatened. In the eyes of foreign investors, the constitution meant "confiscation" of properties, higher taxes, higher costs of operation, and decreased opportunities for large profits in the future. These were powerful groups, and their opposition to making the pro-

16. Wendell C. Gordon, *The Expropriation of Foreign-Owned Property in Mexico* (Washington, D. C., 1941), pp. 103–4.
17. Vicente Lombardo Toledano, "The Labor Movement," *The Annals of American Academy of Political and Social Science*, 208 (March, 1940), 49.

visions of the charter effective was immediate and, as well, both open and undercover. Consequently, the decade of Carranza and his successors was not one of smooth implementation of the document.[18]

After the overthrow of Carranza and the short presidency of Adolfo de la Huerta, General Obregón was inaugurated president in December, 1920. The United States deferred recognition of Obregón in the hope that it would aid negotiations for settlement of the agricultural and oil disputes. Consequent negotiations permitted a temporary quiescence. Oil production greatly increased quite independently of political events and reached nearly 200,000,000 barrels in 1921, notwithstanding cessation of exploration of new fields. This increase resulted largely from the discovery of new rich wells in developed fields and the continued momentum from the war demand for oil as a fuel.[19] "Business was profitable indeed," Millan wrote, "if one can judge by the records of the Mexican Eagle Oil Company (El Águila), founded in 1907 with 30,000,000 pesos as its initial capital. From 1911 to 1920 El Águila showed a net profit of over 164,000,000 pesos, and by the end of that time was paying a sixty per cent dividend to its stockholders."[20] When the Royal Dutch Shell took over the company in 1918 from its independent producer, Weetman S. Pearson, they did not do so because it was a losing enterprise. Shell managed to eliminate its small competitors and, as a result, in 1936 El Águila's activities represented some 59 per cent of the total petroleum production in Mexico.[21] Still, from 1921 on, production declined steadily—in part because of uncertainty by the companies and the turning of their attention to Venezuela, and in part because the frenzied exploitation of wells at full capacity compounded the widespread emulsification by salt water which made its appearance in the wells.[22]

During the administrations of Obregón and Calles (1920–28), the Mexican Supreme Court rendered several important decisions in the matter of injunctions brought by the Texas Company, which had challenged the retroactivity of the Constitution of 1917. The court's decisions were favorable to this contention with respect to properties on which "positive acts" had created vested rights, but not with respect to other properties of which the titles were declared "inchoate" and subject to cancellation by legislation. It is not unlikely, as Person

18. Person, *Mexican Oil*, pp. 41–43.
19. *Ibid.*
20. Millan, *Mexico Reborn*, pp. 216–17.
21. *Ibid.*
22. Person, *Mexican Oil*, pp. 42–43.

felt, that the court responded to requirements of the political situation, for Obregón desired, and was willing to make concessions, to obtain recognition of his administration by the government of the United States.[23] The significant aspect of these decisions was that they marked a shift of the controversy from the military and political toward the judicial field.

The second event of importance was the Bucareli conversations of 1923 between representatives of Mexico and the United States, inspired in part by Obregón's desire for recognition and in part by the decisions in the Texas Company case. These conversations led to informal understandings, first, for mixed commissions for the settlement of claims; second, for broadening of the doctrine of "positive acts" in such manner as to limit severely—as it was believed in the United States—the retroactivity of the Constitution of 1917; and third, for compensation in cash at just value in the event of expropriation. Significant as was the trend indicated by these events, they did not allay the fears of the foreign companies; nor did they satisfy the Mexican people. The companies continued to shift their new investments toward South American fields and did not attempt further exploration and exploitation in Mexico. The Mexican people felt that their reserves were not assured of wise development and conservation. This discontent played a part in the election of Calles in 1924 and led to the enactment, under his administration, of the National Petroleum Law of 1925, which was a definite implementation of Article 27 of the Constitution of 1917, in the light of the Texas Company decisions and the Bucareli conversations. Pertinent parts of this law were: (1) a declaration that ownership of petroleum and associated elements was vested in the nation and that such ownership was not in any manner or under any circumstances alienable; (2) that works required by the petroleum industry might be carried on only under grants expressly authorized by the federal executive; (3) that Mexicans and Mexican companies might obtain such concessions in accordance with Mexican laws and that foreigners might obtain them in accordance with such laws and under additional conditions specified in Article 27 of the constitution; (4) that the following rights would be confirmed without cost and by means of concessions granted in conformity with the law: (a) those arising from lands in which works of petroleum exploitation were begun prior to May 1, 1917, valid for a period of fifty years from the date of the contract, and (b) those arising from contracts with surface owners made before

23. *Ibid.*, p. 43.

May 1, 1917, valid for a period of fifty years from the date of the contract; (5) that such confirmation of rights should be applied for within the period of a year from the effective date of the law, and rights not applied for within the year should be considered as renounced and forfeited; (6) and that forfeiture also should result from lack of actual works in form prescribed by law, failure to make prescribed deposits and pay taxes and failure to observe certain other provisions of the law. This law was not agreeable to the larger foreign oil companies—especially the declaration concerning the ownership of uncaptured petroleum, the time limit on the confirmation of rights, the fifty-year limit, and the equal application of provisions to landowners and to lessees. A campaign for education to stir public opinion was carried on in the United States, and, of more concern to the Mexican government, the companies once more abstained from drilling operations and diverted their investments to fields in other countries. Perhaps it should be noted, however, that the great majority of the smaller companies did comply with the law, for in 1927 the government announced that 125 of the 147 companies had obtained confirmations under it.[24] It may be that the behavior of the major companies was simply further evidence that international capitalism was unable to satisfy the desires of under-developed countries for national independence, and simultaneously to provide for rational use of resources.

The fourth event of significance during this decade was the Morrow-Calles conversations. As a result of these meetings, the Mexican government in 1928 passed certain amendments to the Petroleum Law, in accordance with which a distinction was made between landowners and lessees. Concessions of the landowners were confirmed for an indefinite period, those of the lessees for the term of the contracts. In consequence of the appeasing influence of these amendments, the solidarity of the companies' Association of Petroleum Producers was somewhat weakened, and the government of the United States, although it held unyieldingly to the principle of prompt and fair indemnity for expropriated property, became less firm in its support of other issues.[25]

During the greater part of the period from 1901 to 1935, with the exception of the years immediately following the birth of the C.R. O.M., the workers of the oil industry were without organization and were contracted by agents who gathered them up in the States of Tamaulipas, Nuevo León, and San Luis Potosí, engaging them at

24. *Ibid.*, pp. 43–46.
25. *Ibid.*

rather good wages compared with what they had made in those predominantly agricultural states. The workers were taken in groups and distributed afterwards to the camps and terminals in Tampico. No social services were rendered, and the greater part of the time the workers built their own huts of straw (*jacales*) to protect themselves from the weather. Tampico was growing very rapidly as a result of petroleum development and there was no place to house the new and increasing population. The workers brought from San Luis contracted illnesses and died in great numbers, but there were always more to replace them because, from 1913 to 1935, unemployment in Mexico was great. Vice and gambling were notable in Tampico; the pay of the workers was often thrown away soon after pay day.[26]

After 1915, disorder was extraordinary. Intense struggles took place over the organization of the workers, and the companies used every means available to prevent such organization. "White guards" were used by the companies to make it very unpleasant for workers who evidenced any interest in trade-union activity. There was also diplomatic intervention to prevent the organization of petroleum workers. In July, 1917, Secretary of State Robert Lansing of the United States asked Ambassador Flesher to put an end to the requests for increased wages which, according to the American consul in Tampico, Claudio I. Lawson, were ridiculous. Soon after, a strike was declared, and the United States Department of State gave instructions to Flesher to have the federal government of Mexico uphold the governor of Tampico, who had jailed the three principal leaders of the strike—Srs. A. Berman, Ricardo Treviño, and Andres Araujo—who were taken to the capital city of the state in spite of an injunction obtained from the district judge in Tampico, and the fact that President Portes Gil had asked that the Supreme Court of Mexico uphold the injunction of the district judge. In a strike against El Águila in 1924, the leader of the C.R.O.M., Luis Morones, was repudiated by the oil workers and a conference was arranged with the intervention of Portes Gil. From that date began the rift between Portes Gil and Morones,

---

26. José D. Lavín, *Petróleo: Pasado, Presente y Futuro de Una Industria Mexicana* (México, 1950), pp. 177–78. See also Ramón García Rangel, *El Problema Nacional Petrolero* (México, 1939); Miguel Manterola, *La Industria del Petróleo en México* (México, 1938); José López Portillo, *Exposición Objectiva del Plan Sexenal el Aspecto Técnico del Conflicto Petrolero en México* (México, 1938); Vicente Lombardo Toledano, "El Pueblo de México y las Compañías petroleros," *Futuro* (February, 1938), pp. 20–24; Departamento Federal del Trabajo, *Memoria del Departamento del Trabajo, Septiembre, de 1937–Agosto de 1938* (Mèxico, 1938); Enrique González Aparicio, *Nuestro Petróleo* (México, 1938).

which eventually resulted in the political liquidation of Morones.[27]

As was noted previously, Article 123 of the Mexican Constitution of 1917 was more than an authorization of progressive labor policy; it presented essentially a program. This document was implemented by the Federal Labor Law of 1931, which more specifically defined labor's rights under Article 123, particularly in regard to capital-labor disputes involving an "economic conflict." Article 570 provided for the settlement of a special kind of dispute designated a "conflict of economic order," which related to the establishment of new conditions of labor, suspensions or stoppages of work, that by their special nature could not be resolved under terms set up in Chapter IV of the law. Under the provisions of Article 570, the Board of Conciliation and Arbitration ordered the maintenance of the *status quo* pending an investigation by three experts whom it appointed. Then, after both parties had the opportunity to object to the findings of the experts, the board rendered its decision, which had the binding force of a judicial decision and might change fundamentally the conditions of labor.[28]

In addition to the boost given to organized labor by the Federal Labor Law of 1931, the general climate of opinion toward labor organization changed as Lázaro Cárdenas attained the presidency of Mexico on the program of the National Revolutionary party, whose Six-Year Plan called for the implementation of all provisions of Articles 27 and 123 of the Constitution of 1917. Pertinent sections of the Six-Year Plan included such declarations as:

Faced with the struggle of classes inherent in our system of production, the duty of the government is to strengthen the unions of the working classes. . . .

The National Revolutionary Party declares that during the six years which the present plan covers, the government shall regulate those activities of exploitation of the natural resources and the commerce in the products which signify an impoverishment of our territory, in the following manner: I. The nationalization of the subsoil will be made effective. . . .[29]

27. Lavín, *Petróleo*, pp. 178–79, 180.

28. Victor Manuel Varela (ed.), *Ley Federal del Trabajo: Texto Oficial Conteniendo Todas las Reformas y Adiciones Hasta la Fecha—Notas y Concordancias* (México, 1951), Chapter VII, Article 570.

29. Partido Nacional Revolucionario, *Plan Sexenal del P.N.R.* (México, 1934), pp. 46–56.

The plan further asserted that the masses of country and city workers were the most important element in the Mexican commonwealth, that the hope of making Mexico a great country must be based upon the proletariat, and that labor should enjoy the rights of collective bargaining and union shops.[30]

In the presidential campaign of 1934, Cárdenas declared that he wanted to place the sources of wealth and the means of production in the workers' hands, to end the further exploitation of the subsoil by "usurious foreign capitalists," and to let such exploitation be done by Mexico herself.[31]

In August, 1934, a Worker-Employer Convention was called to meet in Mexico City for the purpose of discussing problems of the collective organization of labor, strikes, lockouts, the collective contract, and the nature and function of the boards of conciliation and arbitration, as well as a social security program. Employers, workers, official representatives of the government, and technical specialists studied all these problems. The employer sector presented a united front, voting always as a bloc. For the first time in conventions of this sort, the worker sector also presented a united front, and "recognizing the high mission of the meeting, avoided the usual sectional strife and jurisdictional disputes."[32]

Prior to this time, there only *appeared* to exist the freedom to strike and other syndical liberties; labor tribunals and the speeches of government officials were always favorable to the interests of labor, but the most important strikes were transformed into failures for the working class. The unions were overpowered by the political influence of the corrupt leaders, and the labor courts decided in favor of private interests against the workers. Beginning in 1935, there were worker conflicts that were decided in favor of the workers, due to the inauguration of a new system of statecraft. President Cárdenas not only initiated a revolutionary interpretation of the laws, but stimulated the unification of workers, which led to the formation of the Confederation of Mexican Workers, the C.T.M., an organization that served to consolidate the gains of the working class and to perfect the unity

---

30. Gilberto Bosques, *The National Revolutionary Party of Mexico and the Six-Year Plan* (Mexico, 1937), pp. 157–58.

31. Standard Oil Company of New Jersey, *The Reply to Mexico* (New York, 1940), p. 31.

32. Alfonso López Aparicio, *El Movimiento Obrero en México: Antecedentes, Desarrollo y Tendencias* (México, 1952), pp. 212–13 (hereafter referred to as *El Movimiento*). See also *Memoria del Primer Congreso Mexicano de Derecho Industrial* (México, 1934), p. 7.

which existed between the people and the government. The strict and inflexible application of the law and respect for the Mexican courts was to result in the expropriation of the petroleum properties; that move was caused by the refusal of the oil companies to abide by the mandates resulting from a labor conflict.[33]

An editorial in *Fortune* (reportedly prepared by Anita Brenner) maintained that the tremendous power of labor in the 1930's sprang from one of the "most amazing combinations on earth: Cárdenas and one Vicente Lombardo Toledano, who controls 600,000 industrial workers through a labor federation called the C.T.M. . . . ."[34] Commenting upon the result of this new combination, the Confederación de Cámaras Nacionales de Comercio e Industria de los Estados Mexicanos (roughly the equivalent of the National Association of Manufacturers in the United States), expressed the feeling that the Federal Labor Law of 1931 and the Minimum Wages Law of 1934 were applied with frankness and certainty under Presidents Gil and Rodríguez, "improving the situation of workers without provoking any commotion in the economic order." Industrial production was increased in all areas; the period of these two presidents, in spite of new relations between employers and workers, resulted in a minimum number of conflicts. "But," the Cámara continued, "at the beginning of 1936 the Government began to demonstrate that it was not satisfied with the relations which then prevailed among workers and employers."[35] In February, 1936, the president delivered his famous speech at Monterrey in which he said that those industrialists who were tired of the social struggle could turn their businesses over to the workers and established the thesis that the demands of the workers had no limit except the economic capacity of the employers.

It was under these conditions, favorable to labor, then, that workers in all the oil companies were called together in the early part of 1936 and organized into the Sindicato de Trabajadores Petroleros de la República Mexicana—referred to hereafter as the Oil Workers' Union.[36] From isolated nuclei formed by nameless "Wobbly" apostles in the days when a discovered organizer was a dead organizer, this powerful union emerged. The early efforts of the Mexican oil workers to organize had met with great difficulties. The companies took ad-

33. Enrique González Aparicio, "Actitud del Gobierno ante el Movimiento Obrero," *Revista de Economía*, III (May–August, 1939), 83–86.
34. "Mexico in Revolution," *Fortune*, XVIII (October, 1938), 75–140.
35. Confederación de Cámaras Nacionales de Comercio e Industria de los Estados Unidos Mexicanos, *Análisis Económico Nacional 1934–1940*, (2nd ed.; n.p., 1940), pp. 33–35.
36. Lavín, *Petróleo*, p. 180.

vantage of all sorts of means—fair and foul—to prevent the unionizing of their workers. When intimidation of organizers by "white guards" of the companies failed to prevent organization, the companies resorted to a different method. Taking the burden of organizing the unions from the workers' shoulders, they began to organize them on their own account; company unions thus came into existence. A period of bitter strife between the bona fide independent unions and those controlled by the companies ensued.[37]

Mexico struggled from 1928 to 1938, following the end of the dispute over oil concessions to the subsoil, to better the condition of labor by controlling the economic and social conditions of industry.[38] Militant labor began to affect the oil industry in the 1930's. The industry contained thirty-five independent oil workers' unions in 1935, but not a single oil company was organized by union labor until that year. At that time, different contracts existed at each refinery and even within the same refinery; there were such contracts with fifteen of the principal oil companies and three shipping companies. Work contracts were not at all uniform as to wages and conditions of labor.[39]

The new Oil Workers' Union affiliated itself with the powerful C.T.M., which felt especially bitter toward the dominating control of Mexican resources by foreign companies, and as this central organization acquired strength it was able to exercise an increasingly strong influence on government policy. Person reasoned that the Oil Workers' Union was in an extremely favorable position with respect to such influence, since it was the union of workers in an industry closely identified with despised foreign interests. Although working conditions in this industry did not compare unfavorably with those elsewhere in Mexico, they were not such as the workers believed the economy of the industry could stand. In addition, the workers held as a grievance the fact that although there had been a marked increase in technical skill among them, advancement went generally to foreigners.[40]

The strength of the new labor movement was relatively great, since in 1935 only 215,003 workers were employed in manufacturing industries with a product value of over ten thousand pesos a year per

37. Carrillo, *The Mexican People and the Oil Companies*, pp. 8–9.
38. Ernesto Enríquez, *Problemas Internacionales: Reclamaciones y Petróleo, Panamericanismo y Derecho Internacional, Cuadernos de Política No. 3* (México, n.d.).
39. José Jorge March, "Mexico and Oil," *Labour Monthly, A Magazine of International Labour*, XXI (March, 1939), 171. See also Silva Herzog, *Petróleo Mexicano: Historia de Un Problema* (México, 1941).
40. Person, *Mexican Oil*, p. 47.

industry. Of these workers, 15,255 were employed in the oil industry, or primarily by the foreign oil companies. In mining, also predominantly foreign, some 42,442 men were employed in 1934.[41] A strike of the workers of the oil company El Águila in 1934, aimed immediately at equalization of wages, led to arbitration by President Rodríguez himself and eventually to the setting up of regional commissions to consider grievances and to make awards. Each commission had three members—a federal labor inspector, a representative of the interested labor organization, and a representative of the company concerned. During 1934, 1935, and 1936, there were numerous strikes, hearings, and awards, all of which signified a broadening of the scope of the workers' demands, integration, and consolidation of the various local petroleum workers' organizations, strengthening of the Oil Workers' Union, and unification of its demands to apply to all companies.[42]

As soon as the new Oil Workers' Union could meet its most pressing problems of internal organization, it called a special convention in July, 1936, to draw up demands for a countrywide collective labor agreement covering all petroleum workers.[43] It was said that the convention took nearly a year in the drafting of this proposed contract; and, on November 3, 1936, it was submitted to the companies—at almost the same time the Expropriation Law was passed by the Chamber of Deputies—under threat of a general strike unless they agreed to begin negotiations on the basis of such draft within ten days.[44] The companies, on November 11, in separate but similar communications, replied, stating that they were not disposed to approve the draft contract because, among other reasons, the existing collective contracts were still in force; but that, notwithstanding this fact, difficulties might be avoided if the Labor Department would call an employer-worker convention at which all the workers and employers of this industry would be represented, with a view to drafting a contract which would subsequently be made obligatory.[45] The companies

41. Manterola, *La Industria del Petróleo en México*, p. 68.

42. Person, *Mexican Oil*, p. 48.

43. J. Richard Powell, "Labor Problems in the Mexican Petroleum Industry 1938–1950," *Inter-American Economic Affairs*, VI (Autumn, 1952), 4.

44. Government of Mexico, *Mexico's Oil*, p. 518; William E. McMahon, *Two Strikes and Out* (Garden City, 1939), p. 73; Compañía Mexicana de Petróleo, "El Águila," S.A., *et al.*, *Mexican Oil Strike of 1937 (May 28–June 9)* (n.p., n.d.), p. 3. In January, 1937, the constitutional term of Supreme Court justices was reduced to six years, identical to that of the president. See Standard Oil Company of New Jersey, *The Present Status of the Mexican Oil "Expropriations,"* (n.p., 1940), p. 36.

45. Government of Mexico, *Mexico's Oil*, p. 518.

stipulated further that neither the draft submitted by the union nor any subsequently presented by any or all of the companies would form the sole basis of negotiation.[46]

At the request of the Labor Department, the union extended the time limit for calling the strike to November 17, and again to November 19, 1936. On this day, the union formally notified the companies in a joint communication that a general strike would be started on November 29 at 11 A.M. if at that time the general collective contract based on the draft of November 3 had been not only discussed but, as well, approved. The Union Draft of Collective Contract contained over 24 chapters, over 240 clauses, and covered some 165 legal-sized pages, of which almost 40 embraced the wage schedule.[47] The Oil Workers' Union alleged as the legal ground for the contemplated action "the discontent of petroleum workers, and the existing lack of economic equilibrium due exclusively to the diversity of working conditions obtaining in the industry," invoking to this end Article 260, Section 1, of the Federal Labor Law.

As the date for the strike approached, without the parties' having reached an agreement, President Cárdenas (who was, at the time, in the Laguna District) communicated by telegram with the head of the Labor Department, instructing him to point out to both parties the advisability of avoiding the strike by means of a special agreement in order that the draft contract might be discussed in a worker-employer convention and to call the attention of the interested parties to the necessity of their arriving at an understanding, thereby avoiding the strike so that the government might devote all its energies to the serious problem of the Laguna area.[48] Despite the fact that several of the individual company contracts had terms of from six months to almost two years to run, the companies accepted the president's suggestion, which was in accord with their reply to the original union demand. The union also acceded to the suggestion, and, as a result, an agreement was signed on November 27, 1936, before the chief of the Labor Department which stipulated that an assembly of representatives of capital and of labor would be held for 120 working days under the auspices of the Department of Labor. This assembly would

46. Compañía Mexicana de Petróleo "El Águila," (*May 28–June 9*), p. 3. The demand was made upon the fifteen leading oil companies in Mexico and three shipping companies.

47. *Ibid.*, pp. 3–4; Project of Approved General Contract at the First Grand Extraordinary Convention of the Syndicate of Petroleum Workers of the Mexican Republic, November 3, 1936. Typescript is in the Library of the United States Embassy, Mexico City.

48. *Ibid.*, pp. 3–4; Government of Mexico, *Mexico's Oil*, p. 518.

seek to formulate a general collective agreement, which would be made, by law, binding upon the whole industry, and the union draft, as well as the companies' counterproposals, would serve as the basis for negotiation. The strike would not be called during such discussions, and all benefits of an economic and social character which might be granted in such an obligatory collective contract would be made retroactive to the date of its approval and signature before the Labor Department.[49]

The worker-employer assembly began, with the first eleven days occupied in drafting rules of procedure; then, discussion of the draft contract of the petroleum workers was initiated, with counterproposals of the companies being presented in accordance with the numerical order of the clauses of the contract. There was early disagreement when the union insisted that the contract mention particulars and specific companies, while the companies wanted a general contract without reference to any particular company. Each party presented its view in writing to obtain the opinion of the Labor Department. The companies wanted a separate chapter—or a contract within a contract—to cover marine, dredging, and river operations, while the union wanted these groups covered by the general contract. In spite of these disagreements, the work of the assembly continued, but without satisfactory results, for, when approximately forty working days remained, only 26 clauses of the total of 248 contained in the labor draft had been approved. For this reason, by agreement between the parties, a new method of conducting the discussions was tried out, according to which the clauses of the draft were divided into three groups, economic, social, and administrative, with the purpose of beginning at once the discussion of the clauses of an economic nature. For this reason, a ten-day recess was agreed upon to give the employers the time necessary to prepare their complete counter-draft to the workers' proposals.[50]

The companies presented their counterproposals, but still no agreement could be reached on economic matters. It was decided to give attention to administrative matters first, since there seemed to be fewer difficulties in this area. Still, no progress was made; this was, however, largely because it was impossible to reach any agreement upon social welfare clauses, etc., until wage scales were known.[51] The companies pointed out that they did not have equal financial capacity; therefore, each should be dealt with separately. (It is possible that this

---

49. Compañía Mexicana de Petróleo "El Águila," (*May 28–June 9*), p. 5.
50. Government of Mexico, *Mexico's Oil*, pp. 518–19.
51. *Ibid.*, p. 519.

position was primarily an attempt to avoid industry-wide collective bargaining.) The union demanded uniform treatment for all companies. Another point was raised: Should the contract contain, with respect to advantages already obtained, the most favorable terms embodied in any of the contracts in force with the separate companies, or should it contain an average of all the benefits taken together, irrespective of the terms of any of the existing contracts in regard to the maximum total of benefits?[52]

Shortly before declaring a general strike in the oil industry, the union presented thirteen points, considered as a minimum to form the basis for a settlement; the employers presented counterproposals to these thirteen points. In the words of the expert commission, later appointed to investigate the dispute, "It was a shifting situation, made up of positions which changed and moved at every moment, because they were based on certain conditions of acceptance by the other party of certain benefits to which the other party did not agree, as upon proposing a given thing, each party did so on condition that the other party desist from certain demands and accept others. In short, it was a question of conditional proposals and counter-proposals, and the conditions were complex and numerous."[53] According to the commission, the draft of collective contract presented by the union contained demands in excess of the financial capacity of the companies, but it was likewise true that after the dispute had begun, the companies did not adopt a conciliatory attitude demonstrating their desire to avoid the conflict. "On the contrary, from the very beginning of the discussions, their attitude showed that they were determined not only not to yield but to impose their authority."[54]

In the draft of collective contract, great attention was given to clauses on social welfare. From a comparison of the draft with the various collective contracts then in force with the different union sections and companies, it may be seen that it was drawn up by taking the most advantageous terms of each existing contract and welding them into the new draft.[55] Insofar as the union demands contained in the draft contract are concerned, the following seem to have been the most significant: (1) a maximum of 114 "confidential employees," plus an unlimited number of legal representatives for each company, all other employees to be controlled by the union; (2) in cases of layoffs, an indemnity to each worker dismissed equal to 90 days' wages

52. *Ibid.*, p. 19.
53. *Ibid.*
54. *Ibid.*
55. *Ibid.*, p. 520.

plus 25 days' wages for each year, or fraction of a year greater than 6 months' employment with the company; (3) establishment of the 40-hour work week; (4) medical service, on a disease-prevention basis, to be furnished at the employer's expense, with the necessary facilities for diagnosis, adequate medical installations, and the elimination of all "humiliating red tape"; (5) in the event of death from nonoccupational causes, the payment of 60 days' wages and funeral expenses, in addition to an indemnity of 25 days' wages for each year the worker had been employed; (6) if death was from occupational causes, an indemnity equal to 1,400 days' wages; (7) 18 compulsory rest days a year, in addition to paid vacations of 25 days a year for workers employed up to 5 years, 40 days for those of from 5 to 10 years' employment, 50 days for those of from 10 to 15 years' employment, and 60 days for those having 15 or more years' employment; (8) establishment of a savings fund, to be made up of a 10 per cent discount from wages, contributed by the workers, and an amount equal to 15 per cent of wages contributed by the employers, to draw interest at 6 per cent per annum; (9) the founding of 45 scholarships for workers or their children; (10) an opportunity for Mexican workers to acquire the experience necessary to replace foreign technicians; (11) the furnishing of sanitary and comfortable housing for all workers, or the payment, in lieu of this service, of 2 pesos daily to each worker; and (12) wage increases totaling 28,149,560 pesos, thus making total increases of annual labor costs under the proposed new contract 65,474,840 pesos, and a total of the annual labor costs under the contract proposed by the union 114,611,460 pesos, according to the union.[56] The companies calculated that the sum of wage increases and social and economic benefits demanded would have increased labor costs to the companies by approximately 500 per cent, or a round sum of 300,000,000 pesos a year.[57]

In the proposed contract, confidential (nonunion) positions consisted almost entirely of the presidents, vice-presidents, chiefs of various departments, general accountants, auditors, sales managers, field superintendents, and heads of legal departments. All workers at the service of confidential employees were to be union men.[58] When analyzing the contract, the companies directed their attention to the three major classifications of union demands, namely, those tending

56. Project of Approved General Contract at the First Grand Extraordinary Convention of the Syndicate of Petroleum Workers of the Mexican Republic, November 3, 1936; Workers' University of Mexico, *The Oil Conflict*, pp.11–13.
57. Compañía Mexicana de Petróleo "El Águila," (*May 28–June 9*), pp. 5–7.
58. "Project of Approved General Contract at the First Grand Extraordinary Convention of the Syndicate of Petroleum Workers of the Mexican Republic, November 3, 1936."

to "abridge the right of company management," social and economic benefits, and the wage schedule. With regard to the first classification, they maintained that the confidential positions were so limited as virtually to turn over the management of the companies to the union. (El Águila was allowed thirty-five such posts; Huasteca, eleven; Pierce, four, etc., in addition to the legal staffs in each case.) No reduction in personnel could be made, even after approval by the proper government authorities, without the consent of the union, and the right to discharge workers was limited solely to grave and infamous causes duly proven by means of an investigation by the companies and the union. All work of any kind, except that of new installations, was to be permanent. No movement of personnel could be made without express consent of the workmen concerned and previous approval of the union. The union was to designate the type and size of houses to be built for workmen, and their location.[59]

Concerning social and economic benefits, the companies pointed out that the union demanded 1,460 days' salary payment for death, while the law stipulated payment for only 612 days (some of the companies at the time were paying from 730 to 1,095 days), and that the union asked 1,825 days' salary payment for total incapacity, whereas the law called for 918 (some companies were paying 1,095 days).[60] The companies called the demands of the union with regard to pensions fantastic, considering them provisional pending the issuance of the Social Insurance Law. They objected to the request for more vacation time, rest days, etc., as well as an increase in the number of scholarships to workers and their children. They called "absurd" the demand of the union that all foreign technicians be removed from employment within a period of one year. As for workers' housing, the companies stated that, taking into account the extremely high cost of furnishing housing in the form stipulated by the draft contract, the acceptance of such a stipulation "would ruin the companies." They proposed that compensation for housing be limited to field workers, on a sliding scale basis, according to the category and wage of the worker; the compensation should be 50 centavos per day to those earning up to 6 pesos, 1 peso per day to those earning from 6.01 to 12.0 pesos, and 1.50 pesos per day to those earning more than 12.0 pesos.[61]

With regard to the wage schedule, Clause 246 of the labor draft contract established eighteen categories as a scale of daily wages run-

---

59. Compañía Mexicana de Petróleo "El Águila," (*May 28–June 9*), pp. 3–7.
60. *Ibid.*
61. Government of Mexico, *Mexico's Oil*, p. 522.

ning from 7 pesos per day for the lowest unskilled labor up to 80 pesos per day for department heads. The following table presents one illustrative category from each classification, together with the corresponding daily salary:

Classification	Category	Daily Salary (*pesos*)
1	General apprentices	4 to 6
2	Special apprentices	5 to 7
3	Unskilled labor	7.00
4	Messengers and janitors	9.50
5	Watchmen	12.00
6	Gaugers	14.50
7	Typists	17.00
8	Chauffeurs	20.00
9	English-Spanish stenographers	23.00
10	Cashiers	26.00
11	Secretaries to Department Heads	40.00
12	Chief clerks	33.00
13	Engineers	43.00
14	General paymasters	50.00
15	General cashiers	55.00
16	Local sales managers	70.00
17	Department heads	80.00

Compañía Mexicana de Petróleo, "El Águila," S.A. *et al., The Mexican Oil Strike of 1937 (May 28–June 9)* (n.p., n.d.).

For the newspaper-reading public, the oil workers enjoyed much better working conditions than those of workers in the other important industries of the country. The oil companies took it upon themselves to inform this public, by means of full-page advertising in the papers, of how these conditions compared with similar conditions in other large industries, such as mining and textiles. As the Mexican government saw it, the companies succeeded in giving a certain impression of exaggeration to the workers' demands; but the public easily saw that these demands represented an increase in wages and an improvement in working conditions that were excessive, perhaps, in relation to other industries, but which would have no other result than to diminish "what the foreign companies take out of Mexico to enrich foreign capitalists."[62] The workers of the other important industries, who, in general, could not hope to obtain such favorable conditions as those of the oil workers, watched with interest the struggle that

62. *Ibid.*, p. 520.

developed over the new contract. In the middle-class sectors of the economy, it was thought that whatever the petroleum workers might obtain should be placed at the disposal of the president of the Republic, to be used to carry out his policies of agrarian credit, public works, education, and health. There was talk of large donations which the oil workers would make to the agrarian program and to scientific and social-welfare institutions.[63]

The companies, after the ten-day recess in negotiations, submitted a complete counterproposal to the union draft—with the single express exception of the wage schedule, which was to be submitted later, as soon as the companies had determined to what extent the obligations incurred with respect to added costs in the other clauses of the contract granting social or economic benefits would come. In this counterproposal, presented on April 12, 1937, confidential positions were divided into four classes: (1) executive positions, including the Board of Directors, managers, assistant managers, representatives, auditors, technicians, accountants, etc.; (2) administrative positions covering superintendents, cashiers, labor agents, paymasters, doctors, etc.; (3) supervising positions, comprising labor and technical inspectors, general and traveling auditors, head watchmen, and (4) secretarial positions, including all labor personnel, and secretaries and other confidential employees of the legal and medical departments, land agents, and all secretaries to executive and administrative heads. This suggestion would have reserved an extensive confidential staff to the companies.[64]

With regard to movement of personnel, employers were to be entitled to move personnel from camps or sales agencies freely within the territorial jurisdiction of the union local. Agreement was to be necessary for the movement of personnel from refineries, terminals, or general offices. Employers were to be permitted to move personnel outside the jurisdiction of the union local, provided such action did not invade the rights of other locals of the same company.[65] The pensioning of able workmen at the age of fifty-five who had from twenty-five to thirty years' service was to be obligatory upon the companies. Annual vacations were to begin on the first working day following the weekly day of rest, the date being mutually fixed. Workers with over one year of service were to have eighteen working days' vacation a year, with full pay, and there were to be seven obligatory holidays and seven and one-half extra holidays with full pay.

63. *Ibid.*
64. Compañía Mexicana de Petróleo "El Águila," p. 11.
65. *Ibid.*, pp. 12–13.

Double, triple, and even quadruple pay was to be given for work performed on these days if they happened to coincide, fall on rest days, or involve a combination of the three.[66]

Employers were to designate the sites for construction of workers' houses and to determine materials, plans, etc., in connection therewith. These homes were to conform to the terms of the Labor Law and the Sanitary Code and were to be furnished workers in recognized oil camps or localities with similar living conditions, as distinguished from population centers. In lieu thereof, rental allowances were to be provided for the workers on the following scale:

Daily Salary (pesos)	Daily Allowance (pesos)
6	0.50
6 to 12	1.00
12 and over	1.50

Compañía Mexicana de Petróleo, "El Águila," S.A. *et al., The Mexican Oil Strike of 1937 (May 28–June 9)* (n.p., n.d.), pp. 13–15.

For purposes of comparison, the following table gives the daily wages for coastal regions proposed by the companies in their wage schedules of May 17, for nine of the same eighteen categories listed in the original labor draft:[67]

Category of Position	Company Offer (pesos)	Union Demand (pesos)
General apprentices	3.60– 4.80	4.00– 8.00
Special apprentices	5.36– 6.32	5.00– 7.00
Unskilled labor	4.80	7.00
Messengers and Janitors	4.80	9.00
Watchmen	4.80	12.00
Gaugers	5.26– 7.44	14.50
Typists	8.33–12.50	17.00
Chauffeurs	6.32– 7.12	20.00
English-Spanish stenographers	15.50–18.83	23.00

Compañía Mexicana de Petróleo, "El Águila," S.A. *et al., The Mexican Oil Strike of 1937 (May 28–June 9)* (n.p., n.d.), p. 16.

According to the company counterproposals for settlement, the offer compared with the 1936 salaries of the workers as follows:

66. *Ibid.,* pp. 13–15.
67. *Ibid.,* p. 16. The companies stated that it was impossible to give the wages for the remaining nine categories listed in the labor draft since these were all administrative and executive positions, generally "confidential," carrying with them direct obligations of responsibility and trust to the company.

Wages Unskilled Labor	1936 *(pesos)*	1937 *Offer (pesos)*
Basic wage (coast)	3.30–3.75	5.00– 5.60
Pay on rest days	0.67–0.77	2.00– 2.24
Savings fund	0.20–0.23	0.70– 0.78
Vacations	0.30–0.34	1.22– 1.35
Housing		0.70– 0.70
Total cash for 8-hour day	4.47–5.09	9.62–10.67
Social benefits	0.22–0.24	0.36– 0.40
Total effective pay	4.69–5.33	9.98–11.07

Compañía Mexicana de Petróleo, "El Águila," S.A. *et al., The Mexican Oil Strike of 1937: The Decision of the Labor Board* (n.p., n.d.), appendices ii and iii.

The salaries offered to the workers by the companies would have meant an increase of 9,500,000 pesos the first year in total cost of production, including 3,500,000 pesos for retroactive salary payments. To the workers of the coast were offered substantial raises, and office workers were offered an average salary of 425.08 pesos per month. The number of permanent workers the contract proposed to cover was 8,284. It proposed to extend a total of 12,750,496.28 pesos for salaries in 1938 and 6,703,095.68 pesos for rest days, vacations, etc.; 1,556,291.21 pesos for the savings fund at 8 per cent interest; 2,047,-650.00 pesos for pensions; 273,372.00 pesos for overalls and laundry. The total was an increase of 23,330,905.17 pesos per year for the workers. The average expenditure by the companies per worker in 1938 was to be 2,816.38 pesos; each month the average worker was to receive 234.70 pesos, for each day of eight hours, 10.90 pesos. In addition, 98.48 pesos for medical expense would be spent for each worker in 1938 and 16.94 pesos for general and cultural benefits, to bring the annual average salary to 2,931.80 pesos, or an average daily salary of 11.35 pesos.[68]

The average daily wage offered the oil worker in the companies' counterproposal compared with the 1936 average of 7.42 pesos very favorably. The average daily wage paid in the mining industry, according to the petroleum companies, was only 4.32 pesos; in light and power, 5.09 pesos; and in the railroad industry in 1936 the average was 4.87 pesos, plus 35 per cent for general social benefits.[69] Work conditions

68. *Proyecto Patronal de Tabulador de Salarios Que Se Presenta a la Asamblea Obrero Patronal Que Discute el Contrato General Obligatorio para Toda la Industria del Petróleo en la República Mexicana* (México, 1937), Appendix i; Merrill Rippy, "El Petróleo y la Revolución Mexicana," *Problemas Agrícolas e Industriales de México*, VI (July–September, 1954), 103.

69. Compañía Mexicana de Petróleo "El Águila," *The Economic Issue*, pp. 56–58.

granted under the employers' counterdraft included a work week of forty-four hours, with straight pay for the remaining four hours up to the legal forty-eight hour limit; time and a half for loading and unloading corrosive acids, dynamite, etc.; double pay for work done at elevators greater than 10 meters, provided the employer did not fulfill the safety requirements of the National Safety Council; double pay for work performed in temperatures from 45 to 55 degrees centigrade (113 to 131 degrees F.), within boilers, stills, etc.[70]

Within twenty-four hours, the labor delegation rejected the companies' counterproposals, both in their entirety and in each and every one of the clauses, except the twenty-nine clauses already agreed upon. The union then demanded that the companies submit their proposed wage schedule, which they reluctantly did. The same afternoon—May 17, 1937—the union formally reminded the companies that the term of 120 working days fixed in the November 27 accord would expire on May 27 at midnight, when, if the discussion and approval of the contract had not been completed, the strike would begin. The communication imputed to the companies the responsibility for the strike, and hence sought to make them, under the law, liable for strike pay, as well as for the costs and expenses incurred therein by the union. The companies replied on May 19, stating that inasmuch as they had submitted both a full counterproposal and a wage schedule which, if accepted, "would place the oil workers on a higher plane than workers in any other industry in Mexico," they disclaimed all responsibility for the strike and, therefore, would not be liable for strike pay or the costs and expenses incurred by the Union in the announced strike movement. They also served notice that they would not continue to pay the wages and expenses of the labor delegates in the convention, and would break off all conversations from the moment the strike began.[71]

With the rejection of the companies' plan by the individual unions to which it was presented, negotiations failed and a strike was called for May 28, 1937, in the entire oil industry. Promptly at midnight of May 27, the union called out all workers, field, refinery, sales, technical, and office, and the long-threatened general strike was on. Despite this, at the instance of the Labor Department, informal conversations were continued between the parties. On Saturday night, May 29, the chief of the Labor Department handed the employers' delegation a copy of a communication from the union in which a "conciliatory" basis for the ending of the strike was proposed. It

70. Compañía Mexicana de Petróleo "El Águila," (*May 28–June 9*), p. 16.
71. *Ibid.*, p. 17.

consisted of thirty-four points, some of which were new, including a peremptory term of ten days for agreement on all clauses of both drafts to which there were no "basic objections" and thirty days for agreement on all other clauses. According to the companies, the only substantial curtailment of the original demands of the Union was the reduction of the minimum wage from seven to six pesos a day. "Quite inconsistently the concessions made in the higher salary brackets were in lesser amounts, so that the highest category was lowered only five centavos from eighty to 79.95 pesos per day."[72]

A comparison of some of the more important clauses of the "thirty-four points" with the original draft of collective contract presented by the union reveals that with regard to confidential employees, instead of El Águila's being allowed thirty-five positions; Huasteca, eleven; Sinclair-Pierce, five, etc., in addition to their legal staffs, the new proposal said "the highest confidential position at present controlled by the Union in any one of its locals to be controlled in future by the Union in all companies, and correspondingly all positions falling below that particular category."[73] In case of payment for lost time for the nonoccupational sickness and accidents, the new suggestion was full pay up to a period of ninety days for each case instead of full pay until the workers were in condition to return to work. If the lost time were due to occupational sickness or accident, the new suggestion was for full pay up to a period of two years, instead of full pay until the workers could return to work. The plan called for eight obligatory holidays and eight extra holidays with full pay instead of eighteen obligatory holidays with full pay, and for thirty working days' vacation with full pay instead of the complicated schedule going up to sixty working days for those with over fifteen years' service.[74]

Beyond these points, the union proposal suggested the formation of a national committee composed of representatives of the workers, the companies, and the government, as in all cases of obligatory collective contracts, for the application of the present contract. This request was not contained in the original union demands. The workers also demanded that all the economic and social benefits, including the wage schedule, to be granted under the contract as and when it was signed, should be made retroactive to May 28, 1937, regardless of other agreements already signed with the companies governing this point. The companies claimed that this new demand violated the Accord of November 27, 1936, which stipulated that the general retroactivity of the contract held good only for the interim between the signing of it

72. *Ibid.*, p. 18.
73. *Ibid.*
74. *Ibid.*, pp. 18–23.

and its publication in the *Diario Oficial*. Further, the companies were to pay full salaries to all union members for all the time that the strike lasted, as well as expenses which might be incurred by the union in connection with the strike.[75]

The union's "thirty-four points" were turned down by the companies on the same night they were received, May 29, 1937, and were characterized by the companies as a "mockery not only to the companies but also to the federal authorities." On Sunday, May 30, 1937, the Labor Board declared a "state of strike to exist," or declared the strike to be legal. The companies appealed to the courts against this decision of the board, alleging that Article 260 of the Labor Law had been improperly applied. This article, they argued, provided that a strike must have as its purpose the reestablishment of equilibrium between capital and labor or the execution of or compliance with a collective labor contract by the employer, or its revision upon expiration. They maintained that none of these three conditions was the case and pointed out that the contract in force would not expire for from six months to two years.[76]

Under a further personal appeal from President Cárdenas that a basis of settlement be found, the companies offered to increase the lower wages and improve certain social-welfare benefits. Their proposal was conditional, however, upon the acceptance of all the points contained in their counterproposal of April 12 and of the wage scale proposed on May 17. The union representatives rejected the counterproposals.[77]

The companies held that the failure of negotiations was attributable to the exaggerated demands of the workers, embodied in the draft contract, which had been approved by all the sections, so that the labor leaders felt obliged to deliver what they had promised the workers. On the other hand, some observers claimed that the companies showed only scant interest in reaching a solution to the conflict, especially since a precedent dangerous for private foreign interests might have been set. The companies published full-page advertisements in the Mexico City press attacking the workers, presenting fantastic figures as to the wages they were earning. The Mexican government felt that the companies believed that the lack of petroleum caused by the strike would provoke public sentiment against the oil workers so that they would yield

75. *Ibid.*, pp. 23–26.
76. Government of Mexico, *Mexico's Oil*, pp. 530 ff. This decision by the Labor Board, in accordance with Mexican labor law, does not imply examination of the merits of the case but merely indicates that all fundamental requisites stipulated by the law have been met.
77. *Ibid.*, pp. 29–30, 519–20.

to the companies.[78] Professor García Rangel, of the National University of Mexico, pointed out that the oil companies, which, since 1931, had practically suspended any publications, spent during the period from June to December, 1936, 220,634.16 pesos; and in the following six months, they spent 546,023.52 pesos, reaching at the culmination of the conflict (January 1 to March 18, 1938), 159,924.80 pesos in only seventy-seven days, thus attempting to sabotage the efforts of the oil workers by showing in various periodicals that they constituted a privileged class among Mexican workers.[79] The companies asserted that it was impossible for them to comply with the workers' demands because they were excessive and far beyond the companies' financial capacity to pay.[80]

On June 2, 1937, the *Mexican Labor News*, organ of the Workers' University of Mexico, commented that after almost a week, the strike was exerting a kind of "slow strangulation on all Mexican industry." Because the government-controlled oil company, "Petromex," was exempted by the union from the strike movement, gasoline and fuel oil were available for the national railroads, but all other transport, and particularly motor transport, suffered severely—as did industrial plants dependent upon petroleum and its derivatives for maintenance of operations. The paper commented editorially, "The strike is without doubt the most important which has ever taken place in Mexico." It went on to say that the companies' plea that the oil workers were the "spoiled darlings" of Mexican industry and that their wage level was far above the average for the country would be irrelevant, even if true, "for the question at issue is not whether the oil workers are already being well paid (they are not) but whether their wages are in any kind of proportion to the profits of their employers."[81] Reflected here was the doctrine of wages based on "ability to pay" enunciated by President Cárdenas in his Monterrey speech.

The labor paper commented further that the companies may have judged a strike not likely to be successful because of a division in the labor movement and the fact that the unions were in some disfavor with President Cárdenas, therefore believing that this was the best moment to provoke a trial of strength. The attitude of organized labor toward the oil companies was summarized in the following bitter terms:

The oil industry, built up in Mexico on a basis of fraud,

78. *Ibid.*, xlii, 519–20.
79. García Rangel, *El Problema Nacional Petrolero*, p. 17.
80. Government of Mexico, *Mexico's Oil*, p. xliii.
81. *Mexican Labor News*, May 26, 1937; *ibid.*, June 2, 1937.

corruption, theft, murder, subvention and of armed revolt, unparalleled in the country's history, is today the spearhead of imperialist penetration and domination. This nation-wide struggle against it is the first forthright battle between the Mexican people and the alien owners of the country's industry.

Even more than a fight for immediate economic improvements for a small section of the working class, the strike is a mighty protest of the popular masses of Mexico, led by the organized workers, against their foreign overlords. As such, whatever its immediate outcome and degree of success, it will have repercussions and reverberations in the months to come that will far transcend the issues at stake at present.[82]

Thus, it became abundantly clear that the oil question was being transformed into something far more than a mere labor controversy between employers and employees in a given industry.

82. *Ibid.*

X. Labor and the
Oil Expropriations:
Part II

On June 7, 1937, the union, undoubtedly after consultations
with the government, appealed to the Federal Board of Conciliation
and Arbitration on the ground that a "conflict of economic order" existed. This move meant that the financial condition of the companies
might be examined and they then might be compelled to accede to the
union's demands, without prejudice to their right to receive the increase of 13,000,000 pesos by way of wage and other benefits, over
their present contracts, which the companies had been forced to con-
cede through "strike pressure."[1] The companies immediately published
a statement making it clear that the 13,000,000-peso offer for the first
year had been conditioned upon the acceptance by the union of all
those clauses of the agreement not so modified, and upon the signature of a final contract to be binding upon the whole industry. They

1. Harlow S. Person, *Mexican Oil: Symbol of Recent Trends in International
Relations* (New York, 1942), p. 50; Compañía Mexicana de Petróleo "El
Águila," *Mexican Oil Strike of 1937* (*May 28–June 9*), pp. 29–30 (hereafter
cited as *Mexican Oil Strike of 1937*). The Constitution of 1917 carried the unusual provision that when a strike involved issues which, by their special nature,
cannot be resolved through the ordinary type of collective bargaining, appeal
to proper authorities may be made on the grounds of a "conflict of economic
order." The Federal Labor Law of 1931 added specific legislative provisions to
the general ones of Article 123.

now withdrew that conditional offer. The Labor Board, by a majority vote, on June 8, 1937, took jurisdiction of the economic issue raised by the union, and urged, as provided by the Labor Law, that the strike be called off. This was done at noon on June 9.[2]

The union's use of the "conflict of economic order" device was to set a precedent for future labor-capital-government relationships. The "economic order" clause had been put into the labor law originally at the behest of the employers, and it was designed for use in case an employer felt he could no longer live up to a union contract so that, lacking any statutory reason, he might allege "economic incapacity." Therefore, the companies denied that such a suit could be brought by the employees. This procedure was used by some mining companies in 1935 and by other employers subsequently, but it remained for the oil fight to permit labor to use the instrument for its own ends. Mexican labor law provides for two types of cases, as pointed out previously: those in "legal" conflicts and those in "economic" conflicts. An example of the first is a worker's filing a claim for unpaid overtime or for violation of a labor contract. This type of case goes to the conciliation and arbitration board as a complaint, just as other cases might go to a justice of the peace. Then follow allegations, answers, presentation of evidence, argument, and a decision by the judge or jury. The second type arises when, in a given industry or in a given region, circumstances of a general nature make it impossible to proceed under the existing conditions of labor-capital relationships. Then, as was seen above, the conciliation board is called on to intervene, as other arms of the government might in a case of public emergency that threatened to paralyze some phase of national life. Thus, in the oil case, the "economic capacity" theory became a boomerang. The labor lawyers argued: If companies could refuse to meet demands on the grounds of economic capacity, then the same theory could be applied to prove that the companies were able to meet demands. The 1936 Expropriation Law, which permitted seizure of the oil properties, was a direct outgrowth of the original "economic capacity" argument. This law was definitely aimed at employers who were closing down their factories, alleging excessive labor demands on the grounds that they lacked "economic capacity" to continue operations. The Labor Law made it possible for the government to

2. *Mexican Oil Strike of 1937*, p. 30; Government of Mexico, *Mexico's Oil: A Compilation of Official Documents in the Conflict of Economic Order in the Petroleum Industry, with an Introduction Summarizing its Causes and Consequences* (Mexico, 1940), p. 530.

take over such properties under the public utility clause.[3]

The Commission of Experts appointed in the oil case commented as follows concerning the procedure used:

> The present economic conflict between the Union of Oil Workers of the Mexican Republic and the oil companies affected by the strike arose under circumstances which in themselves make it outstanding among the labor disputes that have taken place in Mexico. It has in its origin, various factors even aside from the monetary value of the benefits involved. This conflict marks, if not precisely a stage in the relations between labor and the most important industries of the country, at least an experience of considerable significance in the field of social policy.[4]

The suit brought before the Federal Board of Conciliation and Arbitration on June 7, 1937, in the name of the Oil Workers' Union by Eduardo Soto Innes and Carlos G. Flores, included three petitions: first, that the representatives of the union be recognized as bringing suit of an economic nature against eighteen companies; second, that the companies be summoned to appear; third, that the dispute be tried in accordance with the law.[5] In the legal points of the case as submitted, the case was instituted for the establishment of new working conditions. It was asked that these new conditions be made retroactive to May 28, 1937, without prejudice to the right of various sections of the union to claim compliance with agreements or contracts under which the companies obliged themselves to make the new contract effective as of dates prior to May 28. Payment was asked to cover

3. J. H. Plenn, *Mexico Marches* (New York, 1939) pp. 41–44; "Plea of Amparo, December 28, 1937," in Government of Mexico, *Mexico's Oil*, pp. 812–20. See also "Mexican Expropriation Law," *Bulletin of the Pan American Union*, LXXI (1937), pp. 286–88; Mario Sousa and Enrique González Aparicio, *2 Conferencias sobre el Problema Petróleo* (Lectures delivered April 5 and 7, 1938, under the auspices of the Escuela Nacional de Economía of the Universidad Nacional de México) (México, 1938).

4. Government of Mexico, *Mexico's Oil*, p. 517.

5. "Conflict of Economic Order," in Government of Mexico, *Mexico's Oil*, p. 3. The companies named in the action were: Compañía Mexicana de Petróleo, "El Águila," S.A. (Royal Dutch Shell subsidiary), Huasteca Petroleum Co. (Standard Oil subsidiary), Pierce Oil Co., S.A., California Standard Oil Co. of Mexico, Petróleos de México, S.A. (in liquidation), Compañía Petrolera Agwi, S.A., Penn Mex Fuel Oil Co., Standard and Co., Richmond Petroleum Co. of Mexico, Explotadora de Petróleo "La Imperial," S.A., Sabala Transportation Co., Compañía de Gas y Combustible "Imperiod," Mexican Gulf Oil Co., Mexican Sinclair Petroleum Corporation, Consolidated Oil Co. of Mexico, S.A., Compañía Navería "San Cristóbal," S.A., Compañía Navería "San Ricardo," S.A., and Compañía Navería "San Antonio," S.A.

wages during the period between May 28 and the date on which the state of strike was ended, as well as for expenses incurred in the strike. It was also requested that the expert investigation prescribed by Article 572 of the Federal Labor Law be carried out.[6]

Many efforts were made in the press to show that Cárdenas had ordered the question submitted to arbitration. Labor maintained that such was not the case, but rather that the solution was first worked out by the leaders of the Oil Workers' Union and the National Committee of the C.T.M. and submitted to the Oil Workers' Convention on Friday night, June 4, 1937. Although rejected that night, the plan was accepted by a majority of the delegates the following night. On June 8, *El Nacional* carried an editorial to the effect that the president and the National Revolutionary party were not in favor of compulsory arbitration because it would interfere with the right to strike.[7]

In any event, the Federal Board of Conciliation and Arbitration designated a Commission of Experts, as required by law, to investigate the "economic capacity" of the companies named in the suit brought by the Oil Workers' Union and to render a report. The commission's members were Efrain Buenrostro, under-secretary of finance and public credit; Mariano Moctezuma, under-secretary of national economy, and Professor Jesús Silva Herzog, counselor of the Department of Finance and Public Credit. To assist this distinguished group were over one hundred assistant workers, including Lic. Miguel Manterola Flores, Professor Federico Bach, Lic. Moisés T. de la Peña, Ings. José López Portillo y Weber, Manuel J. Zevada, and Gustavo Ortega, as well as Lic. Gilberto Loyo and José B. Durán.[8]

The Committee of Experts analyzed the books of account of the companies, their oil sales and contracts, world market conditions, the historical background of the oil industry, its technical conditions, the problem of transportation and the relations then existing between the companies and their workers. In brief, according to the experts, all the aspects necessary to a complete examination of the dispute and to the answer to the question of whether or not the companies could accede to the demands of their workers were considered. The report, together with the findings, was submitted by the experts to the board on the day on which the term granted by the law expired.[9]

---

6. Government of Mexico, *Mexico's Oil*, p. 530.
7. *Mexican Labor News*, June 9, 1937.
8. "Report of Expert Commission," *El Trimestre Económico*, VII (1940–41), 57; Government of Mexico, *Mexico's Oil*, p. xliii.
9. Government of Mexico, *Mexico's Oil*, p. xliii.

Both sides claimed that the time allowed by the law for the study was too short.

The forty conclusions derived from the reports constituted the most severe indictment that had ever been made of the oil companies operating in Mexico, and in the last of these the commission asserted that the companies were able to increase their disbursements for wages and social services to their workers by the sum of 26,000,000 pesos over and above their costs for the same items during 1936.[10] Professor Silva Herzog insisted that it be pointed out that the increase was not to be 26,000,000 pesos over 1937 figures but rather over those of 1936. In other words, the experts believed that the sum of 49,000,000 pesos spent in 1936 should be increased by 26,000,000— that is, 75,000,000 in all, instead of the 69,000,000 pesos which the companies were willing to give. Consequently, what the experts advised amounted to an increase of only 6,000,000 pesos (about $1,600,000) above what the companies agreed to spend.[11]

The expert commission was unable to accept the data of the company books of account, particularly those of the Compañía Mexicana de Petróleo "El Águila," subsidiary of the Royal Dutch; they impugned the accuracy of these accounts because they found that "in many cases there had been a concealment of profits by means of numerous subterfuges and bookkeeping trickery, undoubtedly with the purpose of evading payment of federal taxes." The books of the companies showed an average annual profit for 1934–36 of about 22,000,000 pesos, whereas the commission held that these profits really amounted to approximately 55,000,000.[12] In reality, as Professor Gordon wrote, the extent to which profits were actually concealed by many devices, including the transfer of the profits to a company incorporated in some other country, is difficult to determine. The company experts argued that it would not have been to the interest of the companies to transfer profits from Mexico to some country in which they would have had to pay a high corporate income tax, such as the United States or England.[13] Nonetheless, as the ex-

10. *Ibid.*, p. xliv.
11. Jesús Silva Herzog, "Mexico's Case in the Oil Controversy," in Institute of Public Affairs, *Mexico and the United States: Proceedings of the Fifth Annual Conference Institute of Public Affairs Auspices Carnegie Endowment for International Peace, 1938*, p. 72 (hereafter referred to as *Mexico and the United States*).
12. Government of Mexico, *Mexico's Oil*, pp. xliv–xlv.
13. Wendell C. Gordon, *The Expropriation of Foreign-Owned Property in Mexico* (Washington, D.C., 1941), p. 112.

perts mentioned, in the directors' reports issued in London to the companies' shareholders in June, 1928, the following statement was submitted: "Following the example of other companies trading internationally, the Directors, as already announced, after serious consideration decided to advise its shareholders to agree to a transfer of certain of its assets, all situated outside Mexico, to a Canadian Company in exchange for shares in that company with a view to overcoming the difficulties of multiple taxation."[14] At a general meeting of the shareholders held on February 28, 1928, the directors' proposal was adopted. The only tax then existing in Mexico to which reference could have been made in the above statement of the board of directors, said the experts, was the income tax levied on profits—a tax which had recently been established in Mexico.[15]

The figures for total net profits for all the companies during the years covered by the report were, as given by both companies and the government, as follows:

Year	Company Figures (in pesos)	Government Figures (in pesos)
1934	20,533,000	51,480,000
1935	27,659,000	61,968,000
1936	20,477,000	55,567,000

Wendell C. Gordon, *The Expropriation of Foreign-Owned Property in Mexico*, p. 111.

Other significant conclusions among the forty reached by the commission of experts included the statements that (1) the principal oil companies operating in Mexico formed part of large North American and English economic units; (2) they never had been fully integrated into the country and that their interests had always been alien—at times, even opposed—to the national interests; (3) they had left in the country only wages and taxes, without, in reality, having cooperated in the social progress of the country; (4) the companies had earned enormous profits; (5) at a conservative estimate, they had recovered their invested capital over a decade earlier; (6) the oil interests had on more than one occasion influenced national as well as international political events; (7) the characteristics of the oil industry in Mexico had been modified in recent years—that is, from 1920 to 1924—and even in subsequent years—the major portion of production was exported, while in 1936 national consumption represented 15.86 per cent of heavy crude oil, 99.9 per cent of light crude, and 43.5 per cent of refined products; (8) nearly 60 per cent of

14. Government of Mexico, *Mexico's Oil*, pp. xliv–xlv.
15. *Ibid.*

Mexican crude oil production and derivatives was exported to the United States and England; (9) "El Águila," together with its affiliated companies, represented, during 1936, 59.33 per cent of total production—thus revealing a tendency toward monopoly; and that (10) the prices of articles of prime necessity which made the "basket of provisions" of a worker's family of five members, in the oil zones, had increased 88.96 per cent in June, 1937, in comparison with the 1934 averages.[16] The companies, in turn, objected that they had no part in establishing the price of the "basket of provisions" and maintained that no important changes occurred in the cost of living between 1934 and 1937 because, if it had, "the Union would already have taken action as provided by Article 423 of the Federal Labor Law."[17] Alejandro Carrillo held that the average daily wage of the oil worker in Mexico had been scarcely more than four pesos and that this very low wage had suffered actual reduction through increase in prices of the necessities of life.[18]

The commission found that the real wages of the great majority of the oil workers were lower than those earned by workers in the mining and railroad industries and that they were also lower than those earned in 1934 by at least 16 to 22 per cent.[19] On the basis of 1934, each peso of the nominal wage of a mining worker was reduced in purchasing power of foodstuffs to sixty centavos by the fall of 1937. That is to say, it would have been necessary for nominal wages to have increased 66.48 per cent during the three years for the workers to have been in a position to maintain their living standards as of 1934. Actually, nominal wages increased during that period by only 46.26 per cent; therefore, concluded the report, mining workers were earning lower real wages. In the case of railroad workers, each peso had been reduced to fifty-five centavos, and to fifty-three centavos in that of the oil workers. So the railroad workers, to enjoy, in mid-1937, the same purchasing power of foodstuffs, would have required an increase of 82.11 per cent in nominal wages during the three years. In reality, nominal wages increased only 26.7 per cent, so that the railroaders earned real wages 30.7 per cent lower. In the case of the oil workers, since the cost of the basket of provisions in their zones increased 88.96 per cent, and nominal wages only 41.28 per cent,

16. "Findings of Expert Commission," in Government of Mexico, *Mexico's Oil*, p. 592.
17. "A Claim of Companies Regarding Experts' Report," *ibid.*, pp. 611–12.
18. Alejandro Carrillo, *Mexico's Resources for Livelihood* (The Hague, 1938) pp. 22–23.
19. "Findings of Expert Commission," in Government of Mexico, *Mexico's Oil*, p. 592; Secretaría de Educación Pública, *Sobre el Petróleo de México: Conferencias* (México, 1938), p. 85.

218   *Labor and the Mexican Revolution under Cárdenas*

there was, therefore, a reduction from 1934 in the purchasing power of necessities of 25.17 per cent.[20]

The companies, on the other hand, claimed that nominal wages in the oil industry were higher than those of either the mining or railroad industry.[21] They held that the average daily wage paid per worker during 1936 reached 7.42 pesos in five major oil companies. "Data on wage scales obtainable from official, public, and private sources all confirm that this is the highest wage scale in the Republic, being almost double the average of daily wage scales paid by other leading Mexican industries," said the companies. They compiled the following table from the "Annual Report of the Department of Labor, 1936" to prove their point:

	Wages (*in pesos*)	
Industry	*Daily*	*Annual*
Petroleum	7.42	2,671.20
Light and Power	5.09	1,832.40
Street Railways	4.55	1,638.00
Mining	4.32	1,555.20
Textiles	3.13	1,126.80

Compañía Mexicana de Petróleo, *The Mexican Oil Strike of 1937* (*May 28–June 9*) (n.p., n.d.), pp. 56–57.

Comparison of rates of pay for common categories of work performed in the oil industry with analogous tasks in other industries was as follows:

Category	*Average Daily Wage in Nation*	*Average Daily Wage in Oil Industry*
Masons	1.89	4.20–8.40
Carpenters	2.05	4.00–8.40
Chauffeurs	2.26	4.80–6.00
Electricians	2.74	6.00–7.60
Stevedores	2.05	3.00
Blacksmiths	1.98	7.25
Unskilled labor	1.13	3.00–3.50

Compañía Mexicana de Petróleo, *The Mexican Oil Strike of 1937* (*May 28–June 9*) (n.p., n.d.), p. 57.

With regard to wages, the company position was that the average daily wage in the oil industry was over 7.42 pesos, while the cost of

20. "Report of the Expert Commission," in Government of Mexico, *Mexico's Oil*, p. 236.
21. *Ibid.*, pp. 612–13.

living in the oil localities for a worker and family of four was only 1.82 pesos per day. Hence they maintained it was obvious that the oil companies "provided a substantial margin of salary which can be employed at the personal discretion and for the personal enjoyment of the individual workers."[22]

Gilberto Bosques presented data that tended to uphold the company position with regard at least to nominal wages in the oil industry during 1934–35, when he found that during those years the average daily wage in the textile industry was 3.13 pesos; in tramways, 4.55 pesos; in mines and metal foundries, 4.32 pesos, and in the oil industry, 5.61 pesos.[23] He commented: "During the years 1934–1935 the legal minimum wage throughout the country varied between 0.75 pesos per day and 3.50. The average was about 1.25 pesos. Minimum wages in Veracruz, where most of the oil industry was located, averaged between 2.00 and 3.00 pesos. As a whole, the oil industry seems to have paid well above the minimum; the same cannot be said of many of the other industries, even assuming that their minimum requirements were lower."[24]

Perhaps it should be noted, however, that the average wage figure is not too meaningful, since, due to the great difference in wages of the skilled and the unskilled workers, the few persons in the industry earning unusually high wages tend to pull the average up considerably above what the majority of workers were actually earning. While it is probably true that nominal wages in the petroleum industry were higher in 1934–38 than nominal wages in other leading Mexican industries, it is also reasonably certain (as the labor officials maintained) that the cost of living was considerably higher and the conditions of work much poorer in the oil regions. In addition, it should be remembered that regardless of the nominal or real wage of the oil workers, their primary contention was that wages were not as high as the oil companies were able to pay.

The commission found that the annual rate of profit on the capital stock of the defendant companies averaged 34.28 per cent during 1934–36 and that the annual rate of profit on the unamortized invested capital of the companies averaged 16.81 per cent during 1934–36. In the United States, however, in 1938, the principal oil companies earned a profit of 7.13 per cent on their invested capital. Furthermore,

22. *Ibid.*, p. 59.
23. "Revista de Investigación Económica," as quoted in Gilberto Bosques, *The National Revolutionary Party of Mexico and the Six-Year Plan* (Mexico, 1937), p. 284.
24. *Ibid.*, p. 85.

the experts maintained, the capital invested in the petroleum industry in Mexico in 1935 represented only 0.73 per cent of the capital invested in the oil industry in the United States, whereas oil production in Mexico represented 4.05 per cent of production in the latter country; an investment of 8.64 pesos was necessary to produce a barrel of crude oil in Mexico as against 48.12 pesos in the United States, so that the investment required in Mexico amounted to 17.96 per cent of that required in the United States.[25] In short, the experts found that ". . . during the last three years (1934–36) the companies have earned very large profits; their financial condition must be considered as being extraordinary in soundness and, as a consequence, it may be asserted that, without prejudice to their present or future condition, at least during the next few years, they are perfectly able to accede to the demands of the Union of Oil Workers up to an amount of approximately 26,000,000 pesos a year."[26]

After submitting a tremendous volume of data and findings, the experts made specific recommendations for clauses to be included in the contract of general application, based upon the labor draft essentially, but with certain aspects not mentioned in that document. Perhaps the most significant of the new suggestions was that the contract should contain precise stipulations fixing the basis of a National Mixed Commission of the Petroleum Industry to be charged with deciding disputes arising between the companies and the workers under the contract. The specific functions of this commission were to be: (1) the study and solution of all disputes arising in the industry, exclusive of strikes, lockouts, suspension and termination of the contract, and claims for occupational hazards; and (2) the drafting of the clauses to regulate the collective labor contract with respect to seniority lists and transportation of workers and with respect to special provisions governing river, maritime, and dredging operations, as well as such other functions as are expressly assigned to it in the

25. Government of Mexico, *Mexico's Oil*, p. 592. In general agreement with these findings was a report of the Secretaría de la Economía Nacional (January, 1936), giving the following data: In the United States, the petroleum industry paid in taxes in 1934 $1,036,149,575 on the production of 908,065,000 barrels of oil for the year, a contribution of $1.14 per barrel, or 4.10 pesos per barrel in Mexican money. On the other hand, in Mexico, the total paid by the oil industry in taxes was $40,500,000 on a production of 38,171,946 barrels, a contribution of $1.06 per barrel, Mexican money, or approximately one-fourth part of that paid in the United States. In the United States, the petroleum industry pays taxes and salaries almost quadruple those paid in Mexico, and the return on investment of capital in Mexico has been almost triple that in the United States. (Secretaría de la Economía Nacional, *Industria y Comercio de México*, I [January, 1936], 11.)

26. Government of Mexico, *Mexico's Oil*, p. 592.

contract. The commission was to be composed of two representatives of the workers, two of the companies, and one of the Federal Labor Department—the latter to have voice and vote in all matters relating to economic and social benefits. In all other matters he was to have voice, but no vote. The Mixed Commission was to be considered the permanent agency for the arbitration of all disputes except those involving strikes, lockouts, suspensions, and termination of the contract. The net effect of this recommendation, it would appear, amounted to compulsory arbitration in all areas except those indicated, the exceptions allowing—at least theoretically—labor the right to strike and management the right to close the plants. The government representative would have the deciding vote in all "economic and social matters" contained in the collective contract which the commission was charged with creating.[27]

Beyond this commission there was to be also a committee formed for the purpose of organizing the leisure time of the workers of the industry—particularly since the forty-hour week created an important problem with respect to the proper use of leisure time, said the experts—to be composed of two employer representatives, two labor representatives, and one official representative—the last-named also to be paid by the companies. Also recommended was a Committee for the Prevention of Occupational Hazards of the Industry.[28] The degree of "paternalism" indicated by these proposals is perhaps astonishing to the worker of the United States, but it is quite understandable if one considers the nature of the historical development of the Mexican labor movement.

Toward the goal of "Mexicanization" of the industry, it was recommended that within a period of two years following the date of the signing of the contract, the employers should agree to fill technical posts with Mexican personnel, with one Mexican apprentice for each foreign technician or specialists to prepare for the transition from foreign to Mexican laborers. Workers immediately subordinate to each technician were to be given preference, provided they had the necessary training and obtained the approval of the Petroleum Board.[29]

Conforming with Section III of Article 111 of the Federal Labor Law, employers were required to furnish workers with comfortable and hygienic housing and to charge rentals which did not exceed one-half of 1 per cent per month of the assessed value of the houses, provided the plants were located within towns and employed more than

27. *Ibid.*, p. 592.
28. *Ibid.*
29. *Ibid.*, p. 593.

one hundred workers. Whenever the employer did not have available the number of houses necessary to satisfy this obligation, he was to pay workmen earning up to 10 pesos daily basic wage 1 peso per day, and those earning from 10.01 pesos upward, 1.50 pesos a day.[30] This regulation gave the greatest housing allowance payments to those earning the largest salaries. With respect to Clause 232 of the draft contract, which asked that the companies supply without charge lands owned or leased by them for cultivation by their workers, in areas up to five hectares per worker, when so requested by the union, the committee opposed this request on the ground that it would be too difficult in most cases to obtain tillable lands close to the industrial working centers and, further, that the oil workers would not have time for engaging in agriculture. In those cases in which such arrangements already existed, however, they were not to be changed to the worker's detriment.[31]

The companies were requested to furnish the facilities necessary for vocational rehabilitation; to dismiss workers properly expelled from the union; to deduct the ordinary or special union dues when so requested (the "check-off"); and to establish a forty-hour week, with the understanding that the workers should work five days of eight hours each—with pay for fifty-six hours. The day was to be divided into three shifts, and all workers required to work overtime were to receive double pay for the extra time.[32]

With regard to savings funds, the experts recommended that the employers deduct 10 per cent of the basic wages of their workers and contribute an equal amount to the savings fund. Interest at the rate of 6 per cent yearly was to be paid only on the amounts deposited by the workers, since these funds belonged to them. In the case of the company contributions, "which must be considered as a share in the profits of the companies," no interest was to be paid. Workers were not to be allowed to withdraw any of their savings before December 15 of each year, and only in cases of serious illness of the worker or of his relatives, or in cases of death, should the employers be authorized to make advances of a maximum of 50 per cent of the total outstanding to the worker's credit. The recommendations in this connection were, further, to require that the contract contain measures indicating precisely the use to which a part at least of these savings might be put, since "it is unquestionable that, in view of the fact that the workers will enjoy two days of rest weekly, *i.e.*, Saturdays and

30. *Ibid.*, p. 596.
31. *Ibid.*
32. *Ibid.*, pp. 596–97.

Sundays, it is to their interest to organize their leisure time, and it is also advisable that a certain percentage of their savings go to matters of collective benefit."[33] Surely, the organization of leisure time represented "paternalism" carried to the extreme.

By the rather unique suggestion that a part of the savings fund be used for "matters of collective benefit" the committee meant that "It likewise seems advisable, on the one hand, that the industrial workers come to the aid of the *ejidatarios*, whose economic and social living standards are extremely low, and, on the other, that stronger ties be established between the urban and the rural working classes."[34]

On the basis of the previous consideration, the experts held that the contract should expressly stipulate that from the savings fund 10 per cent should be taken annually to organize the leisure time of the workers by means of cultural or simply recreational "excursions," and in the fostering of sports, libraries, and other activities socially useful to the workers. Another 10 per cent of the same fund was to be presented each year directly to peasant organizations for the purpose of being utilized in works which "will redound to the economic and social benefit of these rural communities."[35] It might be pointed out that no mention was made in the draft contract of the use to which the savings were to be put; therefore, this is another instance in which the commission imposed a stipulation going beyond anything requested by the workers. In explanation of the recommendation, the experts took the following position:

> One of the fundamental needs the satisfaction of which the country has for many years been demanding and with ever greater insistence continues to demand, is the improvement of the cultural level of the working masses and the physical betterment of the population. The obligation of sparing no effort to meet those needs as fully as possible is not exclusively one of the state but also of the workers themselves and of the companies organized for purposes of profit which have obtained and are obtaining large profits from trade, from the manufacturing industries, or from the exploitation of the country's natural resources.[36]

Clauses with respect to vacations, rest days, layoffs, the furnishing of clothing to the workers, compensation for occupational illness or accidents, and the like, were suggested. These struck something of a

33. *Ibid.*, p. 597.
34. *Ibid.*
35. *Ibid.*
36. *Ibid.*

balance between the demands of the labor draft and the employer offer. On the other hand, in connection with death payments stemming from ordinary illness, the commission recommended a solution foreign to the proposals of either side to the dispute, namely, that the company should pay, in the event of the death of a worker as a result of ordinary illness, the equivalent of thirty days' wages to his family to cover funeral expenses, and that, in addition, the company should issue to each worker an ordinary life insurance policy in the amount of 2,000 pesos, either directly or through some national insurance institution.[37]

A pension system based on the following tabulations was to be instituted:

NOT DISABLED

Age	Years of Employment	Percentage of Wage
50–54	25	65
50–54	30	75
55 up	25	75
55 up	30	85

TOTALLY AND PERMANENTLY DISABLED

Years of Employment	Percentage of Wage
15–19	65
19–24	75
25 up	85

Government of Mexico, *Mexico's Oil: A Compilation of Official Documents in the Conflict of Economic Order in the Petroleum Industry, with an Introduction Summarizing its Causes and Consequences* (Mexico City, 1940), p. 600.

During the five years immediately preceding final qualification for pensions, employers could not discharge workers except for duly proven infamous causes, and they were obliged to reckon seniority for pension purposes from the date on which the workers first entered their employ, without taking into consideration any changes in the name or previous organization of the company.

It was suggested that wages of workers be based on the respective wage scales, with the understanding that the principle of equal pay for equal work, under equal job conditions, working time, and effi-

37. *Ibid.*, p. 599. The union had asked that the companies be obliged to pay sixty days' wages to cover funeral expenses, plus the equivalent of twenty-five days' wages for each year of employment, whereas the companies refused to grant this demand, but offered to pay ninety days' wages.

ciency, should prevail, without establishment of differentials based on age, sex, or nationality.[38] The need for a general increase in wages in the petroleum industry was stated as unquestionable, and the classification of workers made in the company draft of wage scales was decided to be the proper one "because it was drawn up with due consideration of the characteristics, conditions, and importance of each job, in general, of the responsibility which it is possible to assign each worker."[39] The committee further recommended that the National Mixed Commission of the Petroleum Industry designate a Sub-Committee on Wage Scales and Seniority Lists—to be composed of five persons: two company representatives, two labor representatives, and one government representative. To this group the companies and workers were, within a specified period of days, to make their recommendations and objections. The experts considered that the minimum wage of the industry should be 5 pesos a day, and that in cases in which a worker was earning, at the moment of the signing of the contract, a wage higher than the highest contained in the table of wage scales, he should continue to earn such wage. They concluded that, according to their estimates, any increase in cost to the companies, taking as a basis the conditions obtaining in December, 1936, would amount to 26,332,756 pesos.[40] (The union had asked for wage increases totaling 28,149,560 pesos, making the total *increase* of annual labor costs under the proposed new contract 65,476,840 pesos, and total amount labor costs under the contract proposed 114,611,460 pesos.)

The report concluded with the observation that, according to the consolidated balance sheet of the companies, the reserves and surplus amounted, on December 31, 1936, to 77,185,946.23 pesos; therefore, the companies were financially able to make such disbursements arising from the retroactive application stipulated by some of the contracts in force at the time for certain benefits, as well as expenditures for water works, schools, and buildings for medical services. With respect to the wages of the workers during the strike, the experts held that the companies should pay them "in view of their excellent financial condition and for reasons of equity. . . ."[41]

The report was submitted to the Federal Board on August 3, 1937. By August 25, El Águila had issued a denial to all the newspapers of Mexico that it was a subsidiary of Royal Dutch Shell, but made no

38. *Ibid.*, p. 595.
39. *Ibid.*, p. 601.
40. *Ibid.*, p. 602.
41. *Ibid.*

effort to explain why Shell was represented at the New York meeting called by the major companies to discuss the Mexican situation; nor did the statement explain why the English and Dutch ambassadors in Washington suddenly interested themselves in the fate of the oil companies in Mexico.[42] In the meantime, President Cárdenas condemned a local strike which began against El Águila in the Poza Rica field, claiming that the workers were pursuing "suicidal tactics" more calculated to aid capital and the reaction in general than their own interests. Charging "lack of discipline," the president pointed out the hardship the strike was causing not only to industry, the government, and the general public, but also to their fellow workers in other branches of industry. Cárdenas appealed to the workers "not to create new weapons for the capitalist class" by embarking on needless labor conflicts "which furnish labor's enemies precisely the arguments they are seeking for discrediting not only the labor movement but the present administration."[43]

In its first answer to Cárdenas' appeal, the Oil Workers' Union pointed out that the strike of its Section 30 in Poza Rica was not the work of an undisciplined group. Rather, it resulted from a deliberate provocation by the company which, it claimed, was part of a well-planned strategy of increasing the difficulties the public must inevitably have suffered in such a movement, for the purpose of arousing general resentment against the workers. The union claimed that the Poza Rica conflict could have been settled long before had the company been willing to enter into discussions and that the strike was provoked when the Águila refused to abide by the existing signed contract with its workers. Furthermore, the union maintained, the strike was shrewdly provoked by the company to achieve precisely such results as those mentioned in the "present message of the President."[44] After fifty-seven days' duration and while the gasoline supply of Mexico City was slowly drying up, the strike in the Poza Rica field ended, with the workers of Section 30 claiming many important gains, including 75 per cent of their salaries during the strike period, as well as part of the expenses of the strike itself.[45]

On November 11, 1937, in a statement for foreign news correspondents, the companies declared that they would refuse to make any increases in wages or social services to their workers other than the total of 13,500,000 pesos a year they offered at the time of the

42. *Mexican Labor News*, August 25, 1937.
43. *Ibid.*, September 15, 1937.
44. *Ibid.*
45. *Ibid.*, September 22, 1937.

general strike in May, in the event the board handed down an award in excess of that amount.[46] They held that the investigation by the experts lacked a rational and scientific base because it was limited to only three years in which there was a slight improvement in their profit position; for this reason, the companies stated, the commission's report could not reflect the real and permanent situation of the industry, since the years from 1924–29 saw boom conditions throughout almost the entire world, only to be followed (1930–34) by one of the worst depressions known to history. The company position was that no study of the oil industry in Mexico embracing a period of less than ten years could be said to represent a fair retrospective basis for investigation. The companies also claimed it was invalid to compare cost-of-living, wages, or amounts of taxes paid by firms, in countries of widely different habits, traditions, and customs— citing officials of the International Labor Organization as the authority for this position. Further, they objected that the commission had "lumped together" the economic capacity of the total number of companies, though it was certain that the weakest could not meet the payments, while in some cases the strongest could do more. The companies believed that the ability to pay of the weakest should be used, thus preventing the "sanction of the stone-age theory of the survival of the fittest."[47]

With regard to oil prices, the companies said that the prices used in calculations of profits were not real; that they were quoted market prices and not actual sales prices; and that there were many mysteries about the oil game that the experts did not know.[48] As to wage scales, the companies claimed they paid the highest wages in the republic, since they were almost double the average daily wage scales paid by other leading Mexican industries. They compared the scales of pay for certain common categories of work prevailing in the National Railways of Mexico during the year 1936 with those in the petroleum industry and found that in each case considered oil workers' wages were nearly twice as high. The commission claimed, in answer, that the examples did not cover a sufficient number of samples and that the mining and railroad industries paid more than the oil industry. At the same time, the experts admitted that the semiskilled and unskilled workers were better paid by the oil companies, that is, in relation to the railroad companies. The oil companies then took

46. *Ibid.*, November 18, 1937.
47. Government of Mexico, *Mexico's Oil*, p. 609; *The Mexican Oil Strike of 1937*, Vol. I, pp. 41–49; Plenn, *Mexico Marches*, p. 42.
48. Plenn, *Mexico Marches*, p. 43; *The Mexican Oil Strike of 1937*, I, 51.

the position that this statement alone was sufficient to destroy the validity of the assertion in conclusion No. 20 of the findings of the report that workers in the railroad and mining industries were better paid than those in the petroleum industry because, "following the most rudimentary and elementary logic, it must be taken into account that the unskilled and semi-skilled workers constitute the majority within a given industry and that the technical or skilled personnel is in the minority, therefore, it is false to state that the immense majority of the petroleum workers are paid wages inferior to those paid by railroads."[49] It would appear that the company position on this point was correct; however, the essence of the experts' finding in this regard seems to have been that regardless of *nominal* wages, the *real* wages of the oil workers were lower than those in the railroad and mining industries because the cost of living in the oil centers was so much greater.

Finally, the companies recommended that certain "adverse factors" be modified to permit the industry to enjoy a degree of prosperity "which will allow a margin over and above the rate to which so hazardous a venture is legitimately entitled" to the end that such margin be distributed by the way of an excess profits tax "not among the small and already privileged class of oil workers, but among the community as a whole. . . . This would be a wise application of social justice which would have as its objective that great desideratum: a more equitable distribution of the public wealth."[50]

After four months of listening to arguments and objections of both sides, the Federal Board of Conciliation and Arbitration (Group 7) rendered its award on December 18, 1937. The Mexican government claimed that the board accepted "almost in their entirety the opinions contained in the report of the Commission of Experts."[51] A close study of the award reveals, however, that Group 7 provided for less than one-half the original union demands in regard to wages and services, but upheld most of them with respect to participation in management.[52] The award left 49 groups of persons as confidential employees, or about 1,100 workers in the entire industry. It ordered a 40-hour week and 1,000,000 pesos for medical service improvements, with hospitals being maintained for each 1,500 workers. The union demands on pensions and vacations were reduced but ap-

49. *The Mexican Oil Strike of 1937*, I, 57.
50. *Ibid.*, p. 67.
51. Government of Mexico, *Mexico's Oil*, p. xlvi.
52. *Ibid.*, pp. 697–796; Workers University of Mexico, *The Oil Conflict in Mexico, 1937–1938* (Mexico City, 1938), pp. 25–28.

proved, as was its demand for housing. Foreign technicians were to be replaced in three years and scholarships of 150 pesos a month were ordered for 50 workers' children.[53] The average daily wage of the oil worker was increased to 8.83 pesos by the award compared to the 1936 average of approximately 6.97 pesos (or 7.42 pesos, according to the companies) in 1936.[54] According to El Águila, the award of the Labor Board gave unskilled labor the following wages:[55]

Basic wage	5.29	pesos
Rest days	2.12	"
Savings fund	0.74	"
Housing	1.40	"
Vacations	1.71	"
	11.26	"
Social Benefits	0.66	"
Total Effective Pay	11.92	"

Compañía Mexicana de Petróleo, *The Mexican Oil Strike of 1937 (May 28–June 9)* (n.p., n.d.), appendix iv.

The award's total cost, according to Group 7, would be 26,329,393 pesos (7,312,720 dollars); 8,657,647 pesos for wages and 17,641,746 for social welfare benefits.[56] The companies stated their ability to pay had been misrepresented and that the cost of the award had been underestimated, requiring 41,247,032 pesos additional rather than 26,829,393.[57] The 1936 costs of the oil companies, the costs according to the award of Group 7, and the costs of the award according

53. Workers University of Mexico, *The Oil Conflict in Mexico*, pp. 25–28.
54. Sindicato de Trabajadores Petroleros de la República Mexicana, Comité Ejecutivo General, *La Cuestión Petrolera: Sus Diversos Aspectos* (n.p., n.d.), p. 19.
55. Compañía Mexicana de Petróleo, *The Mexican Oil Strike of 1937*, III, appendix iv. Wages had already risen 61.95 per cent since 1934, according to the companies, and 48.53 per cent, according to the Mexican government; *ibid.*, p. 11; Gobierno de México, *El Petróleo de México: Recopilación de Documentos Oficiales del Conflicto de Orden Económico de la Industria Petrolera, con una Introducción que resume sus Motivos y Consecuencias* (México, 1940), p. 190. In spite of these nominal increases in wages, however, Group 7 of the Labor Board found that the real wages of the oil workers had been reduced by at least 88.37 per cent for the three-year period, the decrease claimed by the Commission of Experts. See "Award of Federal Board of Conciliation and Arbitration, Special Group No. Seven," in Government of Mexico, *Mexico's Oil*, pp. 716–17.
56. Standard Oil of New Jersey, *The Fine Art of Squeezing* (n.p., 1940), p. 13.
57. Compañía Mexicana de Petróleo, *The Mexican Oil Strike of 1937*, p. 45.

to the companies compared as follows:[58]

Item	1936 Costs (*pesos*)	Group 7 Award (*pesos*)	Company Estimate of Award Costs (*pesos*)
Payroll	44,622,642	61,691,104	73,111,242
Savings Fund	2,391,000	5,166,576	6,216,320
Social Benefits	1,951,357	6,466,958	7,935,734
Miscellaneous	171,620	2,141,373	3,120,355

Compañía Mexicana de Petróleo, *The Mexican Oil Strike of 1937 (May 28–June 9)* (n.p., n.d.), appendix i.

Total wages and salaries, including allowances for temporary, unhealthful, and overtime work and for vacation holidays and rest days, were to be increased under the award to an estimated 61,000,000 pesos, or more than 35 per cent. In addition there were various wage allowances under special conditions that would increase the total wage and salary cost another 6,000,000 pesos above the 1936 figure.[59]

The award provided for a five-day week of forty hours, each worker to have two rest days a week; if he worked on those days, he was to be paid triple time. It was also required that the companies provide each worker a life insurance policy of 4,000 pesos; this was to be financed by deducting one-half the premium from each employee's wage and matching this with an equivalent contribution.[60] As for housing, the award provided that companies with more than one hundred workers should provide housing or, in lieu of it, 1 peso per day for workers whose daily wages were 10 pesos or less, and 1.50 pesos for workers whose wages exceeded 10 pesos.[61]

Provisions for medical services and pensions were virtually the same as those recommended by the Experts' Commission; however, with regard to a National Mixed Commission for the Petroleum Industry, the board felt that such a commission would, with power to settle disputes, only duplicate its own function, hence it directed that a National Mixed Commission be instituted with duties that would

58. *Ibid.*, appendix i; El Águila declared the 90,383,651 pesos did not include 14,000,000 pesos for retroactive pay to May 28, 1937, 8,000,000 pesos retroactive pay prior to that date, or 1,300,000 pesos strike pay (p. 37).

59. J. R. Powell, "Labor Problems in the Mexican Petroleum Industry 1938–1950," *Inter-American Economic Affairs*, VI (Autumn, 1952), 5.

60. *Ibid.*, pp. 5–6.

61. *Ibid.*, pp. 6–7; Government of Mexico, *Mexico's Oil*, p. 772.

be, rather, the prevention of all conflicts which might arise between workers and employers.[62]

The award required the companies to replace foreign technicians with Mexican technicians within three years from the date on which the new contract became effective; the Petroleum Bureau of the National Economy was to establish the ability of the Mexican technicians.[63] With respect to what they termed "this plea for 'Mexicanization' of industry," the oil companies maintained they had no quarrel and that, on the contrary, they had given evidence of carrying out such a program, as careful perusal of payroll sheets would show how Mexican nationals had been increasingly superseding foreign personnel as rapidly as they could be trained and proven qualified to assume the responsibilities of the highly specialized and technical positions.[64]

Thus, the question became: "What course would the companies follow now that the Board of Arbitration and Conciliation had made its award?" There were several possibilities; the one they chose was to lead to nationalization of the petroleum industry and to consequences for the organized labor movement, for the companies, and for the Mexican government which could not, perhaps, have been foretold with complete accuracy.

Shortly after the board's decision was handed down, the companies announced they would not peacefully submit. Full-page advertisements in the newspapers of December 20 violently attacked the board and its experts' commission as ignorant, incompetent, and partial, and maintained that the commission's report upon which the decision was based was filled with errors of interpretation, judgment, and fact.[65] To the oil companies, the Labor Board award was not the result of over-zealous activity on the part of labor leaders but a deliberate step taken for the nationalization of the oil industry. From 1935, in their view, the constant demands of the workers, encouraged by agitators well-known in the official world, and the threats of strikes against an industry pictured as rapacious, were all the development of a previously-conceived plan to use the proletariat for future ends. As early as August, 1937, after the report of the board of experts was made public, the companies of American capital turned once more to the Department of State of the United States and re-

62. Government of Mexico, *Mexico's Oil*, p. 738.
63. *Ibid.* The Draft of Collective Contract fixed one year as the limit; the Export Commission recommended two years, and the board set the period as three years.
64. Compañía Mexicana de Petróleo, *The Mexican Oil Strike of 1937*, I, 38.
65. *Mexican Labor News*, December 23, 1937.

ported that it was apparent that the objective of Mexico was to take over the oil industry at a low price by reducing the value of the properties through regulation, labor awards, and price fixing.[66] The government of Mexico answered that, in the press campaigns, the companies exaggerated the salaries of the oil workers in an attempt to get public opinion arrayed against the workers in order to "conquer them."[67] To the company charge that the Mexican labor movement was radical and had irresponsible leadership, Alejandro Carrillo answered that (1) from October, 1936 to May 27, 1937, the oil workers patiently awaited the signing of their contract; (2) the oil strike lasted only eleven days when the workers decided to call it off to prove to the government and to the public that, once a conscientious and thorough investigation of the companies' financial and economic conditions was made, the facts would show the workers' demands to be correct and justified; (3) during the long investigation and the time the report was before the labor tribunals, the laborers continued at their jobs and maintained discipline; (4) the workers accepted the board's decision and the Supreme Court's decision; (5) and that in short, the oil workers waited from October, 1936, to March, 1938. He recalled that, in fact, they had waited not years but decades to get at least a small share of the wealth produced, to a great extent, by their efforts in their own country. Finally he denied the company claim that communism was rampant in Mexico and that the workers were taking private property into their hands, disregarding not only national but international law.[68] It is apparent, as Carrillo claimed, that the oil workers did not resort to violence, that they always kept their actions within the framework of the country's constitution and laws, and that, at the end of seventeen months of waiting, they were willing to accept only 50 per cent of what they had originally asked because they had voluntarily left the solution of the conflict in the hands of the labor authorities.

In early January of 1938, the Oil Workers' Union demanded payment of strike wages awarded by the board's decision, but the companies announced they would not pay the amount of approximately 1,300,000 pesos for wages due during the strike of May and June, 1937, on the two grounds that the amounts had been grossly over-

66. Donald R. Richberg, *The Mexican Oil Seizure* (New York, 1939), p. 30.
67. Jesús Silva Herzog, *Petróleo Mexicano: Historia de un Problema* (Mexico, 1941), p. 101.
68. Alejandro Carrillo, *The Mexican People and the Oil Companies* (Mexico, 1938), pp. 16–17.

estimated by the union and that the board itself had no legal jurisdiction in the case and, therefore, its decision was not binding upon
them. They announced that, in view of the fact that they had instituted injunction proceedings in the Supreme Court against the board's
decision, they would not pay the amount asked or any other amount
until the court had rendered its decision.[69] The injunction suit reached
the Supreme Court of Mexico on February 2, 1938; it alleged primarily that it was impossible to comply with the board's award equally
on the basis of the economic burden it would impose and its many
restrictions upon the several company managements with respect to
the administration and maintenance of control, and because of the
lack of the board's authority to render a binding decision, together
with many violations of the Federal Labor Law and the Mexican
Constitution.[70] On March 3, 1938, the Supreme Court denied the
injunction sought by the companies and upheld the decision of the
Board of Arbitration and Conciliation.[71] The companies renewed their
attacks in the press and denied their ability to comply with the board's
order. Further, they objected to the structure, method of appointment, and procedure of the Mexican Supreme Court, claiming that
Cárdenas removed from office those justices who were not in accord
with the defined principles and policies of his administration and
substituted for them justices of his own naming and confidence. They
pointed out that among the five members of the labor group of the
Supreme Court was Justice Xavier Icaza, "an avowed friend of
Lombardo Toledano. . . . and recognized throughout Mexico for his
own espousal of the cause of organized labor and the more radical
principles of socialism."[72] On February 15, the companies challenged
the right of Justice Icaza to sit in judgment upon the case on the
grounds of his "friendship with Lombardo Toledano (to whose potent
C.T.M. the Union of Petroleum Workers belongs) and because of his
constant intervention on the part of the Union in the controversy
between the companies and their workers."[73] On the morning of
March 1, 1938, as the court met to hear the draft of sentence in the

69. *Mexican Labor News*, January 6, 1938.
70. Government of Mexico, *Mexico's Oil*, pp. 809–43; Compañía Mexicana de
Petróleo, *The Mexican Oil Strike of 1937*, III, 39; Workers University of Mexico,
The Oil Conflict in Mexico, pp. 31–35.
71. Government of Mexico, *Mexico's Oil*, pp. 848–71; José Domingo Lavín,
Petróleo: Pasado, Presente y Futuro de una Industria Mexicana (México, 1940),
pp. 183–85.
72. Compañía Mexicana de Petróleo, *The Mexican Oil Strike of 1937*, IV,
15, 22.
73. *Ibid.*

injunction proceedings, Justice Icaza excused himself from participation in the case, stating:

> I, perhaps, will not be able now to participate actively, but I have already done my part. . . . I have intervened continuously, firmly and passionately. I have done this, in spite of being a Justice of the Court, because it is not a conflict of a legal character but a serious conflict of political character; not of a local political nature, nor even national, but international . . . it was, then, a political conflict and for this reason I took part in it, as a man of my times . . . and I am satisfied and even proud of the manner in which I have acted and of the results obtained. . . . Can there be a better pride than to have helped to bring about this campaign against imperialism?[74]

The companies claimed that here again was evidence that the case was considered, not in its "proper aspect of a local employer-labor dispute" to be determined strictly in compliance with the provisions of the labor law and the principles of right, but one of a nationalistic political character from which the oil companies were precluded, and that the suggestion that it was the duty of courts to study and decide such matters with a strictly political, and even "revolutionary," criterion instead of restricting their decision to the fundamental legal questions involved was simply an echo of President Cárdenas in Monterrey in 1936.[75]

On March 8, 1938, the Department of Publicity of the government of Mexico published a note in the country's newspapers to the effect that President Cárdenas had assured the company representatives that he would use all his power to enforce the decision of the court.[76]

Informed of the companies' position, *Mexican Labor News* commented, just eight days before the Expropriation Decree:

> In the opinion of most observers here, the problem in its present stage is less economic than political. The crux of the question now is whether or not the foreign oil companies will submit to Mexican law. So far, their attitude has been one of frank rebellion, and the Government has proceeded with marked forbearance in view of the insolent statements and scarcely veiled threats which have been issuing from the company camp. Present indications, however, seem to point to a settlement within the next day or two, so that drastic measures may not after all be necessary. Should the com-

74. *Ibid.*, p. 25.
75. *Ibid.*, pp. 25–26.
76. *Ibid.*

panies continue to refuse to abide by the Board's order, the next step will probably be the placing of an embargo on all their properties and the appointment of government "interventors" to manage their affairs and to establish the new working and wage conditions ordered by the Board.[77]

The day before expropriation, the same publication reported that, after a week of uncertainty, during which it was not known what attitude the foreign companies would finally adopt with respect to the order to comply with the board's judgment, on March 15, they formally presented a notice to the board that they were unable to meet the terms of its decision. It was felt that this action left the next step squarely up to the government and the workers, and that the Oil Workers' Union would probably petition the board to declare the existing contracts broken, "in view of the companies' defiance of Mexican law and their refusal to continue operations under the terms and conditions laid down by the labor tribunals and upheld by the Supreme Court."[78] There followed what should have been for the oil companies the ominous comments: "In view of the grave national crisis that would be provoked by any suspension of oil production as a result of the companies' refusal to obey the law, it is also possible the government may decide to invoke the Expropriation Act, by which it could nationalize the oil industry in the public interest paying the companies an indemnization based on a court valuation of their properties, over a period not to exceed twenty years."[79]

On Thursday morning, March 17, the union, invoking Section XXI of Article 123 of the constitution and Articles 601 and 602 of the Labor Law, submitted a petition to the board asking that the labor contract contained in the award of December 18, 1937, be decreed as terminated; that the companies be condemned to pay each workman three months' salary; and, furthermore, that the responsibility for the conflict be likewise determined.[80] The board granted the petition in the afternoon of the next day, the ruling being formally communicated to the companies between four and five o'clock. At ten o'clock in the evening of March 18, President Cárdenas addressed the nation, saying:

> To delay the process by further judicial proceedings would prejudice the economic well-being of the entire country— paralyze banking activity, public works, and the existence of

77. *Mexican Labor News,* March 10, 1938.
78. *Ibid.,* March 17, 1938.
79. *Ibid.*
80. Compañía Mexicana de Petróleo, *The Mexican Oil Strike of 1937,* IV, 38.

the government itself would be endangered. . . . I ask the entire Nation to furnish the necessary moral and material support to face the consequence of a decision which we, of our own free will, would neither have sought nor desired.

Another inevitable consequence of the presence of the oil companies, strongly characterized by their anti-social tendencies, and even more harmful than all those already mentioned, has been their persistent and improper intervention in national affairs.[81]

In words that go far toward placing him among the great leaders of our time, Cárdenas concluded:

As a logical consequence of this brief analysis, it was therefore necessary to adopt a definite and legal measure to end this permanent state of affairs in which the country sees its industrial progress held back by those who hold in their hands the power to erect obstacles as well as the motive power of all activity and who, instead of using it to high and worthy purposes, abuse their economic strength to the point of jeopardizing the very life of a Nation endeavoring to bring about the elevation of its people through its own laws, its own resources, and the free management of its own destinies.[82]

The Decree of Expropriation was brief and specific.[83] Company and world reaction to it was to be lengthy and varied. Whatever the economic motives of the action or the long-run repercussions, one thing was certain: "On that day, the Mexican people attained a unity which had never been possible before. An entire nation, accustomed for centuries to the perpetual humiliation of the underdog, reared its head proudly for the first time. Cárdenas gave his people a national consciousness, a sense of historic responsibility and above all else a feeling of pride."[84]

Further interpretative historical analysis was given by Verna C. Millan, when she wrote that there could be little doubt that expropriation signified much more than the conclusion of a labor-management conflict, adding, "For the Mexicans it was a gesture of courage, of confidence in the nation and the beginning of an era of independence in the economic as well as the political sense."[85] Apparently,

81. Government of Mexico, *Mexico's Oil*, pp. 877, 879.
82. *Ibid.*, p. 879.
83. *Ibid.*, pp. 880–81. For a Mexican government analysis of the effect of expropriation, see Secretaría de la Economía Nacional, *Memoria de la Secretaría de la Economía Nacional, Septiembre de 1937–Agosto de 1938* (México, 1938).
84. Verna C. Millan, *Mexico Reborn* (Boston, 1939), p. 199.
85. *Ibid.*

the companies were stunned. Expropriation was followed by an intensive campaign in the Mexican and foreign press which "for sheer distortion of facts has probably never been equalled."[86] The amazing feature of this historic moment was what Millan has called the "attitude of disdain" on the companies' part in that they thought "so little of Mexico that they did not give the enemy even the most rudimentary attention, and therefore all that happened later took them absolutely off guard."[87] On February 22, 1938, just a few weeks before expropriation, the C.T.M. held a general congress in Mexico City, and, in a speech by Lombardo Toledano, evidenced a forecast of the future: "Comrades, it seems to be inevitable that the moment will come when the petroleum companies will have to be replaced by representatives of the State and the Mexican workers in order to maintain petroleum production. We are ready and willing to assume the technical, economic, legal, moral and historic responsibility that befits a nation of free men."[88] The labor leader went farther to predict the almost impossible difficulties the future would surely bring to Mexico when he said:

> But this attitude of ours—there is no other, no other can be possible for us—may bring with it serious consequences for our country. The greatest part of the petroleum that our wells produce in American hands is consumed in Mexico, but that extracted from the wells under British control is used for exportation. To whom shall we sell our petroleum if these two great trusts, the Standard Oil and the Royal Dutch Shell, owners also of all the fleet of tankers, make it difficult for us to market Mexican petroleum? On the other hand, as soon as the industry falls into government hands and those of the workers, to what means will the oil imperialists resort in order to sharpen the artificial economic crisis which they themselves have created and which is now barely beginning?[89]

The possible economic-political repercussions of this state of affairs was considered by Lombardo: ". . . A moment may arrive in which the government will find itself facing a situation so grave that it will have to cut its budget and reduce public works, and this may produce unemployment for thousands of workers . . . . and spread disconcertion in many sections of the populace; . . . which will try to overthrow the government and install in Mexico a regime of oppression of

---

86. *Ibid.*, p. 200.
87. *Ibid.*, p. 204.
88. From speech by Lombardo Toledano, quoted in *ibid.*, p. 204.
89. *Ibid.*

Creole Fascist type in order to turn our national autonomy over to imperialist hands and, at the same time, end the conquests and triumphs of the Mexican Revolution."[90] He continued: "This is why, when the C.T.M., sharing the responsibility with the Union of Oil Workers, initiated the conflict to oblige the companies to sign a general collective contract, it weighed the consequences of its action and on several occasions conferred at length with General Cárdenas."[91]

If these words were not enough to convince the companies that drastic action was about to be taken by the Mexican government, surely they should have been awakened by a resolution passed by the Bloque Nacional Revolucionario in the Cámara de Diputados in a special meeting shortly before expropriation, stating that the situation in Mexico was of international importance and that the "threats of the oil companies to withdraw from Mexico would give Mexico the opportunity to nationalize the industry."[92] Further, in an interview with a group of senators following a series of discussions between the chief executive and the companies' representatives which had proved fruitless in solving the crisis, Cárdenas said: "The Government considers that it is passing through moments of exceptional importance to its economic and social situation, but at the same time we find ourselves faced with a magnificent opportunity for the country to adopt a truly independent economic and political position in opposition to the constant intervention which the Oil Companies have wished to exercise in our affairs."[93]

Virginia Prewett maintained that the decision to expropriate was made on March 10, 1938, when Cárdenas sent a note to Secretario de Comunicaciones Francisco Múgica, requesting that a stirring manifesto be drafted "to touch the hearts of the Mexican people and make them realize the necessity to defend the dignity of Mexico," since, by their disobedience, the oil companies had produced a situation in which the government was required to take over the industry to make the law respected.[94] By March 16, 1938, the C.T.M. had already notified workers and peasants to appear in the capital on March 23 at ten o'clock in the morning to take part in a popular demonstration.[95]

90. *Ibid.*, pp. 204–05.
91. From a speech by Lombardo Toledano, First General Ordinary Congress of the C.T.M., February 22, 1938, in Workers University of Mexico, *The Oil Conflict in Mexico*, p. 41.
92. "Los Diputados Apoyan con Firmeza al Gral, Cárdenas," *El Universal*, March 8, 1938.
93. *Mexican Labor News*, March 17, 1938.
94. Virginia Prewett, *Reportage on Mexico* (New York, 1941), p. 121.
95. "Incidente Sensacional en el Conflicto de los Petroleros," *El Universal*, March 17, 1938.

The Union of Oil Workers placed guards at all offices, terminals, and refineries at four o'clock in the afternoon of March 17, 1938, and stopped the movement of loaded tank cars, except for the railroad's use, together with all other operations in the oil industry.[96] The union then notified all its members to cease work at midnight of March 18.[97]

Mexico was faced, then, with imminent paralysis of a major industry. A high official of one of the oil companies had declared in New York on March 17 that his company had made the greatest concessions possible and that the government could not operate the industry, perform the services, or pay the wages the award required.[98] The chief problem, as Mexico saw it, was different: "It was the abandonment by the companies of exploitation of oil, which industry was a public utility, with the ultimate purpose being the paralyzation [sic] of transport, of industry, and of activities fundamental to the economy —and thus to force a change in government policy."[99] Secretario de Hacienda Eduardo Súarez declared that Mexico's policy toward foreign capital had not changed; that such capital was welcome, but had to obey Mexican laws and cooperate with the state.[100]

The issuance of the Expropriation Decree on March 18, 1938, marked the final act in the long-enduring struggle in Mexico over the subsoil wealth of the nation. A fundamental postulate of the government, nationalization of the subsoil and exploitation of its wealth for the benefit of the nation, had been achieved.[101] Mexican labor regarded the expropriation as the only act possible for Mexico in her life and death battle with oil imperialism; the act began a new drama in which the conquest of the oil companies had to be defended by every means in order to preserve the economic independence of Mexico.[102] Lombardo Toledano declared that the expropriation was not an isolated gesture, nor was it a demagogic act, but a nationalistic

96. "Mexican Oil Move Made in Advance," *New York Times*, March 23, 1938.

97. Workers University of Mexico, *The Mexican Oil Conflict*, p. 85.

98. "La Opinión de las Empresas," *El Universal*, March 18, 1938.

99. Merrill Rippy, "El Petróleo y la Revolución Mexicana," *Problemas Agrícolas e Industriales de México*, VI (July-September, 1954), 115; *Informe Que Rinde al H. Congreso de la Unión el C. Presidente Lázaro Cárdenas sobre Su Gestión de Septiembre de 1937 a Agosto de 1938* (México, 1938), p. 15.

100. Carlos Díaz Dufoo, "El Gobierno y los Capitales Extranjeros," *El Excelsior*, March 5, 1958.

101. Merrill Rippy, "El Petróleo y la Revolución Mexicana," p. 117. See also Secretaría de Gobernación, *Seis Años de Gobierno al Servicio de México 1934–1940* (México, 1940), p. 201; Miguel Manterola, "El Petróleo de México," *El Trimestre Económico*, V, p. 343.

102. Confederación de Trabajadores Mexicanos, *C.T.M. 1936–1941* (México, n.d.), pp. 527–28.

act, a legal act in the revolutionary tradition designed to obtain respect for Mexican institutions and to negate a deliberately premeditated attack on the constitution and public power of Mexico.[103] For Lombardo, the political revolution of a century before had at last produced the economic revolution and Mexico had begun to sense her historic destiny.[104]

The predictions of Lombardo with regard to the serious economic crisis which the oil companies could—and probably would—bring about were not long in coming to pass. The democratic countries were not in the market for Mexican oil; moreover, when Mexico tried to sell her oil elsewhere, there were no tankers available—"The international cartel had seen to that."[105] An Associated Press dispatch from London on May 3, 1938, stated that a complete boycott of Mexican oil had been ordered by Shell, with a threat of refusing to have any further dealings with any concern which shipped, purchased, or otherwise handled Mexican oil. In Mexico, Shell agents began spying to ascertain the movements of tankers, with the purpose of imposing full penalty upon anyone disregarding the boycott. This action was indeed peculiar, coming as it did from a company which had so recently claimed that it had no ties with El Águila. Fearing reprisals from England, the little nations with tankers dared not transport Mexican oil at any freight rate. When a few loads of Mexican oil did arrive at Swedish ports, British agents there claimed the cargo and held up the unloading. United States oil machinery and supply companies that sold to Standard declined to sell the necessary equipment to the Mexicans. They returned certified checks to the Mexican government and frankly said they dared not deal with Mexico for fear of Standard's wrath. In May, 1939, a contract for twenty-eight large trucks to be supplied from American manufacturers was cancelled because of pressure brought by enemies of Mexico. Other companies refused credit. When Mexico had tankers built in Italy, Great Britain would not allow delivery through her blockade; instead, she let them be confiscated by the Italian government after World War II had begun. With no cash and no market, Cárdenas—completely against his desire—had, in the end, to turn to Germany and barter oil for machinery parts. Only the Axis powers would buy Mexico's oil, and they bought well below the world market price. (How reminiscent of the more recent situation, when Castro turned to the Soviet Union! It is little wonder that Mexico, among a few other Latin American states, refused to follow

103. *Ibid.*, pp. 543–46.
104. "Independencia Económica," *El Universal*, March 19, 1938.
105. Hudson Strode, *Timeless Mexico* (New York, 1944), p. 340.

the O.A.S. resolution recommending severance of diplomatic and trade relations with Cuba; her memory of British and U.S. policy during her national crisis is not so short.) According to Strode, in 1939, Mexico's economic survival depended on trade with Germany, Italy, and Japan. "Oil company propaganda had the nerve to denounce the Mexican government bitterly for aiding the Axis war preparations—at the very time that United States boats were groaning under cargoes of scrap iron for Japan."[106] (Again, is there any parallel today when the government of the United States so recently chided Britain for selling buses to Castro while she herself has completed a huge wheat deal with the Soviet Union?)

Nonetheless, moral support for the Mexican labor movement and the government came from some quarters in diverse parts of the world. John L. Lewis cabled: "It is conviction of C.I.O. that both labor and employers should abide by decisions of legally constituted authorities in democratic nations. The C.I.O. has consistently accepted the decision of tribunals to which it has submitted its cases; it expects members to do the same. I see no reason why labor and employers in Mexico should not abide by this principal [sic]. When both sides have submitted their case to the tribunal of the land, then they both should submit to the decision."[107]

The International Federation of Trade Unions, of which the C.T.M. was a member, sent the following response to an appeal from the C.T.M. for aid: "In reply cable regarding long and heroic struggle Mexican oil workers against companies international labour movement expresses wholehearted sympathy and solidarity in struggle stop World workers heartily approve fight of Mexican government supported by whole working population stop Mexico's independence and vital conditions of workers being subordinated to interests international capitalism."[108]

The oil companies claimed that their profits had not been high in Mexico, but that, in reality, the average annual profit from 1927 to 1936 was only 4.25 per cent on the net value of their properties; that Group 7 was a special court that did not consider all the evidence and did not give the proper weight to that considered; that the Supreme Court acted as a political body and not as a court of justice and law, and that the Expropriation Decree was unconstitutional, since it was an act which benefited only one class and not the entire society—in short, that oil was not a public utility. They claimed that the Oil Workers' Union was used by the executive, judicial, and legis-

106. *Ibid.*, pp. 340–41.
107. *Mexican Labor News*, March 24, 1938.
108. *Ibid.*

lative branches of the government to institute a conflict of economic order which put the companies at the mercy of the government and the labor leaders. Further, they claimed to have been denied justice because the decisions of the boards were really the work of Jesús Silva Herzog, "only an economic theorist and by his own acknowledgment a member of the Communist party."[109] On April 4, 1938, the companies presented another plea of injunction in the Federal District Court, alleging that the Expropriation Law of 1936 was unconstitutional.[110] Defending the position that the law was constitutional, Antonio Carrillo Flores held: "There is no doubt that the Mexican Constitution, in spite of its having been drawn up according to the theory of economic liberalism, permits the Mexican State to operate as a modern state in economic matters. The specified limitations upon the activities of the state present no obstacle. . . . And if the modern world has complicated the collective necessities and responsibilities which the people turn over to the state, then the State has the responsibility of carrying them out."[111] On the other hand, López Aparicio maintained that the law was "in all ways illegal because of being in contradiction with Article 27 of the Constitution and with the system of individual guarantees provided by this basic document."[112] Commenting upon this subject, Professor Gordon pointed out that the Petroleum Law of December 26, 1925, had declared the oil industry to be a public utility. Regarding the legal question involved, it would seem that, if expropriation might be made only for reason of public utility, this provision in the 1925 law might well justify expropriation of the oil industry at any time.[113] Certainly, the question of the proper method for deciding which industries shall be considered as public utilities is a complicated one, and even in the United States the question has never been definitely settled. In *Munn* vs. *Illinois*, the ruling was handed down that such a decision was the prerogative of state legislatures; later, the courts reversed this position and took into their own care the right of deciding the question. Recently, however, it would seem that the situation has returned to the philosophy expressed in *Munn* vs. *Illinois* by virtue of the Hope

109. Manuel González Ramírez, *El Petróleo de México: La Expropiación Petrolera ante el Derecho Internacional* (México, 1941), pp. 21–24, 43. See also Compañía Mexicana de Petróleo, *The Mexican Oil Strike of 1937*, IV, 53–55.

110. *Mexican Labor News*, April 17, 1938.

111. Antonio Carrillo Flores, "La Constitución y la Acción Económica del Estado," *Investigación Económica (Revista Trimestral de la Escuela Nacional de Economía Universidad Nacional Autónoma de México)*, I (1941), 296.

112. Alfonso López Aparicio, *El Movimiento Obrero en México: Antecedentes, Desarrollo y Tendencias* (México, 1952), p. 218.

113. Gordon, *The Expropriation of Foreign-Owned Property in Mexico*, p. 120.

Natural Gas decision. In any event, there is no divine edict which decrees that Mexico should follow the example of the United States in this matter, and apparently the Mexican attitude was set forth most clearly in a lecture by Professor Mendieta y Núñez to the Fifteenth National Students' Congress in Oaxaca, when he explained: "If the public interest is evident, and even if the state can't pay immediately, the interest of the community may be placed over that of the individual, under the theory of social utility."[114]

At any rate, the company injunction plea, alleging the unconstitutionality of the Expropriation Law, was denied by the Federal District Court.[115] After considerable litigation, the Mexican Supreme Court, on December 2, 1939, denied the injunction plea brought before it. The court upheld the constitutionality of the Expropriation Law and settled two other questions of immense significance: the companies' claim to ownership of the subsoil petroleum was denied on the grounds that the Constitution of 1917 had vested such ownership inalienably in the Nation; and the Mining Code of 1884 and later legislation, which for the first time departed from that tradition, were either unconstitutional or did not, in fact, grant the surface owner absolute dominion in the subsoil wealth. Finally the court's decision likewise upheld Mexico's right to make deferred compensation, in accordance with the country's own laws, for properties expropriated. The decision meant that the government had the responsibility to pay the companies only the value of their properties—not the value of oil still under the ground, as the companies had asked.[116]

The Mexican government insisted that it did not decide on expropriation in obedience to preconceived plans, "as some ill-informed or unscrupulous persons have asserted"; rather, its decision to expropriate was forced by the "intransigence of the oil companies and because conscious of its enormous historic responsibility that was the sole means by which to defend the decorum and dignity of the country."[117] In a pamphlet answering Standard Oil's publication, *The*

114. Lucio Mendieta y Núñez, "La Expropiación por Causa de Utilidad Pública y el Buen Uso de la Medida," *Jus, Revista de Derecho y Ciencias Sociales*, II (February 15, 1939), 111–12. For an opposing point of view, see Roscoe B. Gaither, *Expropriation in Mexico: The Facts and the Law* (New York, 1940), p. 9.
115. *Mexican Labor News*, June 23, 1938.
116. *Ibid.*, December 7, 1939. For pertinent excerpts from the Expropriation Law, see Government of Mexico, *The True Facts about the Expropriation of the Oil Companies' Properties in Mexico* (Mexico, 1940), p. 83.
117. Government of Mexico, *Mexico's Oil*, p. 1. For a similar analysis of the Mexican Government's position on expropriation, see Banco Nacional de México, *Review of the Economic Situation of Mexico*, January 31, 1940, pp. 14–16.

Mexican Oil Seizure, the Mexican government admitted that the oil companies were always the object of spirited attacks, they being considered as the exploiters of the natural and human resources of the country. It was further explained that the aim of the various governments of Mexico in the last few years had been to place under the control of the nation, for the benefit of the Mexican people, this important industry on which the national economy depended to a large extent. This was to be accomplished, however, "through a slow and gradual process, by creating a national organization to undertake the exploitation of the national reserves," and then gradually to increase the production of the oil lands.[118] The Mexican position was that they were prevented from following this course, however, and were forced to expropriate "as the imperative result of a state of national emergency precipitated by the companies themselves."[119] In the words of Alejandro Carrillo:

> For the first time in our history, a decision of the Supreme Court was publicly disregarded; the oil companies repudiated its decision as they had also repudiated that which was handed down by the National Labor Tribunal. Here was then an evident case of arrogant, powerful foreign trusts, defying the law of the land, making naught of the country's sovereignty and dignity.
>
> No longer was the conflict therefore, one between capital and labor, but one of a very different nature; one between the oil monopolies on the one side, and the Mexican people and their Government on the other. All our people became inflamed with patriotic feelings. We would not tolerate our country's subordination to the Standard Oil and the Royal Dutch Shell.[120]

Still, the route by which the controversy was raised to such a high level was via a labor dispute and the application of the country's labor laws. And the immediate issue in the oil industry under the Cárdenas administration was to be, next to the question of marketing petroleum, how to devise a labor-management relationship under the new structure of public ownership. It is to this somewhat painful reorientation that the next chapter is devoted.

118. Departamento de Información, *Oil, Mexico's Position* (Mexico, n.d.), p. 5.
119. *Ibid.*, p. 8. See also Silva Herzog, *Petróleo Mexicana*, pp. 123–25.
120. Carrillo, *The Mexican People and the Oil Companies*, pp. 18–19.

XI. Labor and the
Oil Industry:
Expropriation to 1940

The role of organized labor in the oil industry, both before
and at the time of expropriation, has been recorded. What was the
nature of Mexican labor's role in operating the nationalized petroleum
wealth during the remainder of the Cárdenas regime? Shortly after
expropriation, President Cárdenas, in a manifesto on the oil question,
sounded an optimistic note and, at the same time, a warning, when
he said:

> Furthermore, the whole of the property of the oil com-
> panies has now been taken over and the management and staff
> has [sic] been selected from among our most capable techni-
> cal men and managers, and also from the more responsible
> members of the Union of Petroleum Workers, so that they
> may direct the course of our new national exploitation; I may
> here and now assert that the integrity of the managers thus
> appointed is absolutely beyond question and that the workers
> have, as a body, responded in a spirit of self-sacrifice which
> the Government is certain will be a factor making for efficient
> co-operation at all times.[1]

1. Lázaro Cárdenas, "Manifesto of Cárdenas on the Oil Question," in *Messages to the Mexican Nation on the Oil Question, 1938* (Mexico, 1938), p. 21.

Labor and the Mexican Revolution under Cárdenas

The chief of the Labor Department, Antonio Villalobos, also made an appeal for harmony in labor relations immediately following expropriation, requesting that workers abstain from exercising all their rights under the law. He was quick to add that abstention did not signify in any manner a renunciation of the ideals of labor or forget the struggle to establish equilibrium between the factors of production; it meant only that time should be given to prove that the government was sincere and, above all, effective. Therefore, the workers should not cause commotion in the national economy, but should remain confident that the labor authorities and the government of the revolution would know how to solve their problems.[2] Events were to prove that the Mexican labor leaders were not entirely content to accept this paternalistic role on the government's part, since many of them, particularly among the oil unions, were strongly influenced by anarcho-syndicalist doctrines and therefore desired that the industry be turned over to the workers entirely. (No doubt they recalled the campaign promises of Cárdenas, noted earlier in this study, in which he expressed his desire "to put the means of production in the hands of the workers themselves.")

The day after expropriation, the Oil Workers' Union sent out a circular to its thirty-two sections, setting forth a program that should be used by the new administration of the industry. Each section was directed to appoint a council composed of the local secretary, the secretary of labor, and a member of the Local Council of Vigilance, to be in charge of the workers of the industry to see that order was not altered. A general council was to be established for the purpose of co-ordinating the work of the local councils and to direct the workers in charge of the administration of the industry. This council was to be composed of persons designated by the state and the necessary members appointed by the general executive committee of the union. Nonunion workers were to remain outside the service, with the union utilizing only those of the nonunion workers whom it considered useful to the industry—such as doctors. This circular concluded:

> We wish to make known to all the sections of the union that the steps taken by Cárdenas toward the economic liberation of the country have the endorsement of all sectors of the country, and that furthermore the oil workers will work with enthusiasm with the state and the army to prevent any acts

2. Antonio Villalobos, "El Jefe del Departamento del Trabajo al Proletariado Nacional," *Revista del Trabajo*, II (March, 1938), 22.

of sabotage, or violence, and will respect the technicians and white-collar workers in the respective jurisdictions.

(Signed) For a society without
classes

Mexico, D.F. 19 March
1938[3]

The Mexican government had entered the oil business as early as 1923, when the Control de Administración del Petróleo Nacional was established, primarily to compete with private companies by drilling wells in the federal zones. In 1933 the Control de Administración was replaced by a more elaborate organization, Petróleos de México, S.A. This organization (Petromex) built a refinery at Tampico and constructed its own distributing outlets. A further reorganization of the government company was made in January, 1937, when the Administración General del Petróleo Nacional was established to explore the national reserves and to produce and refine oil for the government.[4] The day after expropriation, President Cárdenas ordered the founding of the Junta Administrativa del Petróleo, which was to consist of seven men named by the president—three to be selected from the Oil Workers' Union, three from the Secretaría de Hacienda, and one from the former Administración del Petróleo Nacional. The junta was to manage the properties of the expropriated companies and to carry out all operations related to exploration, exploitation, refining, and sale of products concerned with the expropriated companies.[5] The junta was headed by Secretario de Hacienda Eduardo Suárez and Secretario de la Economía Nacional Efraín Buenrostro. The industry itself was operated by the workers through trade-union committees until the national petroleum organization began to function. Trade-union locals were ordered to maintain production at all costs, and former company officials were permitted to remain at their posts if they joined the union.[6]

Eduardo Pérez Casteñeda, twenty-eight-year-old former confidential assistant to the Águila field superintendent, became manager of the rich Poza Rica field. Pérez had been barred from the oil company grounds when it became known he was a member of the union, and,

3. Jesús Silva Herzog, *Petróleo Mexicano: Historia de un Problema* (México, 1941), pp. 144–46.

4. Huasteca Petroleum Company, *Expropriation: A Factual Study of the Causes, Methods and Effects of Political Domination of Industry in Mexico* (New York, 1938), p. 6. (Hereafter cited as *Expropriation: A Factual Study.*)

5. "Petróleo: Sección Oficial," *Boletín de Petróleo y Minas*, IX, 22–23.

6. Nathaniel and Sylvia Weyl, *The Reconquest of Mexico: The Years of Lázaro Cárdenas* (New York, 1939), p. 298.

like so many of the new bosses in the oil industry, he had every incentive in the world to try to show that the Mexicans could manage as well as the foreigners.[7] Other officers of the union were appointed to many high positions in the various branches of the industry. The secretary general of the General Executive Committee of the Petroleum Syndicate became personnel manager of Pemex, and the secretary general of Section 4 became manager of the Atzcapotzalco refinery.[8] From the beginning, Silva Herzog claimed that many of these appointees were incompetent executives.[9]

Criticism from all sides found common ground in pointing up the danger of political control of the oil administration and hence, indirectly, of the Oil Workers' Union. Minor clashes occurred as a result of political appointments to posts in the oil fields and refusal of the union to recognize these appointments. The government established a liaison staff between the union and the oil administration to iron out differences, as there were indications that there would be more of them. One group of critics charged that expropriation was a device to keep the oil fields from passing fully into the hands of the oil workers, as might have happened through the process of an embargo. They charged, further, that (1) nationalization would benefit only the native bourgeoisie and labor leaders, who were getting good jobs in the administration; (2) no indemnity should be paid to the companies because such payment would mean continued subservience to foreign powers in one form or another; (3) the workers were forced to renounce all the concessions they had won from the companies; (4) the union leaders were trying to eliminate class consciousness among the workers and to substitute social patriotism; and (4) that, nevertheless, expropriation deserved the support of workers of the world for the sole reason that it tended to diminish the preponderance of imperialist capital in Mexico and gave the proletariat the possibility of conquering better positions in the struggle for socialism. From another direction came these accusations: (1) the only concrete gain from expropriation was additional prestige for Mexico in Latin America and an increase of Cárdenas' political stature; (2) expropriation was a Standard Oil maneuver to oust British interests and keep the Mexican oil in the ground; (3) payment of indemnity would force increased taxes on other industries; (4) the national economy would be impaired and permanent emergency measures would have to be

7. J. H. Plenn, *Mexico Marches* (New York, 1939), p. 26.

8. J. Richard Powell, "Labor Problems in the Mexican Petroleum Industry 1938–1950," *Inter-American Economic Affairs*, VI (Autumn, 1952), 8–9.

9. Silva Herzog, *Historia de un Problema*, pp. 237–38.

taken to protect the national currency; (5) Mexico's oil reserves would be exhausted at a faster pace than under private exploitation; (6) the Six-Year Plan would have to be sacrificed entirely, with the exception of its section on petroleum; and (7) the nation as a whole would have to postpone social and economic betterment for the exclusive benefit of oil workers and bureaucrats.[10]

Immediately after expropriation, oil production dropped sharply; in April, 1938, production was down 53.4 per cent from March, as pressure was reduced in the wells to alleviate the problem of storage which immediately became serious as daily exports fell from 199,886 barrels in March to 15,216 in April.[11] The income from oil exports declined from $2,500,000 (U.S.) in February, 1938, to only $300,000 two months later, leaving the industry to be supported by the domestic market, only 43 per cent of the expropriated companies' business.[12] The number of wells in production was cut from 981 to 756 immediately after expropriation.[13] The drop in production, both of crude and refined products, was due solely to sales reasons, for the Mexican workers, according to both Kluckhohn and Prewett, proved perfectly capable of operating the industry under difficult conditions and won praise from even their opponents for the way in which production problems were handled.[14] As Millan remarked, "Some people pointed to the lack of technicians, but overlooked one fact: the companies for years paid high salaries in dollars to American officials, who spent a great part of their time in activities that had little to do with oil; the actual bulk of the work fell upon the shoulders of the Mexican 'assistants.' When the showdown came, these 'assistants' were able to carry on the routine work as though the American experts had never been there."[15]

Production was complicated, however, by shortages of technical personnel, materials for refineries, and indispensable equipment for exploiting deposits of oil. The condition of existing equipment, found to be old and in such bad repair that further operation of it was a real danger, was further cause for difficulty in operating the indus-

10. Plenn, *Mexico Marches*, pp. 48–49.
11. Secretaría de la Economía Nacional, Dirección General de Estadística, "Petróleo," *Revista de Estadística*, I (March, 1938), 15. Ten to fifteen million barrels of oil jammed storage facilities at the time of expropriation, according to Frank L. Kluckhohn, *The Mexican Challenge* (New York, 1939), p. 133.
12. Standard Oil of New Jersey, *The Reply to Mexico* (New York, 1940), quoting petition of Petróleos Mexicanos to Labor Board in July, 1940.
13. Secretaría de la Economía Nacional, "Petróleo," p. 15.
14. Kluckhohn, *The Mexican Challenge*, p. 129; Virginia Prewett, *Reportage on Mexico* (New York, 1941), p. 137.
15. Verna C. Millan, *Mexico Reborn* (Boston, 1939), p. 225.

try.[16] Despite company claims of large investments in the industry, the government found the equipment to be antique, in need of repairs, and of deficient quality.[17]

The first major point of difficulty between labor and management in the nationalized industry was over the degree of control to be retained by labor in the attempts to reorganize the industry between 1938 and 1940.[18] Between March and June, 1938, discontent existed among some workers over the discontinuation of double pay for certain types of work, the laying off of some men, and curtailment of some social benefits.[19] Representatives of the companies reported soon after expropriation that workers received only 60 per cent of their former salaries and that some were convinced the properties would have to be returned and were even, on one or two occasions, agitating for such a return and opposing the C.T.M. leadership.[20] Merrill Rippy believed that only union discipline and patriotism held the workers to their jobs until June, 1938, even though the terms of the Labor Board award were not enforced.[21]

By June of 1938, Mexican production settled at about 65 per cent of the pre-March, 1938 level;[22] and on June 7, a decree was promulgated which placed the management of the expropriated oil properties in the hands of a public institution called Petróleos Mexicanos (Pemex), a public corporation to be directed by a Council of Administration composed of nine members, six of whom were to be named by the President of Mexico and the other three by the Oil Workers' Union. The chief executive was to appoint a president, a vice-president, and the secretary of the council from among the nine members, and the members of the council could be removed by agreement between the chief executive and the Oil Workers' Union.[23] At the same time, Cárdenas ordered the creation of a government corporation, Distribuidora de Petróleos Mexicanos to sell oil products

16. Secretaría de Gobernación, *Seis Años de Actividad Nacional* (Mexico, n.d.), p. 315.
17. Secretaría de Gobernación, *Seis Años de Gobierno al Servicio de México, 1934–1940* (Mexico, 1940), p. 206.
18. Powell, "Labor Problems in the Mexican Petroleum Industry, 1938–1950," p. 10.
19. Huasteca Petroleum Company, *Expropriation: A Factual Study*, p. 27.
20. J. H. Carmical, "Strong Stand by Hull Expected in Clash on Mexican Oil Wells," *New York Times*, March 31, 1938.
21. Merrill Rippy, "El Petróleo y la Revolución Mexicana," *Problemas Agrícolas e Industrales de México*, VI (July–September, 1954), 143.
22. Charles A. Thomson, "The Mexican Oil Dispute," *Foreign Policy Association Reports*, XIV, 122–32.
23. Confederación de Cámaras de Comercio e Industria de los Estados Unidos Mexicanos, *Análisis Económico Nacional 1934–40* (2nd ed.: n.p., 1940), p. 62.

belonging to the nation. The executive body of the corporation was a directing council of five members, three named by the President of Mexico and two appointed by the Secretaría de Hacienda, one to be from the Junta Administrativa del Petróleo and the other from the Administración General de Petróleo Nacional.[24]

In August, 1938, when the central administration attempted to remove and replace certain local officials in the Ciudad Madero region, Section 1 threatened a twenty-four hour strike. Even though this threat was not carried out, relations worsened rapidly as the management pressed for industrial reorganization to bring about co-ordination and greater economy of operation, since continued organi-zation of the industry along the lines of the former companies gave rise to serious duplication and waste in sales, advertising, accounting, engineering, and medical services.[25]

In July, 1938, the pay scales of the 1937 award were put into effect, with certain discounts; the workers received a 500,000-peso increase —still 8 to 15 per cent below the Labor Board award. No forty-hour week was established; nor were the welfare provisions of the award enforced. A housing project was begun for workers at Poza Rica, however.[26] In the main, the National Petroleum Administration of-fered the workers the full award given by the Labor Board, to be put into effect little by little, with both the government agency and the workers retaining the old employer-employee relationship. The part of the award pertaining to confidential, nonunion positions was not enforced, and in the entire industry scarcely ten employees were left as nonunion.[27] The provision regarding life insurance policies was not put into effect, but medical services and housing allowances, even above the terms of the award, were eventually paid.[28] The administra-tive employees probably benefited most from the expropriation, since the salaries paid them by Pemex were the highest in Mexico. Since unification of the industry did not leave enough managerial positions, superintendencies were invented in accord with the needs of the union leaders rather than the needs of the industry.[29] Seven sections of the Oil Workers' Union notified the general manager of Pemex that, while their salaries were being cut (in terms of the 1937 award), their leaders were gaining far more than before and wasting money on

24. "Petróleo: Sección Oficial," pp. 22–23.
25. Powell, "Labor Problems in the Mexican Petroleum Industry, 1938–1950," p. 10.
26. Nathaniel and Sylva Weyl, *The Reconquest of Mexico*, p. 304.
27. Silva Herzog, *Historia de un Problema*, pp. 215, 237.
28. *Ibid.*, pp. 228, 262.
29. *Ibid.*, pp. 230, 238.

automobiles and refrigerators.[30] Nonetheless, Pemex maintained, for the rest of 1938, the level of employment and granted most of the social stipulations of the Labor Board award. It painted service stations throughout the country, repaired pipelines, built new houses for workers, purchased four hundred tank cars, bought one tanker, paid full taxes, and lowered prices to the consumers—doing these things on 40 per cent of the former production.[31]

The survival of the industry through the summer of 1938 and its return to the international market, which began in the fall of 1938, made possible a new exploitation of its wealth, for the benefit, primarily, of labor. A surprising enlargement of the labor force began in the industry, although production was still far below the pre-expropriation level.[32] The number of employees, little more than 15,000 in 1934 and 1935,[33] increased to 15,895 in April, 1939, and to 23,073 in October of that year.[34] In the fall of 1938, 20,864 people were drawing wages of 55,000,000 pesos, according to the figures of the Secretaría de la Economía Nacional.[35] The average daily wage rose from 9.58 pesos in 1937 to 10.69 pesos in July, 1938, and to 12.12 pesos in 1939. The total labor bill increased from 56,000,000 pesos in 1937 to 69,000,000 pesos in 1940.[36] The industry operated successfully enough in 1938, despite the increased wage benefits, to enter 1939 with no great burden of deficit, even though in January, 1939, production was 32 per cent lower than in January of the previous year, and there were only 697 active wells.[37]

Employment in the oil industry boomed. In March and April, 1939, according to General Manager Cortés Herrera, employment in Pemex reached 19,316 persons, of whom 15,005 were permanent and 4,311 were temporary workers. Payment of salaries and benefits to the group required 6,500,000 pesos per month, 2,000,000 pesos above expenditures for that purpose in 1938. Cost of production per barrel had risen in the refinery at Minatitlán to nearly three pesos by April,

30. Kluckhohn, *The Mexican Challenge*, p. 222.
31. José Jorge March, "Mexico and Oil," *Labour Monthly, a Magazine of International Labor*, XXI, p. 177.
32. Merrill Rippy, "El Petróleo," pp. 143–45.
33. Miguel Mantolera, *La Industria del Petróleo en México* (México, 1938), pp. 68–70.
34. Silva Herzog, *Historia de una Problema*, pp. 242–43.
35. Secretaría de la Economía Nacional, *Anuario Estadístico 1941* (México, 1943), p. 676, and *Compendio Estadísticio 1947* (México, 1947), p. 312; Gobierno de México, *El Petróleo de México*, p. 119.
36. Powell, "Labor Problems in the Mexican Petroleum Industry, 1938–1950," p. 11.
37. Howard J. Trueblood, "U.S. Urges Mexican Oil Settlement," *Foreign Policy Bulletin*, XXVIII (October, 1948), 2.

1939. By October of that year, permanent workers numbered 16,141 and temporary ones 6,932, a total of 23,073, or 45.16 per cent above the March, 1938 level, according to Silva Herzog, general manager of Distribuidora de Petróleos Mexicanos.[38] At the end of 1938, employment was 22,206. Payments to the employees were 93,692,626 pesos, far above the 75,000,000 pesos recommended by the Labor Board in 1937—but there were many more employees. By October, 1939, payments to employees were at a monthly rate of 8,118,703.76 pesos, an increase of 89 per cent over April, 1938.[39]

The beginning of the European War in September, 1939 put an abrupt end to the ability of the Mexican oil industry to support such an expanded work force. Sales abroad in July, 1939, were more than $2,000,000; in September, they dropped to $800,000. The previous month Pemex had commenced to operate at a loss, and by the end of the year its deficit was 22,000,000 pesos.[40] In spite of the fact that it was apparent that the extreme financial crisis which followed could be traced directly to the drop in petroleum exports immediately following the outbreak of World War II in Europe, Silva Herzog maintained that the managers of the oil industry erred in offering the workers little by little to put into effect the provisions of the Labor Board's award. He continued to say that the error was explicable because it was desired to demonstrate the possibility of realizing what the companies had claimed was impossible—that is, to spend approximately 75,000,000 pesos annually for salaries and the welfare of the workers. Nonetheless, Silva Herzog continued: "Our judgment was in error because the award was given . . . to resolve a conflict at a given moment between the oil companies which operated in Mexico and their workers, imperialist companies which had always operated in Mexico, to get the greatest profits they could without thought of the welfare of their workers or the social progress of the country."[41]

Now, reasoned Silva Herzog, the expropriation and nationalization had put petroleum in the hands of official institutions whose goal was not only to profit but to serve the country; conditions were radically modified, including those that had served as a norm for the relations between workers and employers. By voluntarily accepting the award of the board, the new Pemex management inadvertently contributed to the attitude of the workers that the present union struggle was the

38. Silva Herzog, *Historia de un Problema*, pp. 241–42.

39. *Ibid.*, Secretaría de la Economía Nacional, *Anuario Estadístico 1941*, p. 676.

40. Secretaría de Gobernación, *Seis Años de Actividad Nacional*, p. 402; Silva Herzog, *Historia de un Problema*, p. 244.

41. *Ibid.*, p. 241.

same as had been the case when they were defending their rights against the foreign companies, yet the legal structure of the new in-situations of management was totally different from that of the old companies. The goal of the old companies was to exploit the petroleum wealth of the nation to obtain the greatest profits, while the goal of the new economic institutions was to improve the well-being of the Mexican people, the progress of the nation, and the achievement of economic independence.[42] Silva Herzog, the brilliant economist, rea-soned that now it was logical to expect also to change the nature of the worker-employer relations and to assume that the supreme aspira-tion no longer would be to put into effect the clauses of the award of December, 1937, for, under the system of private ownership, ac-cording to David Ricardo, the profits of the industry would go in major part to the stockholders and not to the workers. But under the new system, the gains would not go to stockholders, but to the nation as a whole, which would be to the interest of the workers, too. Silva Herzog pointed out that the thesis serving as the base of political action of revolutionary syndicalism consists in the affirma-tion that the disorganization of the capitalist system must be accom-plished by means of constant struggle, without rest or truce, since the workers are the only ones who can loosen their chains. This thesis, he maintained, is not applicable to a nationalized oil industry, in which questions of vital general interest are judged. "A public institution whose interest is the improvement of the economic and social life of Mexico should not be treated as a capitalistic business institution."[43] In spite of this "nice logic," it is quite probable that man does not behave as an "economic man," and relations between the mixed administration and the oil workers were not very cordial, despite the representation of the workers on the council.[44] In this connection Gordon noted that the relation of the unions to the gov-ernment administration was a problem difficult to solve since the workers objected to becoming state employees, thus losing the pos-sibility of applying union pressure upon their employers. They pre-ferred that the industry be turned over to them to operate, much as the railroads were turned over to the railway unions.[45] At the con-vention of the Oil Workers' Union, in Mexico City beginning June 1, 1939, the workers appointed a committee to investigate their true

42. *Ibid.*, p. 215.
43. *Ibid.*, pp. 217–18.
44. Confederación de Cámaras de Comercio e Industria, *Análisis Económico 1934–1940*, p. 67.
45. Wendell C. Gordon, *The Expropriation of Foreign-Owned Property in Mexico* (Washington, D.C., 1941), p. 89.

status, as a preparatory step to demanding that the industry be handed over to them if it was found that they were to be classified as government employees.[46] Silva Herzog countered that, "Some union leaders made the grave error of believing that one of their obligations consisted in defending their companions even when they were neither efficient nor honorable."[47] He argued that the failure of Pemex would not be a triumph for the workers but a clear road for the return of imperialistic enterprise in the country, and the industry's workers would not lose their chains but their source of work, their medium of a livelihood, and their revolutionary faith, and that they would acquire an immense historical responsibility. "The grave mistake of the Oil Workers' Union was to consider that Pemex was the same as the workers of the union and that the interests of the union were superior to those of the nation."[48] The professor hoped that the union leaders would in time reorient themselves to a new situation and work constructively for the oil industry and, therefore, defend the conquests made by their comrades.[49] In pointing out that the union leaders constantly affirmed their desire to co-operate with the government of President Cárdenas but would not sacrifice a single conquest already realized because they were forced to protect the temporary gains of their comrades without taking into account the new situation, Silva Herzog touched upon what may well be considered a standard dilemma facing a people in labor-management relations in a newly nationalized industry.

There were, in all likelihood, too many administrative posts, and these were much more highly paid than comparable posts in other, similar, industries. Silva Herzog recommended the abandonment of the Award of December, 1937, as a base for fixing relations between Pemex and its petroleum workers, and urged the formulation of a collective contract of work "not in accordance with what ought to be, but with what is," conforming to the reality of the moment and compatible with the economic capacity of the company, Pemex. He pointed out that the European war had placed the oil industry in a very difficult situation but that there would come better times, when the benefits conferred by the 1937 award could be considered as a minimum aspiration for the oil industry's workers.[50]

In October, 1939, the management announced that it would take

46. *Oil Weekly*, June 26, 1939, p. 46.
47. Silva Herzog, *Historia de un Problema*, pp. 218–21.
48. *Ibid.*, p. 218.
49. *Ibid.*, p. 221.
50. *Ibid.*, p. 222.

measures to unify the various sales agencies under the Distribuidora de Petróleos Mexicanos (the official sales agency established in July, 1938 and headed by Jesús Silva Herzog) so that all wholesale and retail outlets, advertising, and certain other services would be co-ordinated under one control.[51] The financial crisis facing Pemex was presented to Cárdenas in January, 1940, with recommendations being made by the managers for a reduction in expenses through reorganization of the industry.[52] Thus began a dispute among the management of the nationalized oil business and the workers and the Mexican government; this dispute occupied most of 1940. The report calling Cárdenas' attention to the crisis in Pemex was sent by Cortés Herrera, general manager of Pemex, and to the president of Mexico in January, 1940. It charged that (1) lack of discipline among workers resulted in zone and field offices' refusing to send to the central management payroll sheets to justify increased expenditures; (2) workers at the Minatitlán refinery interfered in the operation of the plant according to the director's plan and work was suspended, with resulting damage to the plant; (3) workers in Tampico refused to allow materials in warehouses to be shipped to other refineries, where they were needed; (4) the superintendent of the Tajan field arbitrarily increased his own salary and made the raise retroactive by taking money from funds entrusted to him; (5) medicines applied for in large quantities by the workers at the oil industry dispensaries were, in some cases, sold or bartered for other goods; and that (6) there were instances of pipelines' being tapped by workers, the stolen oil and gasoline then being sold privately.[53] Cortés Herrera ascribed much of the difficulty to the fact that the union controlled hiring and firing of the workers. This situation he held responsible for the continued decline in production.[54] (Later, he said that these charges were true in the summer of 1939, but that the situation had since been rectified.)[55] The Oil Workers' Union issued an official reply to the charges of Cortés Herrera, saying that they were based upon a memorandum addressed by him to the Oil Workers' Convention over six months previously. All the instances of bad administration and

51. *Excelsior*, October 16, 1938.

52. Secretaría de Gobernación, *Seis Años de Actividad Nacional*, p. 402; Silva Herzog, *Historia de un Problema*, p. 244; Confederación de Trabajadores de México, *C.T.M., 1936–1941* (México, n.d.), pp. 1032–33 (hereafter cited as *C.T.M., 1936–1941*).

53. Standard Oil of New Jersey, *Reply to Mexico*, pp. 96–98; Hal Burton, "Mexico Finds Oil Grab Was Gigantic Flop," *New York Daily News*, May 24, 1940; *New York Times*, January 6, 1940.

54. Gordon, *The Expropriation of Foreign-Owned Property in Mexico*, p. 89.

55. *New York Times*, January 7, 1940.

management mentioned in the memorandum referred to the period of confusion immediately following expropriation before it was possible to perfect the centralized system for the operation of the industry—when it was necessary to rely upon local and largely autonomous management councils which frequently conflicted with other, similar groups in adjacent zones. The union claimed that these conditions had totally disappeared by 1940. As for the charges of theft of oil, gasoline, and materials, the union stated that in all such cases the guilty workers had been punished by the loss of their jobs and, at times, by criminal prosecution. The union charged that publication of the report was an obvious example of bad faith on the part of the managers responsible for the purpose of discrediting the government-worker management of the industry.[56] On January 18, an afternoon paper of Mexico City published, under eight-column headlines, what it presented as an attack by the workers of Section 22 of the Oil Workers' Union against Cortés Herrera. The supposed complaint declared that the general manager was responsible for the failure of the Mexican government's administration of the oil industry and that Pemex had lost 15,000,000 pesos through corruption and inefficiency. Simultaneously, with the publication of this attack in Mexico City, the National Broadcasting Company announced by radio from New York that the Mexican petroleum industry had completely broken down and that General Juan Andreu Almazán, conservative candidate for the presidency, was preparing to launch a rebellion.[57]

Both Cortés Herrera and the Executive Committee of the Oil Workers' Union issued new statements refuting the story published by the Tampico and Mexico City press. The union declared that the report against the petroleum administration could not have originated in either its central committee or in that of any of its sections, and that it therefore repudiated the story. In commenting on the incident, *El Popular*, labor daily published in Mexico City, said that the whole affair was a part of a general conspiracy to slander Mexico's management of the oil industry in favor of the current campaign of the foreign oil companies to recover their properties. In support of this thesis, it pointed out the circumstances that the report was simultaneously issued by the anti-labor press in Mexico and by radio in the United States; that it was timed to coincide with the pamphlet on the Mexican oil conflict prepared by Donald Richberg, representative of the companies, and distributed by Standard Oil; that the daily paper, *El Mundo*, of Tampico, in which the story originally appeared, was

56. *Mexican Labor News*, January 11, 1940.
57. *Ibid.*, January 25, 1940.

founded by an "adventurer" named Villasana, "who received the machinery for the paper he edited as a gift from the Huasteca Petroleum Company."[58]

Late in February, 1940, after studying the situation in the petroleum industry, Cárdenas called a meeting of officers of the Union of Oil Workers and the managers of Pemex, reading to them a memorandum that suggested a reorganization of the industry to reduce its budget to its gross income.[59] The president expressed his sympathy and bond with workers of cities and farms, and referred to the co-operative spirit shown by the petroleum workers. He said, however, that the oil workers had at times confronted the management of Pemex and the General Administration of National Petroleum with an attitude similar to that shown toward the expropriated companies. This, he felt, was a mistake resulting from the failure by certain union leaders to recognize that the profits of the industry now belonged to the nation and the union and that attempts to injure the industry would injure the union itself.[60] The president then outlined the needs of the industry and stated that if the budget was to be balanced, it was evident to all that drastic cuts would be necessary in labor costs. In 1936, labor costs had amounted to about 20 per cent of sales; in 1938, they had risen to more than 35 per cent of sales, and in 1939 stood at 42 per cent. That the president considered labor costs to be the chief contributing factor to the unbalanced financial position of the petroleum industry was shown by the nature of his fourteen specific recommendations. This statement correlates with the previously held one that decreased sales of oil after expropriation accounted for the industry's difficulties. The same volume of labor costs loomed as a much larger percentage of the reduced volume of sales.

Cárdenas, in addressing the union leaders, went on to say that it was the obligation of the government to specify the measures necessary to reorganize the industry and put it on a sound financial basis. To achieve that goal, he recommended fourteen measures as absolutely essential and undeferrable: (1) to reduce the number of permanent employees to that prevailing on March 18, 1938, and to hire temporary employees only for special work and upon the recommendation of the Board of Directors; (2) to eliminate unnecessary positions; (3) to reduce administrative salaries to a more equitable level, taking into

58. *Ibid.*

59. Roscoe B. Gaither, *Expropriation in Mexico: The Facts and the Law* (New York, 1940), pp. 176–77; Silva Herzog, *Historia de un Problema,* p. 245; *C.T.M. 1936–1941,* p. 1030.

60. Silva Herzog, *Historia de un Problema,* pp. 245–53.

account that administrators in Pemex enjoyed greater compensation than in comparable positions in other industries; (4) to reduce the number of temporary employees to not more than 10 per cent of the number of permanent employees; (5) to increase the efforts of labor during regular working hours until conditions in the industry improved so that unnecessary expenditures for overtime could be avoided; (6) to suspend for whatever time was necessary the payment of rental allowances to employees receiving more than ten pesos a day; (7) to suspend the labor award of December, 1937, until such time as the industry could pay off the indemnification and modernize its equipment; (8) to relax rigid seniority requirements in filling indispensable vacancies arising from temporary absences or vacations; (9) to give the administration discretionary power in designating what positions were indispensable and necessary to fill when temporarily vacant; (10) to give the administration freedom to move personnel among zones or to new offices where their services were most needed; (11) to revise the administrative assignments to adapt the ability of personnel to the duties of the offices; (12) to weight ability heavily in promotions so that incentives for advancement could be maintained; (13) to reorganize the Union of Petroleum Workers to conform to the new nationwide organization of the industry and thus reduce the number of local sections, and (14) to include in the collective contract being negotiated a provision to give the administration complete freedom in choosing field superintendents.[61]

In many ways the recommendations of the president curtailed gains achieved by the Oil Workers' Union, particularly with respect to the surrender of some coveted powers of management acquired by labor; therefore, it is not surprising that the Union delayed its answer until April, when it replied point-by-point to Cárdenas' recommendations.[62] Among the most important of the union contentions were the following: (1) the difference in employment figures was attributable largely to differences in methods of classification, and also it was impossible to specify any definite number of employees to be hired, since this depended upon the extent of the developmental work in the industry; (2) indiscriminate elimination of unnecessary positions would damage legitimately acquired interests of workers; (3) administrative salaries should be reduced, but that the savings realized as a result should go toward putting into effect the Labor Board award of

61. Powell, "Labor Problems in the Mexican Petroleum Industry, 1938–1950," pp. 14–15.
62. Silva Herzog, *Historia de un Problema*, pp. 255–60. See also *Excelsior*, April 5, 1940.

December, 1937, rather than abandoning that award; (4) there should be no limitation on the "vested rights" in seniority; (5) the administration's power in filling vacancies and moving personnel should be determined by collective agreement; and (6) ability was largely a consequence of experience—therefore, the incentives for advancement were not subverted by seniority rules. The union agreed that (1) over-time should be reduced to the indispensable minimum; (2) the Labor Board award should be the minimum aspiration of labor, but they were reluctant to delay putting its provisions into effect; (3) changes in administrative assignments were acceptable if seniority rights were safeguarded; and that (4) the recommendation to simplify the structure of the Union would be referred to the component sections.[63]

With the union's reply to the fourteen points of Cárdenas was its own plan for reorganization of the industry—a plan suggesting that (1) the administration of the industry be centralized in one agency; that all connections with ministries of the government be eliminated from the administration of Pemex; (2) the union be given majority representation on the executive board of Pemex; (3) the provision for government representatives on the board of directors be appealed; (4) the Oil Workers' Union participate in every respect in the reorganization of the industry, and that (5) the discounts in workers' wages be ended after the reorganization.[64] Pemex presented its plan for the industry, modeled on the plans of the government, at the beginning of May, 1940.

Cárdenas met with the representatives of the union on May 25, and read a message in which he declared that, since the purpose of the reorganization of the industry was to make possible economies, it could not do so by raising the salaries of the workers by ending the discounts which kept wages below the level of the December, 1937, award.[65] The president agreed that Pemex should be placed under single management, but stated that the proposal could not be effected until exports became normal and legal arrangements could be made. With regard to placing a majority of union representatives upon the administrative board of Pemex, Cárdenas maintained that such a plan was not feasible because it would imply renunciation by the government of its responsibility to the country and the turning over to the

---

63. *Ibid.*; Powell, "Labor Problems in the Mexican Petroleum Industry, 1938–1950," pp. 16–17.

64. Silva Herzog, *Historia de un Problema*, pp. 260–61.

65. Oil workers' salaries were still 8 to 25 per cent below the level of the sums specified in the 1937 award, according to Hal Burton, "Capital Flees Iron Squeeze of Mexican Labor," *New York Daily News*, May 26, 1940.

union of an industry belonging to the entire people, *i.e.* the nation.[66] He proposed again that the union agree to suppress positions shown by experience not to be necessary, to accept a small cut in wages of administrative workers and laborers who earned over 700 pesos monthly, to consent to a suppression of overtime except in unusual cases, to permit the reduction of temporary employees until a reasonable number corresponding with the development of the industry was reached, to concur in giving general managers authority to shift workers to any part of the republic, and to end the creation of new positions without consent of the administrative council.[67]

The following day—May 26, 1940—the general managers of Pemex and the representatives of the oil workers on the administrative council began a series of conferences to work out details of the administration of Pemex, but no agreement was reached. Throughout June there were several conferences, but little agreement as to a program of action. Apparently labor opposition and resentment toward the administration of Pemex and the government grew stronger, and the issues were further complicated by a threat of schism developing in the Oil Workers' Union when workers of the general administration of National Petroleum raised objections to fusion of that organization with Pemex for fear of losing their jobs.[68]

In the meantime, the financial condition of Pemex became more serious. By June 1, 1940, its income for the year was 143,000,000 pesos, while its expenses were 211,000,000 pesos.[69] Production in the first four months of 1940 averaged only 110,000 barrels daily, and refineries were operating far below capacity. At the Mata Redonda refinery in Tampico, 60 per cent of the workers were involved in maintenance rather than production. According to one newspaper correspondent, the Poza Rica field was a hotbed of intrigue, suspicion, and even sabotage.[70] Finally, on July 15, 1940, Cárdenas ordered the management, unless the industry remedied its situation at once, to pay the savings funds due the workers in December, 1940, not in cash but in bonds and to suspend the payment of housing allowances for all workers earning from ten to twenty pesos a day. Overtime was ordered reduced to a minimum, and unnecessary positions were to be eliminated; wage scales were to be reduced, and administrative salaries of over seven hundred pesos a month were to be cut 10 per cent. Vaca-

66. Silva Herzog, *Historia de un Problema*, pp. 261–66.
67. *Ibid.*; *Excelsior*, May 21, 1940.
68. Silva Herzog, *Historia de un Problema*, p. 268.
69. *Ibid.*, pp. 265–268.
70. Burton, "Mexico Finds Oil Grab Was Gigantic Flop." See also Silva Herzog, *Historia de un Problema*, p. 190.

tions were to be six days each year, and a few minor reductions were also suggested.[71] In short, the order contained virtually the fourteen points recommended by Cárdenas in February.

When the President's orders were read to the administrative council, the workers' representatives left the room, but the remaining members constituted a quorum and ordered the execution of Cárdenas' decree. Cortés Herrera and Silva Herzog decided that the only way to carry out the wishes of Cárdenas was to bring a "conflict of economic order" before the Labor Board. They declared that expenses for Pemex had risen, that wages had been paid at the cost of suspending payment of federal taxes, not replacing materials needed for operations, stopping needed repairs and new work, ending royalty payments, and not filling contract obligations. Actually, they informed the board that bankruptcy faced the industry unless virtually all the recommendations in Cárdenas' order were put into effect. In addition, they asked authority to dismiss 25 per cent of the permanent working staff.[72] On July 27, the Labor Board, complying with the request of the general managers, suspended all existing work contracts, put the reorganization into effect provisionally and set a bond to be put up by Pemex to cover wages in case the reorganization was subsequently denied.[73] No experts to study the case were appointed until the end of September, and their report was privately made on October 31, 1940.[74]

An attempt by the Oil Workers' Union to obtain an injunction against the temporary award of the Labor Board failed on the grounds that a remedy was provided, since the award was only provisional. The union then began a campaign against the boards of directors of the three government petroleum agencies. It answered the charge that the poor organization of the industry was largely the union's fault by saying: "The Union declares itself openly against those high administrative employees who, forgetting their own origin, have attempted to conserve their own privileged position at the expense of the workers. . . . The real problem in the petroleum industry is the obvious incapacity of the administrators, the exorbitant salaries of functionaries, burdensome sales contracts, loss of markets, lack of attention to the domestic market, and ruinous purchase of materials."[75]

71. *Ibid.*, pp. 268–70; Standard Oil of New Jersey, *Reply to Mexico*, pp. 105–07.

72. *Ibid.*, pp. 109–13, quoting petition of Pemex to Labor Board. See also *Excelsior, El Universal, El Nacional,* July 26, 1940.

73. *El Universal*, July 27, 1940.

74. Silva Herzog, *Historia de un Problema*, pp. 271–72, 285.

75. *Mexican Labor News*, August 25, 1940.

The union openly accused the General Managers of Pemex and the Distribuidora of underhanded tactics in influencing President Cárdenas.[76] It ordered a twenty-four hour protest strike but retracted the order when the C.T.M., at the insistence of Lombardo Toledano, intervened in the dispute. In an executive meeting of the C.T.M., he favored the Presidential plan of reorganization and accused the expropriated companies of inciting the labor trouble.[77] After Lombardo took this position, the General Executive Committee of the Oil Workers' Union became more cautious. Many local sections, however, were irritated by the stand of the C.T.M. and by the apparent approval of it by their own General Executive Committee. Demonstrations of protest broke out, evidenced by sabotage and threats against the lives of the general managers.[78] Cárdenas accepted the resignation of Jesús Silva Herzog as general manager of Distribuidora and appointed Manuel Sánchez Cuen to replace him.[79] Silva Herzog was reported to have remarked that he was unwilling to deal with the "ruffians" in the Oil Workers' Union.[80] He claimed that some of the labor unrest could be attributed to machinations of agents of the former companies. A report to the subsecretary of state in July, 1940, declared that a leader of the oil union conferred in Cuernavaca with confidential agents of Standard Oil of New Jersey, Standard Oil of California, and El Águila, and it was agreed that the union leader should receive weekly sums of money in return for fomenting opposition among workers to reorganization of the industry, reduction of salaries, etc. Reportedly, large sums were offered to union leaders if a total strike in the industry were made effective. Company agents were said to be busy again among the workers in the oil fields. Reported actions of sabotage in the Mexican oil industry were investigated by the British government's intelligence service, since by 1940 Mexican oil was involved in World War II.[81]

On August 8, 1940, Cárdenas revoked the decree establishing Distribuidora de Petróleos Mexicanos and the Administración General del Petróleo Nacional, turning the work of both over to Petróleos Mexicanos. Pemex was now to be operated by a council of nine men, five to be named by Cárdenas and four to be named by the Oil Work-

76. *Excelsior*, July 27, 1940.
77. Silva Herzog, *Historia de un Problema*, pp. 275–76.
78. *El Universal*, August 4, 1940.
79. *Mexican Labor News*, August 12, 1940.
80. Prewett, *Reportage on Mexico*, p. 217.
81. Silva Herzog, *Historia de un Problema*, pp. 277–79; Betty Kirk, *Covering the Mexican Front: The Battle of Europe Versus America* (Norman, Oklahoma, 1942), pp. 175–76.

ers' Union. The president was to name the general manager and his assistant.[82]

The caution of the General Executive Committee of the Oil Workers' Union threatened to produce further schism in the ranks of the petroleum workers, since a number of the local sections wanted the committee to handle the reorganization problem, while other sections wanted to call a special convention to deal with it.[83] Some sections insisted that in the reorganization all "white collar" employees hired since March 18, 1938, be discharged.[84] Apparently the objective of this recommendation was the removal of all nonunion confidential employees whom the administration had appointed gradually to replace many confidential employees installed by the union immediately upon expropriation, when those of the companies had been barred from their offices. It would seem that the management groups took advantage of the favorable attitude of the General Executive Committee of the Oil Workers' Union, and with the aid of the secretary of labor they reached a conciliatory agreement to modify the Labor Board's temporary award of July 27, 1940. Given official status as an award by the Labor Board, this agreement gave the committee more power in the reorganization proceedings and provided for the appointment of four commissions to study the temporary reorganization and the application of reorganization procedure, economies proposed by the union, rules for filling vacancies, and the transfer of workers by the administration.[85] The announcement of this compromise agreement was not met favorably by some sections of the union, and their repeated demand for a special convention brought from President Cárdenas a declaration opposing such a convention as an attempted obstruction to reorganization.[86]

For some reason, the Labor Board, on September 11, rescinded its award of August 7 and reverted to the presidential plan of reorganization of July 25.[87] This development met with the opposition of the locals in the Federal District, and within a few days these groups met

82. "Decreto Que Deroga Los Que Crearon la Distribuidora de Petróleos Mexicanos y la Administración General del Petróleo Nacional y Modifica El Creó la Institución Denominado Petróleos Mexicanos, México, D.F., 8 de Agosto de 1940," *Boletín de Minas y Petróleo*, October 1939–June 1941, pp. 238–39.

83. *Excelsior*, August 2, 7, 1940; Powell, "Labor Problems in the Mexican Petroleum Industry, 1938–1950," p. 21.

84. *Excelsior*, August 7, 1940.

85. Powell, "Labor Problems in the Mexican Petroleum Industry," p. 21; *Excelsior*, August 10, 1940.

86. *Excelsior*, August 13, 1940.

87. *Ibid.*, September 23, 1940.

in a general assembly and agreed to strike against Pemex for not carrying out the reorganization in accordance with the agreement of August 7, 1940.[88] They claimed that the reorganization plan of July 27 discriminated against workers in the lower categories and that the problems of the industry were attributable to political considerations rather than the business background of the general manager of Pemex. The general assembly declared in favor of forming a central strike committee, separating from the C.T.M. if support was not received, and creating a new petroleum union in the central zone by divorcing themselves from the existing Oil Workers' Union. In the meeting, reportedly punctuated by cries against Lombardo Toledano and the C.T.M., the general secretary of the union, Rafael Suárez, pointed out that without any doubt such a strike as that advocated would be declared illegal, but that the Executive Committee was willing to follow the will of the majority.[89]

President Cárdenas condemned this strike movement as unjustified, and his position was supported by the C.T.M. and the major industrial unions, which united in opposition to the leaders of the Oil Workers' Union, specifying certain conditions to be met by the union before it would receive aid in the reorganization fight.[90] These conditions included remaining in the C.T.M. and submitting the conflict to that organization for solution—rather clear evidence of Lombardo Toledano's role in supporting the position of President Cárdenas in the dispute. Many members of the Executive Committee of the Oil Workers' Union had taken places in the nationalized oil industry and the new Executive Committee that followed had removed itself from close ties with the C.T.M. For a year or more, the C.T.M. had no information concerning developments between Pemex and the Oil Workers' Union. With the action of the Oil Workers' Union in the fall of 1940, however, the C.T.M. decided to intervene in the dispute, since it had originally aided the oil workers in their struggle to nationalize the industry and the national union organization did not feel that the problem was exclusively that of the oil workers.[91]

Because of the opposition to the strike movement by the government and the C.T.M., and, further, because of the lack of support from sections in the northern and southern zones, the strike was called off and, in its stead, a conference, attended by Lombardo Tole-

88. *Ibid.*, September 14, 1940.
89. *La Prensa*, September 14, 1940; Powell, "Labor Problems in the Mexican Petroleum Industry," p. 23.
90. *El Nacional*; *Excelsior*, September 21, 1940.
91. C.T.M., *C.T.M. 1936–1941*, pp. 1030–34.

dano, the Executive Committee of the Petroleum Workers' Union, and executive secretaries of unions affiliated with the C.T.M., was called.[92] A special commission of the C.T.M. was formed to co-operate in the reorganization of the oil industry "toward the interests of both the petroleum workers and the financial necessities of the industry itself." *Mexican Labor News* commented editorially that there was no question that the industry had to pare down operating expenses or go bankrupt, despite the fact that such economizing would result in the dismissals of some union workers who might be justified, from the individual viewpoint, in objecting to the shake-up. "But this problem boils down to one of considering the greatest good for the greatest number."[93] The announced objective of the special commission was to plan a detailed method of reorganization that would ". . . place the least possible burden upon the backs of the rank-and-file workers" and the results of the study were to be submitted to President Cárdenas, the oil workers' union, the industry executives, and the approaching national extraordinary session of the oil workers.[94]

The commission interviewed Cárdenas, presenting evidence of bad administration in Pemex, and obtained permission to make its own study of Pemex to see if interference with the workers' savings funds, rent allowances, and vacations could be avoided. The study found that Pemex's budget included unusually large estimates of expenses for the second half of 1940 and for capital investments in the same period. It revealed that the Mexican government received 53.4 per cent of the gross income of Pemex for taxes, capital works, and amortization of the expropriation debt. Large amounts were spent in amortization of capital in a single year. Further, the commission found that if investments for capital expansion were deducted from the deficit, Pemex showed a profit of 4.9 per cent. As a result of the study, the commission proposed that taxes should be collected in a fair proportion to the industry's income, that the industry should be operated on a commercial rather than a governmental basis, that a program co-ordinated with the economic situation of the industry should be worked out for capital improvement, and that contracts for low-priced sale of oil should be cancelled. The plan was presented to Cárdenas, who authorized its discussion by the commission with Pemex and the Department of Labor. Pemex agreed that the savings fund, house rent, and vacations should be retained, but insisted on a

92. *Mexican Labor News*, September 20, 1940.
93. *Ibid.*, September 27, 1940.
94. *Ibid.*

cut of five thousand persons in the working force. The commission's counterproposal was a reduction of four thousand workers from the number after March 18, 1938, the cut to be made by Pemex and the Department of Labor without intervention by the Oil Workers' Union.[95] Agreement was reached on the basis of the negotiations, and the immediate crisis appeared to have passed.

In spite of the efforts for a smooth settlement, however, the discharge of workers during the early phases of reorganization resulted in sporadic strikes in the Federal District.[96] President Cárdenas again intervened in the conflict, giving the Oil Workers' Union ten days to propose a better plan of reorganization.[97] The union appeared to be resorting to a system of delaying tactics which were designed to improve its bargaining situation as Cárdenas' term neared its end and his power weakened.[98] The petroleum management was asked to reinstate all workers "who were unjustly fired in the recent reduction in personnel," although this did not mean any reduction in the percentage of dismissals. Also, management was to present its lists of scheduled dismissals to the Oil Workers' Union twenty-four hours before they took place so that such dismissals as were in error could be corrected.[99]

While direct negotiations were proceeding between Pemex, the government, and the C.T.M., the committee of experts appointed at the end of September, 1940, was making its study. On October 31, its report (not made public) was presented to the Labor Board.[100] The committee, composed of Enríque Sarro, director of economic studies in the Banco de México, Miguel Manterola, economist and public accountant, and José López Portillo y Weber, petroleum engineer, declared that (1) new explorations were necessary to assure the life of the industry, which was exhausting existing pools of oil;[101] (2) the division of the industry into numerous districts, regions, and groups, was not justified in the nationalized form, (3) the percentage of crude treated in refineries from 1938 to 1940 was below that of 1936 to 1939; and that (4) total exports of crude and derivatives decreased 27.5 per cent in 1938–40 below that of 1936. The crude exports in

95. C.T.M., *C.T.M. 1936–1941*, pp. 1035–39.
96. *El Universal*; *Excelsior*, September 29, 1940.
97. *Excelsior*, October 4, 1940.
98. Silva Herzog, *Historia de un Problema*, p. 284.
99. *Mexican Labor News*, October 4, 1940.
100. Silva Herzog, *Historia de un Problema*, pp. 285–92.
101. This conclusion would seem to support the contention of Silva Herzog, former director of Distribuidora, that huge capital expenditures were necessary for further exploration and modernization of plant.

1936 were only 27.8 per cent of total petroleum exports but were 68 per cent in the first six months of 1940, and exports of refined gasoline decreased from 17 per cent of those in 1936, to 0.1 per cent in January–June, 1940. It is quite possible, however, that a partial explanation of the foregoing situation was the increase of domestic consumption, since the use of petroleum products within Mexico increased 34.2 per cent by January–June, 1940, over 1936. Gasoline consumption alone increased 53.2 per cent in that period.[102] The report stated that prices received for oil products within Mexico were virtually the same as before expropriation, while prices received for exported oil were considerably below the pre-expropriation level— at times, as much as 55 per cent below the former level.[103]

While the profits of Pemex had fallen from 15,000,000 pesos in 1938 to losses of more than 21,000,000 pesos in 1939, personnel had increased 45.16 per cent from April, 1938, to October, 1939, and was still 25.10 per cent above April, 1938, in September, 1940. By early 1940, wages and benefits to workers had risen 110 per cent above April of 1938.[104] At the same time, imposts on exported oil products increased from 11,000,000 pesos in 1936 to 21,000,000 pesos in January–June, 1940. Total sales were 256,234,501.06 pesos in 1936, while in 1939 sales for Pemex were 234,098,180.37 pesos —only 8.64 per cent below the companies' level; yet, the companies earned a profit of 53,235,265.29 pesos in 1936, while Pemex, in 1939, lost 21,574,279.54 pesos.[105] Because of the difficult financial condition of Pemex, payments of taxes and royalties had ceased.[106]

While the Labor Board was considering the report of the experts' committee, President Cárdenas announced that 25 per cent of the annual income from the petroleum industry would be turned over to the workers and that an additional 25 per cent would go into a reserve fund.[107] Commenting upon this action, *El Popular,* organ of the C.T.M., said in an editorial:

102. Silva Herzog, *Historia de un Problema*, pp. 285–92.
103. *Ibid.* It is likely that prices on exported oil products declined because of the decreased foreign demand for Mexico's oil from the democracies, resulting from the foreign company tactics mentioned previously.
104. Silva Herzog, *Historia de un Problema*, pp. 285–92.
105. *Ibid.* It may be, however, that these figures are not too meaningful in that the profit return has an entirely different significance in a nationalized industry from that in a privately owned one. Nevertheless, the difficult situation of Pemex was attributed by the committee not to a decline in income, but to increasing expenditures—particularly increasing labor costs. See Powell, "Labor Problems in the Mexican Petroleum Industry, 1938–1950," p. 24.
106. *Ibid.*, p. 24.
107. *Mexican Labor News*, November 15, 1940.

The reform decree concerning the petroleum industry which President Cárdenas has presented to the Chamber of Deputies reveals his constant efforts to safeguard national rights and recompense the working class as much as is possible in these times.

The C.T.M. approved from the beginning the President's attitude on the reorganization of the petroleum industry, because it believes that technical organization on the basis of strict justice for the workers constitutes a guarantee not only for the development and stability of the industry, but also for the workers themselves and for the economic independence of Mexico.[108]

The award of the Labor Board was rendered on November 28, 1940, upholding in its most essential aspects the administration of Pemex with respect to reorganization procedure; but, with regard to pay scales and allowances, it upheld the union's position.[109] A reduction of personnel to the level of that of April, 1938, was ordered by the board, and in addition there was to be a reduction of 10 per cent in the salaries of all workers earning over 700 pesos a month. Temporary employees were to be dismissed at the end of the period for which they were hired, without further responsibility by Pemex; the listing of confidential positions as given in the award of 1937 was to be followed: Pemex was to have full freedom in filling temporary vacancies without regard to seniority; the work week was to be forty-four hours; and workers could be moved freely during the reorganization. More pleasing to the union were the provisions that vacations were to continue at twenty-one days a year for workers with more than ten years' seniority; Pemex was to continue paying rent allowances of 30 pesos a month to workers earning ten pesos a day and of 45 pesos a month for workers earning above 10 pesos a day; the savings were to be paid in cash when due in December, 1940; and the petition of Pemex for a collective contract was denied.[110]

Although many problems were left to be settled by the incoming administration of Ávila Camacho,[111] the several investigations of Pemex produced by the end of 1940 a general "meeting of the minds"

108. *Ibid.*
109. Silva Herzog, *Historia de un Problema*, pp. 294–300.
110. *Ibid.*
111. For a discussion of these labor problems, such as the dismissal by the new Pemex management of 3,500 workers in the northern zone, and the signing of a collective contract in May, 1942, see Powell, "Labor Problems in the Mexican Petroleum Industry 1938–1950," pp. 26–29.

concerning the difficulties of the industry.[112] Despite the effects of controversy and war, Pemex in 1940 enjoyed a productive year. The value of exports, as well as of internal sales, increased. Investments in refining almost doubled and new drillings expanded to thirty-three holes, of which twenty-three were productive. The volume of crude treated in refineries continued to decline, reaching a level sixty-one points below the 1937 index; and employment dropped slightly at the end of 1940 to 21,309.[113]

In looking back over the events leading from the demand by the Oil Workers' Union for a new collective contract, through expropriation, and, finally, to the development of new modes of administration and labor-management relations in a nationalized petroleum industry, what can one conclude about the role of government and labor in these revolutionary events? Demonstrating a complete lack of comprehension of the historic moment of this stage of the Mexican Revolution were the oil companies, which apparently could think of no policy except to call on their governments to aid them in their attempt to maintain the nineteenth century *status quo*.

Organized into a rather homogeneous group, and affiliated with the powerful central, the C.T.M., the oil workers played a key role in presenting a draft of collective contract to the foreign-owned petroleum companies, in carrying the case to the Federal Board of Conciliation and Arbitration through the procedure of a "conflict of economic order" and in running the oil industry after expropriation.

By the end of 1940, the Oil Workers' Union still remained very powerful, although by this time it was quite noticeably influenced by the C.T.M. In labor-management relations after expropriation, it was apparent that the leaders of the petroleum workers were disappointed in their failure to get complete control of the industry and felt that President Cárdenas had not carried out his campaign pledge "to place the means of production in the hands of the workers."

In spite of this situation, however, the individual workers in the oil industry, between expropriation and the end of 1940, enjoyed a high level of employment, an increasing wage level, improved medical and social services, and they were able, even under many adverse circumstances, to know that in 1940 Pemex enjoyed a productive year.

In the words of López Aparicio, President Cárdenas not only initiated a revolutionary interpretation of the laws but stimulated the

112. Merrill Rippy, "El Petróleo," p. 150.
113. Secretaría de la Economía Nacional, *Compendio Estadístico 1947*, p. 312; *Anuario Estadístico 1941*, p. 676; League of Nations, *Monthly Bulletin of Statistics*, XXII, p. 365.

unification of workers, which led to the formation of the Oil Workers' Union and the C.T.M. These organizations, among others, served to consolidate the gains of the working classes and to unite more closely the people and their government.

The strict application of law, as they saw it, and respect for the Mexican courts, resulted in expropriation of the petroleum properties, a move caused by the refusal of the oil companies to abide by a decision stemming from a labor conflict. Thereafter, the dispute was of a very different nature; it became one between the oil companies, on one side, and the Mexican people and their government, on the other. The issue of national sovereignty was at stake.

For Lombardo Toledano and the organized labor movement, the political revolution of a century before had at last produced at least the beginning of the economic revolution, and Mexico had begun to sense her historic destiny. Nonetheless, the conflicts between the management of the newly nationalized industry and the union over reorganization reveal that the issues of job security, wages, and fringe benefits may be no more easily settled under socialized forms of production than under private ownership and management. The dictum of the Webbs that unions would still be needed to represent worker interests even in publicly owned industry was surely borne out in the sense of the application of it to the Mexican petroleum industry.

XII. Summary and Conclusions

Summary

The inauguration of Lázaro Cárdenas as President of Mexico marked a culminating phase in the revolt in that country against an economic policy based on classical liberalism, international capitalism, and colonialism.[1] Cárdenas and his followers accepted the postulate of the "class struggle" as inherent in the capitalist system of production, although it became evident, as economic policy unfolded, that they did not mean a battle to the death between the two contending parties—capitalists and workers—in the Marxian sense of the phrase. Rather, they saw the workers as struggling in a society of competing groups and maintained that the function of the modern state was intervention in behalf of labor as the weaker of the parties. In the view of "Cardenismo," to do otherwise was neither to act equitably nor to promote social justice. According to the pronouncements of the Six-Year Plan and the speeches of the Cárdenas wing of the P.N.R., the final goal of this policy was to be "socialization" of the means of production, although it was not clear whether productive property

---

1. Oscar Lewis, "Mexico Since Cárdenas," in Richard N. Adams *et al., Social Change in Latin America Today: Its Implications for United States Policy* (New York, 1960), pp. 285–86. See also Howard T. Young, "Mexico: A Revolution Gone Bankrupt," *The New Republic*, CXLII (April 4, 1960), 13–15.

was to be turned over directly to the workers to own and operate or whether the state was to own the property to be managed by and for the working class. As a matter of fact, both of these, as well as other, solutions became a part of the economic policy which evolved.

By the time Cárdenas took office as president, Lombardo Toledano had withdrawn from the Morones-dominated C.R.O.M. (Confederación Regional de Obreros Mexicanos) and organized a new labor central known as the C.G.O.C.M. (Confederación General de Obreros y Campesinos de México), which embraced some of the most effective trade unions of Mexico. After noting the campaign declarations of Cárdenas, the unions of this central intensified their organizing activities and began demanding wage increases and other improvements in working conditions; when these were not granted, work stoppages followed. In the first year of the Cárdenas government, the number of strikes against such industries as the Mexican Tramways Company, the Huasteca Petroleum Company, the Rafael Paper Mills, and the Mexican Telephone Company reached such proportions that the Calles-dominated wing of the P.N.R. issued, through a public declaration by Calles himself, a strong protest against the labor movement.

Labor reaction to this outburst of opposition from Calles was to issue a stinging reply and to form The National Committee for the Defense of the Proletariat—later to grow into the C.T.M. (Confederación de Trabajadores de México)—to support Cárdenas and his policy of encouraging continued trade-union activity. When Cárdenas replied to the Calles statement, he made it abundantly clear that the policy of his administration would be to support organized labor in its efforts to improve the living conditions of the Mexican masses, and he urged the workers to unite into one great national organization. From this moment on, the labor movement was wedded to Cárdenas, and he, in turn, to the labor movement. Cárdenas and labor supported each other; but the government kept, always, the upper hand. Few have characterized the marriage between Cárdenas and the labor movement more aptly than Hanson, who wrote: "In bolstering the position of labor, the government had strengthened itself against the influence of foreign interests in the economy, projected a powerful instrumentality in the form of the trade union to offset the emerging strength of locally controlled industry, but at the same time it had maintained its control over the instrumentality. The union was another vehicle of growing central control of the economy, to be used as the government saw fit.[2]

Soon after the break between Cárdenas and Calles, a labor-management conflict broke out in the industrial center of Monterrey, having its origin in a dispute at the glass factory there. Disagreement between the Lombardo-influenced labor leaders and the employers of Monterrey became so serious that President Cárdenas intervened personally in the conflict, setting a precedent that was to be followed many times afterward. In the now famous Monterrey speech, Cárdenas again insisted upon the complete and voluntary unification of the workers into a grand central with which the government would deal to the exclusion of other minority worker groups. The president introduced "fourteen points" which he considered to be the basis of his labor philosophy and policy. Among these principles were the ideas that (1) once in unions, workers should bargain collectively with employers (themselves organized) until all workers were covered by collective contracts; (2) wages should be based upon the economic capacity of the companies to pay; (3) the labor courts should render "revolutionary interpretations" of the laws; and that (4) employers who were weary of the "social struggle" should turn their plants over either to the workers or to the government.

About the time of the Monterrey episode, a Congress for the Unification of the Labor Movement was held in Mexico City, and the outcome was the formation of the C.T.M., a central federation composed of independent national trade unions, primarily industrial in structure. The outstanding figures in this new organization were Vicente Lombardo Toledano, a first-rate intellectual and veteran labor leader, and Juan Gutiérrez, head of the powerful Railroad Workers Union, both of whom had been active in the C.G.O.C.M., and the Committee for the Defense of the Proletariat. Although the organization was composed of unions of diverse strengths, philosophies, and tactics, it reflected, in general, the qualities of its head, Lombardo Toledano. The organization claimed to embrace no single socio-

2. Simon G. Hanson, *Economic Development in Latin America: An Introduction to the Economic Problems of Latin America* (Washington, D.C., 1951), p. 503. In this connection, see also Howard F. Cline, *The United States and Mexico* (rev. ed., enl.: Cambridge, 1963), especially Ch. 11, and *Mexico: Revolution to Evolution 1940–1960* (London, 1962). According to Cline, a considerable part of his material on Mexican labor is drawn from an unpublished manuscript of about thirty pages by Dr. Ben F. Stephansky, written in 1957 and called "The Mexican Labor Movement: An Interpretation of a Political Labor Movement." Stephansky was at the time a labor attaché in Mexico.

economic philosophy but to be merely a popular front of labor unions designed to strengthen labor's condition through both collective bargaining and the support of "revolutionary" political leaders. The C.T.M., containing perhaps a million workers, became the dominant labor central of the Cárdenas era, but it was not allowed to organize and attach the peasant organizations, who were organized by the P.N.R. into Leagues of Agrarian Communities, joined in the C.N.C. (Confederación Nacional de Campesinos), or the National Confederation of Peasants.

In addition to the regular trade-union activities, Lombardo Toledano and the C.T.M. leaders planned to establish a popular front with other groups in the nation with the C.T.M. as the focal organization. In this move, however, President Cárdenas took the initiative and reorganized the old P.N.R. into the new P.R.M. (Partido de la Revolución Mexicana)—a "popular front" party based upon the support of industrial labor, the peasants, government employees, the army, and the so-called middle class, or small businessmen. It is interesting to note that the labor wing of the "front" was separated into three distinct groups and was never unified under the C.T.M. In 1938, under the auspices of the C.T.M., a congress from which sprang the C.T.A.L. (Confederación de Trabajadores de América Latina) was held in Mexico City. This international group, composed of member labor centrals from the leading countries of South America, was headed by Lombardo Toledano and had the warm endorsement of the C.I.O. during the latter part of the 1930's and the war years of the 1940's.[3]

During the 1936–40 period, the organized labor movement of Mexico grew rapidly, and its influence in national economic affairs became quite apparent. Capital-labor disputes in many basic industries led to collective agreements, usually accomplished only after intervention of the Department of Labor and the rendering of decisions through arbitral awards which were generally in favor of labor and, in three notable cases, involving the National Railways Company, land in the Laguna district, and the foreign-owned oil properties; labor disputes culminated in serious strikes and resulted in expropriation and nationalization of these properties and their operation in greater

3. For a discussion of the change in the C.T.A.L., after the World War II years, see John Coe, "Recent Labor Disputes in Mexico and the Caribbean," *Inter-American Economic Affairs*, I (March, 1948), 55–70. "John Coe" is the pseudonym of a well-known analyst of Latin American labor.

or lesser degree by organized labor. In disputes with the Mexican Light and Power Company, the American Smelting and Refining Company, the Mexican Telephone and Telegraph Company, the British-owned Tramway Company, and the Cananea Cooper Company, labor unions achieved collective agreements that increased wages and improved working conditions. In the sugar and textile industries, as well as the baking industry of the Federal District, after the personal intervention of President Cárdenas, collective contracts raised to the status of "contract law" were signed. This situation was possible under Mexican labor law when two-thirds of the employers and employees in a given industry and region voluntarily agreed to such an industry-wide contract. In a few cases, such as the El Mante Sugar Mill, the Zacatepec Sugar Mill, and the lumber mills of El Chaparro—not of extreme importance from the point of view of the national economy—properties were expropriated and turned over directly to the workers organized into co-operatives to own and operate. This procedure, rather favored at times by Cárdenas, was not considered a solution to the labor problem by Lombardo Toledano and economists of influence in the government. In the vast majority of labor-management conflicts, settlements were reached by arbitral awards after voluntary submission of the disputes to the labor authorities.[4]

A different solution was attempted, however, after a strike of the railroad workers in May, 1936. Although a labor board declared the strike illegal, continued unrest on the lines resulted. In June, 1937, in an executive decree issued pursuant to the Expropriation Law of 1936 (which provided nationalization of properties for purposes of "public utility") the National Railways Company was expropriated. This move had the approval of both the railroad union and the C.T.M., and at the time, President Cárdenas promised to turn the nationalized properties over to the workers to operate, although title to them was to remain with the state. In April, 1938, the National Workers Administration of the Railroads was established and the Railroad Workers Unions took charge of management of the lines, but with several restrictions, concerning financial matters especially, held by the government.

Judgments differ as to the success of worker administration of the railroads during the period, but it is likely that many of the difficulties

4. For an authentic discussion of this development, see Research Center in Economic Development and Cultural Change of the University of Chicago, an article by Dr. Adolf Sturmthal, "United States Business and Labor in Latin America," U.S. Congress, Senate 86th Cong., 2nd Session, Document No. 125, Study No. 4. United States-Latin American Relations (Washington, 1960), pp. 277–97.

encountered resulted from factors developing long before labor management of the lines as well as being due to contemporary influences outside the province of the Railway Union. In the first place, the lines, when taken over by the workers, were in deplorable physical and financial condition, and no real national network of railroads had been developed. Secondly, the status of railroad workers under the Labor Law was a constant source of question, and within the Railroad Workers' Union there was never any real agreement as to the manner in which the properties should be handled. Finally, a series of serious accidents on the lines, followed by several changes in personnel and the structure of railroad management, gave an unfavorable press the opportunity to shape public opinion in opposition to the worker administration. It is a moot question whether somewhat improved conditions of the lines in later years, following a complete reorganization of management of the lines, was a result of the new direction or of generally more favorable economic conditions fostered by the outbreak of World War II in Europe and the resulting increased level of freight activity. If the entire set of circumstances at work in Mexico at the time is considered, the difficulties of the National Railways could not fairly be attributed solely to worker administration of the lines.

Even before nationalization of the railways had occurred, a general strike of peasants of the Laguna district in August, 1936, had led to intervention by President Cárdenas and to a decree in October of that year applying the Agrarian Code to the area; this resulted in a complete change in the system of property ownership and use by breaking up the previously foreign-owned landed estates into smaller, independently owned farms and into collectively run agrarian communities, or *ejidos*. This move was hailed as the first voluntary experiment in communal farming on a large scale in the modern epoch, and unquestionably it did represent a triumph for the various peasant organizations in the area which had struggled for years, against almost insurmountable obstacles, to achieve a new status for agricultural workers on the private *haciendas*.

After Cárdenas' inauguration, organizing activity in the Torreón region was intensified by Lombardo followers as well as by other groups. When landowners refused to sign a collective contract covering all the peasants in the area, the groups called a general strike, which was halted only after Cárdenas had promised to apply the Agrarian Code by October, 1936.[5] The president justified his pro-

5. For the thesis that the developments in the Laguna region were largely the work of organized labor, see Dorothy W. Douglas, "Land and Labor in Mexico," *Science and Society*, IV (Spring, 1940), 127–152.

cedure on the grounds of special climatic, financial, and technical circumstances pertaining to the raising of cotton and wheat in the area. It is clear that insufficient rainfall made irrigation on a large scale necessary and that this meant that small, independent peasants operating individually could have neither the financial resources nor the necessary experience to make individual farming for everyone a possibility.

In view of these circumstances, the new system was based on granting title to land to communal villages, the land to be cultivated in common, under the technical direction and with the financial assistance of the National Bank of Ejido Credit and/or its branch bank in the city of Torreón, the center of the Laguna district. Each community had its Ejidal Credit Society, in theory the local center of agricultural activity. A work chief, elected by the peasants themselves and subject to removal by them, directed day-to-day farming activities. The bank advanced roughly 1.5 pesos a day to cover expenses involved in planting seeds and the performance of normal farming operations and, after marketing the crops, any income remaining when the bank loans were repaid was divided as profit among the workers, according to the amount of labor performed.

With regard to the success of the system, opinions vary widely, as in the case of the railroad nationalization. As explained in the chapters on "Labor and the Laguna Experiment," an evaluation of the Laguna policy on the basis of production and income figures alone suffers major limitations in view of such factors as weather conditions, obstacles placed in the way of the program by the former private owners, the haste with which the new program was implemented, the method of allowing private owners to retain a limited amount of choice land (usually near the water supply), and lack of experience of the peasant organizations themselves. Some writers charge that the peasants simply changed masters—the Ejidal Bank replacing the *hacendado*. In any case, it is apparent that the workers had more control over the new master than they did over the old; that their consumption of better homes, clothes, food, pure water, and medical services was greatly increased; and that they had no desire to return to the old system.

In the case of the oil properties, workers in all the oil companies joined, in the early part of 1936, in the Sindicato de Trabajadores Petroleros de la República Mexicana (Union of Oil Workers of the Mexican Republic), which affiliated itself with the powerful C.T.M. Shortly after meeting its most pressing problems of internal organization, the Oil Workers' Union called a special convention in July, 1936, to draw up demands for a countrywide collective labor agreement covering all petroleum workers and presented the draft of the contract to the oil companies early in November, at approximately the same time as the passage, by the Mexican Congress, of the Expropriation Law. The union threatened to begin a general strike in the oil industry on November 10, later extending the time to November 29, and alleged "the discontent of petroleum workers, and the existing lack of economic equilibrium due exclusively to the diversity of working conditions obtaining in the industry."

The oil companies, on November 11, in separate but similar communications, declined to approve the draft of collective contract submitted by the Oil Workers' Union, but suggested that the Department of Labor call an employer-worker convention with a view of drafting a contract which might subsequently be made obligatory for the entire petroleum industry. Following a request by President Cárdenas, an agreement was signed on November 27, 1936, before the chief of the Labor Department, calling for an assembly of representatives of capital and labor which had as its purpose the formulation of a general collective contract, to be made binding by law upon the entire industry. On its part, the union agreed that no strike would be called for the duration of the session, and it was stipulated that all benefits of an economic and social character which might be granted under the proposed contract would be made retroactive to the date of its approval and signature before the Labor Department.

Progress was extremely slow, and there seemed to be a series of proposals and counterproposals, with the conditions complex and numerous. According to the Expert Commission appointed to study the dispute, the union demanded more than the companies were financially able to grant, but at the same time, the companies demonstrated no desire to avoid the conflict that was looming. The major points of difference seemed to concern which party should control the "confidential employees" and, consequently, the seat of policy-making in the industry; the demand of the union for replacing foreign technicians with Mexicans within a period of one year; and the clause providing that the companies furnish housing facilities. On the afternoon of May 17, 1937, the union formally reminded the companies that the term fixed in the November accord would expire on May 27 at midnight, when a general strike within the petroleum industry would begin if the discussions had not produced a contract. Upon the rejection by individual unions to which it was presented of a company counterplan, negotiations failed, and a strike was called for May 28 in the entire oil industry. At midnight of May 27, the Union called out all workers—

field, refinery, sales, technical, and office—and the long-threatened general strike began.

On Sunday, May 30, 1937, the Labor Board declared the strike legal; the companies appealed to the courts, alleging that Article 260 of the Labor Law had been improperly applied. In the press, the companies claimed it was impossible for them to comply with the Union demands because they were beyond the companies' financial capacity to pay. On June 7, 1937, probably after consultation with the government, the Oil Workers' Union instituted before the Federal Board of Mediation and Arbitration a "conflict of economic order," under Section I of the Federal Labor Law. This move meant that the union claimed that "economic equilibrium" was no longer being maintained and that the financial condition of the companies would be examined to see if they should be compelled to accede to the Union's demands, at least in part. The Federal Labor Board assumed jurisdiction of the economic issue, and the strike was called off at noon on June 9, 1937. A commission of experts was appointed, as required by the pertinent section of the Labor Law, to investigate the "economic capacity" of the companies and to render a report upon which the board was authorized by the law to make an award materially changing the conditions of work in the industry. The forty conclusions derived from the report constituted the most severe indictment that had ever been made of the oil companies operating in Mexico, and in the last of the conclusions the commission asserted that the companies were financially able to increase their payments for wages and social services to the workers by the sum of 26,000,000 pesos over and above their costs for the same items during 1936. They also found that the prices of articles of prime necessity which made up a "basket of provisions" for a worker's family of five members, in the oil zones, had increased 88.96 per cent in June, 1937 in comparison with the 1934 averages. The commission claimed that the real wages of the great majority of the oil workers were lower than those earned by workers in the mining and railroad industries and that they were also lower than those earned in 1934 by at least 16 to 22 per cent.

The companies made several objections to the experts' report and held that the procedure of instituting a "conflict of economic order" applied only to employers. Nonetheless, after four months of considering the case, the Federal Board of Conciliation and Arbitration rendered its award, which provided for less than one-half the original union demands in respect to wages and services but upheld most of them concerning participation in management. An injunction suit was brought by the companies before the Supreme Court on February 2;

the suit alleged, primarily, that it was impossible to comply with the award equally on the basis of the economic burden it would impose and of its many restrictions upon the several company managements respecting administration and maintenance of control, and because of the lack of authority of the board to render a binding decision inasmuch as there had been many violations of the Federal Labor Law and the Constitution of Mexico. The following month, the Supreme Court handed down its decision, denying the injunction asked by the companies and upholding the decision of the Federal Board of Conciliation and Arbitration.

The companies renewed their attacks upon the Mexican government and upon the Supreme Court itself. It became clear that the problem had become less and less economic and more and more political, and that it was international, rather than national, in its scope. On March 15, after the companies formally presented notice to the board that they were unable to meet the terms of the decision, the question was left to the government and the workers. Two days later, the Oil Workers' Union, invoking a clause of the Federal Labor Law, submitted a petition to the board which asked that the labor contract contained in the award of December 18, 1937, be decreed terminated; that the companies be condemned to pay each worker three months' salary; and that the responsibility for the conflict be likewise determined. The board granted the petition on the afternoon of March 18, and at ten o'clock that evening President Cárdenas addressed the nation, announcing the expropriation of the oil properties.

In such fashion, the Mexican labor movement and the government of Lázaro Cárdenas, supporting each other, rendered another—and perhaps the most important—stroke for the Mexican revolution in the rebellion against the policies of economic liberalism.

All the economic and diplomatic power of the oil companies was brought to bear against the nationalized oil industry of Mexico, but the outbreak of war in Europe and the policies of the Roosevelt administration in the United States toward the Mexican nation were the deciding factors that finally swung events more favorably toward the efforts of the Mexican labor movement and governmental policy. Soon, the problem became an internal, national one, restricted to the question of adjusting the great disturbances occasioned by the new relations of the factors of production in the oil industry. The focus of attention was bound to be brought to bear on the questions concerning the seat of decision-making power, exactly the goals to be sought by the petroleum industry under the new arrangements, and the methods for achieving them. On these vital questions it would have been surprising indeed had the government, the labor movement, and the Mexican public been able to realize the unity of opinion and action which had characterized the era of expropriation.

Antonio Villalobos, chief of the Labor Department, appealed for harmony in labor relations, requesting that workers "abstain from exercising their rights under the law, as well as from striking and other natural syndical actions." He assured the workers that they "should remain confident that the Labor Authorities and the Government of the Revolution will know how to solve their difficulties." As would have been expected, however, organized labor in Mexico was not entirely content to accept this extreme degree of paternalism on the part of the government. The day after expropriation, President Cárdenas ordered the founding of the Junta Administrativa del Petróleo, which consisted of seven men named by the president of the republic, three to be selected from the Oil Workers' Union, three from the Secretaría de Hacienda, and one from the former Administración del Petróleo Nacional. The Junta was to manage the properties of the expropriated companies and to carry out all operations related to exploration, exploitation, refining, and sale of products related to the expropriated companies.

The first major point of difficulty between labor and management in the nationalized industry was over the degree of control to be retained by labor in the attempts to reorganize the industry between 1938 and 1940. There was some labor opposition to various efforts of the national oil administration to reorganize the industry and to eliminate certain wastes, which were unnecessary under the unified oil organization. In the main, the national petroleum administration offered the workers the full award given by the Labor Board, to be put into effect little by little, with both the government agency and the workers retaining the old employer-employee relationship. The part of the award pertaining to confidential, nonunion positions was not enforced, and in the entire industry scarcely ten employees were left as nonunion. The provision with respect to life insurance policies was not adopted, but medical services and housing allowances were paid eventually, even above the terms of the award. Average daily wages for workers rose from 1938 to 1940, in spite of the fact that production fell by approximately one-third. The union representatives on the executive board of the oil company opposed efforts to reduce the working staff, and apparently the oil workers preferred that the industry be turned over to them to operate, much as the railroads were turned over to the railway union; and at a convention of the Oil Workers' Union in Mexico City, beginning June 1, 1939, the workers appointed a committee to investigate their true status as a preparatory step to demanding that the industry be handed over to them if it was found that they were to be classified as government employees. In pointing out that the union leaders constantly affirmed their desire to co-operate with the government of President Cárdenas, but they would not sacrifice a single conquest already realized, because they were forced to protect the temporary gains of their comrades without taking into account the new situation, Silva Herzog touched upon what may well be considered a standard dilemma facing a people in labor-management relations in a newly nationalized industry.

Most of 1940 was taken up with recommendations and counter-recommendations concerning the reorganization of Pemex, and President Cárdenas was convinced that the major item in the great increase of costs in the industry was the increase in labor costs. Therefore, his recommendations for reducing the expenses of Pemex dealt primarily with the curtailment of labor benefits. The Oil Workers' Union, Pemex management, and the government presented separate plans for the industry's reorganization. In mid-July, 1940, Cárdenas ordered the management, unless the industry immediately remedied its situation, to put into effect virtually the program he had recommended. Thereupon, Pemex management instituted a "conflict of economic order" proceeding before the Labor Board, claiming that bankruptcy faced the industry unless the recommendations of the president were put into effect and asking, in addition, authority to dismiss 25 per cent of the permanent working staff. On July 27, the Labor Board suspended all existing work contracts and put the reorganization plan into effect provisionally. Experts to study the case were not appointed until the end of September, and their report was made privately on October 31, 1940. The Oil Workers' Union had, in the meantime, begun an active campaign against the managers, making it clear that they desired an arrangement which amounted to a type of *syndical socialism*; the government of Cárdenas, backed by the C.T.M., desired a system which could be more properly characterized as *state socialism*. In August, 1940, Cárdenas, with the support of Lombardo Toledano, united the administration of the industry into one agency, a council of nine men. Five were to be named by the president and four by the Oil Workers' Union. The new management reached a compromise agreement to modify the Labor Board's temporary award of July 27, 1940, but the Oil Workers' Union was apparently dissatisfied with this arrangement and there were repeated demands for a special convention and for separation from the C.T.M. At a special conference attended by Lombardo Toledano, the executive committee of the Oil

Workers' Union, and executive secretaries of unions affiliated with the C.T.M., however, a special commission of the C.T.M. was formed to co-operate in the reorganization of the oil industry "toward the interests of both the petroleum workers and the financial necessities of the industry itself." The report of the commission upheld several of the charges leveled by the Oil Workers' Union against the former management of Pemex, and when the plan was presented to Cárdenas. he authorized its discussion by the commission with Pemex management and the Department of Labor. Pemex agreed that the savings fund, house rent, and vacations should be retained, but insisted on a reduction of five thousand in the labor force. The commission countered by proposing a reduction of four thousand workers from the number after March 18, 1938, the cut to be made by Pemex and the Department of Labor without intervention by the Oil Workers' Union. Agreement was reached on the basis of these negotiations, and the immediate crisis appeared to have passed. Despite the efforts for a smooth settlement, however, the discharge of the workers during early phases of reorganization resulted in sporadic strikes in the Federal District.

On November 28, 1940, the award of the Labor Board in the suit of "economic order" was rendered; it upheld, in its most essential aspects, the administration of Pemex with regard to reorganization procedures, but, with respect to pay scales and allowances, it upheld the Union position. Still, the petition of Pemex for a collective contract was denied. Although many problems were left to be settled by the incoming administration of Ávila Camacho, the several investigations of Pemex produced by the end of 1940 resulted in a general "meeting of the minds" between labor, the government, and the management of Pemex concerning the difficulties of the industry.

Conclusions

Jack Barbash said of the organized labor movement in the United States, "It was only through the wholesale intervention of government in its behalf that unionism could overcome the overpowering disabilities that an antagonistic environment had contrived."[6] This observation applied equally well to the labor movement of Mexico. Under the Cárdenas regime, the Mexican labor movement attained its highest form of organization, prestige, and influence in national economic policy. Among other things, workers assumed direction of the National Railway Company, co-operated in the management of the

6. Jack Barbash, *Labor Unions in Action: A Study of the Mainsprings of Unionism* (New York, 1948), p. 7.

nationalized petroleum industry, and were a potent force in bringing about application of the agrarian laws to important commercial agricultural districts.[7] In the view of Silva Herzog, "The government of General Cárdenas . . . was the culminating moment of the Mexican Revolution. Never before had land been distributed at such a rapid rate; never before had the labor movement been so encouraged from above."[8] And, as was so aptly said by Tannenbaum, ". . . the trade union became an instrument for the reduction of power of private industry and for making the state the arbiter of the nation's economy."[9] At the same time, the labor movement, through trade union organization, exercised considerable power in the state; therefore, it became one of the principal agents of the state in its march to a more significant position in the evolution of Mexican economic and social life.

The lines along which labor policy was to develop were clearly outlined early in his term of office by Cárdenas in the "fourteen points" speech at Monterrey, and a definite pattern for dealing with the labor-management problem emerged, based on the provisions of the Constitution of 1917 and the Federal Labor Law of 1931, as amended from time to time. Specifically, the government encouraged—even sponsored—the unification of industrial workers into a central confederation (the C.T.M.) with which it dealt to the exclusion of other central groups save for the national organization of peasants (the C.N.C.). The direction and integration of peasant activity were considered the special province of the official party, a fact Cárdenas made perfectly clear to Lombardo immediately following the Monterrey affair. When he learned that the C.T.M. planned to organize and attach the peasant organization, Cárdenas drew the line and stated in an interview that organization of agricultural workers was strictly the task of the government party. (The organization of another group, government employees, was under the more or less personal supervision of the chief executive; these workers, governed by a special law, were never allowed to unite with the C.T.M. or to enjoy the same privileges of unions belonging to that group.) In this manner, perhaps by design, the administration divided the labor wing of its "popular front" party and effectively curtailed the power of the Lombardo Toledano-led worker movement.

In the second place, the administration urged that, once organized

7. "Llega a su Final el Período Revolucionario 1934–1940," *México Agrario*, II (October–December, 1940), 251.

8. Jesús Silva Herzog, *La Revolución Mexicana en Crisis* (México, 1944), p. 18.

9. Frank Tannenbaum, *Mexico: The Struggle for Peace and Bread* (New York, 1950), p. 114.

into trade-unions, workers bargain with management (also organized into employer associations) to the end that every worker in the country be covered by a collective contract. Strikes in the bargaining process, when declared legal by the appropriate boards of arbitration and conciliation, occurred relatively frequently during the early period of the Cárdenas regime; however, a definite policy of intervention on the part of the Department of Labor, attempting to reach a settlement before work stoppages became actualities, was soon established. While in both theory and law, arbitration of labor disputes was purely voluntary, the unions, because of the lack of economic strength as well as of generally favorable arbitral awards, came to agree to arbitration. Management, apparently because of the possibility of a suit of "economic order" being instituted, entailing a thorough investigation of the business and the final possibility of expropriation, was coerced into accepting arbitration as the most acceptable alternative. Hence, by far the majority of significant disputes between labor and management over terms of collective contracts were settled by arbitral awards handed down by officials of the Labor Department or even by the chief executive himself.

With regard to collective agreements signed, when two-thirds of the employers and employees in a given industry and region so agreed, the contract was, by executive decree, raised to the status of "contract law." Such industry-wide agreements were reached notably in the sugar industry, in textiles, and in the baking industry of the Federal District.

In the third place, the wage theory enunciated by Cárdenas was that wages should be based upon the "ability of the companies to pay." If the economic capacity of an industry could not be agreed upon in the course of the procedure described above, either party could, under the Federal Labor Law, in cases involving questions of "economic equilibrium," bring a suit of *economic order* before the Federal Board of Conciliation and Arbitration. In the latter half of the Cárdenas era, this procedure became an established pattern and was utilized by both labor and management—notably in the petroleum controversy. Under this provision of Mexican labor jurisprudence, when either party felt that economic circumstances made it impossible to continue operations under the terms of the existing contract because of a fundamental change in economic circumstances, it could petition the labor boards for a suit of "economic order." If the labor board (composed of representatives of capital, labor, and the government, with the last having a majority vote) accepted the plea, it appointed a commission of experts to investigate the structure and financial capacity of the industry. Upon the basis of the report of the commission, the board made an award, upholding either the union or the company, or, as often happened, a decision not granting either party its full demands, but, rather, entailing a compromise. Thus, the board had the power, in such cases, to terminate the old contract and construct a new one for those concerned.

Either party could appeal the award of the board to the appropriate section of the Supreme Court through an *amparo* (roughly, the equivalent of an injunction in the United States), and this practice was another technique evolved for settling labor conflicts. Since, under Cárdenas, the Supreme Court's members were appointed by the president and their terms of office coincided with that of the chief executive, most decisions of that body were, as Cárdenas suggested, based on a "revolutionary interpretation" of the laws. These rulings, generally favorable to labor, were characteristic not only of the Supreme Court, but of the labor boards and the lower echelons of the judiciary.

Finally, for those employers "tired of the social struggle" and refusing to co-operate within the frame of reference outlined above, it was suggested that they either turn their properties over to the workers or to the government to operate for the workers. In considerable numbers of instances, the government expropriated properties under the Expropriation Law of 1936 and turned them over to the workers—organized into co-operatives for ownership and operation. Examples of this procedure were the sugar mills of El Mante and Zacatepec, as well as the lumber mills of El Chaparro. The same general method was utilized in the case of lands of the Laguna District by application of the Agrarian Code, dividing the previously foreign-owned private estates among the peasants to own and operate collectively.

In the case of the National Railways Company, the government, while retaining ownership of the lines, turned their management over to the Railroad Workers' Union. And in the nationalized oil industry, the government maintained title as well as control of management, although allowing the Oil Workers' Union minority representation on the directive board.

The pattern developed for dealing with the labor problem clearly demonstrates that the labor movement of Mexico during the Cárdenas period was under the tutelage of the benevolent hand of government with regard to both organization and trade-union activities. At the same time, the segment of organized labor led by Lombardo Toledano (representing the vast majority of industrial workers), possibly because of the lack of a better alternative, supported the government of General Cárdenas, and consequently achieved a position of influence over national economic policy never before realized. This arrangement, however, may have meant that organized labor came to depend too much on government patronage rather than upon its own economic power and, under succeeding administrations, not so favorably disposed toward labor, was to suffer a relative loss of influence.

In more general terms, the statecraft of Cárdenas consisted in devising a national economic policy based upon government intervention, directed toward achieving a greater degree of economic independence for Mexico. The program was designed to obtain the support of a popular front of industrial and peasant workers, the military, government employees, and the small businessmen. The worker sector of the popular front remained divided, perhaps by government design, between the agricultural laborers—sponsored by the official government party, the federal government employees—sponsored more or less directly by Cárdenas himself, and the industrial workers—organized under the leadership of Lombardo Toledano and joined in the C.T.M. While this division of the labor sector might not have been exactly the arrangement desired by the labor leaders, or even the workers themselves, they apparently agreed to it for the dual reasons of the ever-increasing threat of fascism on both national and international scenes and the fact that the labor movement was not yet sufficiently strong and united in purpose to do otherwise. It is interesting, but fruitless, to speculate on the course that might have been taken by Cárdenas and Lombardo had war not begun in Europe in the fall of 1939.

Even though the Cárdenas government and the labor movement were joined in opposition to the system of economic liberalism, still the program formulated to replace it represented a type of interventionism that cannot properly be classified with any of the identified "isms." The fundamental lack of theoretical unity, or consistency, goes far in explaining the different approaches to reform during the Cárdenas regime, as evidenced by government-labor policy in the Laguna region, in the railroad expropriations, in the oil controversy, and in the several instances of minor importance (from the viewpoint of the national economy), in which the instruments of production were turned over to the workers to own and to manage. In the important commercial agricultural districts of Laguna and Yucatán, the agrarian laws were applied and systems of collective farming on communally owned *ejidos* were established. The National Railways Company was expropriated and, although owned by the state, was turned over to the Railroad Workers' Union to manage. The nationalized oil industry was not managed exclusively by the Oil Workers' Union, but the workers were represented on the board of directors of the government-owned oil company. In each of these instances, government action against the privately owned, foreign interests was prompted by labor disputes, usually involving a serious strike. In the majority of industries, however, such as mining, textiles, electric power, and urban transportation, even though foreign owned, the properties were not nationalized after serious labor disputes; instead, important concessions were gained for labor through intervention of the Labor Department after collective bargaining procedures had broken down.

Lack of agreement over both end-in-view and tactics was apparent not only among government officials, but also among unions affiliated with the C.T.M.—not to mention the differences among the C.T.M., the C.R.O.M., the C.G.T., and the several independent unions of the country. Considering these circumstances, the marvel is that an effective program of any kind was devised, much less one that could achieve the general support of the various contending interests and could maintain itself in the face of disrupting influences both inside and outside Mexico.

Regardless of the name given by various students of the Mexican scene to the socio-economic system developed during the Cárdenas administration, it would seem abundantly clear that organized labor, under the tutelage and sponsorship of the government, played a role never before achieved in the history of Mexico. While, on balance, the material situation of the working masses was improved during the last half of the decade of the 1930's, the primary achievement of Cárdenas and organized labor lay, rather, in the field of obtaining for the workers of Mexico a position of dignity in the national life and in making the organized labor movement an important influence over national economic policy.

At the end of the Cárdenas era, Lombardo Toledano proclaimed: "We have not made a socialist revolution; we have barely achieved a popular revolution by getting rid of the vestiges of feudalism and taking the first steps towards economic independence."[10] In one of his last public addresses as Secretary General of the C.T.M., shortly before retiring to turn over the leadership of the organization to Fidel Velázquez, Lombardo declared before the Petroleum Workers' Convention:

> The majority of the workers of all countries pursue the same end, the transformation of society and the present regime into a system without exploiters or exploited, but the work-

10. *Mexican Labor News*, July 19, 1940.

ing class is divided on the method of achieving this final aim. . . . The workers of Mexico, a semi-colonial country, can best achieve their aims by allying themselves with the people. Only the alliance of the best forces of the people, among whom the working class is the nucleus and the vanguard, can guarantee domestic peace, our sovereignty, and the realization of the program which the Mexican Revolution has been working for.[11]

At least, in the short view (possibly disappointing to Marxists, Fascists, and classical liberals alike), the labor theory of the Cárdenas era involved no more than the creation of a unified, organized worker movement, under the tutelage of the government, the unions agitating for collective contracts, with wages based on the economic capacity of each industry to pay. When employers refused to comply with these standards, the plants might theoretically be, and occasionally were, taken over, either by the workers themselves or by the government. Labor policy was carried out through a program supported by a popular front composed of organized workers, the army, the government bureaucracy, and small businessmen, within the framework of a government-regulated, predominantly private-ownership economic system largely freed from the domination of foreign interests.

11. *Ibid.*, December 20, 1940.

Appendixes

Appendix A
National Unions Affiliated with
the C.T.M., February, 1941[1]

Union	Sections
Sindicato de Trabajadores Petroleros de la República Mexicana (Oil Workers' Union)	32
Sindicato de Trabajadores Ferrocarrileros de la República Mexicana (Railroad Workers' Union)	34
Sindicato de Trabajadores de la Industria Azucarera y Similares de la República Mexicana (Sugar Workers' Union)	106
Sindicato Nacional de Trabajadores de la Industria Textil y Similares de la República Mexicana (National Textile Workers' Union)	126
Sindicatos Industrial de Trabajadores de Artes Gráficas de la República Mexicana (Printers' Industrial Union)	45
Sindicato Industrial de Trabajadores del Alijo, Estiba, Cargaduría y Similares en Fuertos y Zonas Maritimas y Fluviales de la República Mexicana (Industrial Union of Longshoremen)	66
Sindicato Nacional de Telefonistas (Telephone Workers' Union)	31
Sindicato Industrial de Trabajadores del Transporte Maritimo, Fluvial y Lacustre de la República Mexicana (Industrial Union of Maritime Workers)	82
Sindicato de Trabajadores de la Enseñanza de la República Mexicana (Teachers' Union)	34
Sindicato de Trabajadores de la Industria Cinematográfica, Similares y Conexos de la República Mexicana (Union of Workers of the Moving Picture Industry)	44

1. Confederación de Trabajadores de México, *C.T.M., 1936–1941* (México, n.d.), p. 1105.

Sindicato de Trabajadores de Hoteles, Restaurantes, Cantinas, Cafés y Similares de la República Mexicana (Hotel, Restaurant, and Cafe Workers' Union)	61
Sindicato de Trabajadores del Banco Nacional de Crédito Agrícola de la República Mexicana (National Bank of Agricultural Credit Workers' Union)	10
Sindicato de Trabajadores de la Industria Paperlera (Paper Workers' Union)	7
Federación Nacional de Trabajadores de la Industria Eléctrica (National Federation of Electrical Workers)	—²
Federación Nacional de Uniones Teatrales y Espectáculos Públicos (Actors' Union)	7
Federación Nacional de Auto-Transportes (National Teamsters' Union)	—³

2. This union has 48 sections and 9 co-operatives.
3. *Ibid.*

Appendix B
Unification of Peasants,
September, 1935, to August, 1937[1]

Ejidos	Date	Number of Delegates	Number of Peasants Organized	Number of Villages Reported
D.F.	9/8/35	164	35,475	82
Morelos	10/6/35	440	39,575	220
Aguascalientes	10/20/35	250	22,554	125
Zacatecas	10/24/35	1170	105,500	585
San Luis Potosí	11/2/35	1274	109,810	637
Tamaulipas	11/6/35	1000	38,628	550
Monterrey, N.L.	11/24/35	886	46,599	443
Chihuahua	12/8/35	1668	88,642	534
Durango	1/26/36	1142	97,094	571
Saltillo, Coah.	2/10/36	1300	83,518	504
Jalisco	3/2/36	1480	170,608	740
Conima, Col.	3/4/36	152	10,785	76
Querétaro, Qro.	3/29/36	532	35,678	266
Pachuca, Hgo.	12/7/36	996	135,385	498
Sinaloa	2/14/37	1354	76,163	677
Sonora	2/31/37	800	42,387	400
Veracruz	3/28/37	5120	259,688	2560
Total			1,397,889	

1. *Memoria del Departamento Agrario, Estados Unidos Mexicanos Apéndice Estadístico 1935–1936* (n.p., n.d.), pp. 142–43.

Appendix C
Investment of Ejidal Funds
in Works of "Collective Benefit"[1]

Project	Sept. 1935 to Aug. 1936	Sept. 1936 to Aug. 1937	Increase
Schools	352,294.85	760,388.74	408,093.89
Buildings	86,286.21	270,970.62	184,684.41
Roads	55,207.48	128,464.85	73,257.37
Laundry Places	17,121.53	42,893.07	25,771.54
Bath Houses	15,181.51	41,713.53	26,532.02
Mills	38,178.52	116,317.05	78,138.53
Irrigation Works	145,564.94	268,729.59	123,164.65
"Campos Deportivos"	60,328.90	81,956.01	21,627.11
Outside Theaters	35,589.31	43,595.31	8,006.00
Machinery and Implements	401,620.49	611,938.69	210,318.20
Pure Water	31,840.60	40,854.61	9,014.01
General Expenses	87,207.26	154,711.49	214,918.75
Total	1,326,421.60	2,736,948.08	1,410,526.48

1. *Memoria del Departamento Agrario, Estados Unidos Mexicanos Apéndice Estadístico 1935–1936* (n.p., n.d.), p. 124.

Appendix D
I
Number of Unions in Federal District, Selected Years[1]

Year	Number of Unions	Number of Workers
1934	750	200,000
1935	900	237,500
1936	900	270,000
1937	1,000	312,500
1938[2]	1,000	325,000
1939	1,100	325,000
1940	1,100	325,000

1. Secretaría de Gobernación, *Seis Años de Gobierno al Servicio de México 1934–1940* (México, 1940), p. 388.
2. In February, 1938, the C.T.M. claimed a membership in the entire country of 945,913 individuals in 3,594 affiliated organizations (C.T.M., *Informe del Comité 1936–1937*) (México, 1938).

II
Number of Strikes and Workers Involved, Selected Years[1]

Year	Number of Strikes	Number of Workers
1934	200	15,000
1935	650	145,000
1936	675	115,000
1937	575	64,000
1938	325	15,000

1. Secretaría de Gobernación, *Seis Años de Gobierno al Servicio de México 1936–1940*, p. 386; Secretaría de la Economía Nacional, Dirección General de Estadística, *Anuario Estadístico de los Estados Unidos Mexicanos 1938* (México, 1939), 144–45.

Bibliography

Bibliography

Acuña, Ramos Rafael. "Fundamento Económico-Jurídico de la Constitución de los Tribunales del Trabajo." Thesis, National University of Mexico, 1946.

Adams, H. "Agrarian System of Mexico," *American Review,* VII (1936), 409–21.

Adams, Richard N., et al. *Social Change in Latin America Today: Its Implications for United States Policy.* New York: Vintage Books, 1960.

"Administración Obrera de los Ferrocarriles Nacionales de México," *Revista Mexicana del Trabajo,* X (April–May, 1938), 316–19.

Alba, Víctor, "El Movimiento Obrero en la América Latina— Presente y Futuro," *Cuadernos Americanos* (May–June, 1953), pp. 33–51.

———. *Esquema Histórico del Movimiento Obrero en América Latina.* México: B. Costa-Amic, 1957.

———. *Historia del Frente Popular: México, 1959. Análisis de una Táctica Política.* México: Libro Mex Editores, 1959.

———. *Historia del Movimiento Obrero en América Latina.* México: Libreros Mexicanos Unidos, 1964.

———. "Significado del Movimiento Obrero Latino Americano," *Humanismo* (September, 1953), 44–51.

Alexander, Robert J. *Communism in Latin America.* New Brunswick: Rutgers University Press, 1957.

———. *Labor Parties in Latin America.* New York: League for Industrial Democracy (L.I.D. Pamphlet Series), 1942.

———. *Labor Relations in Argentina, Brazil, and Chile.* New York: McGraw-Hill, 1962.

———. *Organized Labor in Latin America.* New York: The Free Press, 1965.

———. *A Primer of Economic Development.* New York: Macmillan, 1962.

———. *Prophets of the Revolution: Profiles of Latin American Leaders.* New York: Macmillan, 1962.

Almada, Pedro J. *99 Días en Jira con el Presidente Cárdenas.* México: Ediciones Botas, 1943.

Alvarez, Oscar. *La Cuestión Social en México.* México: Mundiales, 1950.

"Amendment of the Labour Act in Mexico," *International Labour Review,* XLV (July, 1941), 67–68.

Amoros, Robert G. *Derecho de Clase 1.* México: Secretaría de Educación Pública, Departamento de Educación Obrera, D.A.P.P., n.d.

————. *Derecho de Clase 2.* México: n.d.

"An Interview with President Cárdenas," *Modern Mexico,* VI (May, 1935), 3.

Andrade Valderrama, Vicente. "Panorama Social Latinoamericana," *Nuevo Mundo* (January 15, 1954), 31–38.

Anguiano Equihua, Victoriano. *Lázaro Cárdenas: Su Feudo y la Política Nacional.* México: Editorial Erendira, 1951.

Ashby, Joe C. "Labor and the Philosophy of the Argentine Revolution," *Inter-American Economic Affairs,* V (Summer, 1951), 71–96.

————. "Labor and the Philosophy of the Mexican Revolution Under Lázaro Cárdenas," *The Americas* (October, 1963), 158–99.

Askinasy, Siegfried. *El Problema Agrario de Yucatán,* México: Ed. Botas, 1936.

Association of American Owners of Land in Mexico. *Mexico's Agrarian Laws: How the Titles to Lands Owned by Americans Are Affected and Their Right to Acquire Lands Restricted—Expropriation Authorized* (n.p., n.d.).

Bach, Federico. "México en la Cooperación Económica Pan-Americana," *Revista de Economía,* IV (January, 1941), 5–19.

————. "The Nationalization of the Mexican Railroads," *Annals of Collective Economy: International Review in Four Editions,* XV (1939), 70–93.

Bahamonde, Antonio. *México es Así.* México: Editorial "México Nuevo," 1940.

Banco Nacional de Crédito Ejidal, S. A. *Breves Informaciones Sobre la Organización, Funcionamiento y Resultados de los Sociedades Locales Colectivas de Crédito Ejidal en el Comarco Lagunera.* México: Talleres Gráficos de la Nación, n.d.

————. *Informe que Rinde el Consejo de Administración del Banco Nacional de Crédito Ejidal, S. A., a la Tercera Asamblea General de Accionistas, por el Ejercicio de 1938.* México: Talleres Gráficos de la Nación, 1939.

————. *Informe que Rinde el Consejo de Administración del Banco Nacional de Crédito Ejidal, S. A., a la Cuarta Asamblea General de Accionistas, por el Ejercicio de 1939.* México: Talleres Gráficos de la Nación, 1940.

————. *Informe que Rinde el Consejo de Administración del Banco Nacional de Crédito Ejidal, S. A., a la Quinta Asamblea General de Accionistas, por el Ejercicio de 1940.* México: Talleres Gráficos de la Nación, 1941.

————. *Legislación Agraria Mexicana.* México: "La Impresora," 1938.

Banco Nacional de México. *Review of the Economic Situation of Mexico,* January 31, 1940, pp. 14–16.

Bandera Molina, Juan. "La Situación Económica y Social de los Trabajadores Henequeneros de Yucatán," *Revista de Economía,* VII (October, 1944), 10–13.

Barbash, Jack. *Labor Unions in Action: A Study of the Mainsprings of Unionism.* New York: Harper Bros., 1948.

Barrera Fuentes, Florencio. *Historia de la Revolución Mexicana. La Etapa Precursora.* México: n.p., 1955.

Beals, Carleton. "Cárdenas Organizes Capitalism," *Current History,* XLVI (May, 1937), 47–54.

"Behind Mexico's Oil Seizure," (editorial). *Christian Science Monitor,* March 24, 1938, p. 14.

Bernal, Antonio, Jr. "De Como y Porqué se Formó la Confederación General de Obreros y Campesinos de México y su Primer Congreso Ordinario," *Futuro,* II (December, 1934), 3–7.

Berrón Mucel, Raúl. *Actual Jurisprudencia del Trabajo.* México: Porrúa Hnos. & Cía., 1936.

Beteta, Ramón. *Economic and Social Program of Mexico.* Mexico: n.p., 1935.

————. *The Mexican Revolution: A Defense.* Mexico: D.A.P.P., 1937.

————. *Pensamiento y Dinámica de la Revolución Mexicana: Antología de Documentos Político Sociales.* México: Editorial México Nuevo, 1950.

————. (ed.). *Programa Económico y Social de México (Una Controversia).* México: n.p., 1935.

Bishop, Edwin W. Comments in the Labor Section of the *Handbook of Latin American Studies.* Gainesville, Florida: University of Florida Press, No. 24, 1962.

Blanco Macias, Gonzalo. "The Ejido at Work Down Mexico Way," *Land Policy Review,* III (November, 1937), 18–22.

Blanco Moheno, Roberto. *El Cardenismo*. México: Libro Mex Editores, 1963.

Blanksten, George I. "Latin America," Almond, Gabriel A. and James S. Coleman (eds.). *The Politics of the Developing Areas*. Princeton University Press, 1960.

Bosques, Gilberto. *The National Revolutionary Party of Mexico and the Six-Year Plan*. Mexico: Bureau of Foreign Information of the National Revolutionary Party, 1937.

Botella Asensi, Juan. *La Expropiación en el Derecho Mexicano: El Caso del Petróleo*. México: Ed. Moderna, n.d.

Branch, H. N. (tr.) *The Mexican Constitution of 1917 Compared with the Constitution of 1857*. Philadelphia: The Academy of Political and Social Science, 1917.

Brenner, Anita. *The Wind That Swept Mexico: The History of the Mexican Revolution 1910–1942*. New York: Harper & Bros., 1943.

Brown, Ed J. "Hemisphere Journey," *American Federationist* (October, 1943), 20–21.

Bulnes, Francisco. *Los Grandes Problemas de México*. México: Ediciones de "El Universal," 1926.

Bureau of Information of the Mexican Government. *Oil, Mexico's Position*. Mexico: Bureau of Information of the Mexican Government, n.d.

Burgin, Miron. "Research in Latin American Economics and History," *Inter-American Economic Affairs*, I (December, 1947), 3–22.

Cabello Branott, Samuel. "Economía Dirigida en México. Estudio Sobre el Contenido y Resultados del Primer Plan Sexenal," Thesis, Universidad de Chile, 1942.

Cabrera, Luis. *Un Ensayo Comunista en México*. México: Editorial Poles, 1937.

Callcott, Wilfred Hardy. *Liberalism in Mexico, 1857–1929*. Stanford University Press, 1931.

Capistrán Garza, René. "El Problema del Obrero en México," (Editorial) *Vida*, October 10, 1945, pp. 753–59.

Cárdenas, Lázaro. *Address Made Before the First National Congress of the Confederation of Mexican Workers, February 24, 1938*. Mexico: D.A.P.P., 1938.

————. *Condiciones Económicas de México*. México: D.A.P.P., 1937.

————. "General Cárdenas' Platform: Address to the Nation on the Eve of his Election, by President-elect Cárdenas, June 30, 1934," (translated by Robert H. Murray), *Modern Mexico*, V (August, 1934), 9–10.

————. *Los Ejidos de Yucatán y el Henequén.* Mérida: Talleres Gráficos del Sudeste, n.d.

————. "Manifesto," *Revista del Trabajo*, II (March, 1938), 7–16.

————. "Manifesto of Cárdenas on the Oil Question," *Messages to the Mexican Nation on the Oil Question, 1938.* Mexico: D.A.P.P., 1938.

————. *Mensaje de Año Nuevo, 1938.* México: D.A.P.P., n.d.

————. "Mensaje al Proletariado Lagunero," Sindicato de Trabajadores de los Talleres Gráficos de la Nación. *Despertar Lagunero: Libro que Relata la Lucha y Triunfo de la Revolución en la Comarca Lagunera.* México: Talleres Gráficos de la Nación, 1937.

————. *A Message to the Mexican Nation on the Solution of the Agrarian Problem of La Laguna.* Mexico: National Revolutionary Party, Foreign Information Bureau, 1937.

————. *Message to the Mexican Nation on the Oil Question.* Mexico: D.A.P.P., 1938.

————. *Realización del Plan Sexenal 1935–1936.* México: Publicaciones Oficiales de la Secretaría Particular de la Presidencia de la República, No. 1, Talleres Gráficos de la Nación, 1936.

Carrillo, Alejandro. *The Mexican People and the Oil Companies.* Mexico: D.A.P.P., 1938.

————. *Mexico's Resources for Livelihood.* The Hague: International Industrial Relations Institute, 1938.

Carrillo, Flores, Antonio. "La Constitución y la Acción Económica del Estado," *Investigación Económica, Revista Trimestral de la Escuela Nacional de Economía, Universidad Nacional Autónoma de México*, I, 1941.

Carrillo, Rafael. *Ricardo Flores Magón, Esbozo Biográfico.* México: n.p., 1945.

Carrión Simbrello, Joaquín. "Concepto y Naturaleza Jurídica del Contrato Colectivo de Trabajo. Algunos de sus Aspectos en la Legislación Mexicana," Thesis, National University of Mexico, 1950.

Caso, Antonio. *El Acto Ideatorio: Las Escencias y los Valores.* México: n.p., 1934.

Castorena, José de Jesús. *Manual de Derecho Obrero. Ensayo de Integración de la Doctrina Mexicana del Derecho Obrero.* Segunda edición. México: n.p., 1949.

Chapoy Bonifaz, Dolores Beatriz. *El Movimiento Obrero y el Sindicato en México.* México: n.p., 1961.

Chase, Stuart. *Mexico: A Study of Two Americas*. New York: The Macmillan Co., Reprint, 1946.

"Claims of Companies Regarding Experts' Report," in Government of Mexico. *Mexico's Oil: A Compilation of Official Documents in the Petroleum Industry, with an Introduction Summarizing its Causes and Consequences*. Mexico City: Editorial Cultura, 1940.

Clark, Marjorie Ruth. "Historical Background of Mexico's Labor Movement," *Mexican Life*, XI (November 1936), 18–20; 45–53.

————. *Organized Labor in Mexico*. Chapel Hill: The University of North Carolina Press, 1934.

Cleven, N. Andres. "Some Social Aspects of the Mexican Constitution of 1917," *Hispanic American Historical Review*, IV (August 1921), 474–85.

Cline, Howard F. "Mexico: A Matured Latin American Revolution, 1910–1960," *The Annals of the American Academy of Political and Social Science*, CCCXXXIV (March 1961), 89–94.

————. *Mexico. Revolution to Evolution, 1940–1960*. London: Oxford University Press, 1962.

————. *The United States and Mexico*. Rev. ed., enl. Cambridge: Harvard University Press, 1963.

Cobos D., Bernardo. "El Movimiento Obrero en México," *Revista Mexicana del Trabajo*, III (November–December, 1956), 44–58.

Coe, John (pseud.), "Recent Labor Developments in Mexico and the Caribbean," *Inter-American Economic Affairs*, I (March, 1948), 55–70.

Combined Mexican Working Party, The International Bank for Reconstruction and Development. *The Economic Development of Mexico*. Baltimore: John Hopkins Press, 1953.

Comisión Nacional de Irrigación. *La Obra de la Comisión Nacional de Irrigación Durante el Regimen del Sr. Gral. de División Lázaro Cárdenas, 1939–1940*. México: n.p., n.d.

"Comments on the Economic Situation," *Modern Mexico*, IX (August, 1937), 13.

Compañía Mexicana de Petróleo "El Águila," S.A., et al. *The Mexican Oil Strike of 1937 (May 28–June 9)*. Printed in U.S., n.d.

————. *The Mexican Oil Strike of 1937: The Decision of the Labour Board*. Vol. III. N.p., n.d.

————. *The Mexican Oil Strike of 1937: The Economic Issue*. N.p., n.d.

————. *The Mexican Oil Strike of 1937: The Expropriatory Decree*. Vol. IV. N.p., n.d.

Compendio de Derecho del Trabajo. Tercera ed., 2 vols. México: Ed. Aedor., 1940.

Confederación de Cámaras Nacionales de Comercio e Industria de los Estados Unidos Mexicanos. *Análisis Económico Nacional 1934–1940.* Segunda edición, n.p., 1940.

Confederación de Trabajadores de América Latina. *Por un Mundo Mejor: Diario de una Organización Obrera Durante la Segunda Guerra Mundial.* México: n.p., 1948.

————. *Reunión de Montevideo, Febrero–Marzo de 1944.* Montevideo: Impresa Central, 1944.

Confederación de Trabajadores de América Latina. *Estatutos.* México: n.p., 1938.

————. *Presente y Futuro de la América Latina.* Cali, Colombia, n.p., 1944.

————. *Segundo Congreso General de la Confederación de Trabajadores de la América Latina. Cali, Colombia, 1944.* México: n.p., 1945.

Confederación de Trabajadores de México. *C.T.M. 1936–1941.* México: Talleres Tipográficos Modelos, n.d.

————. *5 Años de Vida de la C.T.M.* México: n.p., n.d.

————. *La C.T.M. y la Carestía de la Vida.* México: n.p., 1937.

————. *IV Consejo Nacional.* México: n.p., 1937.

————. *Informe del Comité Nacional 1936–1937.* México: n.p., 1938.

————. *El Problema de la Laguna: Antecedentes, Soluciones.* México: n.p., 1937.

Confederación de Trabajadores de México, Confederación Campesina Mexicana. *A Todos los Trabajadores de la República.* México: D.A.P.P., 1938.

Confederación Regional de Obreros Mexicanos. *Memoria, 1935.* México: n.p., n.d.

"Conferencia de Prensa del Secretario General del P.P.S.," *Avante,* XXV (May, 1962) 9–24.

Conferencia Sindical Latinoamericana de Trabajadores, Intervenciar de Vicente Lombardo Toledano, Presidente de la Confederación de Trabajadores de América Latina. México: n.p., 1962.

"Conflict of Economic Order," Government of Mexico. *Mexico's Oil: A Compilation of Official Documents in the Conflict of Economic Order in the Petroleum Industry, with an Introduction Summarizing its Causes and Consequences.* Mexico City: Editorial Cultura, 1940.

Congreso Obrero Latino-Americano, Ciudad de México, 5 al 8 de Septiembre de 1938. México: n.p., n.d.

"Congress Extraordinary of the Confederation of Latin American Workers (C.T.A.L.) Meeting in Paris, on 10–12 October, 1945," *International Labour Review*, LII (November 1945), 557–60.

"Contrato Colectivo de Trabajo Celebrado entre los Ferrocarriles Nacionales de México, S.A., y Lineas Administradas y el Sindicato de Trabajadores Ferrocarrileros de la República Mexicana," Departamento Federal del Trabajo. *Revista Mexicana del Trabajo*, VII September–October, 1936), 185–228.

"Contrato Colectivo de Trabajo Celebrado entre los Ferrocarriles Nacionales de México, S. A., y Lineas Administradas y el Sindicato de Trabajadores Ferrocarrileros de la República Mexicana, en Vigor desde el Día 1° de Abril de 1937," Departamento Federal del Trabajo. *Revista Mexicana del Trabajo*, VIII (April–May, 1937), 262–316.

Cormack, Joseph M. "Operation of the Mexican Labor Law," *Southwestern Law Journal*, VII (Summer and Fall, 1953), 301–26; 464–95.

——— and F. M. Barker. "The Mexican Labor Law," *Southern California Law Review*, VII (March 1934), 251–94.

Correa, Eduardo J. *El Balance del Cardenismo.* México: Talleres Linotipográficos "Acción," 1941.

Corro Viña, J. Manuel. *El Presidente Cárdenas: ¿Nos Lleva Hacía la Dictadura del Proletariado?* México: Editorial "Orientación," 1936.

Cortés, Roberto A. "El Movimiento Obrero de México es Autenticamente Libre," *Revista Mexicana del Trabajo*, IV (November–December, 1957), 54–56.

Cortina, Alfonso. "The Agrarian Problem in Yucatán," *Annals of Collective Economy: International Review in Four Editions*, XV (January–April, 1939), 209–22.

Cronon, E. David. *Josephus Daniels in Mexico.* Madison: University of Wisconsin Press, 1960.

"Cost of Living of Working-Class Families in Mexico City," *Monthly Labor Review*, XLIII (January, 1936), 794–97.

Cuéllar, A. B. "Railroad Problems of Mexico," *Annals of the American Academy of Political and Social Science*, CLXXXVII (September, 1936), 193–206.

Cueva, Mario de la. *Derecho Mexicano del Trabajo.* I. México: Porrúa Hnos. y Cía., 1938.

———. *Derecho Mexicano del Trabajo.* Tercera edición, 2 vols. México: Porrúa, 1949.

Cumberland, W. W.; Joseph Thorning; and R. A. McGowan. *Economic and Social Program of Mexico*. México: n.p., 1936.

Davis, Harold E. *Makers of Democracy in Latin America*. Washington, D. C.: Inter-American Bibliographical and Library Association, 1945.

Davis, Horace B. "Numerical Strength of Mexican Unions," *Southwestern Social Science Quarterly*, XXXV (June, 1954), 44–55.

De la Peña, Moisés T. "El Crédito Agrícola en la Economía Mexicana," *El Trimestre Económico*, VII (April–June, 1940), 96–115.

————. "La Administración Obrera de los Ferrocarriles Nacionales de México," *Revista de Economía*, II (September–December, 1938), 683–702.

————. "La Expropiación de los Ferrocarriles Nacionales de México," *El Trimestre Económico*, IV (June, 1937), 195–226.

———— and Alfredo Navarrete. "Reorganización de los Ferrocarriles Nacionales," *El Trimestre Económico*, VII (January–March, 1940–41), 616–34.

De María y Campos, Armando. *Múgica: Crónica Biográfica*. México: Compañía de Ediciones Populares, S. A., 1939.

De Mendizabel, Miguel Othon. "The Agrarian Problem of La Laguna," *Annals of Collective Economy: International Review in Four Editions*, XV (1939), 163–208.

"Decision of Supreme Court," Government of Mexico. *Mexico's Oil: A Compilation of Official Documents in the Conflict of Economic Order in the Petroleum Industry, with an Introduction Summarizing its Causes and Consequences*. Mexico City: Editorial Cultura, 1940.

Decision Rendered by the Supreme Court of Mexico in the Oil Expropriation Case. (Translated from Spanish by Attorney Oscar Rabasa.) México: Talleres Gráficos de la Nación, 1940.

"Decree of Expropriation, March 18, 1938," Government of Mexico. *Mexico's Oil: A Compilation of Official Documents in the Conflict of Economic Order in the Petroleum Industry, with an Introduction Summarizing its Causes and Consequences*. Mexico City: Editorial Cultura, 1940.

"El Decreto del 6 de Octubre de 1936," Liga de Agrónomos Socialistas. *El Colectivismo Agrario en México: La Comarca Lagunera*. México: Talleres de Industrial Gráfica, S.A., 1940.

"Decreto que Deroga los que Crearon la Distribuidora de Petróleos Mexicanos y la Administración General del Petróleo Nacional y Modifica el que Creo la Institución Denominado Petróleos Mexicanos, México, D. F., a 8 de Agosto de 1940," *Boletín de Minas y Petróleo* (October, 1939–June, 1941), 238–39.

Del Vayo, J. Alvarez. "Mexico, Left and Right," *The Nation*, CLVIII (May 13, 1944), 560–63.

Departamento Autónomo de Prensa y Publicidad. *Revista de Estadística*, I (March, 1938), 15.

──────. *Revista del Trabajo*, III (April, 1939), 55–59.

Departamento de Información, *Oil, Mexico's Position*. Mexico, D.A.P.P., n.d.

Departamento de Petróleo. *Legislación Petrolera: Leyes, Decretas, y Disposiciones Administrativas Referentes a la Industria del Petróleo*. México: D.A.P.P., Tomo Décimoctavo, 1938.

Departamento del Trabajo, *Policies of the Present Administration of Mexico* (Mexico, 1936).

Departamento Federal del Trabajo. *Demanda para que se Declara Obligatorio el Contrato Colectivo de Trabajo Celebrado entre Patrones y Obreros de la Industria Textil en el Ramo de Lana*. México: *Diario Oficial* (Sección Segunda), June 12, 1937.

──────. *El Departamento del Trabajo en 1938*. México, D. F., D.A.P.P., n.d.

──────. *Directorio de Agrupaciones Obreras y Patronales de Jurisdicción Federal y Local*. México: D.A.P.P., 1939.

──────. *La Obra Social de la Actual Administración que Preside el G. Lázaro Cárdenas* (México, 1936).

──────. *Memoria del Departamento del Trabajo, Septiembre de 1937–Agosto de 1938*. México: D.A.P.P., 1938.

──────. *Memoria del Departamento del Trabajo, Septiembre de 1938–Agosto de 1939, Presentada al h. Congreso de la Unión por el Jefe del Departamento, Lic. Antonio Villalobos*. México: D.A.P.P., 1939.

──────. *Prontuario de Organización Sindical*. México: Talleres Gráficos de la Nación, Manuales D.A.P.P., Serie "Trabajo," 1937.

Deyrup, Felicia J. "Organized Labor and Government in Underdeveloped Countries: Sources of Conflict," *Industrial and Labor Relations Review*, XII (October, 1958), 104–12.

Díaz Cárdenas, León. *Cananea: Primer Brote del Sindicalismo en México*. México: Publicaciones del Depto. de Bibliotecas de la Secretaría de Educación Pública, 1936.

Dios Bojórquez, Juan de. *Directorio de Asociaciones Sindicales de la República*. México: Departamento del Trabajo, 1936.

Dirección General de Estadística. *La Reforma Agraria en México*. México: D.A.P.P., 1937.

"Dónde y Cómo Terminará la Guerra?" *Futuro*, LX (February, 1941), 3–4.

Dorfman, Adolfo. *El Desarrollo Industrial de América Latina*. Santa Fe: Imp. de la Universidad Nacional del Litoral, 1942.

Dorothy W. Douglas, "Land and Labor in Mexico," *Science and Society*, IV (Spring, 1940), 127–52.

Durán, Marco Antonio. "Exotismo y Revolución Agraria," *México Agrario*, II (July–September, 1940), 225–29.

"Economic Review of Mexico," *Modern Mexico*, VII (October, 1935), 20.

Efrón, David. "Latin American Labor Comes of Age," *Annals of the American Academy of Political and Social Science*, CCXL (July, 1945), 116–30.

Enríquez, Ernesto. *Problems Internacionales: Reclamaciones y Petróleo. Panamericanismo y Derecho Internacional. Cuadernos de Política No. 3*. México: n.p., n.d.

Enríquez, Ignacio C. *Democracia Económica*. México: Porrúa Hnos. y Cía., 1945.

Escoffié Z., Oscar. "Otro Experimento en Yucatán," *Economista*, VIII (November 16, 1942), 14–16.

Estandia Cano, Alfonso. *La Reglamentación de la Huelga*. México, n.d.

"Estatutos de la Confederación de Trabajadores de México," C.T.M., *C.T.M. 1936–1941*. México: Talleres Tipográficos Modelos, n.d.

"Federal Labor Law," *Diario Oficial*, August 28, 1931, p. 51.

Fernández del Castello, Germán. *El Problema Social en México*. México: Ed. Polis, 1939.

Fernández y Fernández, Ramón. "El Comercio del Trigo en la Comarca Lagunera," *México Agrario*, II (January–March, 1940), 19–54.

———. *El Problema Creado por la Reforma Agraria de México*. México: Banco Nacional de Crédito Agrícola, n.d.

———. "La Reforma Agraria Mexicana," *Revista de Economía* (September–December, 1938), 703–15.

Ferrer Mendioles, Gabriel. *Historia del Congreso Constituyente de 1916–1917*. Instituto Nacional de Estudios Históricos de la Revolución Mexicana, 1957.

Ferrocarriles Nacionales de México. *Justicia para los Ferrocarriles*. México: Depto. de Publicidad de los F.C.N. de Méx., 1938.

Fiérez, Margarita. "El Problema Obrero en la América Latina," *Latinoamérica* (October 1, 1952), 450–59.

Figuerola, José. *La Colaboración Social en Hispanoamérica.* Buenos Aires: Editorial Sudamericana, 1943.

"Findings of Expert Commission," Government of Mexico. *Mexico's Oil: A Compilation of Official Documents in the Conflict of Economic Order in the Petroleum Industry, with an Introduction Summarizing its Causes and Consequences.* Mexico City: Editorial Cultura, 1940.

"First General Congress of the Confederation of Latin American Workers," *International Labour Review,* XLV (February, 1942), 211.

Flores Magón, Ricardo. *Land and Liberty: Mexico's Battle for Economic Freedom and its Relation to Labor's Worldwide Struggle.* Los Angeles: n.p., 1913.

Foix, Pere. *Cárdenas: Su Activación, Su País.* México: Ediciones Fronda, 1947.

Fourth Period of Conferences on Collective Cooperative Farming in the Laguna Region. Torreón, 1941, mimeo. (A collection of addresses presented at the conference sponsored by the Banco Nacional de Crédito Ejidal at Torreón, August 4, 5 and 6, 1941, dealing with operations of the Laguna Region.)

Frank, Waldo. "Cárdenas of Mexico," *Foreign Affairs,* XVIII (October, 1939), 91–101.

El Frente Único en México. Habana: Ed. Marcos Díaz, 1938.

Frola, Francisco. *El Cooperativismo y la Clase Obrera.* México: Talleres Gráficos de la Nación, n.d. (Published also in *Revista del Trabajo,* VII, pp. 29–93)

———. "Los Ejidos Colectivos en México," *América* (Habana), XIX (July, 1943), 39–41.

Fuentes Díaz, Vicente. "Desarrollo y Evolución del Movimiento Obrero a Partir de 1929," *Ciencias Políticas y Sociales.* V (July–September, 1959), 325–48.

———. *Los Partidos Políticos en México.* 2 vols. México: n.p., 1954 and 1956.

Gaither, Roscoe B. *Expropriation in Mexico: The Facts and the Law.* New York: William Morrow and Company, 1940.

Galarza, Ernesto. "Labor—Leaven of Democracy," *Survey Graphic* (March, 1941), 169–71, 208. (Chief, Division of Social and Labor Information, Pan American Union.)

Galenson, Walter (ed.). *Labor and Economic Development.* New York: John Wiley & Sons, Inc., 1959.

———. *Labor in Developing Countries.* Berkeley: University of California Press, 1962.

Gámio, Manuel. "An Analysis of Social Processes and the Obstacles to Agricultural Progress in Mexico," *Rural Sociology*, II (June, 1937), 143–47.

García Rangel, Ramón. *El Problema Nacional Petrolero*. México: Ediciones Encuadernables, 1939.

García Treviño, Rodrigo. "Los Sindicatos en la Administración de las Industrias," *Revista de Economía*, III (January–April, 1939), pp. 33–45.

Garizurieta, César. *Realidad del Ejido*. México: Editorial Dialéctica, 1938.

Germán Parra, Manuel. *La Industrialización de México*. Mexico City: Impresa Universitaria, 1954.

Glenn, J. B. "Present Economic Trends in Mexico," *Modern Mexico*, VIII (July 1936), 11–15.

Gobierno de México. *El Petróleo de México: Recopilación de Documentos Oficiales del Conflicto de Orden Ecomómico de la Industria Petrolera, con una Introducción que Resume sus Motivos y Consequencias*. México: Editorial Cultura, 1940.

Gómez, Gudelia. *El Artículo 123 Constitucional y los Sindicatos*. México: Talleres Gráficos de la Nación, 1954.

Gómez, Marte R. *La Región Lagunera*. México: Germinal. (Sociedad Agronómica Mexicana, Bol. Técnicos, Serie A: Cuestiones Sociales, No. 2), n.d.

González Aparicio, Enrique. "Actitud del Gobierno ante el Movimiento Obrero," *Revista de Economía*, III (May–August, 1939), 83–86.

————. "New Forms of Industrial Organization in Mexico," *Annals of Collective Economy: International Review in Four Editions*, XV (1939), pp. 94–106.

————. *Nuestro Petróleo*. México: Ed. Masa, 1938.

————. "El Problema Ejidal en Yucatán," Sociedad Agronómica de México. *Primer Ciclo de Conferencias (de Octubre a Noviembre de 1937)*. México: D.A.P.P., 1938, pp. 85–96.

González López, Guillermo. "La Huelga y el Arbitraje en México," Thesis at The National University of Mexico, 1950.

González Navarro, Moisés. "La Ideología de la Revolución Mexicana," *Historia Mexicana*, X (April–June, 1961), 628–36.

González Ramírez, Manuel. *El Petróleo de México: La Expropiación Petrolera ante el Derecho Internacional*. México: Editorial América, 1941.

————. *La Revolución Social en México*. México: Fondo de Cultura Económica, 1960.

Gordon, Wendell C. *The Economy of Latin America.* New York: Columbia University Press, 1950.

————. *The Expropriation of Foreign-Owned Property in Mexico.* Washington, D.C.: American Council on Public Affairs, 1941.

Government of Mexico. *Mexico's Oil: A Compilation of Official Documents in the Conflict of Economic Order in the Petroleum Industry, with an Introduction Summarizing its Causes and Consequences.* Mexico City: Editorial Cultura, 1940.

————. *The True Facts about the Expropriation of the Oil Companies' Properties in Mexico.* México: Talleres Gráficos de la Nación, 1940.

Graciadas, Carlos L. *Esencia Imperativa del Artículo 123 Constitucional. Los Debatas en Querétero como Imprescindible Fuente del Derecho Obrero en México.* México: Unión Linotipográfica de la República Mexicana, 1948.

"El Grave Problema de los Ferrocarriles Mexicanos," *Acción Social,* II (April 9–11, 1941), 20.

Guerra Cepeda, Roberto. *El Ejido Colectivizado en la Comarca Lagunera.* México: Talleres Gráficos de la Nación, 1939.

Halperin, Ernst. *Communism in Mexico.* Cambridge: Massachusetts Institute of Technology, 1963.

Halperin, Maurice. "Inside Mexico," *Current History,* XLV (February, 1937), 83–87.

————. "Mexico, the Incredible. What's Happening Over the Border and Why They Like It," *Current History,* XLV (November, 1936), 47–52.

Hammond, W. J., "Mexican Labor and World Affairs," Institute of Public Affairs. *Mexico and the United States: Proceedings of the Fifth Annual Conference Institute of Public Affairs Auspices Carnegie Endowment for International Peace, 1938,* pp. 89–104.

————. "Some Aspects of International Labor Relations Between the United States and Mexico," *The Southwestern Social Science Quarterly,* XXV (December, 1944), 208–21.

Hanke, Lewis. *Modern Latin America: Continent in Ferment.* Vol. I. Princeton: D. Van Nostrand Co., Inc., 1959, An Anvil Original.

Hanson, Simon G. *Economic Development in Latin America: An Introduction to the Economic Problems of Latin America.* Washington, D.C.: The Inter-American Affairs Press, 1951.

Harker, Mary Margaret. "Organization of Labor in Mexico Since 1910," Ph.D. Dissertation, University of Southern California.

Hernández, Manuel A. "The 'Ejido' is Not Mexico's Way Out," *Mexican-American Review,* IX (March 1, 1941), 12–14.

————. "Están Ahora los Trabajadores Petroleros Mejor que Antes de la Expropiación," *Economista*, IV (April 1, 1942), 608, 38–40.

————. "Observaciones Adicionales al Informe del Gerente de Petróleos Mexicanos," *Economista* (May 1, 1943), 28–30.

Herring, H. "Cárdenas in Mexico," *Harper's Magazine*, CLXXVII (October 1938), 489–502.

————. "Cárdenas' Triumphs in Mexico," *Current History*, XLII (September 1935), 636–38.

————. *Good Neighbors: Argentina, Brazil, Chile and Seventeen Other Countries*. New Haven: Yale University Press, 1941.

————. "Mexico Claims its Own," *The Nation*, CXLVI (April 16, 1938), 440–42.

————. "Mexico's President Defies Calles," *Current History*, XLII (August 1935), 524–26.

————. "The Unconquerable Mexican," *Harper's Magazine*, CLXXV (June 1937), 46–56.

Hill, Rachel Newborn. "A Sketch of the Mexican Labor Movement," M.S. Thesis, Columbia University.

Hinojosa, Roberto. *El Tren Olivo en Marcha*. México: Talleres Gráficos de la Nación, 1937.

Horner, John. *Labour's Struggle in Latin America*. London Research Press Publications, 1945.

Huasteca Petroleum Company. *Expropriation: A Factual Study of the Causes, Methods and Effects of Political Domination of Industry in Mexico*. New York: Mail and Express Printing Co., Inc., 1938.

Ibañez, Bernardo. "Inter-American Labor and Democracy," *American Federationist*, LV (June 1948), 10–11, 24–25.

Icaza, Xavier. *El Nuevo Derecho Obrero Mexicano*. México: Publicaciones de la Universidad Obrero de México, 1936.

"If you Hire Labor in Mexico," *Modern Mexico*, VIII (September 1936), 4.

Infield, Henrik E., and Kike Freier. *People in Ejidos: A Visit to the Cooperative Farms of Mexico*. New York: Frederick A. Praeger, Inc., 1954.

"Informe del Comité Nacional de la C.T.M., Al Segundo Congreso General Ordinario de la Misma Institución," C.T.M., *C.T.M. 1936–1941*. México: Talleres Tipográficos Modelos, n.d.

Informe que Rinde al H. Congreso de la Unión el C. Presidente Lázaro Cárdenas sobre su Gestión de Septiembre de 1937 a Agosto de 1938. México: D.A.P.P., 1938.

Inman, Samuel Guy. "Economic and Social Progress in Latin America," *Latin American Viewpoint* (1942), 36–55.

————. *Latin America: Its Place in World Life*. New York: Harcourt, Brace and Co., Rev. Ed., 1947.

————. "Observations on Labor, Politics and Religion in Northern Mexico," *World Affairs*, XCIX (September, 1936), 177–79.

————. "Spirit of the Mexican Revolution," Institute of Public Affairs. *Mexico and the United States: Proceedings of the Fifth Annual Conference Institute of Public Affairs Auspices Carnegie Endowment for International Peace, 1938*, pp. 1–28.

"Inter-American Confederation of Workers," *International Labour Review*, LVIII (December, 1948), 795–98.

Isserman, Abraham J. "El Trabajo en México," *Revista del Trabajo*. (January, 1939), 75–87.

Jáquez, Fernando. "El Ejido Como Institución Básica de Nuestra Economía," *México Agrario*, I (November–December, 1939), 215–20.

Jellinek, Frank. "Mexican Industrialization Problems," *Mexican-American Review*, XIII (July, 1945), 50–52, 137.

————. "Mexican Labor's Changing Currents," *Mexican-American Review*, XV (April 1947), 10–15.

Jones, Chester Lloyd. "If Lewis Sits Down in Mexico," *American Scholar*, VI (Autumn, 1937), 471–80.

Jordan, Henry P. "Labor and Social Security in Latin America," *American Labor Conference on International Affairs, International Postwar Problems*. New York: n.p., 1945.

Kassalow, Everett M. (ed.). *National Labor Movements in the Postwar World*. Evanston: Northwestern University Press, 1963.

Kawage Ramie, Alfredo. *Con Lombardo Toledano: Un Hombre, Una Nación, Un Continente*. México: n.p., 1943.

Keen, Benjamin (ed.). *Readings in Latin-American Civilization*. Boston: Houghton Mifflin Co., 1955.

Kirk, Betty. *Covering the Mexican Front: The Battle of Europe versus America*. Norman: University of Oklahoma Press, 1942.

————. "Current Social Movements in Mexico," *Sociology and Social Research*, XVI (May 1931), 403–16.

Kluckhohn, Frank L. *The Mexican Challenge*. New York: Doubleday, Doran & Co., Inc., 1939.

"Labor Legislation and Collective Bargaining in the Americas," *Industry and Labour*, XXV (April 1961), 254.

"Labor Under Cárdenas. Welfare of Workers Comes into Conflict with Effort to Change Economic System," *Journal of Commerce*, CLXXXV (August 27, 1940), 319.

"Labor Unrest Faces Mexico," *Christian Science Monitor* (March 30, 1938), 1, 6.

Laborde, Hernán. "Cárdenas, Reformador Agrario," *Problemas Agrícolas e Industriales de México*, IV (January–March, 1952), 57–86.

————. "Primero de Mayo," *Todo*, México, May 2, 1946, p. 16.

"The Labour Conference of American States which are Members of the International Labour Organization, Santiago de Chile, 2–14, January 1936," *International Labor Review*, XXXIII (April, 1936) 479–98 and (May, 1936) 646–684.

Langnas, Isaac. "Mexico Today. Aspects of Progress since the Revolution," *The World Today* (Royal Institute of International Affairs) London: Oxford University Press, April 1961, pp. 158–167.

Laski, H. J. *Trade Unions in the New Society*. New York: The Viking Press, 1949.

Lastra y Villar, Alfonso. *Las Leyes del Trabajo de la República Mexicana Interpretadas por la Suprema Corte de la Nación*. México: n.p., 1936.

"Laudo Arbitral: El Dictado por el C. Presidente de la República, Gral. de Div. Lázaro Cárdenas en su Calidad de Arbitro Arbitrador Designado por las Partes, en el Conflicto Suscitado entre el Sindicato de Trabajadores Ferrocarrileros de la República Mexicana y la Empresa de los Ferrocarriles Nacionales de México," Departamento Federal del Trabajo. *Revista Mexicana del Trabajo*, V (September–October, 1935), 189–253.

Lavín, José Domingo. "Mexico Descubre un Sistema Económico," *Humanismo*, V (September–October, 1956), 107–16.

————. *Petróleo: Pasado, Presente y Futuro de una Industria Mexicana*. México: Edición y Distribución Ibero-Americana de Publicaciones, S.A., 1950.

League of Nations. *Monthly Bulletin of Statistics*. Vol. XVIII, XIX, XX, XXI, XXII.

Lewis, Oscar. "Mexico since Cárdenas," Richard N. Adams, et al. *Social Change in Latin America Today: Its Implications for United States Policy*. New York: Vintage Books, 1960.

Leyva Neri, Benigno. *El Contrato Colectivo de Trabajo en el Derecho Obrero Mexicano*. México: n.p., 1946.

Liga de Agrónomos Socialistas. *El Colectivismo Agrario en México: La Comarca Lagunera*. México: Talleres de Industrial Gráfica, S. A., 1940.

————. *Los Sofismos de la Reforma Agraria*. México: n.p., 1939.

"Llega a su Final el Período Revolucionaria 1934–1940," *México Agrario*, II (October–December, 1940), 251.

Lombardo Toledano, Vicente. *Al Pueblo Mexicano: Defender a Cuba es Defender a México y a la América Latina*. México: n.p., 1961.

———. *Causas de la Elevación del Espíritu Humano*. México: n.p., 1960.

———. "Como Surgió la Federación Sindical Mundial," *El Movimiento Sindical Mundial*, VI (June, 1960), 3–5.

———. *Contrato Sindical de Trabajo*. México: n.p., n.d.

———. *Cristianos y Socialistas Unidos Contra la Regresión*. México: n.p., 1943.

———. "Debate, en pro," *Futuro*, II (October, 1934), 50–63.

———. "Discurso de Clausura," C.T.M., *C.T.M. 1936–1941*. México: Talleres Tipográficos Modelos, n.d.

———. "Discurso del Lic. Lombardo Toledano," *América Latina*, I (April 1, 1939), 8–10.

———. Discurso Pronunciado en la Sesión Inaugural del Congreso Económico de la C.T.M., Reunido del 29 al 31 de Enero de 1941 en el Palacio de Bellas Artes," *Importantes Resoluciones al Congreso Económico de la Confederación de Trabajadores de México*. México, 1941.

———. "El Cooperativismo y los Trabajadores," *Futuro*, IX (January, 1938), 16–24.

———. "El Drama de México," *Nuestras Grandes Problemas Económicas*. México: n.p., 1954.

———. *El Estado y la Iglesia; La Revolución y la Religión; Progreso y Retroceso*. México: n.p., 1943.

———. *El Nueva Programa del Sector Revolucionario de México*. México: n.p., 1944.

———. "El Pueblo de México y las Compañías Petroleras," *Futuro*, IX (February, 1938), 20–24.

———. *En Qué Consiste y a Cuanto Asciende la Fortuna de Vicente Lombardo Toledano*. México: n.p., 1940.

———. *Escritos Filosóficos*. México: n.p., 1937.

———. *5th Column in Mexico*. New York: Publication of the Council for Pan American Democracy, n.d.

———. *Idealismo vs. Materialismo Dialéctico: Caso-Lombardo*. 2nd ed. México: Universidad Obrera de México, 1963.

———. *Importantes Resoluciones al Congreso Económico de la Confederación de Trabajadores de México*. México: Talleres de "El Popular," 1941. (Also appeared in *México Agrario*, III [April–June, 1941], 91–135).

————. "Informe Rendido por el . . . presidente de la Confederación de Trabajadores de América Latina al Congreso General de la Propia C.T.A.L. el Día 22 de Noviembre de 1941," *México Agrario,* III (October–December, 1941), 387–433.

————. "The Labor Movement," *The Annals of the American Academy of Political and Social Science,* CCVIII (March, 1940), 48–54.

————. *La Batalla de las Ideas en Nuestro Tiempo.* México: Universidad Obrera de México, 1963.

————. "La Comarca de La Laguna en Cifras," Confederación de Trabajadores de México. *El Problema de la Laguna: Antecedentes, Soluciones.* México: n.p., 1937.

————. *La Doctrina Monroe y el Movimiento Obrero.* México: n.p., 1927.

————. *La Doctrina Socialista y su Interpretación en el Artículo 3°.* México: n.p., 1934.

————. *La Evolución de México durante la Primera Mitad del Siglo XX.* México: n.p., 1956.

————. *La Filosofía y el Proletariado.* México: n.p., 1962.

————. *La Libertad Sindical en México.* México: n.p., 1927.

————. "La Perspectiva de México: Una Democracia del Pueblo," *Problemas Agrícolas e Industriales de México* (April–June, 1955), 247–80.

————. *La Revolución Rusa—la Revolución Mexicana: Pasado, Presente y Porvenir.* México, n.p., 1943.

————. *La Sucesión Presidencial de 1958.* México: n.p., 1957.

————. *La Universidad Obrera de México y la Educación Política del Proletariado.* México: n.p., 1943.

————. *Las Corrientes Filosóficas en la Vida de México.* México: Universidad Obrera de México, 1963.

————. *Lenin, el Genio.* México: n.p., 1942.

————. *Los Problemas Principales de la Agricultura y de la Economía del Continente Americano.* México: n.p., 1942.

————. *Mensaje al Proletariado de la América Latina.* México: n.p., 1936.

————. "No es la Hora de Buscar Culpables," *Siempre!* CCCCLXV (May 16, 1962), 18–19.

————. *Objetivos y Táctica del Proletariado y del Sector Revolucionario de México en la Actual Etapa de la Evolución Histórica del País.* México: n.p., 1947.

————. *Por Vez Primera en la Historia Contemporanea de México la Revolución Está en Oposición al Gobierno.* México: n.p., 1952.

————. *Presente y Futuro*. México: n.p., 1952.

————. "Primera Reunión del Comité Central del Partido Popular Socialista: Informe al Comité Central," *Avante*, VI (April, 1961), 1–12.

————. *Teoría y Práctica del Movimiento Sindical Mexicano*. México: n.p., 1961.

————. *The C.T.A.L., The War and the Postwar*. México: n.p., 1945.

————. *The United States and Mexico: Two Nations—One Ideal*. New York: n.p., 1942.

————. *Un Viaje al Mundo del Porvenir*. México: n.p., 1936.

————. *What Does the C.T.A.L. Mean? "Latin American Federation of Labor."* México: n.p., 1944.

Lombardo Toledano, Vicente with Xavier Icaza, et al., *Marxismo y Anti-Marxismo*. México: n.p., 1934.

López, Gustavo S. *Legislación Obrero-Patronal*. Tercera edición. México: Tip. Hispano-Mexicana, n.d.

————. *Curso de Historia Económica de México*. México: Escuela Nacional de Economía, Universidad Nacional Autónoma de México, 1963.

López Aparicio, Alfonso. *El Movimiento Obrero en México: Antecedentes, Desarrollo y Tendencias*. México: Editorial Jus, 1952.

López Cárdenas, Fernando. "Lo de la Reversión a los Hacendados Henequeneros Yucatecos," *México Agrario*, IV (January–March, 1942), 21–24.

López Mateos, Adolfo. *El Desarrollo Económico de México durante un Cuarto del Siglo, 1934–1959*. México: Nacional Financiera, 1959.

López Portillo, José. *Exposición Objetiva del Plan Sexenal, el Aspecto Técnico del Conflicto Petrolero en México*. México: "Sag.," 1938.

López Rosado, Diego. *Ensayos sobre Historia Económica de México*. México: Imprenta Universitaria, 1957.

López Zamora, Emilio. "El Parcelamiento Ejidal. Promesa del Nuevo Gobierno," *Revista de Economía*, IV (January, 1941), 20–30.

————. *La Situación del Distrito de Riego del Mante*, México: n.p., 1939.

Lorwin, L. L. *The International Labor Movement*. New York: Harper & Bros., Inc., 1953.

Macmahon, Arthur W. and W. R. Dittmar. "The Mexican Oil Industry since Expropriation," *Political Science Quarterly*, LVII (March, 1942), 28–50.

McMahon, William E. *Two Strikes and Out.* Garden City: Country Life Press, 1939.

Maddox, James G. *The Growth of the Mexican Economy.* New York: Report by the American Universities Field Staff, June, 1956.

Maestri, Raúl. "De las Economías Nacionales a una Economía Continental," *América ante la Guerra.* Habana: Instituto de Previsión y Reformas Sociales, n.d., pp. 54–71.

Magner, J. A. "Strong Men in Mexico," *The Commonweal,* XXIX (November 18, 1938), 94–96.

Mancisidor, José. *Historia de la Revolución Mexicana.* México: El Gusano de Luz, 1958.

"Man with a Mission," *Time Magazine,* XXXIX (April 13, 1942), 18.

Manterola, Miguel. "El Petróleo de México," *El Trimestre Económico,* (October, 1938), 343–74.

———. *La Industria del Petróleo en México.* Mexico City: Secretaría de Hacienda y Crédito Público, 1939.

———. "La Situación Actual de la Industria del Petróleo en México," *Revista de Economía,* IV (January, 1941), 31–34 and (February, 1941), 119–27.

March, José Jorge. "Mexico and Oil," *Labour Monthly, a Magazine of International Labour,* XXI (March, 1939), 171–77.

Marrett, R. H. K. *An Eye-Witness of Mexico.* London: Oxford University Press, 1939.

Martin, Michael Rheta and Gabriel Lovett. *An Encyclopedia of Latin American History.* New York: Abelard-Schuman Co., 1956.

Martin, R. L. "Mexican Prospects," *Yale Review,* XXV (March, 1936), 511–36.

Martínez Báez, Antonio et al. *La Constitución de 1917 y la Economía Mexicana. Cursos de Invierno, 1957. Conferencias.* México: Universidad Nacional Autónoma de México, Escuela Nacional de Economía, 1958.

Martínez Mezquida, Ignacio. "Concepto del Despido en la Legislación Mexicana del Trabajo," *Revista del Trabajo,* XXX (June, 1947), 13–30.

Matthews, Herbert L. (ed.). *The United States and Latin America.* 2nd ed. Englewood Cliffs: Prentice-Hall, Inc., 1959.

Medina, Hilario. *Interpretación Económica de la Constitución.* México: La Justicia, 1957.

Memoria del Primer Congreso Mexicano de Derecho Industrial. México: Talleres Gráficos de la Nación, 1934.

Memoria del Departamento Agrario. Estados Unidos Mexicanos Apendice Estadístico 1935–1936. n.p., n.d.

Mendieta y Núñez, Lucio. "The Balance of Agrarian Reform," *The Annals of the American Academy of Political and Social Science,* CCVIII (March, 1940), 121–31.

————. "La Expropriación por Causa de Utilidad Pública y el Buen Uso de la Medida," *Jus, Revista de Derecho y Ciencias Sociales,* II (February 15, 1939), 111–12.

————. *El Problema Agrario de México.* 4th ed. México: Porrua, 1937.

"Mexican Conservatives and Labor Break," *Christian Science Monitor,* March 10, 1941, p. 5.

"Mexican Expropriation Law," *Bulletin of the Pan American Union,* LXXI (1937), 286–88.

Mexican Government. *The Mexican Government and the Solution of the Agrarian Problem in La Laguna District.* Mexico: D.A.P.P., n.d.

————. *Policies of the Present Administration of Mexico.* Mexico: Government Printing Office, 1936.

"Mexican Labor in Hemisphere Politics," *The American Analyst,* Pilot Copy No. 4 (October 15, 1946), 24–34.

"Mexican Labor to Fight to Save Cárdenas' Gains," *Christian Science Monitor,* January 20, 1941.

Mexican Liberal Party. *Land and Liberty: Mexico's Battle for Economic Freedom and its Relation to Labor's World-Wide Struggle, Selected from the Writings of Ricardo Flores Magón, A. de P. Araujo and William C. Owen.* Los Angeles: Mexican Liberal Party, 1913.

"Mexico in Revolution," *Fortune,* XVIII (October 1938), pp. 75–140.

Millan, Verna Carleton. "La Laguna: An Experiment in Communal Farming," *Mexican Life,* XV (September, 1939), 15–17.

————. *Mexico Reborn.* Boston: Houghton Mifflin Co., 1939.

Millen, Bruce H. *The Political Role of Labor in Developing Countries.* Washington, D.C.: The Brookings Institution, 1963.

Millon, Robert Paul. *Mexican Marxist—Vicente Lombardo Toledano,* Chapel Hill: The University of North Carolina Press, 1966.

Ministry of Foreign Relations. *The Mexican Government in the Presence of Social and Economic Problems: Presidential Plan for Incorporation of Federal Territories—Ideology and Work of National Revolutionary Party—Mexico and Spain, and the League of*

Nations—The Agrarian Problem in the Laguna Region, No. 6. Mexico: Press of the Ministry of Foreign Relations, 1936.

————. *The Mexican Government in the Presence of Social and Economic Problems: The President's Message to Congress, No. 5.* Mexico: Press of the Ministry of Foreign Relations, 1936.

————. *The Mexican Government in the Presence of Social and Economic Problems: The Religious Question—The President's Reply to the Memorial From the Employers—Mexico's Economic Situation Rapidly Improving, No. 2.* Mexico: Press of the Ministry of Foreign Relations, 1936.

————. *The Mexican Government in the Presence of Social and Economic Problems: Tour of the President of the Republic, Monterrey—Tampico—Guadalajara, No. 1.* Mexico: Press of the Ministry of Foreign Relations, 1936.

Molina Enríquez, Andrés. "Mexico's Defense, Action in Agrarian Reforms and Expropriation of Oil Lands," *Atlantic Monthly,* CLXII (March, 1939), 378–84. (Trans. by Virginia Prewett.)

————, Félix F. Palavicini, and Enrique González Aparicio. *El Ejido en Yucatán.* México: Ed. México Nuevo, 1937.

Molina Enríquez, Renato. "La Evolución Histórica del Ejido y Sus Transformaciones," *Revista Banco Obrero,* XI–XII (October–November, 1938), 1–3.

Molina Font, Gustavo. *La Tragedia de Yucatán.* (Prólogo by Luis Cabrera). México: Jus, 1941.

Montagu, I. "Mexico on the March," *Labour Monthly,* XX (1938), 437–42.

Moore, Wilbert E. *Industrialization and Labor: Social Aspects of Economic Development.* New York: Cornell University Press, 1951.

Morales Jiménez, Alberto. *Historia de la Revolución Mexicana.* México: Instituto de Investigaciones Políticos, Económicos y Sociales del Partido Revolucionario, Institucional Cooperativo de Trabajadores de los Talleres Gráficos de la Nación, 1951.

Moreno, Daniel. *Los Hombres de la Revolución.* México: Libro Mex Editores, 1960.

Moreno, Jean. "Labor Creeps Forward," *Modern Mexico,* XIII (August, 1940), 11–12.

Moreno-Sánchez, Manuel, et al. *Política Ejidal.* México: Universidad Nacional Autónoma de México, 1960.

Mosk, Sanford A. *Industrial Revolution in Mexico.* Berkeley and Los Angeles: University of California Press, 1950.

Mujal Barniol, Eusebio. "América Latina y los Trabajadores," *Mundo del Trabajo Libre* (August, 1957), 21–24.

Munguía, E. "Agrarian Problems in Mexico," *International Labour Review*, XXXVI (January, 1937), 49–85; 200–38.

Naft, Stephen. *Labor in Latin America*. New York: Confidential Report No. 22, News Background, 1947.

Nathan, Paul. "México en la Época de Cárdenas," *Problemas Agrícolas e Industriales de México*, VII (July–September, 1955), 17–176; 177–262.

"National Agreement in Cotton-Textile Industry in Mexico, 1939," *Monthly Labor Review*, L (May 1940), 1140–46.

"National Legislation on Hours of Work in Latin American Countries," *Monthly Labor Review*, XLIII (November, 1936), 1243–50.

Nelson, Eastin. "Some Recent Developments in Economic Thought in Mexico," *Intellectual Trends in Latin America*. Austin: The University of Texas Press, 1945.

Neumann, William L. "Rivalry for Control of Latin American Labor," *American Perspective*, II (April 1948), 15–25.

Novo, Salvador. *La Vida en México en el Período Presidencial de Lázaro Cárdenas*. México: Empresas Editoriales, S. A., 1964.

"Un Nuevo Gobierno," *Futuro*, LVIII (December, 1940), 1–52.

Oil Weekly, June 26, 1939, p. 46.

O'Neil, F. E. "Mexico Has a New Deal," *Modern Mexico*, VIII (February, 1937), 6; 23.

Ortíz, Andrés. "Los Ferrocarriles Nacionales de México," *Investigación Económica*, IV (Third Quarter, 1944), 241–70.

Owen, Eugene D. "Recent Latin American Labor Codes," *Inter-American Quarterly*, III (January 1940), 68–79.

———. "Sources of Information on Social Problems in Latin-America," *Inter-American Bibliographical Review*, I–II (Summer, 1941), 91–97.

Pan American Union. Bulletin of the Pan American Union, LXXI (September, 1937), 726–27.

———. *Labor Trends and Social Welfare in Latin America: 1939–1940*. Washington, D.C., Pan American Union, Division of Labor and Social Information, 1941.

Parkes, Henry Bamford. *A History of Mexico*. Rev. ed. Boston: Houghton Mifflin Co., 1950.

Parra Hernández, Enrique. *Tribunales de Trabajo en México*. México: Universidad Nacional Autónoma de México, 1939.

Partido de la Revolución Mexicana. *En Defensa de la Soberanía Nacional, 18 de Marzo* Mexico, n.d.

———. *Pacto Constitutivo, Declaración de Princípios Programa y Estatutos*. México, 1938.

————. *Partido de la Revolución Mexicana.* México, 1938.

Partido Nacional Revolucionario, México. *Constitución del P.N.R.,* n.p., n.d.

————. *The Mexican Government's Six-Year Plan, 1934–1940; Along with Cárdenas' Nomination Address,* Mexico: n.p., 1934.

————. *Plan Sexenal del P.N.R.* México, 1934.

————. *Second Six-Year Plan, 1941–1946.* n.p., n.d.

Partido Popular. *Razón Histórica, Programa y Estatutos del Partido Popular.* México: n.p., 1948.

————. *Tesis Sobre México.* México: n.p., 1958.

"El Partido Popular Socialista y El Movimiento de Liberación Nacional." *Avante: Documentos,* I (July, 1962), 2–11.

Pemex. *Informe Anual,* March 18, 1941.

Pendergast, L. O. "American Money in Mexico," *The Nation,* CXLV (November 7, 1937), 585–87.

————. "Growing Pains of Mexican Labor," *The Nation,* CXLIV (June 12, 1937), 671–74.

Peralta, Carlos M. "El Gran Ejido Yucateco," *México Agrario,* III (January–March, 1941), 15–25.

Pérez Leirós, Francisco. *El Movimiento Sindical de América Latina.* Buenos Aires: Imprenta "La Vanguardia," 1941.

Person, Harlow S. *Mexican Oil: Symbol of Recent Trends in International Relations.* New York: Harper & Bros., Publishers, 1942.

"Petróleo: Sección Oficial," *Boletín de Petróleo y Minas,* IX (January, 1938), 22–23.

Phillips, Henry Albert. *New Designs for Old Mexico.* New York: Robt. M. McBride & Co., 1939.

Piña, Roberto. "Mexico's Runaway New Deal," *American Mercury,* XLVI (February 1939), 176–82.

Pineda, Salvador. *Presencia de Cárdenas.* México: Libro Mex, 1959.

"Plea of Amparo," Government of Mexico. *Mexico's Oil: A Compilation of Official Documents in the Conflict of Economic Order in the Petroleum Industry, with an Introduction Summarizing its Causes and Consequences.* México: Editorial Cultura, 1940.

Plenn, J. H. *Mexico Marches.* New York: The Bobbs-Merrill Co., 1939.

Poblete Troncoso, Moisés. "The Enforcement of Labor Legislation in Latin America," *International Labour Review,* XXXII (November, 1935), 637–64.

————. "Influencia de la Legislación del Trabajo en los Ramos Tradicionales del Derecho. Tendencia a la Codificación de la Legislación Social en América Latina," *Revista Mexicana de Sociológica,* III (July–September, 1941), 53–62.

————. "The Second Labor Conference of the American States, Habana, November 21–December 4, 1939," *Bulletin of the Pan American Union*, LXXIV (March, 1940), 173–80.

————, and Ben G. Burnett. "Latin American Labor Law: A Synthesis," *Inter-American Economic Affairs*, XII (Autumn, 1958), 3–18.

————. *The Rise of the Latin American Labor Movement*. New York: Bookman Associates, 1960.

Pond, Randall. "Toledano and Mexico," *The Commonweal*, XXIV (June 12, 1936), 173–74.

Porter, Charles O. and Robert J. Alexander. *The Struggle for Democracy in Latin America*. New York: The Macmillan Co., 1961.

Powell, J. Richard. "Labor Problems in the Mexican Petroleum Industry 1938–1950," *Inter-American Economic Affairs*, VI (Autumn, 1952), 3–50.

————. *The Mexican Petroleum Industry, 1938–1950*. Berkeley: University of California Press, 1956.

Presidencia de la República (Cárdenas). *Informe que Rinde al H. Congreso de la Unión el C. Presidente Lázaro Cárdenas, sobre su Gestión de Septiembre de 1937 a Agosto de 1938*. México: D.A.P.P., Talleres Gráficos de la Nación, 1938.

Prewett, Virginia. *Reportage on Mexico*. New York: E. P. Dutton and Co., Inc., 1941.

Price, John. *The International Labour Movement*. London: Oxford University Press, 1945.

Priestly, Herbert I. "The Contemporary Program of Nationalization in Mexico," *Pacific Historical Review*, VIII (March, 1939), 59–80.

"Project of Approved General Contract at the First Grand Extraordinary Convention of the Syndicate of Petroleum Workers of the Mexican Republic, November 3, 1936," Typescript copy is in the Library of the United States Embassy in Mexico City.

Proyecto Patronal de Tabulador de Salarios Que se Presenta a la Asamblea Obrero Patronal Que Discute el Contrato General Obligatorio para Toda la Industria del Petróleo en la República Mexicana. México: n.p., 1937.

Quintana, Miguel A. *Economía Social*. México: Talleres Gráficos de la Nación, 1937.

"Railroads," Banco Nacional de México, S. A., *Review of the Economic Situation of Mexico* (August 31, 1940), p. 17.

Ramírez Cabañas, Joaquín. *La Sociedad Cooperativa en México*. México: n.p., 1936.

Ramírez y Ramírez, Enrique. *La Obra y la Lucha de Vicente Lombardo Toledano*. México: n.p., 1952.

————. "Vicente Lombardo Toledano, un Militante de la Clase Obrera de México," *Futuro*, LXI (March, 1941), 35–42.

Ramos, Samuel. *Profile of Man and Culture in Mexico*. Austin: The University of Texas Press, 1962.

Ramos Malzarraga, Javier. "Las Grandes Huelgas Victoriosas de la C.T.M.," *Futuro*, LXI (March, 1941), 31–33, 79.

Ramos Pedrueza, Rafael. *La Lucha de las Clases a Través de la Historia de México*. México: n.p., 1934.

"Recommendations of Expert Commission," in Government of Mexico. *Mexico's Oil: A Compilation of Official Documents in the Conflict of Economic Order in the Petroleum Industry, with an Introduction Summarizing its Causes and Consequences*. México: Editorial Cultura, 1940.

"Report of the Expert Commission," in Government of Mexico. *Mexico's Oil: A Compilation of Official Documents in the Conflict of Economic Order in the Petroleum Industry, with an Introduction Summarizing its Causes and Consequences*. México: Editorial Cultura, 1940.

"Report of the Expert Commission," *El Trimestre Económico*, VII (1940/41), 57.

Research Center in Economic Development and Cultural Change of the University of Chicago. "United States Business and Labor in Latin America," in U. S. Congress. Senate 86th Congress. 2nd Session. Document No. 125. Study No. 4. *United States-Latin American Relations*. Washington, D.C.: G.P.O., 1960, pp. 277–97.

Retinger, Joseph H. *Morones de México: Historia del Movimiento Obrero en Ese País*. México: Biblioteca del "Grupo Acción," 1927.

Revista del Banco Obrero. (Organo del Banco Nacional de Fomento Industrial.) México: n.p., 1938.

Revueltas, José. *Ensayo sobre un Proletariado sin Cabeza*. México: Editorial Logos, 1962.

Reyes Pimental, José. *La Cosecha*. México: D.A.P.P., n.d.

————. *Historia de las Luchas Proletarias de México, 1923–1936*. México: Editorial Avante, 1958.

———— (ed.). *Despertar Lagunero. Libro que Relata la Lucha y Triunfo de la Revolucíon en la Comarca Lagunera*. México, 1937.

Richberg, Donald R. *The Mexican Oil Seizure*. New York: Arrow Press, Inc., 1939.

Rippy, J. Fred. *Latin America and the Industrial Age*. New York: G. P. Putnam's Sons, 1944.

Rippy, Merrill. "El Petróleo y la Revolución Mexicana," *Problemas Agrícolas e Industriales de México*, VI (July–September, 1954), 9–180.

Riso Alvarez, José Germán. "Las Cuestiones de Competencia en Materia de Huelga," Thesis at the National University of Mexico.

Rivera Solana, Manuel. "La Obligatoriedad del Contrato Colectivo en el Derecho Obrero Mexicano," *Jus, Revista de Derecho y Ciencias Sociales*, XV (October, 1939), 343–50.

Rodríguez Adame, Julián. "El Banco Nacional de Crédito Ejidal, S. A., y la Reforma Agraria," *Agricultura*, II (May–June, 1939), 3–7.

Rodríguez Meza, Venustiano. "La Limitación del Derecho de Poro General o Lackout en La Legislación Mexicano del Trabajo," *Revista Mexicana del Trabajo*, XXXI (March, 1948), 71–90.

Rodríguez Pérez, Felipe. "Algunos Aspectos sobre las Sanciones en el Derecho del Trabajo," Thesis at the National University of Mexico.

Roel, Santiago. *La Ley del Trabajo: Apuntes y Breves Comentarios*. Monterrey: Talleres J. Cantú Leal, 1931.

Romualdi, Serafino. "Labor and Democracy in Latin America," *Foreign Affairs*, XXV (April, 1947), 477–89.

Rosado de la Espada, Diego. "El Ejido y la Pequeña Propiedad," *México Agrario*, I (July–August, 1939), 15–23.

Rottenberg, Simon. "México: Trabajo y Desarrollo Económico," *Foro Internacional, El Colegio de México*, II (July–September, 1961), 85–113.

Saint Albans, Mary. "What about the Laguna?" *Modern Mexico*, XI (June 1939), 9–13 and 22–24.

Salazar, Rosendo. *Historia de las Luchas Proletarias de México, 1923–1936*. México, 1958.

————. *La Carta del Trabajo de la Revolución Mexicana: Fundamentos de Una Revolución*. México: Libro Mex, 1960.

————. *La C.T.M. Su Historia, Su Significado*. México: Ediciones Modelo, 1956.

————. *Líderes y Sindicatos*. México: Ediciones T. C. Modelo, S.C.L., 1953.

Santibáñez, Felipe. *Legislación sobre Trabajo*. México: Información Aduanera de México, 1937.

Sarames, George N. "Third System in Latin America: Mexico," *Inter-American Economic Affairs*, V (Spring, 1952), 59–72.

Schmitt, Karl M. *Communism in Mexico*. Austin: The University of Texas Press, 1965.

Scott, Robert E. *Mexican Government in Transition*. Urbana: University of Illinois Press, 1959.

"Second General Congress of the Confederation of Latin American

Workers," *International Labour Review*, LI (February 1945), 236–43.

Secretaría de Educación Pública. *Sobre el Petróleo de México: Conferencias*. (Speech by Alejandro Carrillo.) México: D.A.P.P., 1938.

Secretaría de Gobernación. *Diario de los Debates del Congresso Constituyente de 1916–17*, I.

———. *Seis Años de Actividad Nacional*. México: Talleres Gráficos de la Nación, n.d.

———. *Seis Años de Gobierno al Servicio de México 1934–1940*. México: Talleres Tipográficos La Nacional Impresora, S.A., 1940.

Secretaría de Industria, Comercio y Trabajo. *Monografía Sobre el Estado Actual de la Industria en México*. México: n.p., 1930.

Secretaría de la Economía Nacional, Dirección General de Estadística. *Anuario Estadístico de los Estados Unidos Mexicanos, 1938*. México: D.A.P.P., 1939.

———. *Anuario Estadístico de los Estados Unidos Mexicanos, 1941*. México: N.P., 1943.

———. *Compendio Estadístico, 1947*. México: n.p., 1947.

———. *Industria y Comercio de México*, Vol. I, Enero de 1936.

———. *Memoria de la Secretaría de la Economía Nacional, Septiembre de 1937–Agosto de 1938*. México: D.A.P.P., 1938.

———. *Memoria de la Secretaría de la Economía Nacional, Septiembre de 1938–Agosto de 1939, Presentada al H. Congreso de la Unión por el C. Secretario del Ramo, Efraín Buenrostro*. México: D.A.P.P., 1939.

———. *Memoria de la Secretaría de la Economía Nacional, Septiembre de 1939–Agosto de 1940*. México: D.A.P.P., 1940.

———. *México en Cifras, Atlas Estadística*. México: D.A.P.P., 1934.

———. *Revista de Estadística*, III (México, 1940).

———. *Segundo Censo Ejidal de los Estados Unidos Mexicanos, 1940. Resumen General*. México: Talleres Gráficos de la Nación, 1949.

Senior, Clarence. *Democracy Comes to a Cotton Kingdom: The Story of Mexico's La Laguna*. México: Centro de Estudios Pedagógicos e Hispanoamericanos, 1940. Distributed in the United States by the League for Industrial Democracy, New York.

———. *Land Reform and Democracy*. Gainesville: The University of Florida Press, 1958.

———. *Mexico in Transition*. New York: League for Industrial Democracy, 1939.

———. "Reforma Agraria y Democracia en la Comarca Lagunera," *Problemas Agrícolas e Industriales de México*, VIII (April–June, 1956), 3–174.

Shapiro, Samuel. *Invisible Latin America*. Boston: Beacon Press, 1963.

Silva Herzog, Jesús. *Apuntes sobre Evolución Económica de México*. México: n.p., 1927.

——. *Breve Historia de la Revolución Mexicana: La Etapa Constitucionalista y la Lucha de Facciones*. México: Fondo de Cultura Económica, 1960.

——. *Colección de Folletos para la Historia de la Revolución Mexicana*. México: n.p., n.d.

——. "La Cuestión del Petróleo en México," *El Trimestre Económico*, VII (1940/41), 1–74.

——. *Historia de la Expropiación de las Empresas Petroleras*. 3rd ed. México: Instituto Mexicano de Investigaciones Económicas, 1964.

——. *Historia de la Expropiación Petrolera*. México: Cuadernos Americanos, 1963.

——. "Lo Humano, Problema Esencial," *Cuadernos Americanos*, I (January–February, 1942), 9–16.

——. *El Mexicano y su Morada y Otros Ensayos*. México: Ediciones Cuadernos Americanos, 1960.

——. "Mexico and the Oil Companies," *Annals of Collective Economy*, XV (January–April, 1939), 55–69.

——. "Mexico's Case in the Oil Controversy," Institute of Public Affairs, *Mexico and the United States, Proceedings of the Fifth Annual Conference Institute of Public Affairs Auspices Carnegie Endowment for International Peace*, 1938, pp. 67–77.

——. *El Pensamiento Económico en México*. México: Fondo de Cultura Económica, n.d.

——. *Petróleo Mexicano: Historia de un Problema*. México: Fondo de Cultura Económica, 1941.

——. *La Revolución Mexicana en Crisis*. México: Cuadernos Americanos, 1944.

——. "Rise and Fall of Mexico's Revolution," *Mexican-American Review*, XVII (December, 1949), 34–35; 112–16.

——. *Trayectoria Ideológica de la Revolución Mexicana; 1910–1917: Del Manifesto del Partido Liberal de 1906 a la Constitución de 1917*. México: Cuadernos Americanos, 1963.

Simpson, Eyler N. *The Ejido: Mexico's Way Out*. Chapel Hill: The University of North Carolina Press, 1937.

Simpson, Lesley B. *Many Mexico's*, 4th ed., rev. and enlarged. Berkeley: University of California Press, 1966.

Sindicato de Trabajadores Petroleros de la República Mexicana,

Comité Ejecutivo General. *La Cuestión Petrolero: Sus Diversos Aspectos.* n.p., n.d.

Sociedad Agronómica de México. *Primer Ciclo de Conferencias (de Octubre a Noviembre de 1937).* México: D.A.P.P., 1938.

Soule, George, David Efrón and Norman T. Ness. *Latin America in the Future World.* New York: Farrar and Rinehart, 1945.

Sousa, Mario. "Nuevas Orientaciones de Política Económica," *Investigación Económica,* I (3rd Quarter, 1941), 323–40.

————, and E. González Aparicio. *2 Conferencias sobre el Problema Petrolero.* México: Imp. Universitaria, 1938.

Standard Oil Company of New Jersey. *Empty Promises.* n.p., 1940.

————. *The Fine Art of Squeezing.* n.p., 1940.

————. *The Present Status of the Mexican Oil "Expropriations."* n.p., 1940.

————. *The Reply to Mexico.* New York: n.p., 1940.

Starr-Hunt, Jack. "Mexico's Collective Farms Show Profit," *Modern Mexico,* IX (November 1937), 15–16.

Stewart, M. S. "Our Mexican Colony," *The Nation,* CXLI (September 18, 1935), 323–24.

Stocking, George Ward. "Mexican Expropriation—The Mexican Oil Problem," *International Conciliation,* No. 345, December 1938.

————. "The Mexican Oil Problem," Institute of Public Affairs, *Mexico and the United States: Proceedings of the Fifth Annual Conference Institute of Public Affairs Auspices Carnegie Endowment for International Peace,* 1938, pp. 45–66.

Strode, Hudson. *Timeless Mexico.* New York: Harcourt, Brace and Co., 1944.

Sturmthal, Adolf. "United States Business and Labor in Latin America," U.S. Congress, 2nd Session, Document 125, Study 4. Washington, D.C., 1960, pp. 277–97.

Tannenbaum, Frank. "Cárdenas—That Is the Way He Is," *Survey Graphic,* XXVI (August, 1937), 425–27.

————. "Lázaro Cárdenas," *Historia Mexicana,* X (October–December, 1960), 332–41.

————. *Mexico: The Struggle for Peace and Bread.* New York: Alfred A. Knopf, 1950.

————. *Peace by Revolution.* New York: Columbia University Press, 1933.

Teja Zabre, Alfonso. *Guide to the History of Mexico: A Modern Interpretation.* Mexico: Press of the Ministry of Foreign Affairs, 1935.

————. (ed.). *Ley Federal del Trabajo.* México: Ediciones Botas, 1940.

Terán Gómez, Luis. "Las Clases Trabajadoras de la América Latina y su Necesario Bienestar," *América*, XXVIII (April–June, 1946), 55–57.

Thomas, A. B. "Mexico's New Economics," *Southwestern Review*, XXIII (July 1938), 373–91.

Thomas, Charles A. "Agrarian Reform in Mexico," Institute of Public Affairs, *Mexico and the United States: Proceedings of the Fifth Annual Conference Institute of Public Affairs Auspices Carnegie Endowment for International Peace*, 1938, pp. 29–44.

————. "Land for Peons . . . Agrarian Reform in Mexico," *Southwest Review*, XVIII (January, 1938), 148–66.

————. "The Mexican Oil Dispute," *Foreign Policy Reports*, XIV, 122–32.

————. "Mexico's Social Revolution," *Foreign Policy Association Reports*, XIII (August 1, 1937), 114–24.

"Toledano Faces Labor Revolt," *World Report*, December 31, 1946, p. 30.

Townsend, William Cameron. *Lázaro Cárdenas: Mexican Democrat.* Ann Arbor: George Wahr Publishing Co., 1952.

"The Trade Union Movement in Latin America," *International Labour Review*, LVI (September, 1947), 355–61; (October, 1947), 489–97.

"The Trade Union Movement in Mexico," *International Labour Review*, LIII (April, 1941), 463–64.

Translation of Agrarian Code of the Mexican United States. México: Asociación de Empresas Industriales y Comerciales, 1940. (Published in *Diario Oficial* of October 29, 1940.)

Treviño, Ricardo. *El Espionaje Comunista y la Evolución Doctrinaria del Movimiento Obrero en México.* México: n.p., 1952.

————. *El Movimiento Obrero de México no es Marxista.* México: Reveles, 1937.

————. *El Movimiento Obrero en México, su Evolución Ideológica.* México: n.p., 1948.

"Trouble Below the Border," *The Atlantic Presents*, July, 1938, pp. 1–64.

Trueba Barrera, Jorge. *El Juicio de Amparo en Materia de Trabajo.* México: Editorial Porrúa, S.A., 1963.

Trueba Urbina, Alberto (ed.). *Constitución Política de los Estados Mexicanos (Anotada). Textos Vigentes y sus Limitaciones durante el Estado de Guerra.* México: Editorial Porrúa, S.A., 1944.

————. *Evolución de la Huelga.* México: Botas, 1950.

———. *Ley Federal del Trabajo Reformada.* México: Porrúa Hnos., 1960.

———. *El Nuevo Artículo 123.* México: Editorial Porrúa, S.A., 1962.

United States Bureau of Labor Statistics. "Cooperatives in Mexico in 1940," *Monthly Labor Review*, LIII (September 1941), 657–61.

United States Tariff Commission. *Economic Controls and Commercial Policy in Mexico.* Washington: Government Printing Office, 1946.

Universidad Obrero de México, 1936. México: n.p., 1936. (Catalog of Courses and Professors.)

———. *Vicente Lombardo Toledano: Curriculum Vitae.* México: n.p., 1961.

Uruchurtu Gil, Alfredo. "La Política Estatal Frente a la Asociación Profesional de Trabajadores," *Revista Mexicana del Trabajo*, II (September, 1949), 31–39; (October, 1949), 23–32.

Valencia, Hugo. "Algunas Reflexiones Acerca de la Administración Pública del Trabajo en México," *Revista de Derecho Social Ecuatoriano* (January–December, 1959), pp. 13–16.

Vance, John T. and Helen L. Claggett. *A Guide to the Law and Legal Literature of Mexico.* Latin American Series No. 6, Washington: Library of Congress, 1945.

Varela, Victor Manuel (ed.). *Ley Federal del Trabajo: Texto Oficial Conteniendo Todas las Reformas y Adiciones Hasta la Fecha— Notas y Concordancias.* México: Ediciones Cicerón, 1951.

Vargas, Elvira, *Lo Que Vi en la Tierra del Petróleo.* México: "México Nuevo," 1938.

Vargas Macdonald, Antonio. "Agrarian Reform in Mexico," *Annals of Collective Economy: International Review in Four Editions*, XV (Geneva, 1939), pp. 120–41.

Vavasour Noel, John. "Yucatán Resurgent," *Mexican Life*, XV (February, 1939), 22, 24.

Vera Estañol, Jorge. *La Revolución Mexicana. Orígenes y Resultados.* México: Ed. Porrúa, S.A., 1957.

Villalobos, Antonio. "El Jefe del Departamento del Trabajo al Proletariado Nacional," *Revista del Trabajo*, II (March, 1938), 21–22.

———. "La Expropiación Petrolera, un Servicio a la Patria," *Revista del Trabajo*, III (April, 1939), 55–59.

Wallace, Colonel Irving Speed. *Mexico Today.* Boston: Meador Publishing Co., 1936.

Walling, William E. *The Mexican Question: Mexico and American-*

Mexican Relations Under Calles and Obregón. New York: Robins Press, 1927.

Waugh, Evelyn. *Mexico: An Object Lesson.* Boston: Little, Brown and Co., 1939.

Werlin, Joseph S. "Mexico's Unity," *The Yale Review,* XXXIII (December, 1943), 268–81.

Weyl, Nathaniel and Sylvia. *The Reconquest of Mexico: The Years of Lázaro Cárdenas.* New York: Oxford University Press, 1939.

Whetten, Nathan L. *Rural Mexico.* Chicago: University of Chicago Press, 1948.

Wilgus, A. Curtis (ed.). *The Caribbean at Mid-Century.* Gainesville: University of Florida Press, 1951.

"Workers' Organizations in Mexico," *Monthly Labor Review,* LVII (September, 1943), 535–36.

"The Workers Run the Railroads," *Modern Mexico,* X (December, 1938), 6–11.

Workers University of Mexico. *Mexican Labor News.* Published three times a Month by the Press Department of the Workers University of Mexico. 1936, 1937, 1938, 1939, 1940.

————. *The Oil Conflict in Mexico, 1937–1938.*

Yllanes Ramos, Fernando. "Nuestra Problema Social," *Revista Mexicana del Trabajo* (May–June, 1954), 9–25.

Young, Howard T. "Mexico: A Revolution Gone Bankrupt," *The New Republic,* CXLII (April 4, 1960), 13–15.

NEWSPAPERS:

Christian Science Monitor. 1938, 1941.

El Nacional. Mexico City: 1936, 1938, 1939, 1940.

El Popular. Mexico City: 1939, 1943, 1947.

El Universal. Mexico City: 1935, 1938, 1939, 1946.

Excelsior. Mexico City: 1938, 1940, 1941, 1942, 1950.

La Prensa. Mexico City: 1940.

Lux. Mexico City: 1935, 1939.

Mexican Labor News. Mexico City: 1936, 1937, 1938, 1939, 1940.

New York Daily News. 1940.

New York Times. 1938.

Index

Index

and labor, 245–71 *passim*; administration after nationalization, 245–71, 281–82; employment, 252; expropriation, 287
Oil marketing, after expropriation, 250–51, 256
Oil strike, 1937, 211–12
Oil workers, 79; 1901–35, 190–91; living conditions, 191; demands, 199–202, 206–8, 209
Oil Workers' Union, 63, 130, 179, 195–96, 213–14, 226, 232, 235, 247, 248, 250–71 *passim*, 278–84, 287, 288; United States, 94
Olvera, Augustín, 82
Organized labor, 20, 32; anti-Calles meeting, 27; 1936–40, 31; rights of, 62, 193; management and ownership of industry, 63
Orizaba, 6, 7, 107, 108–9, 111, 113
Ortega, Gustavo, 214
Ortíz Rubio, Pascual, 17; strikes during administration, 99
Overtime, 58, 102

P

Padilla, Eziquiel, 26, 40
Padilla, Mariano, 76
Palace of Fine Arts, 23
Palavicini, Felix, 11, 60
Pan-American Labor Federation, 14, 94
Pan-American trade-unity, 93–94
Parasites, 65, 66
Parras, 150
Partido de la Revolución Mexicana (P.R.M.), 37, 42, 52, 81, 82, 275; principles and program, 41; composition of, 89–90; and middle class, 140
Partido Laborista, 12, 13
Partido Nacional Revolucionario (P.N.R.), 17, 19, 20, 37, 41, 51, 52, 57, 80, 82, 86, 272, 273; principles and policies, 58; and peasant organizations, 80–81; and popular front, 86–89; and Mexican socialism, 130; and middle class, 140
Peasant Co-operative for Ejidal Medical Services in the Laguna district, 167
Peasants, 14, 15, 27, 28, 32, 51, 70, 72, 73, 79, 80–82, 86–88, 96, 148–79 *passim*, 275, 277–78, 285, 287;

and industrial unions, 80; organization of, 81–82, 179
Pearson, Weetman S., 188
Pemex (Petróleos Mexicanos), 248–70 *passim*, 283, 284
Peña, Lázaro, 53
Pérez, Casteñeda, Eduardo, 247
Pérez Leirós, Francisco, 53
Pérez Medina, Alfredo, 15
Perón, Juan, 35
Person, Harlowe S., 184, 188–89, 195
Peru, 95
Petróleos de México. *See* Petromex
Petromex, 209, 247
Petroleum Board, 221
Petroleum Bureau of the National Economy, 231
Petroleum industry, 98, 183. *See also* Oil industry
Petroleum Law, 1925, 242
Petroleum Workers' Convention, 289
Piño Suárez, José María, 4
Plan of San Luis Postosí, 8
Plantation economy, 151
Police, 91, 102, 185
Political boss, ejido, 173
Political parties, 8
Political status, localities, 153–54
Popular front, 39, 41–42, 50–52, 66, 70, 74, 85–90, 97, 144, 155, 275, 288
Popular University, 77
Portes Gil, Emilio, 17, 80, 86, 99, 191, 194
Post Office Department, 101
Postal Workers' Union, 101
Poza Rica, 226, 247, 251, 261
Presidential Succession, The, 7
Prewett, Virginia, 80, 88, 90, 92, 238, 249
Printers, 16, 75
Printers' Union, 16
Private capital, 95
Private enterprise, 54, 56, 73
Private land holdings, 21
Private property, 39, 42, 46, 47, 60, 66, 67, 69, 71, 72, 96, 143–47
Productive machinery, ownership of, 68
Profit motive, 43
Profits, oil companies, 215–16, 219–20, 241
Profit sharing, 61
Propaganda, oil companies, 241
Proletariat, 42, 48, 49, 50–51, 65, 87–88, 125, 141